NEXT YEAR IN JERUSALEM

NEXT YEAR IN JERUSALEM

Jews in the Twentieth Century

Edited by Douglas Villiers

HARRAP   LONDON

FRONTISPIECE: The Western Wall. Photo by Micha Bar Am.

To Lena, Charlotte, and Ann
and
to Chaim Bermant, who helped
translate my initial ideas
into practical reality

First published in Great Britain 1976
by GEORGE G. HARRAP & CO. LTD
182-184 High Holborn, London WC1V 7AX
© *Douglas Villiers Publishing Ltd* 1976
All rights reserved. No part of this publication may
be reproduced in any form or by any means without
the prior permission of George G. Harrap & Co. Ltd

ISBN 0 245 52844 X

First published in the United States 1976
by The Viking Press, New York, in association with
Douglas Villiers Publishing Ltd, London

Made in the United States of America

Contents

Foreword

During 1972 and 1973 I invited a group of authors, critics, and commentators on Jewish life to write a series of articles on what interested them particularly about the Jew in this century—his occupations, talents, pleasures, and foibles, and the areas in which he has best expressed himself and made the most valuable contribution. Each was given the basic theme: why, after prolonged periods of relative obscurity and quiescence, the impact of Jewish intellectualism and originality should have surfaced so dramatically at this time rather than at any other. In most cases the decision as to subject was left to the author.

Each article was written without the authors' having access to one another's material. This method of working has had the advantage of spontaneity, but necessarily many areas of Jewish activity have been omitted, and many prominent individuals have not been mentioned even within the context of an article dealing with their professions.

For the purposes of this book a Jew was considered to be a person with at least one Jewish parent rather than the more formal rabbinic definition, which states that a Jew is a child of a Jewish mother or a convert to Judaism. No consideration was given as to whether he practiced the faith or not. In some instances individuals discussed in the text either actively rejected the religion of their fathers or were baptized by their parents, which was a tactic frequently used to protect the child from anti-Semitism.

Without men like Einstein, Marx, Freud, Wittgenstein, and Schönberg, without the Jewish presence in physics, medicine, psychology, law, business, music, literature, theater, film, and the visual arts, Western society would be immeasurably poorer today. What makes these contributions so remarkable is that the Jews comprise less than one-half of one per cent of the world's population.

I have become increasingly aware that the Jew differs from his gentile counterpart in many fundamental respects. It is not that he has a patent on originality or the creative process, but that his history has influenced his method of thought and of working out problems. A more radical view is that there is some underlying hereditary factor involved. My own view is that the Jews are trying to live out the role they were historically offered: they are attempting to become the chosen people by a conscious effort of choosing themselves. Several of the contributors tackled this question, and their answers may be more convincing than mine.

There are many people to whom I owe a debt of gratitude for their help in making this book possible:

To Nicholas Faith for the many hours he spent discussing the theme of the book with me, and for his valuable advice and encouragement during its production.

To Thomas H. Guinzburg of The Viking Press for his part in publishing this book, and to Bryan Holme and Michael A. Loeb, who were responsible for the design and editorial elements of the finished book. It was a great pleasure and very instructive to work with them.

The photographs are the result of patient research by Yvonne Freund and Mike and Regina Edelson.

London, 1975   Douglas Villiers

The Creation of Israel

Richard Crossman

Anyone interested in the determinist view of history should study the history of Zionism to see how an idea can become an accomplished fact. The concept of a Jewish national homeland, launched in 1896 by Theodor Herzl, an emancipated Viennese Jew, became a reality fifty-two years later. There was nothing inevitable about the rebirth of the Jewish state, and even after it did come into existence, in the most unfavorable circumstances, its chances of survival were desperately small. Yet it has continued to exist.

In none of the other revolutionary changes of the twentieth century—and for good or for ill the creation of Israel constitutes a revolutionary change—has personal leadership counted for more, faced longer odds, and overcome more adverse circumstances. In the first period of this story—up to the Balfour Declaration in 1917—Herzl's idea was sustained by a quarrelsome and ineffective Zionist organization, which never represented more than a tiny fraction of world Jewry. In the second phase, when the British mandate, at least in its early years, provided a real opportunity, world Jewry failed to provide more than a trickle of support—whether support is measured by the size of contributions that Jews made or the number of them who settled in Palestine. It took the impact of the Nuremberg Laws in Germany— followed a few years later by the revelation of the holocaust, to convert the majority of Jews throughout the world to the need for a Jewish state. During this second phase—both in Palestine and in the Diaspora— the foundations for a state were laid by a Zionist organization, still small and inadequate, but led by two remarkable, conflicting personalities—Chaim Weizmann and David Ben Gurion.

What caused the upheaval that transformed a mystical belief in the return to Zion into a political ideology intent on making Palestine the home of a reborn Jewish nation? Much is uncertain in the history of Zionism, but its origin is not in doubt. The first links in the chain of events that culminated in the 1948 Declaration of Independence were the oppression of Russian Jewry by successive Czarist governments and the Dreyfus affair. Without these, the Jews of the West, along with other religious and ethnic minorities, might well have been content to enjoy the civil rights they slowly gained in the age of post-Napoleonic emancipation—although they never were free from sporadic anti-Jewish movements. Liberated from their ghettos and sharing the fruits of economic expansion, they could have freely decided between total assimilation and peaceful retention of religious differences, while the Jewish communities of the Orient and North Africa could have lived on at peace with their Arab neighbors. If Herzl's personal conversion to Jewish nationalism was the result of the Dreyfus case, Zionism as a movement emerged as a reaction to the persecution of Russian Jewry.

Searching for the past—an excavation in Jerusalem. Photo by Cartier-Bresson.

Building a new nation, by hand and by machine. Photos by Robert Capa and Leonard Freed.

The German author and physician Max Simon Nordau (1849–1923), as an early and avid Zionist, urged the creation of a Jewish settlement in East Africa.

Theodor Herzl (1860–1904), an Austrian, wrote *Der Judenstaat* when he was thirty-six years old and spent the balance of his life advocating the establishment of a Jewish state in Palestine. Pictured with his mother.

The first of the Czarist anti-Jewish measures was the decree that established the Pale of Settlement in 1791. In the following years the area was greatly expanded after each partition of Poland. Not allowed to own land, the Jews lived alongside the Russian peasant, sharing many of his miseries, understanding his weaknesses, but cut off by the difference in language and religion. The vast majority knew little Russian, using Yiddish in their everyday lives and learning to read and write Hebrew in the religious schools, the only form of education. Russian Jews had neither minority status, as did the Oriental Jews of the Ottoman empire, nor the emancipation increasingly enjoyed by the Jews of Western Europe. They were treated as a strange race in someone else's country.

They differed from the rest of world Jewry in that they retained their essential Jewishness in all its medieval purity. Those who were able to move westward quickly adopted Western standards, and many soon excelled in business, politics, and every aspect of Western culture and civilization, including art, literature, and music. Away from the Pale, the Jews became consummate actors who could assume any national disguise and play any professional role. But in the Pale they were allowed only one role—that

of the ghetto Jew tethered in his place of exile. They played it in their intense, closed community with a unique mixture of pride and humility, humor and pathos, innocence and cunning. In so doing they evolved a self-governing community with its own codified laws and rules of behavior and its unique respect for learning and the exegesis of the Torah as the highest activities of man. Toynbee used to rebuke Jewry for possessing only a petrified civilization. He was absurdly wrong about the Jews of the West, whose fault was a dangerous adaptability. But he was right that the Jews of the Pale, like the Jews of the Yemen, had a petrified way of life—though he failed to note that stone survives the crushing weight of oppression better than unprotected human flesh and blood.

Even so, this intense, inward-looking culture of the *shtetl* did not remain completely unaffected by the spirit of the Enlightenment. The Haskalah, which emanated from Germany, was the Jewish equivalent of Protestantism in the Christian world; it was a revolt against rabbinical tyranny over the mind. Newspapers and magazines began to appear in Hebrew, heretofore used only for religious purposes, as did geography and history books, novels and poetry. Groups met in secret to read Schiller's poetry or popularizations of Darwin's theory in Hebrew, while others read novels depicting the Jews as proud, fiery, independent —far from the resignation approved by the *shtetl*. Even the smallest town probably harbored at least one of the *maskilim*, an enlightened one who read a newspaper and provided the news to villagers, who were shocked by his iconoclasm.

Because the language of the Haskalah was the sacred language, the use of it preserved the separateness of the chosen people, but at the same time it taught the new thrilling way of being a modern man while remaining a loyal Jew. Thus it opened the mind of a vigorous nonconformist minority to political consciousness.

During the reign of Alexander II, Russia experienced a mild wave of liberalization. Rights of residence beyond the Pale were granted to certain classes of the Jewish population, and the restriction on Russian education for Jews was slightly eased. This period of comparative relaxation came to an abrupt end in 1881, when Alexander II was assassinated and his son, Alexander III, ascended the throne. The "May Laws" passed by the new regime expelled the Jews from the cities once again, prohibited new Jewish settlements both in and out of the Pale, and granted the Russian peasants the right to demand the expulsion of Jews who lived among them. These measures were brutally enforced by the local authorities and were accompanied more and more frequently by pogroms, usually abetted by the police, culminating in the infamous Kishinev pogrom of 1903.

The economic conditions of the Jews of the Pale were harsh indeed. Excluded from agriculture, the main activity of their Russian neighbors, they went into commerce or the crafts (for the most part, tailoring and cobbling).

The first reaction to the persecution of the 1880s was not resistance but mass flight. The Jewish population of the Pale had quadrupled during the nineteenth century, and the new government regulations, which not only continued to exclude them from agriculture but also excluded them from the new industrial cities, made the problem of survival almost insoluble. After 1880 a huge stream of emigrants began to pour into Western Europe, across the Channel to Britain, and on to the New World. The Jewish population of the United States had been a paltry 15,000 in 1840. By 1880 it had grown to 280,000, owing to a German-Jewish immigration that was part of the great German emigration following the revolt in 1848. After 1880 most Jewish immigrants came from the Pale, and the pace increased with each decade.

During this same period the Jewish population of Palestine increased from about 24,000 in 1882 to about 85,000 in 1914. Of this total, 50,000 were either Oriental Jews or pious indigenes dependent on charity. Only 35,000 were new settlers—and they had no legal or civil rights there under Turkish rule. The strength of Zionism before the outbreak of World War I can be measured by a comparison of these two sets of figures. It was thus not the agitation of a strong Zionist movement that extracted the Balfour

Jews, whose ancestors had been barred from owning land in many parts of Europe throughout the nineteenth century, turned the desert of Palestine into productive farmland. Photo by Ted Spiegel.

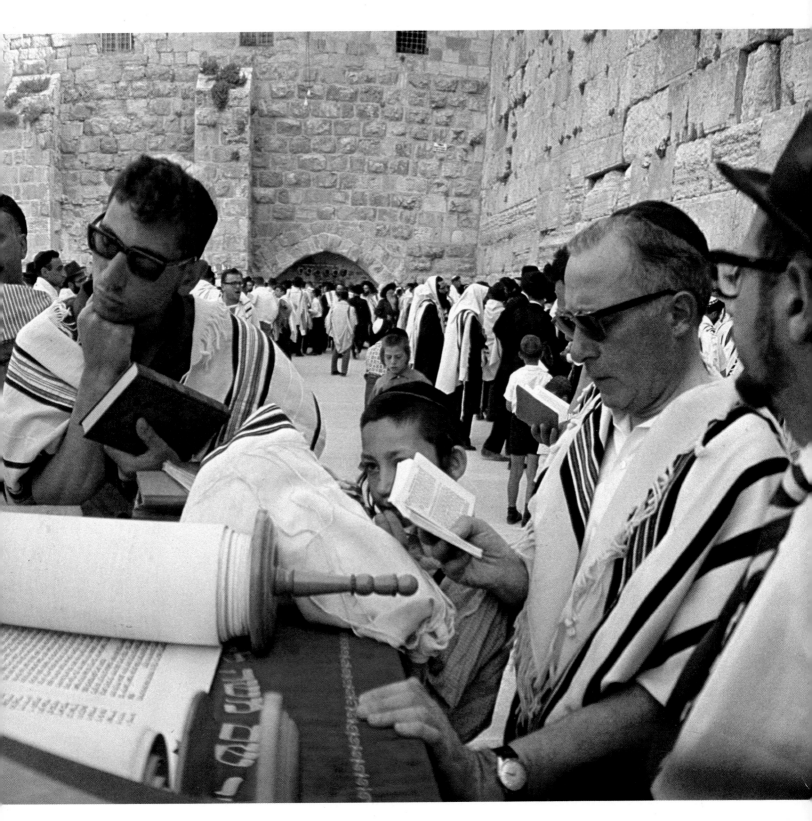

A torah reading at the Western Wall. Photo by Ted Spiegel.

Declaration from a reluctant British government. It was the Balfour Declaration itself that created for the first time the conditions for large-scale Zionist organization in the Diaspora.

The concept of the ingathering of the exiles little appealed to the suffering Jews of the Pale so long as other escape routes from Russian anti-Semitism remained wide open, particularly the route that led to a new world of civil liberties and unlimited possibilities.

There were two special reasons why Zionism had little appeal in the Pale. In the first place, unlike the *maskilim,* whose program of enlightenment remained within the tradition of Jewish learning, the Zionists accepted from Herzl a Western political ideology that, at least up to 1914, most Russian Jewry regarded as crass and impious heresy. To them, Herzl was translating a Messianic concept of the return to Zion into a crude political program, which seemed to encroach on God's prerogative to accomplish His will regarding the chosen people in His own way and in His own time. So, too, by accepting the whole European theory of nationalism and national self-determination and applying it crudely to the Jewish people he downgraded the chosen people to the level of any gentile nation.

The second reason was the emergence of Marxist socialism as the doctrine of the Russian Revolution. The social democrats offered young Jewish intellectuals a movement in which they would be accepted as equals by the Russian intelligentsia. To the workers they offered a trade unionism in which racial prejudice would be a crime. It is not surprising that the sons of the *maskilim* lost their enthusiasm for the Hebrew literary renaissance when they were so warmly accepted as comrades in a workers' movement that did not differentiate between gentile and Jew and that, in its illegal activities, offered so many opportunities for heroism and self-sacrifice.

The chances of creating a mass movement among the Jews of the West were equally slim. In Germany, France, and Britain the long-established Jewish communities were at least as patriotic if not as chauvinistic as the *goyim* among whom they now lived on (almost) equal terms. They were increasingly aware that Russian anti-Semitism was breeding in Western Europe a new variety of anti-Semite, who demanded stringent restrictions on aliens, designed (though this was rarely publicly admitted) to steer the Russian Jews to someone else's shores. In each country the old Jewish establishment regarded these new immigrants as an utterly foreign, disturbing element, for which it was necessary to provide while desperately trying to restrict its entry.

Zionism, therefore, by the time of the Balfour Declaration, had failed to achieve either of its two main objectives. It had not created a mass movement in the Diaspora supporting a national home in Palestine. Nor had it solved the practical problems of large-scale settlement.

These failures were, of course, not admitted by the Zionist leaders, who were bound to keep up their own spirits and those of their followers by looking at the best side of things. Nonetheless their weakness throughout this period is undeniable, and Zionist internationalism went the way of socialist internationalism when World War I broke out. Unwilling to go underground and fight the Czarist regime alongside the Marxist revolutionaries, the Zionists found themselves fighting for a regime they detested. In Western Europe and in Great Britain each Zionist national organization put its principles at the disposal of its national government and broke off all communications with the enemy. An unsuccessful effort was made to keep some neutral Zionist organization going, first in Copenhagen and then in Holland, and across the Atlantic the American Zionists set about performing the same function. But it was soon clear that the best possibilities for Zionist diplomacy were within the political system of each of the major belligerents. What mattered was how much Zionism could offer to the Western allies or to the Triple Alliance in winning the war.

In this competition it was soon clear that the German Zionists were at a grave disadvantage, since their country was allied with Turkey, which maintained an implacable hostility to Zionist settlement in Palestine. German Zionists did what they could to alleviate the fate of the unfortunate Jewish settlers who, until the occupation of Palestine by British forces, were at the mercy of a hostile and suspicious Ottoman

The Holy Land. Photo by Marvin E. Newman.

Foreign Office,
November 2nd, 1917.

Dear Lord Rothschild,

I have much pleasure in conveying to you, on behalf of His Majesty's Government, the following declaration of sympathy with Jewish Zionist aspirations which has been submitted to, and approved by, the Cabinet

"His Majesty's Government view with favour the establishment in Palestine of a national home for the Jewish people, and will use their best endeavours to facilitate the achievement of this object, it being clearly understood that nothing shall be done which may prejudice the civil and religious rights of existing non-Jewish communities in Palestine, or the rights and political status enjoyed by Jews in any other country".

I should be grateful if you would bring this declaration to the knowledge of the Zionist Federation.

Arthur James Balfour (1848–1930), speaking for His Majesty's Government as World War I drew to a close, declared support for a national Jewish home in Palestine.

administration. But there was little prospect of persuading the imperial German government to adopt the creation of a Jewish national home as a German war aim.

The prospects in Paris were not much better. The great majority of native-born French Jews and the official organization of the Jewish community were actively hostile to the Zionist program, fearing that their status acquired in the great emancipation would be placed in jeopardy. Moreover, it was clear that Zionist interests conflicted with French national interests in the Middle East.

Arab delegates with others at the Paris Peace Conference (1919). Second from the right in the middle row is Thomas Edward Lawrence of Arabia, a leader of the Arab revolt against the Turks.

In Britain the attitude of Anglo-Jewry was equally hostile. But here Zionism had a real opportunity, thanks to the peculiar attitude of gentile public opinion, in particular the Anglican Church and the Non-conformist chapels. This attitude stems from the Commonwealth period, when Cromwell tacitly tolerated the re-creation of a small Jewish community in London and his most ardent supporters tried to reintroduce the Mosaic law as the law of the land. They looked forward to the return to Zion as a pre-condition of Christ's second coming.

Those who gathered in the desert to draw lots for building sites in 1909 would be struck dumb at the sight of their Tel Aviv (at right) sixty-five years later. Early photo by Abraham Soskin.

If the excesses of Puritanism were driven underground by the Restoration, the British people retained, at least until the 1930s, a belief that they were a people of the Bible. Their habit of regular Bible-reading made them as familiar with the topography of Palestine as with that of their own country. To them there was nothing bizarre in the concept of a Jewish national home; on the contrary, they regarded the return of the Jews to their own country as an aim worthy of support by any British government. Palmerston was the first statesman to introduce this theme into British Middle-East policy, and the precedent he set was followed at the turn of the century by another rumbustious imperialist, Joseph Chamberlain. In offering Uganda to Herzl as a place for immediate Jewish settlement, he made it perfectly clear that he would welcome a national home in Palestine when favorable circumstances developed in Turkey.

These circumstances came in 1914 when Turkey entered the war on the side of Germany. It is not surprising, therefore, that when Weizmann asked for a British declaration in support of a national home in Palestine, he found himself pressing at an open door. If the war ended, as it almost certainly would, with the collapse of the Ottoman Empire, Britain must share control of the Middle East with her allies. To extend her influence north from Egypt and to secure the Suez Canal against attack she needed to prevent French influence from penetrating farther south than Syria. What was more natural than for the British government to accept the role of protecting power for a Jewish national home?

The Asquith cabinet was already giving serious consideration to such a policy within a few months after the declaration of war—prompted by a cabinet paper drafted by a Jew with no Zionist connections, Herbert Samuel. This first proposal foundered, and was only renewed when Lloyd George became prime minister and appointed Balfour his foreign secretary. Weizmann, who had been completely excluded from the previous round of discussions, now had his chance since he was acquainted with both men. It took five months of patient persuasion for Weizmann to convince each cabinet member that support of the national home would ensure that coincidence of expediency and morality which is always the aim of British statesmanship. This was one of those cases where providence made sure that doing the right thing would earn dividends. A British government that assumed the responsibility for redressing the long-standing injustice suffered by the Jews would find its imperial interests had been richly served.

In order for the Lloyd George government to make any convincing claim for the control of Palestine, it had to look as though the government was acceding to an urgent Jewish request. It was here that Weizmann's role was indispensable. First he had to mold a respectable body of Jewish support in Britain and so make the opponents, who actually represented the main traditional Jewish establishment, appear a fractious Jewish minority. Second, although the Balfour Declaration was a letter addressed to Lord Rothschild, it was necessary to have a leader who could accept the declaration on behalf of the Jews. From the British point of view such a Jewish leader had to be as personally committed to a British mandate in Palestine as the British government itself, and he also had to be able to impose his authority in the first instance on the Zionist movement and ultimately on world Jewry. In 1917 no such leader of the Zionist movement, far less of world Jewry, existed. Weizmann recognized that the Balfour Declaration was his appointment with destiny, his chance to make himself the true successor to Herzl. He donned the prophetic mantle and from then on spoke as the prince of his people. In order to do so he had to permit the part he played in obtaining the Balfour Declaration to assume legendary proportions. It was not Weizmann's greatness that achieved the declaration but the declaration that made him great.

It was confidently predicted that an era of mass Jewish immigration would begin once the mandate had been taken over by the British government, but this did not happen. Immigration to Palestine was but a trickle. The explication is not far to seek. During the 1920s the forces that had made Zionism so unpopular among world Jewry before 1914 were still at work. Quite apart from the failure of all but a negligible minority to settle in Palestine, the Jews of the West failed to insure the flow of capital without which mass settlement leads to mass unemployment. If only world Jewry had contributed in the 1920s a tenth of what it gave in the 1960s! But a sense of duty to assist the ingathering of exiles began to operate only after Israel had proved her military might and become an established success as a nation-state. During the interwar period, year after year, Weizmann had to drop the mantle of prophecy and adopt the role of the beggar for dollars.

This was the first—and also the last—chance of unlimited immigration under the British mandate. It was hopelessly missed because world Jewry was too slow in realizing that the era of Jewish emancipation had been finally ended by World War I. No country of Western Europe was completely immune to anti-Semitism, and in the new democracies of Central Europe created by the Treaty of Versailles it was an endemic and ever-spreading disease. Instead of Czarist pogroms the Jews were now exposed to persecution by a variety of ultra-nationalist movements—fascists, national socialists, iron guards. The United States, in 1924, had passed the Johnson Act, which, by substituting quotas for unlimited immigration, had closed that door.

By the beginning of the 1930s both the Zionist analysis and the Zionist conclusion began to make sense, particularly to the Jews of Poland and Rumania, who were again feeling the lash of persecution and came to realize they could no longer dream of building a new life in the old world or the new. Before

The British High Commissioner celebrates the King's birthday with a garden party in Jerusalem (1934). Photo by Zvi Orron.

1914 it had been easy to laugh at the Zionist who claimed that anti-Semitism was not a criminal Czarist activity but a disease endemic in the Christian nations of Europe and that no Jew could really be safe from persecution except in a Jewish state in Palestine. Now what had once sounded like a narrow sectarian dogma began to make sense in terms of everyday life. For the first time Zionism began to win mass support in Central Europe and a sympathetic hearing among the older and wealthier Jewish establishment in the United States.

This changed attitude enabled Weizmann in 1929 to achieve the establishment of a Jewish agency that would involve world Jewry and in particular American Jewry in the building up of a national home. But by now Weizmann was faced with a British administration that was discovering to its cost that the commitment to the Jew was bringing none of the imperial advantages confidently expected of it. The Arab riots of 1929, fomented by the Grand Mufti Amin el-Husseini, were the turning point in the history of the mandate. Until then the British administrators, though for the most part personally pro-Arab, had worked on the assumption that the interests of the Jewish and Arab communities could be reconciled in a binational state under British supervision. Now they realized that these interests were incompatible. It was impossible to permit the Jews to build up a majority in Palestine and create a Jewish state without condemning a sizable number of Arabs to permanent second-class citizenship. It was equally impossible to satisfy the perfectly reasonable Arab demand for immediate self-government without transforming the national home into a Jewish minority encapsulated in an Arab state.

Ironically, Arab resistance to Zionism might well have been substantially less if the Zionist colonists had been true white settlers comparable to the *colons* in Algeria or the British in Kenya and Rhodesia. The rich Jewish plantation in Rehovot fitted into the pattern of Arab life, whereas the kibbutz (collective farm) or the *moshav* (cooperative village) was a living affront. Where Arabs worked for the Jews they were paid good wages, and they had other social benefits as well, unavailable in the rest of the Arab world.

Between the beginning of 1933 and the end of 1936, 164,000 Jews were allowed into Palestine by the immigration authorities. They were Zionists not by conviction but by compulsion, a quarter of them assimilated Jews, leaders in their trades, industries, and professions. They brought with them an influx of capital. This skilled manpower and scarce capital was Hitler's contribution to the establishment of the state of Israel.

In the early years of the mandate the Arabs had been too disorganized to resist a firm British decision to impose a large Jewish community on the country. But when that decision was not taken, violence began. It soon became clear that in any crisis extremists on both sides would be able to frustrate any compromise solution proposed by the administration, even when it was supported by a mass of moderate Arab and Jewish opinion.

The interaction of Jewish and Arab nationalism put successive high commissioners in a peculiar difficulty. In the years between World War I and World War II every British colonial administrator saw it as his task to advance the peoples for whom he was responsible as rapidly as possible toward local self-government as a stage on the way to complete independence. But in Palestine any such proposals were resisted for different reasons by the leaders of both communities: the Arabs because the proposals fell short of the immediate independence they demanded as of right; the Jews, though they were reluctant to admit this publicly, because it would automatically give the Arab majority control of immigration.

When in 1937 a royal commission headed by Lord Peel recommended partition into a large Arab and a small Jewish state, the Arabs opposed the plan and the Jews accepted, however reluctantly.

As extremist Arabs resorted more and more to terrorism, British policy vacillated until in 1939 a White Paper was issued restricting Jewish immigration for a five-year period to 75,000 a year—at a time of increasing need for a place of refuge for those fleeing Nazi oppression—and limiting the amount of land Jews could buy. In addition it stated that after a ten-year transition period the mandated administration would be replaced by an independent government with an Arab majority.

The politics of the Yishuv (literally, settlement) was dominated by an elite of Russian Jews who ran the Labor party—many of whom had started work on the soil of Eretz Israel before 1914. Through their determined efforts they had succeeded in making a reality of the vision of Jewish settlement in Palestine. On the land and in the trade unions a political and military elite was emerging under whose leadership the refugees could be molded into a Jewish nation ready to prove its nationhood by winning the war of survival.

Revolutionary action has never been taken by moderate majorities, and Palestine was no exception to this rule. The moderate majority in the Yishuv was horrified by this prospect, and many were prepared to postpone the achievement of a Jewish majority in order to avoid it. But the men who ran the labor movement were unrelenting in their refusal to compromise on the immigration issue. The Yishuv must be built up as fast as possible, if necessary by illegal immigration. Their resolution was stiffened by the fanaticism

A mild form of European anti-Semitism at the beginning of the twentieth century.

PUCK.

A HINT TO THE HEBREWS.
HOW THEY MAY MAKE THEMSELVES INDEPENDENT OF THE WATERING PLACE HOTELS.

The exodus to America. Jews, among other immigrants, first set foot on American soil at Ellis Island, New York (above, in 1907). The means of getting there: a crowded ship, such as the S.S. *Westernland*, 1890, shown at right.

of Arab nationalism and the outbreaks of violence by which the Arabs expressed their opposition to any form of compromise with the Zionists. In the strictest sense of the word, theirs was "reaction" against Jewish nationalism. While the Zionist labor movement was a democratic political organization united by common ideals and fighting for a political program, Amin el-Husseini, who led the Arab extremists throughout the mandate, relied on the politics of stealthy violence and mass agitation. His main aim was to browbeat into submission any body of Arab public opinion ready to cooperate with the British and reach a settlement with the Jews.

Under the mandate the Yishuv developed institutions of self-government and learned to manage its economic and social affairs. Most of the efforts of the mandatory authority were concentrated on trying to bring the Arab living standards up to those of the Jews. The Jews were expected to manage and finance their own education, social insurance, and health and welfare services, and to pay the cost of integrating their new immigrants. Though this seemed unjust at the time it was a godsend to the Yishuv, since it was forced to be completely self-reliant. The Jewish community became a state within a state with its own system of justice and its own defense force, the Haganah, which included an excellent intelligence network inside the British Army and the British administration as well as a large resistance movement, by means of which illegal immigrants were brought into the country.

OVERLEAF: The holocaust begins in 1934. Hitler is honored at Bueckeberg Party day.

This ability to maintain self-governing institutions and the habit of expecting no favors had been acquired during generations of suffering in the Pale. But in Russia these had been combined with a deferential acceptance of orders and a strange combination of carefree optimism and fatalistic acceptance of injustice that discouraged collective efforts at self-defense. In the conditions of Palestine the Jew soon learned to be a fighter. That the old tradition dies hard is shown by the firmness with which the Jewish authorities imposed the policy of *havlagah*, or self-restraint, upon the Jewish defense forces during the Arab rioting in the years 1936 to 1939. Attacks by Arabs—who were armed by the Nazis—were to be answered in self-defense, but counterattacking or retaliation was forbidden.

That there was such means of self-defense was largely unknown in the outside world, including the Jews of the Diaspora. Like the British government, they continued to think that military defense depended on the troops of the protecting power.

Inevitably a split developed between the policies advocated by the politicians of the Zionist organization in the Diaspora and those practiced by the leaders of the Yishuv, and this division was personified in the struggle between Weizmann and Ben Gurion. Ben Gurion was able to accept Weizmann's leadership when the problem was how to maximize immigration, how to raise the capital for land purchase and industrial development, how to activate world Jewry and stiffen the British into the necessary resistance to Arab pressure. Weizmann was no socialist, but he was not shocked by any proposal, however extreme, if it could possibly assist large-scale settlement on the land. Many Jewish leaders in the West were appalled by the idea of the kibbutz and wrote off collective settlements as rank communism. Weizmann backed the kibbutz enthusiastically as a method of turning Jewish intellectuals into pioneers and because he realized that a form of ownership must be found for farming land on which no profit could be shown for many years. His support for the Histadrut, the trade-union organization, was equally pragmatic. As a practical Zionist he concentrated on the job of supervising the training of the pioneers, persuading Western Jewry to provide the finances necessary to settlement, and preventing the British government from reneging even on their ambiguous support for the national home provided in the Balfour Declaration.

Often it was a heartbreaking job. Right up to 1933—and indeed beyond—world Jewry was only mildly responsive to the possibilities of the national home, and active Zionists, though no longer a derisory splinter group, particularly in America, were still a small, quarrelsome minority movement. As for the British government, the exalted sense of imperial destiny that had united the war cabinet soon collapsed and was followed by a revulsion against foreign entanglements and a determination to slash government spending and in particular to run the security forces and the colonies on the cheap.

Weizmann had done everything to deepen and clarify the exalted vision of the Lloyd George cabinet. Indeed during the years that led up to the Balfour Declaration he had begun to believe that the British empire and the Jewish people were mysteriously linked by a common destiny which in time would make the Jewish state a seventh dominion. By 1921, when the mandate was finally assigned to Britain, he had committed himself body and soul to this idea and had become not merely the spokesman of world Jewry in its dealings with Britain but the mediator between the two.

It is sometimes suggested that Ben Gurion and the other leaders of the Mapai, the Labor party, disapproved of Weizmann's pro-British attitude. But in fact they were in no sense anti-British. If there had to be a mandatory power, Britain was very much the best choice in their eyes, and under British tutelage they accepted gladly a large part of the British way of life—and administration. As social democrats staunchly opposed to Russian communism, they felt themselves closer to the British trade unions and Labour party than to any other European labor movement. But once it was clear that the British Foreign

21 August 1942. "It is lovely weather and in spite of everything we make the most we can of it by lying on a camp bed in the attic, where the sun shines through an open window." The words and the window are Anne Frank's. Photo by James Caccavo.

Office had decided that the Yishuv should remain a minority in an Arab state, Weizmann's inside position became a weakness and his inability to face a break with Britain an embarrassment to colleagues in Palestine who were already making contingency plans for armed resistance to the occupying power.

The rift between Weizmann and the Yishuv deepened during World War II when he spent four years in Britain and America trying rather unsuccessfully to repeat the scientific contribution to the war effort that had earned him such high political dividends in World War I. In 1945, when he at last arrived in Palestine, the only solid achievement to his credit was the British decision to create a Jewish brigade— four years too late. The effective power in the Yishuv had already passed to Ben Gurion and the young leaders of the Haganah.

Both leaders had reluctantly accepted the principle of partition in 1937. Both had been slow to commit themselves publicly to the demand for a Jewish commonwealth in Palestine, which was for the first time incorporated as official Zionist policy at the Biltmore Conference of 1942. There their agreement ended. Whereas Weizmann, the aging diplomat, dismissed the Biltmore Proclamation as a statement of maximum demand, Ben Gurion accepted it as an immediate program of political action. Directly the war against Hitler had been won, the Yishuv must turn its attention to the British and extract from them a guarantee for the creation of a Jewish state in Palestine, in complete control of its own immigration policy.

The chances of a quick and peaceful triumph were far more favorable than in 1918. As the Anglo-American and Soviet armies moved into Germany and the extermination camps were revealed, a shudder went through Western Jewry and Western Christendom as well. In recruiting support for the Zionist program among gentiles as well as among Jews, the holocaust had an even greater effect than Hitler's Nuremberg Laws a decade previously. For the first time Weizmann's contention that anti-Semitism was endemic in Western civilization and that a Jew could only be safe in his own independent state in his own country received a new significance in the gentile mind when it was argued against the background of Belsen and Auschwitz. By 1945 the Zionists were no longer trying to turn a minority thesis into a majority program but were riding the wave of a mass movement that would at last unify world Jewry behind Herzl's demand that the Great Powers should grant a charter for the Jewish state.

In addition to the guilty consciences of the victorious governments and the readiness of world Jewry to assume financial responsibility, there were two other factors favoring a separate state. First, the supply of suitable settlers, which had been so small after World War I, now seemed inexhaustible. As the refugee camps in occupied Germany were emptied, they were quietly refilled by other refugees escaping from Eastern Europe. And if this source was stopped, as it probably would be by a Russian ban, it would be replaced by a stream coming out of the Arab countries. Second, most of the Arab governments—whose contribution to victory had been undistinguished—were in such disarray that they could not form any united resistance to a clear-cut pro-Jewish policy if it were announced by the Great Powers.

With the Russians as well as the Americans not unsympathetic, all depended on the attitude adopted by Britain, the mandatory power. Under the Churchill wartime government some cabinet consultations had been begun and a committee had even gone so far as to suggest a reconsideration of partition. But after the murder in Cairo of Lord Moyne, British resident minister in the Middle East, by Stern gang terrorists, Churchill ordered these consultations to stop. When the Labour party won the 1945 election the ground was clear for a new declaration of British socialist policy for the Middle East. A few months previously the long-standing Labour support of Zionism had been confirmed by the insertion of a detailed commitment into the election manifesto, and it was expected that the new British policy would include at least a firm repudiation of the 1939 White Paper (whose policy was still in force) as well as a short-term policy of relaxing controls on immigration and land purchase and a long-term commitment to work out a new partition plan.

Ernest Bevin, however, would have none of it. Within a few weeks after entering the Foreign Office he had decided that the new government policy in Palestine must still be based on the White Paper, although this would require the repudiation of the party's solemn pledges to the Jews and a major row

The exodus continues. At the Tel Aviv airport a Russian Jew is greeted, after many years of separation, by his sister. Photo by Sherry Suris.

with the United States. In coming to this conclusion he seems to have been influenced chiefly by the strategic conclusions presented by the Foreign Office and the Chiefs of Staff. The Foreign Office maintained that the Nazi threat during the war, though remote, had only just been warded off. The postwar Soviet threat was much nearer and more acute. No action therefore must be undertaken which would push the Arab governments into the arms of the Russians. Since a partition of Palestine favorable to the Jews would certainly outrage the Arab governments, it could not be contemplated. Along with this general argument the Chiefs of Staff added that, since the Anglo-Egyptian treaty would soon run out, it was necessary to plan the evacuation of the Suez base and transfer it to Palestine. The political regime most suited to a British base

Ernest Bevin (at left) as head of the Foreign Office in the Labor Government (1945), based British policy on the 1938 White Paper, which repudiated the Balfour Declaration. A bitter series of battles led to the establishment of the independent state of Israel, announced in 1948 by David Ben-Gurion (at right), appropriately standing beneath a picture of Theodor Herzl. Photo by Robert Capa.

Chaim Weizmann (1874–1952) (below), a Russian-born Jew who was president of the World Zionist Organization for eleven years and then president of the Hebrew University in Jerusalem, voted in the first national election (1950). He became Israel's first President. Photo by Robert Capa.

OVERLEAF: David Ben-Gurion and Golda Meir led Israel from the 1950s into the 1970s. Ben-Gurion was born in Poland and moved to Israel when he was ten years old. He became Prime Minister in 1949 and continued in that post, with only one brief absence, for fourteen years. Mrs. Meir, born in Kiev, raised in Milwaukee, Wisconsin, and Denver, Colorado, chose Israel as her homeland and followed David Ben-Gurion as Prime Minister in 1963. Photo by Dave Rubinger.

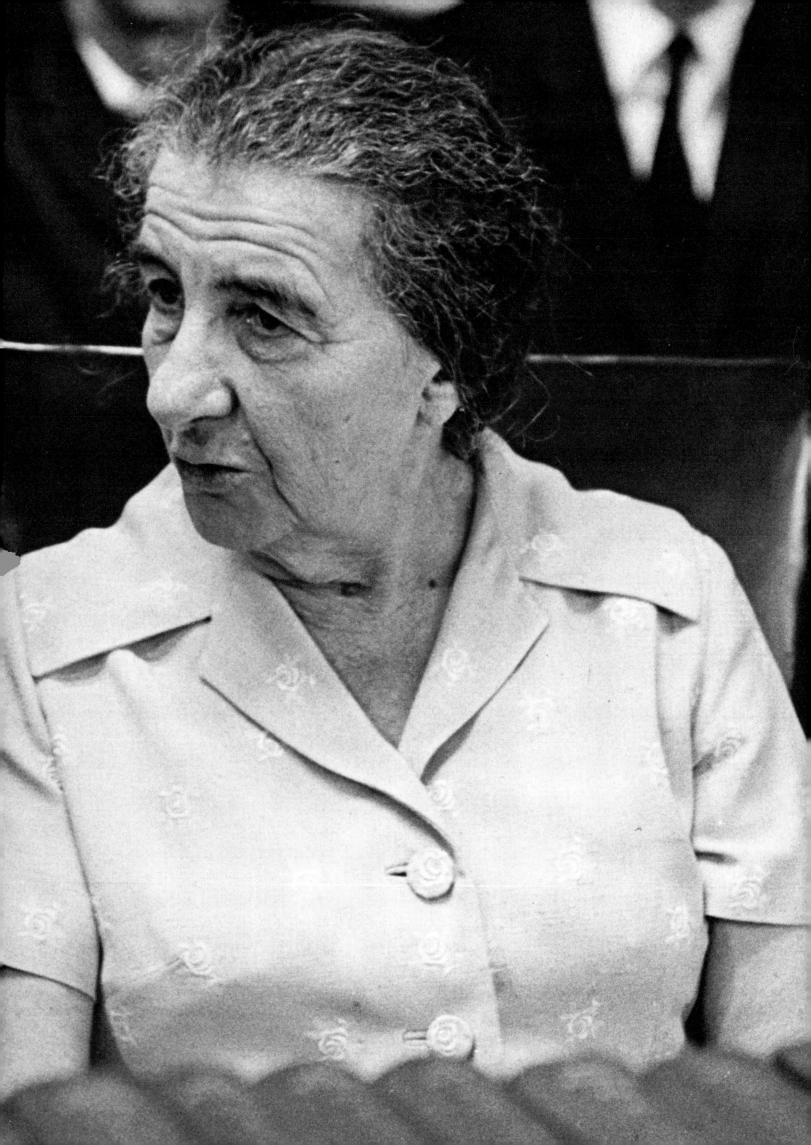

would be an Arab constitutional monarchy run by King Abdullah of Jordan, with the Jews as a national minority inside it.

Realizing how the Americans would react to such proposals, Bevin persuaded President Truman to set up a committee consisting of six Americans and six Englishmen to consider the problem. Since they were for the most part completely uncommitted on the issue, Bevin apparently was confident that they would find for him. But in fact, while recommending that the mandate should continue, they urged that 100,000 refugees should immediately be admitted to Palestine and the land laws abrogated. When these proposals were accepted by the White House and disowned by the British cabinet, the rift between London and Washington was publicly revealed and the British government started an armed campaign to impose its will by smashing the Palestine resistance movement. This produced Jewish reprisals, and it soon became clear that a policy of ruthless repression would be opposed by the Russians as well as the Americans and would leave a weak and economically exhausted Britain in an isolation the country could ill afford.

It was this realization that persuaded Bevin to throw in his hand and transfer the problem to the United Nations. There President Truman, with the whole of American influence behind him, was just able to obtain the necessary two-thirds majority for the partition proposals made by the U.N. Special Committee on Palestine (UNSCOP). The arrangement suggested was impractical and was rendered unworkable by the mandatory government's refusal to assist the United Nations in its implementation. Instead, Bevin announced an end of the mandatory government and a total withdrawal of British forces, and he arranged this in such a way as to give the maximum advantage to the Arabs and cause the maximum chaos on the Jewish side. On the day that the mandate ended and the last British soldier was withdrawn, Palestine was invaded from all sides by Arab armies equipped by Britain and in the case of the Jordanian army officered by the British as well.

Once again we must observe the role in Israel's pre-history played by the force of accident and the force of personality. In terms of the balance of political power at the end of World War II, the stage seemed set in 1945 for the peaceful creation of a Jewish state guaranteed by the victor powers and imposed against the outraged protests of a weak and disunited Arab world. That this peaceful solution was frustrated was the handiwork solely and exclusively of the British government of the time.

The dynamic that enabled the Yishuv to survive the war of independence and become the Israeli nation-state came partly from within the Yishuv itself and partly from the Diaspora, and once again this dynamic was given flesh and blood in the persons of Weizmann and Ben Gurion.

The role of Ben Gurion in the war of independence has already been well established and has been documented in his own autobiographical writings. It was he who took the two vital military decisions, proclaiming first the strategy of no retreat and then, when the vital time had been won, insisting, whatever the risk, that Israel must go on the offensive and hold the initiative throughout the rest of the war. But these military decisions were by no means his most important contributions.

When the six Arab armies invaded Palestine there was no Israeli army but only a resistance movement under divided political control. The Haganah was obedient to the new civil power represented by the cabinet. The Irgun Zvai Leumi and the Stern gang were not. And when the *Altilena,* manned by the Irgun and laden with arms and ammunition, anchored off Tel Aviv, the new state was confronted with a crisis of authority that could have destroyed it. It was Ben Gurion's personal decision that the Irgun must be crushed even at the risk of jeopardizing that priceless cargo, thereby establishing the rule of law in Israel and insuring that the democratic development of the Jewish state should not be impaired by the growth of a terrorist tradition. In order to value Ben Gurion's achievement, we have only to compare the later history of the Irish Republic, where terrorism remained a part of its revolutionary tradition, with that of Israel, where it was crushed at birth. Of all the new states created since World War II, Israel is the only one where military force is completely subject to civilian control.

Mayor of Jerusalem since 1965, Teddy Kolleck is well acquainted with other cities: Vienna, where he was born in 1911; Haifa, to which he emigrated with his parents in 1934; the kibbutz Ein Gev, which he helped found; Istanbul, where during World War II he worked with the Jewish underground and the American and British intelligence organizations; New York, where he bought arms for the Haganah; Washington— he served as Israel's first Minister to the United States. He started the Israel tourist office in 1952 and as Board Chairman developed the Israel Museum in Jerusalem. Photo by Arnold Newman.

The nature of a modern state is such that the state never breaks away completely from its origins. The revolutionary upheaval out of which it emerges remains part of its national tradition and profoundly influences its codes of social behavior and political ethic. It was Ben Gurion who made sure that the new nation, forged in the fire of war, would remain true to the central principle of its Zionist faith. When the war tension was momentarily relaxed and Israel's government found time to formulate its first development plans, the economic position of the country was desperate. Huge areas of cultivated land and citrus groves were going to ruin, deserted by their Arab owners. The export industries were virtually nonexistent, and the economy was being geared almost entirely to war production. In these circumstances it would have been natural for the government to demand a period of respite in order to prepare for the ingathering of the exiles. Ben Gurion would have none of it. From its first day the new Jewish state must accept the flood of refugees, come what may. The economy must not be planned to receive the number of immigrants it could sustain; immigration, whatever its dimensions, must determine the economic policy. This was an act of faith that was against all expert advice and professional economic anticipation. This is what provided the dynamic without which Israel's astonishingly speedy development would have been impossible.

The mass immigration on the scale that Israel accepted in its first ten years would have been utterly disastrous if it had not been accompanied by an influx of capital sufficient to finance the programs of housing, agricultural development, and industrial expansion. In 1948 this influx could come from only one source—the United States. Unless the largest and richest Jewish community in the world mobilized its skill and its wealth to finance the ingathering of the exiles, Israel would suffer speedy economic collapse. But more was required than Jewish assistance. The American government also had to be prepared to give its full backing to the new struggling state.

It is easy to assume that this twofold American support for Israel was inevitable; in fact it was by no means inevitable. The forces in Washington opposed to American recognition of Israel were very formidable, and it was only by a hairbreadth that the plans of the Pentagon and the State Department for abandoning partition and restoring British rule under the Trusteeship Council were thwarted. Second, though at the Biltmore Conference in 1942 American Jewry had committed itself for the first time to the Jewish state, this was an abstract pledge given before the United States had begun to feel anxious about the Russian threat to the Middle East and the future of its own oil supplies. For Israel to survive in 1948 a military victory against the Arabs was not enough. A firm guarantee by the United States was also required to enable the new state to increase its 650,000 inhabitants to the 2 to 3 million necessary for economic and military power.

Weizmann was already old and ailing by 1948. But it was then that he achieved his greatest single diplomatic triumph by winning the moral respect of President Truman and holding him to the course he had set when almost every other pressure in Washington was against him. Inevitably in Israeli history the military victories of Ben Gurion will loom larger than the diplomatic achievements of the man he had ousted from the leadership of the Yishuv. Yet in retrospect we can see that Ben Gurion's victories in the field would have been Pyrrhic indeed if Israel had not been formally anchored to the United States. It is one of the ironies of history that Weizmann, who staked his whole reputation on achieving a Jewish state under British protection, should have consumed his last efforts in building the basis of the American-Israeli alliance.

Israel today:

RIGHT: The Arab quarter of Jerusalem. Photo by Bhupendra Karia.

OVERLEAF: A street scene in Tel Aviv. Photo by Cartier-Bresson.

A Purim celebration in Haifa. Photo by Leonard Freed.

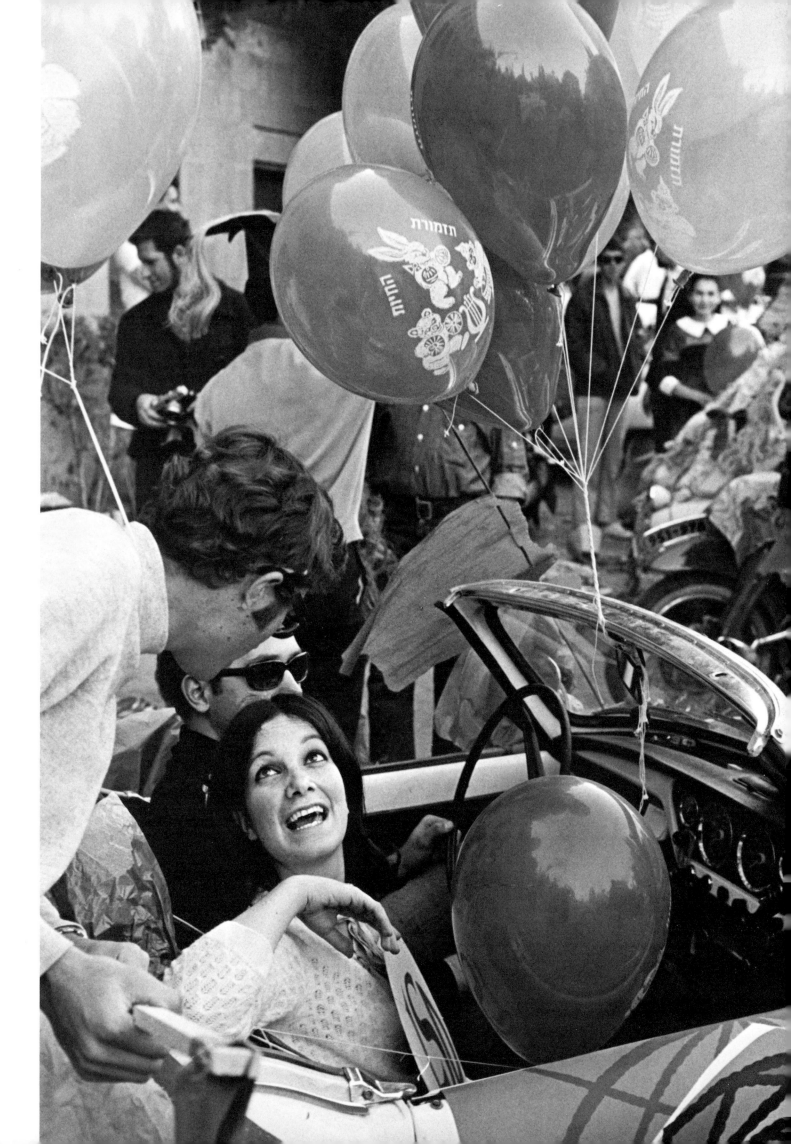

The Israeli Soldier

Photo by Micha Bar Am.

Photo by Franz Goess.

Photo by Boris Carmi.

Photos by Micha Bar Am.

Photo by David Perlmutter.

Yiddish, the Language of Exile

Isaac Bashevis Singer

It is an accepted tenet in both our religious and secular literature that the exile was a calamity for the Jewish people. "And because of our sins we have been exiled from our land." Three times a day the Jew prays that his eyes may see God's return to Zion. Some of the extreme Zionists have expressed the opinion that the almost two-thousand-year period of the Diaspora was nothing more than an error and a void in our history. Others have even tried to belittle what the Jew has created in exile: the Talmud, the Midrash, the Commentaries, the Zohar. Of course, the religious Jew would never concur. The exile might have been a punishment or a state of imprisonment, but within this frame great spiritual works were produced. The ghettos teemed with saints, mystics, men of genius.

I was brought up in an exceedingly orthodox home. My father was the rabbi in the Polish *shtetl* of Leonczyn, where I was born. Later he became the head of a yeshiva in Radzymin, and still later a rabbi in Warsaw on Krochmalna Street. In our house, being a Jew and a man were synonymous. When my father wanted to say, "A man must eat," he would say, "A Jew must eat." It was not chauvinism as we understand it today. My father did not begrudge the nations their lands, their cities, their armies and navies. But since Esau and Ishmael had an opportunity to receive the Torah and repudiated it, they surrendered the best of everything to the Jews. In our house, the yearning for the Messiah and the Holy Land constituted the very air we breathed. The Temple would rise and the holy tongue would be spoken again. Atheism would disappear. The dead would be resurrected. Our risen forefathers would teach Torah to Jewish children and reveal secrets to them which could not be found in any Kabbalistic book. The good gentiles would share in paradise and learn the truth.

The pious Jew could not view the exile as a void or an error. The exile was a link in religious evolution. Even if the exile was its weakest link, it is known that a chain is as strong as its weakest link.

Actually, the exiled Jew had to employ a great deal of his inventiveness to adjust the ideas of the Bible to those of his time. Subconsciously he thought of the Biblical period as an adult thinks of his childhood. Abraham with his two wives, Sarah and Hagar; Isaac, who favored Esau because of the delicacies Esau prepared for his palate; Jacob with two sisters as wives and two concubines; the tribes who sold their brother Joseph into slavery; Simon and Levi, who murdered the people of Shechem; Yehudah, who went to a harlot and in so doing copulated with his daughter-in-law; King David and his passion for Bathsheba and Abigail; Solomon with his thousand wives, one of whom was a daughter of a Pharaoh— all these heroes of the Bible were oddly out of tune with the concepts of holiness that the Jews in exile had developed. The Talmud and Commentaries continually had to explain and defend the behavior of the Biblical heroes, their primitivism, their lust for life, and their "gentile" traits.

Photo by Izis.

As a pupil in the *cheder*, the Hebrew school, raised in a house where the notion of righteousness signified the curbing of one's appetites, the immersement in Torah, prayer, Kabbalah, and Hasidism, I never could comprehend why the great men of the Bible were so bodily oriented, so warlike, so paganly hot-blooded. I was still very young when I assailed my parents with questions about those Biblical ancestors who were supposed to be super-saints but in reality seemed not much better than the goyim of our times. My parents constantly assured me that the stories of the Bible were nothing more than fables and that they should not be interpreted literally. Even the Christians of later epochs were embarrassed by the infantile hedonism of the patriarchs, their greed for the flesh, their clannishness, and most of all by the fact that life after death and resurrection were never mentioned in the Old Testament. Christian theologians could never make peace with the idea that the Song of Songs was nothing more than a love poem. In my later years it became clear to me that only in exile did the Jew grow up spiritually. A people who never ceased to fight off their belligerent neighbors could not keep all the commandments of the Torah, and certainly could not have taken upon themselves the countless restrictions that the rabbis had added generation after generation. Moses' demand that the Jews create a kingdom of priests and a holy nation could not have become reality in ancient Israel. The Bible testifies again and again that from a purely religious point of view our history was a failure. Our prophets kept on bemoaning this fact. Our kings, with a few exceptions, served idols and indulged in the abominations of their iniquitous neighbors. The truth is that a people who must fight for its existence and be ever prepared for war cannot live by high religious ideals. The division between the aggressor and the attacked is seldom clear-cut. Christianity has failed not because the Christians are by nature hypocrites, but because they have never abandoned the ambitions of statehood. The kingdom of heaven and the kingdom of earth simply could not go together. The preacher of love and the bearer of the sword are the greatest contrasts the human mind can entertain. Even fighting for a just cause must turn into evil, since so often the innocent are punished for the misdeeds of the guilty.

Jewishness would never have reached its religious heights had the Jews remained in their land. Ceaseless wars and ever-repeating raids and occupations by stronger neighbors would eventually have transformed the Jews into an Arabic tribe. This is a terrible statement to make but a true one nevertheless. If in the eight hundred years of independence ten tribes of Israel were lost, three thousand years of independence would have destroyed or crippled our spiritual heritage. The Jew was able to reach the acme of his religiosity only because for many centuries he was not drafted into any army and did not need to take part in the murderous battles of his captors; because he was almost completely isolated from the nations among whom he subsisted as a despised stranger. Only because the Jews enjoyed a minimum of worldliness could they acquire a maximum of saintliness. The Jew was aware of this and he never aspired to be restored to his former state. His Messianic hopes meant a pan-Jewishness, where all nations would recognize God and submit to His reign. In all the religious disputes between Jews and Christians, the Jew's answer to his adversaries was that if Jesus were really the Messiah, he would have brought to an end bloodshed among his followers. The fact that even popes waged war and instigated battles among Christians was the Jew's mightiest argument against all Christian contentions that Jesus had saved the world. The Christians have never found an answer to this and never will.

I was born and brought up in a time when the Enlightenment had its greatest victory among the Jews. In a sense, Poland was the last fortress of what the gentiles call the Talmudic Jew. The Enlightenment came to the Jews in Germany and even to Lithuania scores of years before it reached Poland. Hasidism preserved the piety of the Polish Jews for the longest period. But in my time Hasidism was already on the wane, and the ever-encroaching Enlightenment succeeded it in its two schools—the one that preached assimilation and the other that encouraged a new form of Jewish nationalism. Zionism was a product of the latter.

Yiddish theater in New York. George Jessel (1898–   ) stars in *The Jazz Singer*—a 1925 poster. He had Walter Winchell as his first singing partner and toured with Eddie Cantor in Gus Edwards' Vaudeville Acts before he was twelve. Jessel appeared in dramas, wrote and appeared in musicals, worked with Twentieth Century-Fox for twenty years as producer and writer, and became the most wanted MC and toastmaster.

דער סוקסעם פון ניו־יארק - באסטאן - שיקאגא!

אלבערט לואים צוזאמען מיט סעם העבריים פרעזענטירען

דזשארדזש דזשעסעל

אין

דער דזשעזז זינגער

א קאמעדי דראמא פון אידישען לעבען אין אמעריקא

פון שמשון רייפעלסאן

נעשפילט צו אוזספארקופטע הויזער א גאנצען סיזאן אין קארם טהעאטער, ניו יארק

OVERLEAF: Hasidic children gather in Brooklyn's Prospect Park. Photo by Leonard Freed.

Since at an early age I forsook the code of laws according to which I was raised, and assimilation never appealed to me, I became a Zionist automatically. But I always realized that Zionism was and must remain a secular movement. Regardless of how much a Jewish state would tolerate the religious Jew, it would not be the Jewish state he has prayed for in the long night of exile. The proud Jew who defends his country, defies his enemies, seeks friends among the nations, and tries to emulate their cultures brings the Jew back to his Biblical beginnings, not to the End of Days. He is compelled to make an end to his isolation, to his feeling of uniqueness, his abhorrence of the pagan world and its pleasures, which sustained him for the last two thousand years of his history. There is a contradiction between Jewish exile and Jewish statehood that can never be ignored or glossed over. Even though I have never been an active Zionist, I have been bothered by this historical paradox.

Being brought up as an exiled Jew, I never felt that I was to blame for the actions of my gentile co-citizens. Until I was about twelve years old, I was a citizen of Russia. It never occurred to me that I was responsible for the Czar's conquests in Middle Asia or for the war with Japan. When Poland gained its independence I never felt that I was guilty for the way the Polish government acted toward the Ukrainians, White Russians, and certainly not for their mistreatment of us Jews. I identify myself with the United States more than I ever did with the Russians or Poles, but even here I do not have the feeling that it is I who took California away from the Mexicans.

To the exiled Jew, politics was unkosher. I was happy as a boy when I read about Kerenski's revolution in Russia and the downfall of the Czar, but it never dawned on me for a minute that it was *my* revolution. Later on came the October Revolution, the pogroms in the Ukraine, the Communists' persecution of all Jews who did not agree one hundred per cent with their program, and all that I could feel was the eternal Jewish revulsion for violence.

The revolution in Russia and the Balfour Declaration came almost at the same time, and this was also the time that I decided my fate as a writer. In the city of Warsaw where my father was a rabbi, Russian, then German, and Polish had been the official languages since the time of my birth, but I did not speak one of them properly. My choice had to be between Yiddish and Hebrew, but neither of them was then a worldly language in the accepted sense of the word. In 1918, Hebrew was still a language of prophets, of religious books, and of authors who preached nationalism, worldliness, and secularism in a Biblical language and style. Hebrew had many festive and solemn idioms but not enough everyday words and no technological ones. After many trials I decided that I could not convey in Hebrew a conversation between a boy and a girl on Krochmalna Street or even the talk used by the litigants who came to my father's courtroom. I turned to Yiddish, but I soon realized that this language had limitations and peculiarities inherent perhaps to no other language. Yiddish was never spoken by military men, police, people of power and of influence. It was the language of the tailor, the storekeeper, the Talmud teacher, the rabbi, the matchmaker, the servant girl, but never of the engineer, the scientist, the army officer, the judge, the *grande dame*. No one could have written a *War and Peace*, an *Anna Karenina*, or even a *Crime and Punishment* in Yiddish because no counts, ranking officers, or even university students used Yiddish in their everyday life. Yiddish, however, was the language of the Ashkenasic Jewish exile. It was remarkably appropriate not only to my experience but also to my spirit. Yiddish had a *Weltanschauung* of its own. It was saying, one cannot go through life straight and directly, one can only sneak by, smuggle one's way through it. The leitmotif of Yiddish was, that if a day passes without a misfortune it is a miracle from heaven. This is how the Jew in Eastern Europe thought and felt whether he was rich, half poor, or a pauper. The poverty lies in the very marrow of this tongue. It is the language of those who are afraid, not of those who arouse fear.

During the years when I was becoming a writer, both Hebrew and Yiddish made an effort to free themselves of their linguistic boundaries. In the last fifty years Hebrew has become the official language of a state, a language used in universities, in laboratories, in an army and navy, by bankers and diplomats, and even by Israeli Arabs. In half a century the language has become rejuvenated and worldly. Hebrew words no longer draw associations from the Bible, the Mishnah, the Midrash. It is no longer a holy tongue but a language as secular as English, Russian, or French.

60

Avoiding the camera. Photo by Douglas Villiers.

The leftist Yiddishists tried to identify Yiddish with the social revolution. For a short time modernized Yiddish waved the red flag in Russia, in Poland, and in the United States; it preached materialism, bloody uprisings, barricades. In their jargon a rabbi became a clerical; a merchant, a bourgeois; a wealthy man, an exploiter; a peasant, a kulak. Russia had promised its Jews a Yiddishist cultural autonomy and even an autonomic republic—Birobidzhan. The works of Marx, Lenin, Bukharin, and Stalin were translated into Yiddish. The Hebrew words used in Yiddish were written phonetically. A number of letters of our old Jewish alphabet were liquidated. In Yiddish, which was for hundreds of years the language of the *shtetl*, poems and essays were published that condemned the *shtetl* and its culture to oblivion. But the powers that decide the fate of things decided that this kind of Yiddish flourishing should not endure. Stalin's anti-Semitism and the Russian policy of supporting the enemies of the Jews all over the world finished, once and for all, the hopes of the Yiddish Communists in Soviet Russia and everywhere else. It seems to be the destiny of Yiddish to remain what it always has been, a language of exile.

If one chooses to, one can say that Hebrew succeeded and Yiddish failed, but for me Yiddish is far from being a failure. By discarding its foreign entrappings, its worldly chaff, and preserving the vitamins and hormones that nourished it for generations, Yiddish is again slowly becoming what it was in its beginning—a language of Jewishness, the expression of those who still view human behavior from the point of view of kosher and non-kosher, permitted and forbidden.

For me and for many other Jews, both in Israel and in the Diaspora, the exile and its various cultural media are still fulfilling their historical mission. Without two thousand years of total dedication to our heritage, neither Jews nor Israelis would exist today. As for Yiddish, it was and still is the language of study in a great many yeshivahs all over the world. It is still spoken by the Hasidim in the Mea' Shearim quarter of Jerusalem and by many other Ashkenazic Jews who adhere to the teachings of the Talmud and the *Shulchan Aruch*, to the wisdom of Mussar and the mysteries of the Kabbalah. To many Jews to whom Hebrew will remain forever a holy tongue to be used only in religious ceremonies, Yiddish may serve as the everyday language of *Yiddishkeit*. As a matter of fact, Yiddish may become an esoteric language. At the time when the Talmud was written Aramaic was considered a secular language. According to the Talmud, the angels don't understand Aramaic. But in the Middle Ages, when Hebrew was known to many and Aramaic to a few, the latter became the linguistic medium of the Kabbalist and therefore also of the angels, seraphim, cherubim, and *arelim*. It is quite possible that the Moshe de Leon of the future may choose to write his "Zohar" in Yiddish.

Strange as this may sound, Yiddish literature has better chances to remain Jewish in content and form than modern Hebrew literature, which tries so hard to follow the literary vogues of the gentiles and to take over all their idiosyncrasies. As a Jewish writer, I am shocked to see modern Hebrew literature becoming more and more worldly. The modern Jew's ambition to be "like all nations" at a time when the nations themselves are becoming a hodgepodge of cultures, a generation like that which built the tower of Babel, deprives his literature of the very juices that sustained its vitality.

Like my pious ancestors, I am waiting for a miracle, for a messiah and a redemption. Powers must arise that will instill a new purpose in our lives, a new faith, and new reservoirs of individuality. An order must come in which peoples will cooperate economically and still uphold their individual traditions. A time must arrive when cultures will have no need of armies to maintain their uniqueness and when the majorities will no longer attempt to swallow up the minorities. I cling to Yiddish because this language conveys my disbelief in worldly achievements and expresses my hope for redemption. When all nations realize that they are in exile, exile will cease to be; when majorities discover that they too are minorities, the minority will be the rule and not the exception. The Yiddish-speaking Jew, his fear of physical and spiritual effacement, his desperate effort to sustain the values and the languages of his history, his struggle for independence and his actual dependence on the good will of others—this Jew symbolizes to me the whole human species. Man must be both himself and an integrated part of the whole, loyal to his own home

Dancing at an orthodox wedding—Williamsburg, New York. Photo by Leonard Freed.

and origin and deeply cognizant of the origin of others. He must possess both the wisdom of doubt and the fire of faith. In a world where we are all basically strangers, the commandment "And thou shalt love the stranger" is not just an altruistic wish but the very core of our existence.

Jewish art in general, and Yiddish art in particular, must express these truths. To the Yiddish artist yesterday is as actual as today. Those who died are not dead. Destroyed cities still throng with life. For me and those like myself, the two thousand years of exile have not been a dark passage into nowhere but a grand experiment in upholding a people only on spiritual values. Even though we have attained the land we longed for and revived the Hebrew language, this experiment is far from being concluded.

The Hitlers, the Mussolinis, and the Stalins turn to dust, but the works of the spirit are ever imbued with new life. Such mighty empires as the Assyrian and the Babylonian left nothing to posterity but their names and some crumbling artifacts, but the children of Israel have been creative for thousands of years and have even performed the miracle of national rebirth. To me, the Jew and his history lead the way for the future.

I am not exaggerating when I say that, of all Jews, those who spoke Yiddish were and still are the least known. But the very fact of acknowledging that for generations Yiddish was despised should serve as a sign that great treasures of folklore, wisdom, and uniqueness are hidden in it. Yiddish shared and is still sharing the lot of the Jew who resigned from the promises of this world, its vanities, and its wickedness. He will remain hidden until there will be justice for all. A lot of what is to be learned about this Jew can be found in Yiddish literature.

Some "Meta-Rabbis"

George Steiner

Generalizations in intellectual history and sociology are always vulnerable. This is even more the case when we are dealing with a phenomenon as complex, as innerly diverse, as the legacy of the Diaspora. But if one puts forward a generalized hypothesis concerning the special genius of the Jewish contribution to the substance and emotional climate of modern culture, it is not with any aim to rigorous proof. One hopes to bring certain elements into a possible configuration, if only to make our doubts more fruitful and our questions more sharply focused.

I want to ask whether certain ethnic constants, certain characteristic similarities of voice and intellectual supposition, are common to the major political, psychological, philosophical systems and visions of reality put forward by Jews in the later nineteenth and twentieth centuries. Underlying this question is the fact, at once flattering and problematic, that the Jewish element has been largely dominant in the revolutions of thought and of sensibility experienced by Western man over these last one hundred and twenty-five years. Without Marx or Freud, without Einstein or Kafka, without Schönberg or Wittgenstein, the spirit of modernity, the reflexes of argument and uncertainty whereby we conduct our inner lives, would not be conceivable.

Marcel Proust (1871–1922), twenty-one years old, at Neuilly (RIGHT). Twenty-one years later the first book of *Remembrance of Things Past* was published.

The opening of the ghetto brought on by the Enlightenment, by the French Revolution, and above all by Napoleonic intervention released intense nervous and cerebral energies. A millennium of ingathering, of intellectual and psychological compression, was broken open, almost explosively, in a few decades. The space of habit, the customs of feeling and self-definition, which separated Marx and Heine from their grandparents were literally vast. Baptism was often no more than an external, in certain respects trivial, symptom of an abrupt emancipation and entry into the gentile world. Yet however dramatic the break—and in many individual lives it provoked bitter, nearly schizophrenic instabilities—the emancipated Jew carried with him powerful and characteristic burdens or privileges of inheritance. It is these, I suggest, that determine, though often in an indirect, perhaps parodistic way, the direction and quality of the Jewish intellectual achievement after 1850.

The culture of the ghetto was doubtless more complex and locally varied than any but the specialist realizes. Life in the Jewish quarter of Venice, where the term "ghetto" originated, obviously differed from that in the *Altstadt* of Prague. There were, nevertheless, shared characteristics and styles of consciousness. Barred from political-social action, its very identity and survival riveted to the transmission of Torah and Talmud, the life of thought and of feeling in the Jewish community was primordially verbal and textual. The written word and the ever-proliferating but vital context of commentary and critique that surrounded the canonic statement concentrated the essential energies of Jewish being. The analysis, the elucidation of speech-acts, many of them immensely old and obscure, was the natural mode of moral and intellectual doing. The dramas of personality, the violence, the attainment of fame, which attended political, military, and artistic deeds in the Christian world, had their counterpart in Judaism. But that counterpart was, to an overwhelming degree, verbal. Thought was action; critique was creation. Exiled from the material temple, the Jewish community gathered and survived in the indestructible house of words.

That the Diaspora developed strong local roots is beyond question. The history of Polish Judaism, of the Rhineland Jewish centers, of Jewish life in the Provence—each is a case in point. It is nonetheless true to say that Jewish existence, even during periods of physical safety and material progress, turned on a central tradition of exile. Unreal, allegoric as it might seem, the notion of a true home elsewhere, of a return to that home under Messianic dispensation, deeply marked the Jewish temper. Thus, in a manner singular to itself, the Judaism of the Diaspora cultivated roots not in space—all space outside Israel being that of banishment, of temporary ostracism—but in time. The Jewish homeland was not a piece of ground but a continuity of history. Very nearly by definition, the thinking Jew could not be at home in the present. "Now" was always alien. He was domiciled either in the distant past or in the promise of the future—hence a particular Jewish affinity to the exercise of remembrance, of etiology (the effort of intellect and sensibility to locate distant antecedents), and to the prophetic mode. For the Jew of the ghetto, native ground was one of remembrance and futurity.

Under the stress of altering historical conditions, Jewish law and practice had to be expanded, qualified, adapted via an incessant process of "translation" and interpretative metamorphosis. The intelligence of the Diaspora evolved by virtue of a constant interplay, often sophistic and agonizingly over-ingenious, between the canonic propositions of eternal truths and the imperative requirement of local, circumstantial application. But the vision remained a totality. To the believing Jew no aspect of life—economic, social, psychological—could be immune from the reach and pertinence of the Law. At whatever price of mental agility, the novelties and challenges of a changing world had to be comprehended within the bounds of a unified, unalterably coherent vision. What is more: the new had in some way to be seen as foretold, as logically consequent on the rubrics of the past. Like the ghetto itself, Judaism, however physically confined, was a systematic unity, an organic whole giving a universal valuation to individual life and event, or it was nothing.

An intense, perhaps pathological concentration on the life of the word, a profound historicity and bias to historical diagnosis, a commitment to analytic totality, to the ordering of all phenomena under unifying laws and principles of prediction—these three traits accompanied the Jewish intelligentsia as it entered gentile culture. They were, in crucial respects, to inspire and characterize the formidable contributions of Jewish thinkers, scholars, and artists to the sum of the modern. These traits, moreover, form a basis of analogy among Jewish accomplishments in fields that are otherwise evidently and necessarily different: in political theory and in logic, in linguistics and in music, in mathematics and in fiction.

The relations of Marxism and revolutionary socialism to Judaism, relations so frequently self-destructive, are being looked at elsewhere in this volume. It is both obvious and of primary significance that the utopian eschatology of Marxism, its theory of history and promise of a kingdom of justice for man, are, from Marx himself to Trotsky and Ernst Bloch, shot through with the idiom and sensibility of the Messianic. When Marx, in the 1844 manuscripts, envisions a system in which man will not exchange material counters but "love for love and trust for trust," he is all but paraphrasing Deutero-Isaiah. When Bloch, in the *Geist der Utopie* (1918), speaks of the meaning of history and the human condition as compacted in the mystery of the future tense and the enigma of hope, he is closely echoing both orthodox and Kabbalist thought. But the point I want to make here is a narrower one. In Marx's life and practice, in the ironic distaste for direct physical action that marked his relations to Lassalle and Bakunin, we observe the obsession with the written word that characterizes and indeed typifies a rabbinic inheritance. Marx made of the reading room of the British Museum his empire. From his writing desk, amid accumulations of political pamphlets, factory-inspection reports, parliamentary blue books, parish registers, law records, local agricultural and industrial surveys, he poured out an inexhaustible legion of words—crabbed, spiky, encumbered—but informed even at their most technical or polemic by a kind of Talmudic trust in the supreme dignity of text and exegesis. Furniture and clothing were often in pawn; Jenny Marx went to prison for debt. But when the life-saving five-pound note came from Engels, Marx took off to hunt for more books. The composition of a master text, the analysis and critique of man's historical destiny, the achievement of a total, logically knit code and creed for social behavior—these were the aims of dialectical materialism, as they had been the aims of the Torah and of the legislative, predictive commentaries it generated. Even Marx's notorious "final solution," his wish to see the Jew absorbed into the anonymity of mankind, is only a parodistic inversion of the prophetic image of a last gathering and confluence of all men at the hour of redemption.

Psychoanalysis is defined, of course, both by its focus on language and by its "radical" historicism —that is, by its endeavor to trace the genesis of current reality back to the roots of a remote past. The belief that the externals of language form a deceptive surface, that there are successive levels of meaning leading to an authentic, deep-buried core, is not, to be sure, exclusive to Judaism. It has its pronounced role in Gnosticism and Christian scholasticism. But Talmudic exegesis and the elaborate investigations of the Kabbalists into the polysemic nature of the human word, indeed of the individual alphabetic sign, have given the whole technique of "deep reading," of "listening in depth," a distinct strength. Whether there are forty-nine planes of signification to every word or seventy-two, one fact is utterly obvious in the Kabbalistic tradition: true meaning lies far below the surface of discourse and text, but it can be teased out, in part at least, by assiduous decipherment. On a less mystical, less literalist or numerological basis, the same view underlies the constant scrutiny, the reinterpretative commentary on and analytic paraphrase of the Law in the rabbinic practice and in the daily personal existence of the observant Jew. The maneuver from "this is what it says" to "but what does it mean, what is it *really* trying to tell us or to hide from us?" was ingrained in the Jewish cast of mind, as was also the intuition that seemingly casual or enigmatic modes of utterance—jokes, riddles, puns, the apparently accidental collocation of letters and syllables in names— might contain profound, elusive sense.

Psychoanalysis seeks to give to this view of human speech a methodological, scientific framework. It attempts to locate the ambiguous, pluralistic, often self-deceiving nature of what we say, to others as well

Two who changed the world. Karl Marx (1818–
1883), German political philosopher; Sigmund
Freud (1856–1930), Austrian neurologist and
psychoanalyst (at right).

as to ourselves, in the vertical architecture of consciousness. Like the Talmudic exegetist, like the Kabbalist bent over the word so as to catch its inner, vital energies of secret truth, the analyst listens to the rush or limp of the patient's speech, endeavoring to pierce its illusory surface and decode. The analyst too has been (with a few striking exceptions) or still is a Jew. From Freud to the present, the entire psychoanalytic movement has been overwhelmingly Jewish, not only in its personnel but in its habits of expression, personal behavior, and wit. Freud was acutely and uncomfortably aware of the fact. The bitter complexity of his relation to Jung was that of a Jew who had hoped to find a commanding ally, a successor perhaps, in the gentile camp. Centrally conscious of his own Jewishness but resolved to break the mold of that condition in order to achieve an objective, universally applicable therapeutic and theory of man, Freud performed characteristic evasive moves. In the preface to the Hebrew edition of *Totem and Taboo* (1930) he declared himself "completely estranged from the religion of his fathers," yet his answer to the question, "What is left in you that is Jewish?" would be, "A very great deal, and probably its very essence." What was this essence? "The scientific mind," said Freud, the insistence on a rational analysis and account of reality. One recalls the strange formulation in the *New Introductory Lectures to Psychoanalysis:* "Our best hope for the future is that intellect—the scientific spirit, reason—may in process of time establish a dictatorship in the mental life of man."

Although a passion for rational insight and abstraction is undoubtedly a part of the Jewish mentality, Freud's statement is patently defensive. His "essential" Jewishness was of a much deeper, more troubling

intensity. It found expression in his mimetic relationship to the figure of Moses, the sovereign but solitary leader marshaling a great movement toward a promised land of human liberation and truth but being plagued on the way by mutiny, calumny, and betrayal by those closest to him. It found expression, above all, in the character of psychoanalysis itself, which is not an objective science with a verifiable basis in neurophysiology but a hermeneutic, an art of linguistic critique and decipherment, and which leads to an archaeology of the human spirit. Freud's account of the psyche as a product and a carrier of tragic antecedents—the murder of the father in the primal horde, the crime of incest—is a scarcely concealed translation into anthropological terms of the Biblical view of the fall of man. Freud's unmasking of dreams is, as he himself remarked, as old as Joseph and Daniel. Nor could anything be more innately Judaic, more antithetical to libertarian enlightenment, than Freud's somber conviction that the destiny of the individual is largely determined by forces, by energies of remembrance and responsibility, out of an ancient, possibly tribal past. When he put forward the conjecture that Moses was in fact an Egyptian, Freud, subconsciously perhaps, was attempting to shift away from himself and his own people the fatal burden of a unique clairvoyance and of a tragic historicity. But by then it was 1938.

If we dissociate the psychoanalytic movement from the towering but also idiosyncratic presence of Freud, it is legitimate to see psychoanalysis as a special branch of a much wider intellectual, psychological argument. This argument—one might fairly call it "the language revolution"—may well impress future historians as the most important intellectual achievement outside the physical and mathematical sciences (with which it is at some points cognate) of the twentieth century. It involves nothing less than a fundamental investigation of the logical foundations and social structure of speech. It connects the linguistics of Roman Jakobson to the cultural criticism of Karl Kraus; it relates the philosophical language theories of Ludwig Wittgenstein to the art of Franz Kafka and Paul Celan, the master of German poetry after Rilke. It includes the poetics of Walter Benjamin and the transformational generative grammars of Zelig Harris and Noam Chomsky. All of these men are Jews or of Jewish origin. Their work constitutes a second principal chapter, as it were, in the decisive interaction between Judaism and the genius of the spoken and written word.

Fritz Mauthner's *Beiträge zu einer Kritik der Sprache* of 1901–1902 is the seminal text. Educated in the Jewish and "German academic" tradition of reverence for the philosophic or literary *opus*, Mauthner came to experience a radical distrust of language. How could the word adequately comprise and convey the opaque, ever-changing nature of existing things? Was grammar in some manner an anatomy, a just simulacrum of reality, or was it, on the contrary, a rigid and arbitrary screen interposed between ourselves and the dynamic, non- or even anti-logical substance of life? How could an individual communicate facts of feeling and perception obviously singular to himself, obviously rooted in private impulse, when the syntax and vocabulary available to him were public, endlessly shopworn, and eroded into cliché? With an insistence bordering on genius, Mauthner asked the questions to which the most important literature and philosophic speculation of the twentieth century appear to be fragmentary answers. In the year in which the *Kritik* was issued, Hugo von Hofmannsthal—one of that spiritual family of half or baptized Jews who so decisively shaped modern European sensibility—published his *Letter of Lord Chandos*, an inspired fictional statement of the fatal gap between consciousness and word, between the poet's experience of the world and the tyrannical inertness of conventional speech. A few years later Kafka began to compose and (rarely) publish his several "silences." Kafka's close formal kinship with Hasidic parables and the open-ended allegorical techniques of Talmudic and Kabbalistic exegeses has been thoroughly documented. What is less clearly understood is his vital affinity with the general movement of language criticism and grammatically oriented philosophy. Kafka's haunted irony regarding the "indecency" of conventional locutions, his obsession with the abyss of fear or falsehood that underlies the dog-eared formulas of our daily idiom, precisely parallel the language polemics of Kraus. Wittgenstein's celebrated recommendation of silence at the end of his *Tractatus* is exactly concordant with a dozen pronouncements in Kafka's diaries, letters, and fables. When Walter Benjamin, adapting a Kabbalistic trope, defines meaning as that which is enacted "between the lines" of a text, he is echoing Kafka and the grim warning of Kafka's parable on the Sirens that Odysseus may have survived their singing but that no man will escape their silence.

This motif was taken further by Hermann Broch, another key figure in the confrontation between the Judaic tradition and the moral, ethical problems of language. In his *Death of Virgil* (1945), Broch asked whether it was possible for a poet—that is, for any responsible artist—to continue to use words to create beauty when so many of these same words were being used for political lies and bestiality. In the latter part of his life Broch turned increasingly to mathematics, which, together with music, might represent a purer, morally intact code of communication. It would, indeed, be worth inquiring whether there are affinities of a spiritual and cultural order between the revolution in mathematics of Georg Cantor, the musical language of Schönberg, and the linguistic-philosophic achievement of Jewish writers, linguists, and logicians, but I am not competent to do so.

The theme of the destruction of language through inhumanity culminates in the poetry of Celan, a Jew of Rumanian origin, deeply at home in the Hebraic and Talmudic traditions of speech and symbol. Only Celan has, to some degree, been able to find an articulate form in which to enact the experience of the holocaust. In one or two poems—he himself called them "narrows"—the world of Auschwitz finds oblique but just representation. The price is, however, extreme. Celan shivers normal German syntax and breaks individual words into hermetic fragments. Though he stands among the greatest of poets in the German tongue, Celan (who committed suicide at the height of his powers) is also an "anti-poet," an obsessed destroyer of the language in which millions of Jews had been jeered and harried to their deaths. That Jews, traditionally eminent in their regard for the word, hereditary guardians of the text, should become advocates of silence, or "word-breakers," symbolizes the ironic catastrophe of the relations between Jew and German.

But it is not only in the revaluation of language through literature that Jews have played a radical role: it is also in linguistics, properly speaking. From Jakobson to Chomsky, the Jewish element in the language sciences has been large, perhaps predominant. Moreover, it exhibits fascinating links with the exegetic and Kabbalistic past. In the concept of normative universals—of formal structures and constraints, which are the single bedrock of all human tongues however diverse their outward shape—we find a notion central to Jewish speculations on the mystery of Babel. The syntax of Adam was immediate and universal; no ambiguities intervened between the Adamic word and the object or living creature it designated. The rudiments of that original speech lie buried, as it were, under the ruins at Babel. It is the task of the linguist to find these lineaments of an ancient oneness—that is, to determine the phonetic, grammatical, semantic universalities that explain the generation of all tongues from a few primary, necessary molds. As it happens, I believe that this approach has been grossly inflated, that the "universals" so far proposed by transformational generative grammarians are trivial or uncertain. The monistic abstraction of the entire method seems to run counter to the social, locally contingent, idiolectic nature of actual human speech. But the influence and stimulus of Chomsky's ideas and of the movement associated with the new linguistics are enormous—and very obviously Judaic in coloration. This is so not only at the level of biography and professional milieu —Chomsky's first work deals with aspects of Hebrew grammar but fundamentally. Linguistic universalism reflects a belief, old as Akibah, that all meaning is potentially present in a very few primal units—in the signs of the alphabet, in the letters of His name, in the one letter, perhaps, that marks the beginning of Genesis. There is in Jewish feeling an intoxication with oneness and total explanation.

In man's relations to the world, writes Claude Lévi-Strauss, "a simple logical structure underlies and antedates the subsequent complexities of sensory perception." Nature itself "appears more and more made up of structural properties undoubtedly richer although not different in kind from the structural codes

Ludwig Wittgenstein (1889–1951), philosopher. Born in Vienna, educated in Berlin and Cambridge, England, he became a professor at Cambridge University.

Noam Chomsky (1928–   ), theoretical linguist. Born in Philadelphia, a professor at the Massachusetts Institute of Technology.

Claude Lévi-Strauss (1908–   ), anthropologist. Born in Belgium, he studied in France and now teaches there.

Franz Kafka (1883–1924), author. He lived and worked in Prague, Czechoslovakia.

Herbert Marcuse (1898–   ), political philosopher. Born in Berlin, he has lived in the United States since the rise of the Nazis.

Sketches by David Levine.

in which the nervous system translates them, and from the structural properties elaborated by the understanding in order to go back, as much as it can do so, to the original structures of reality." We recognize familiar themes: the presumption of a unitary logical structure underlying the seeming plurality of natural forms, the endeavor of the intellect to move back through history to the archaic, fundamental sources of reality, the proud intimation that mind and world are in essential concordance. These themes constitute the main lines of Lévi-Strauss's anthropology. Like no anthropologist before him, he has taken the word in its generic total sense: Lévi-Straussian anthropology is, literally, the science and logic of man. It builds, selfconsciously, on the foundations laid by Marx and by Freud but declares itself as more comprehensive than either of these two great models of the social and psychological. Going beyond Freud, the *anthropologie structurale* would anchor the dynamics of human consciousness, the rules of feeling and of thought, in the actual neurophysiological architecture of the brain. Transcending Marx, it would include in its systematic analysis of social evolution not only the literate, historically conscious, technological cultures of the West but the entirety of the race. Once more we come up against the hunger of the intellect for rational wholeness, for a model of man as unified and explanatory as was that of the theological contract.

The masters of Claude Lévi-Strauss were Emile Durkheim and Marcel Mauss. Together these three thinkers on man represent that complex tradition of French-Jewish genius to which we also owe Henri Bergson and, on his mother's side, Marcel Proust. There are in this "cluster" not only actual kinships (by marriage) but suggestive affinities of style. In their works the current of analytic ethics characteristic of Judaism seems to reinforce the heritage of the French *moralistes. Tristes Tropiques*, Lévi-Strauss's masterpiece, is immediately related to the normative-moralistic anthropology of Diderot and Rousseau; but the technique of many-leveled decipherments of myth that makes up the massive fabulation of *Mythologiques* is often strikingly Midrashic. Increasingly, moreover, Lévi-Strauss is giving expression to an apocalyptic teleology. *Mythologiques* closes on a vision of utter desolation, of the earth made lifeless by human folly and spinning inert in the indifferent cold of eternity. In a harrowing play on words, Lévi-Strauss suggests that "anthropology," the science of man, will necessarily become "entropology," the science of entropy and of the run-down of the vital energies of our world. But this somber projection is, in fact, a moral judgment. Reflecting on man's wanton massacre of animal species, on his indiscriminate destruction of the ecology, on the hideousness he has made of his environment, Lévi-Strauss anticipates, indeed he appears to long for, retribution. It is as if man, after being banished from the Garden of Eden, has set out in vindictive folly to lay waste on the earth all other "Edens," all other landscapes and "primitive" cultures, which might remind him, however distantly, of a paradise lost. It is a vision instinct with vengeful prophecy, and we recognize its spiritual, stylistic background.

The political economy of Marx, the psychology of Freud, the language philosophy of Kraus and Wittgenstein, the linguistics of Chomsky, the development of a socio-anthropological model of man from Durkheim to Lévi-Strauss—each of these movements has its own structure and limitations. They cannot be confounded in any facile scheme. All I would suggest is that they show certain parallel attributes and impulses rooted in the Jewish past and, more specifically, in the explosive, fatally unstable admixture of that past with the secular emancipation from the ghetto. One might, most usefully, consider these different achievements under a rubric that Freud proposed to Einstein when he wrote: "It may perhaps seem to you as though our theories are a kind of mythology. . . . But does not every science come in the end to be a kind of mythology?" In each of the cases I have cited, the mythological element—in the true sense of the word, meaning an articulate, imaged, self-consistent narrative diagnosis of the origins and shapes of human experience—is paramount. The Marxist myth is one of a long march of oppressed humanity toward the promised land of social justice. Without the Oedipal myth, the myth of the primal patricide in *Totem and Taboo*, or the final mythologizing of Moses into a member of the house of Akhnaton, it is difficult to imagine either Freud's personal fulfillment or the vocabulary of psychoanalysis. Lévi-Strauss describes his own work as a mythology of myths or, by virtue of logical transformation, a myth of all mythologies. Behind these ambitious constructs of intellect seems to lie, though at a great distance, a Hasidic conjecture dear to Kafka, that God created man in order to tell stories.

Yet whatever their structural analogies to theology and exegesis, whatever their hardly disguised borrowings from the metaphors and legends of the Law, these political, therapeutic, philosophic, or anthropological summations of man and history are explicitly agnostic or even anti-religious. And in many crucial instances their Jewish begetters rejected, denied, or simply ignored Judaism. Marx's anti-Semitism is notorious. Freud's attitudes toward Judaism were profoundly ambivalent. So far as I am aware, Lévi-Strauss would repudiate any attempt to relate his anthropological theories and menacing vision to a Jewish identity, which he seems to treat as wholly contingent. Chomsky is, one supposes, resolutely agnostic, and his hostility to Israel borders on the hysterical. If Kafka and Celan made of their Jewishness the active core of their genius as writers, Kraus or Hofmannsthal found their heritage an irrelevance or a positive embarrassment. Indeed, one may argue that from Heine to Proust and Pasternak many of the decisive moments in the modernist movement represent maneuvers of rejection by Jews of their Jewish past.

However strenuous these maneuvers were, they nevertheless marked their man. Jewish self-hatred, the alert instability of an artist or thinker homeless between two worlds, the stress of the convert, the corrosive nostalgia for a repudiated past that may assail the ex-Jew or the "non-Jewish Jew" (Isaac Deutscher's phrase) under pressure of private or public catastrophe—each of these has contributed vividly to the quality of twentieth-century European and American intellectual, artistic sensibility. Marina Tzvetayeva's well-known dictum that "every poet is a Jew" and Jean-Paul Sartre's assertion that the Jew is simply man in an extreme, representative condition of "man-kind" are attempts to express the complex yet graphic overlap between Judaism as a typology of mind and temperament on the one hand and modernism on the other.

But from the Jewish point of view, properly speaking, the consequences, however brilliant, are fatally ambiguous. The genius of the Diaspora has largely determined the directions of contemporary thought. Every thinking man today has come after Freud and Marx, whatever his explicit attitude to their doctrines. Much of Western philosophy is, at present, a set of elaborative or critical footnotes to Wittgenstein. Lévi-Strauss dominates anthropology as Jakobson and Chomsky dominate linguistics. The waiting-rooms of bureaucracy, the opaque terrors in which millions conduct their political existence, are variants on Kafka. But the Jewishness of these acts of spirit lies outside the observance of Judaism. For the educated, speculative individual in the modern West they have made such observance even more unreal. Hence a drastic, unresolved tension and ironic dialectic between the achievements of modern Jews and the inevitably defensive posture of religious or traditionally educated Jews. In rare figures, such as Gershon Scholem, this tension seems to have found resolution or creative poise. In most cases the edges stay raw and self-lacerating.

What is implicit is the subtle but undeniable mechanism of the economy of intellectual resources and investment. The great builders of words and thought to whom I have referred are "meta-rabbis" (though some, particularly with regard to Marx, might even call them false or parodistic messiahs). They are teachers and commentators, they are masters of meaning—but outside the Law. And this externality signifies more than departure or self-banishment. It has meant that the Jewish religious communities they left behind were crucially impoverished. The gifts of diagnosis and of vision that have gone into revolutionary socialism, into psychoanalysis, into transformational linguistics, into social anthropology, might well, under pressure of containment in the ghetto and traditional community, have gone into the further evolution of the Jewish religious and moral substance. They might, as physics would put it, have acted implosively rather than explosively. We do not know. Conceivably it was only the release from Jewish religiosity and the unstable meshing of emancipated Jew with gentile that released the creative forces in a

Marx, a Freud, or a Lévi-Strauss. But the means of an ethnic and social unit are not limitless. What is expended in one way cannot be harnessed in another. The relative thinness of the modern phase in Jewish religious thought, the stasis that seems to affect so many aspects of the intellectual and symbolic life of the practicing Jew, may be an inevitable concomitant of the wealth and impetus of the Jewishness outside Judaism: "meta-rabbis" instead of rabbis, rational mythologists in the place of expositors of the Law. But, as Kafka's parable of the gates of the Law states unsparingly, the loss is twofold. Whatever their personal eminence and creative reach, the "meta-rabbis" have remained outsiders, men who are, at decisive junctures, only guests in their own skin. Much in their work, even at its finest, shows this distortion ("alienation" is Marx's password) and the extremism that comes of being, to some degree, stranger to one's own shadow. The very condition of Western Judaism was one of exile. But the high masters of modernity have been exiles twice over: from their Jewish past and, therefore, from a fundamental strain in their own being. There is a Diaspora within the Diaspora. It has proved to be one of the most creative but also tragic episodes in the history of the Jew and of rational man.

Of that of which one cannot speak one must be silent, urged Wittgenstein. There has always been a Jewish alternative: of that of which one cannot speak one must sing.

Albert Einstein (1879–1955), German-Swiss theoretical physicist.

The Revolutionaries

Walter Laqueur

For about a century and a half Jews have played a leading role in the revolutionary movement in Europe and, more recently, in the United States. The list is long—it includes Karl Marx and Moses Hess, Ferdinand Lassalle, Eduard Bernstein, and Rosa Luxemburg, many leaders of the radical left in Russia, many American anarchists, socialists, and communists, most of the leaders of socialism and communism in Austria, Hungary, and other East European countries. Even in France, Italy, and Holland, Jews have played a prominent part in the party of the revolution. In our time many of the thinkers idolized by the New Left, such as Georg Lukács, Ernst Bloch, and Herbert Marcuse, have been Jews. The facts are abundantly known but they have been differently interpreted. The anti-Semites have traditionally regarded this high incidence of Jews in the revolutionary movement as proof of a world-wide conspiracy to subjugate the gentiles. Their view is in a way less surprising than the fact that most Jews have preferred to ignore the phenomenon, or, at best, approached it self-consciously and with great reluctance.

One can think of various reasons for this strange omission. Most Jewish revolutionaries have regarded their Judaism as an accident of birth; they had not the slightest interest in Jewish affairs or, like Marx, had been baptized at an early age. As far as they were concerned, they were citizens of the world, fighters in the international revolutionary movement with no parochial ties or predilections. The fact that their enemies harped on their Jewish origin seemed to them sheer malevolence and demagoguery, which indeed it frequently was. The non-revolutionary Jews on the other hand were usually embarrassed by the exploits of their lapsed coreligionists, and since these had dissociated themselves so clearly from the Jewish community, they were in no hurry to claim them, as they would identify with Einstein or Freud.

What were the motives that made so many Jews join the radical left and play a prominent role in its leadership? Was there a specific Jewish predisposition toward the left, quite irrespective of "class interest"? It is a complex question, difficult to tackle with detachment, and even the benefit of historical hindsight is only of limited value. What is not really in doubt is the fact that it has always been essentially a phenomenon of the Jewish intelligentsia; while Jews were numerous among the radical left, most Jews were by no means revolutionaries. Once the walls of the ghettos came down, Jews found their way to the forefront of many political parties—left, right, and center. The first major ideologist of the German conservatives, Friedrich Julius Stahl, was born a Jew; so was the most outstanding leader of the Tories in the last century, Benjamin Disraeli. Jews were prominent among the German liberals, the Austrian pan-Germans; they were outstanding in the Hungarian struggle for national liberation and even in the Italian risorgimento. It is beyond doubt, furthermore, that Jews have disappeared by and large from

Student leaders sing the "Internationale" at the Karl Marx memorial in London (1968). Danny (the Red) Cohn-Bendit with Karl Dietrich Wolf of Germany and Tariq Ali of England on his right and Yasuo Ishii of Japan at his left.

leading positions in the Communist parties both East and West, though there are still many of them today among the marginal groups and the sectarians, the short-lived New Left factions and the Trotskyites. This is an interesting process with an inner logic of its own, though one would wait in vain for comments on the subject by those involved. But even if Jews have disappeared or were squeezed out of central positions on the radical left, there is still a great deal of sympathy for the party of revolution among Jews, and since this is quite unconnected with their position in society—the American-Jewish intelligentsia is far more open to radical ideas than the Jewish working-class—this phenomenon is of more than historical interest.

The reasons that made young Jewish intellectuals join the left in the early part of the last century are obvious and hardly need further elaboration. The French Revolution had bestowed freedom on them, but the conservative parties of the right opposed the granting of full civil rights. The economic position of the Jews in Central and Western Europe improved rapidly during the first half of the nineteenth century, but their social and political standing rose much more slowly. The right-wing parties, by and large, still excluded them from their inner circles. The choice of a young Jew who wanted to be active in nineteenth-century politics was limited from the beginning to the left and liberal parties unless he converted, which indeed not a few of them did. In the empire of the czars, where one-half of the Jewish people lived, the choice was even more clear-cut; yet the revolutionary movement among the Jews appeared relatively late—later than among the Russians, the Armenians, the Georgians, and even the Ukrainians, for the simple reason that the Jews were cut off, socially and culturally, from their environment. But once the Jews began to enter the main stream of Russian politics and culture, there was not the slightest doubt that the place for an idealistic Jewish student was on the radical left, not among the liberals. For given a desperate disease —the national and social oppression of the Jewish masses—only a radical cure would do. The only question was whether he (or she) would espouse the cause of world revolution or whether he would find his way into the Jewish revolutionary movement.

The situation west of Russia was different. When a young Jewish intellectual opted for socialism, anti-Semitism hardly seemed to play an important part in his decision. It is more than likely that Marx and Lassalle in their younger days were exposed to an occasional anti-Semitic remark; when Marx asked for the hand of Jenny von Westphalen her family was probably not too happy about the *mésalliance*. In the internal struggles of nineteenth-century socialism Marx was exposed more than once to anti-Jewish attacks, but he shrugged them off, just as Lassalle did, and suffered no lasting political damage. Moses Hess in his younger years had suffered a painful rebuff when an anti-Semite put him in his place after Hess, in a sudden fit of hurrah patriotism, had composed a nationalist hymn. But Hess forgot the incident, or repressed it, and it was only twenty years later, when he had started work on "Rome and Jerusalem," that he suddenly remembered it.

What had begun as a trickle became a stream within a few decades. Soon Jews constituted a majority in the inner councils of Austrian and Hungarian socialism and in Russian social democracy. It was precisely at this time, just before the turn of the century, that outside observers began to study the phenomenon. Was there something peculiar to the Jewish tradition and mental make-up that made them receptive to radical ideals? Wilhelm Liebknecht, the elder statesman of German social democracy, thought there were sound historical reasons. Summarizing the debate on anti-Semitism at the party's annual convention in 1893, Liebknecht said:

> Slavery demoralizes, but it also acts as a purgatory and gives an uplift to those who are strong, it creates rebels and idealists. And so we find precisely as a result of their past experience intense feeling for freedom and justice among Jews and there is more idealism among them, proportionally at any rate, than among non-Jews.

Writing in 1898, Léon Blum, the future leader of French socialism, went even farther back in his search for a specifically Jewish motivation. The central idea of the Jewish religion, he wrote, was that of justice, just as the central idea of Christianity was love and charity. Insofar as the Jews had a collective will, it was toward revolution, for they were strict rationalists and would turn against any idea, any tradition, that could not be justified by reason. Their Messiah was the symbol of eternal justice, and socialism, the transformation of the social order according to reason and justice, was Messianism secularized.

Gustav Mayer, the distinguished historian of German socialism, compared Marx's analysis of early industrial capitalism, with its ravages and inequities, with Isaiah's dire predictions. Gustav Landauer, the prophet of anarchism in Germany, also emphasized the central role of the Messianic idea in this context: "An innermost voice tells us that redemption for the Jews will only come with the redemption of all mankind, and that to wait for the Messiahs and to be the Messiahs of the peoples is one and the same thing."

In our own age Isaac Deutscher has noted the phenomenon of the "non-Jewish Jew": the heretics such as Baruch Spinoza, Heinrich Heine, Karl Marx, Rosa Luxemburg, and Leon Trotsky who found Jewry "too narrow, too archaic, and too constricting." Deutscher's basic idea was not new; fifty years earlier Karl Kautsky had expressed it in an aphorism: the Jews have become an eminently revolutionary factor, but Judaism itself a reactionary force. Deutscher did not believe in a specific Jewish genius but assumed that individual Jews had attained revolutionary eminence not because of any innate inclination but because of their historical position as the outsiders *par excellence:* "They were born and brought up on the borderlines of various epochs," they were of society and yet outside it, and thus able to throw off with less difficulty the shackles of outworn traditions and beliefs. For the very same reason these heretical Jews were the natural pioneers of internationalism. As they had no state of their own they found it easier to accept that the nation-state was becoming an anachronism.

The witnesses quoted so far were, with two exceptions, all Jews; they all assumed that there was something like a Jewish predisposition toward the revolutionary movement, and that it was rooted by and large in the specific Jewish sense of justice and other idealistic motives.

Non-Jewish writers have frequently taken a less sanguine view. Commenting some eighty years ago about the role of Jews in politics, Guglielmo Ferrero, the great Italian historian, noted a curious mixture of idealism and fanaticism that propelled Jews toward revolution. A non-Jewish biographer of Lassalle observed the same phenomenon: when the Jews discarded their religious beliefs, they were likely to turn to the other extreme, to atheism and materialism. Yet another nineteenth-century biographer of Lassalle actually used the term chutzpah, which, for the benefit of non-Jewish readers, he defined as "presence of mind, impertinence, audacity, intrepidity, insolence."

Robert Michels, one of the pioneers of modern political science, was puzzled by the prominence of Jews among the left-wing parties. The Jews had been persecuted for many centuries, and social discrimination against them continued even after they had been given full legal rights. They were highly adaptable, intellectually curious and active, and thus more open than others to embrace new ideas. But this alone was not sufficient to explain the inclination of Jewish intellectuals to join revolutionary parties. Hence he too came to believe in a specific "Jewish predisposition" based on a mixture of motives: moral indignation vis-à-vis individual acts of injustice, which was transformed into a revolutionary urge to change the world; the prophetic element; great self-confidence; consummate dialectical ability—but, on the other hand, great personal ambition, the urge to demonstrate one's talents and achievements, and also rootlessness.

Werner Sombart, the economic historian, went beyond this in his search for specific Jewish motives. He did not deny the high ethical sensitivity of the Jews and their fanatical belief in justice, their Messianic hopes for redemption from evil in this world rather than the next. But it was also true, he said, that the ghetto had bred a one-sided, rootless type of man, thinking and living in abstractions. The modern Jewish *litterateur* who joined the revolutionary movement was the Talmudic Jew in modern attire; they were both essentially strangers to this world. True, the rootlessness made the Jew less self-conscious toward historical tradition, but it also made him less responsible, more inclined to think in logical principles,

81

OVERLEAF: Leon Trotsky (1879–1940), born Lev Davidovich Bronstein, organized the Communist army in 1917, was defeated for party leadership by Stalin in 1924, and was assassinated while in exile in Mexico. Photo by Robert Capa.

doctrinaire systems, rational constructions. But the world was not as the Jewish intellectual thought it was; mankind did not exist in the abstract. It was constituted of individuals and peoples, each with a specific, unique past. Since the Jewish revolutionary had no sense for what had organically developed over a long time, he found it easier than others to criticize the existing order. Since this order had usually not been very good to him, and often treated him as a pariah, it was easy to understand that Jews hated this order and were more eager than others to see it destroyed. Friedrich Nietzsche had once defined this Jewish hate as the worst possible hate. It created ideals and transformed old values. Hence the conclusion that the Jews were fated to play a dual role in modern history. On the one hand, they were the strongest advocates of justice; on the other, they were blind, despite all their intellectual acumen, to the fact that there were limits to the perfection of mankind and its institutions—at least in the foreseeable future.

There is a surprising measure of unanimity among the observers we have quoted about the reasons that induced Jews to join the revolutionary camp. Even the contradictions among them are more apparent than real. When Léon Blum wrote about the Jewish "race" (using the term in the French sense) and its specific inclinations, and when Deutscher denied the existence of a specific "Jewish genius," they really meant one and the same thing—namely, that under specific historical conditions certain traits and attitudes had developed among the Jews. When Sombart wrote about Jewish rootlessness and Deutscher about the vulnerability of Jewish revolutionaries, they again were referring to the very same phenomenon. The only difference was that Sombart regarded it as a weakness and Deutscher as something positive. The Jews might have been uprooted cosmopolitans in the eyes of the average German and Russian, Deutscher would maintain, especially at a time of crisis when nationalist passions were running high. But the Jewish revolutionary was deeply rooted in the highest ideals of mankind, its eternal values. This raises the question whether these revolutionaries would not have been better advised, and ultimately more effective, if they had devoted their considerable energy to the ideology rather than the practice of revolution.

To sum up this part of the argument: many non-Jews and some Jews have mainly attributed discreditable motives to the Jewish intellectuals who joined the revolutionary movement and attained leading positions in it. In their view, they acted out of hurt pride, resentment, thirst for power, and similar motives. Such an appraisal is at best one-sided, at worst grossly unfair; the decisive motive force was the specific Jewish urge for justice together with the questioning, skeptical attitude of Jewish intellectuals toward the established order, their unwillingness to put up with the world as it is as the best of all possible worlds. However, there is no denying that the historical disposition that induced Jewish intellectuals to join revolutionary parties was in some respects a source of weakness. Jewish revolutionaries, more than their non-Jewish comrades, all too often lacked the feeling for the imponderables in politics. They had a tendency to give abstract answers to concrete questions, and they expected internationalism to prevail, where, in actual fact, the trend was toward nationalism. They regarded nationalism as an anachronism; why could men not behave rationally and give up outdated beliefs that presented major obstacles on the road to universal peace and justice? On an abstract level such indignation was perfectly justified, but what good was it to launch a frontal assault against something that was not in their power to change?

The rate of failure and the incidence of personal misfortune among Jewish revolutionaries has been astonishingly high. It could be argued that it was sheer accident that Trotsky, Rosa Luxemburg and Kurt Eisner, Hugo Haase and Leo Jogiches were assassinated, that Otto Bauer, Rudolf Hilferding, and so many others were persecuted and exiled, that two successive generations of Jewish Communists—from Gregory Zinoviev and Leo Kamenev, Karl Radek, Béla Kun, and Heinz Neumann, to Rudolf Slansky and Anna Pauker—were arrested on trumped-up charges by their own comrades and ultimately liquidated, that Paul Levi and Adolf Joffe committed suicide, that Mátyás Rákosi, Hilari Mine, and countless others, after many years of faithful service to the cause of their party, became unpersons from one day to the next. It could be sheer accident, but it is highly unlikely. The fact that most Jewish revolutionaries have come to grief sooner or later does not disprove their beliefs. Perhaps these Jewish revolutionaries were destined to be *dor hamidbar*—those who were not to live to see the promised land. Perhaps they were to be the martyrs, and their blood the seed of the new religion. Seen in this light, their failure had tragic grandeur and will be a source of comfort to the later-day true believer. But it is not at all certain whether this is the correct explanation for what really took place.

The facts are not in dispute. In the 1920s the proportion of Jews among the leadership of the Soviet Communist party was very high: in the 1970s not a single Jew is left in the supreme decision-making bodies of the party. The same applies, *grosso modo,* to Poland, Czechoslovakia, Rumania, and the other East bloc countries. There are very few Jews left in leading positions in Communist parties outside the Soviet bloc. To a certain extent this was a perfectly natural process; it was only to be expected that native elites would sooner or later replace the Jews. Seen from the point of view of the "Jewish masses," the disappearance of the Rákosis, Slanskys, and Anna Paukers was not necessarily an unmitigated disaster. But what matters in the present context is the simple fact that while the Jews played an important role in the early revolutionary struggle, their presence and collaboration were less and less needed once the "building of socialism" came under way.

Anti-Semites may point to this fact as triumphant confirmation for their old thesis about the essentially destructive character of the Jewish race and its inability to play a creative, constructive role. But this is no more true than Deutscher's theory about the "special vulnerability" of Jewish revolutionary leaders, in view of the deeply ingrained anti-Semitic prejudices of the masses, which Communists describe as the evil heritage of capitalism. That such prejudices exist no one will dispute, but their importance is frequently overrated. They did not prevent the soldiers of the Red Army from following Trotsky un-questioningly into the battles of the Russian civil war, just as they did not prevent Disraeli from becoming prime minister or, in our age, Bruno Kreisky from being made chancellor of what was once one of Europe's most anti-Semitic countries, Austria. Jews have been vulnerable, but not only under capitalism; on the contrary, it was precisely in the liberal societies of the nineteenth and twentieth century that they attained the greatest measure of freedom. A Jew could become prime minister in Britain or France; it is quite inconceivable that a Communist of Jewish origin could attain a position of similar eminence in Eastern Europe in the 1970s.

If the political career of Jewish revolutionaries has so often ended in failure and tragedy it is not only the fault of anti-Semitism; Jewish revolutionaries have often failed because of their own shortcomings. It is easy to think of important theoreticians among them, of effective speakers and writers, but their record as national leaders has been anything but impressive. Statesmanship in contrast to theoretizing or agitating involves political instinct, common sense, and foresight as well as other such qualities, and in this respect many Jewish revolutionaries have been found wanting. Their blindness has led them time and again into belittling patriotism, and it has beclouded their judgment as to what was, and what was not, possible to attain in a given situation. Rosa Luxemburg is perhaps a perfect illustration, precisely because she was so gifted, in most respects head and shoulders above her contemporaries in German social democracy. Yet on the essential point she was mistaken, and for that reason her career would have ended in failure even if she had not been assassinated by right-wing terrorists in 1919. She simply did not understand that a revolution as she envisaged it was impossible even in a defeated Germany. With all his intellectual brilliance, Trotsky was so often wrong; up to the end of his life he refused to accept that Stalin had ousted him in the struggle for power with such ease because Stalin was the more accomplished politician.

What so many Jewish revolutionaries lacked was not intelligence but instinct, and they did not even realize their weakness. They were firmly convinced that what mattered above all in political life was a solid grounding in revolutionary theory, analytical ability, effective speechmaking, and rational debate. Not having had a state of their own for two thousand years, it would have been a miracle had Jews shown the political instinct, the responsibility and maturity, particular to other men descending from a sovereign people with centuries-old traditions of statecraft. A few individual geniuses could perhaps overcome this handicap, but a generation of Jewish revolutionaries could not do so. It is just conceivable to imagine a Jewish Rembrandt or Leonardo straight out of the ghetto, having no predecessors, no roots in a past

Rosa Luxemburg (1870–1919), German socialist leader who was killed while under arrest.

tradition, a lonely star on the firmament—there is no accounting for individual genius. But a Jewish school of painting comparable to the Flemish school or the *cinquecento* would have been simply unthinkable. And the same, *grosso modo*, refers to Jews in politics.

The real tragedy of the Jewish revolutionary was not, however, his personal failure. To have been defeated, to have died on behalf of a great cause, is no disgrace. The real tragedy was that the new order that emerged on the ruins of the old system brought little joy to those who lived to see it, and it found its most violent critics among Jewish revolutionaries. Was this the great new world they had fought for? Jews were in the first ranks of the Polish thaw of 1955–56, of the Hungarian freedom fighters of 1956, of the Czech spring of 1967, and of the Soviet liberal opposition of the 1960s. But again, how easy it was for the Communist establishment to isolate and defeat them precisely because they had no popular support. More recently a generation of Jewish revolutionaries found its way to the New Left and the various Trotskyite sects as ideologists, leaders, and militants. But no great gift of prophecy is needed to understand that if by some miracle the New Left or the Trotskyite sects turned into mass movements, they would be squeezed out of them too.

What has been the attitude of the Jewish revolutionary to the people from whom he descended? There have been, broadly speaking, two traditions: on the one hand, Bundism and left-wing Zionism fighting for the realization of their socialist aims from within the Jewish community; on the other, the heritage of Trotsky and Rosa Luxemburg, Jewish revolutionaries who wanted to have as little as possible to do with it. It has been said that the former tradition has mainly prevailed in Eastern Europe, whereas the non-Jewish Jew is a specifically West European phenomenon. But this is less than a half truth. The most eloquent appeals for the huddled, the downtrodden masses of East European Jewry came from West European revolutionary leaders, such as Moses Hess, Bernard Lazare, and Gustav Landauer. On the other hand, most emphatic in their renunciation of specific Jewish preoccupations were East European Jewish revolutionaries half a generation out of the ghetto, such as Rosa Luxemburg and Trotsky, and even before them some of the *Narodniki*, who justified the pogroms as a regrettable necessity. How feelingly did Rosa Luxemburg write about the swallows she watched from her prison cell, how compassionate she was for all men and women suffering hardship and deprivation, but when a friend tried to enlist her sympathy for some persecuted Jews she was told sternly: "Why do you come with your special Jewish sorrows? I feel just as sorry for the wretched Indian victim in Putamayo, the Indian in Africa. . . . I cannot find a special corner in my heart for the ghetto." Trotsky in his autobiography related that from his earliest childhood nationalist passions and prejudices were incomprehensible to him, producing in him a feeling of loathing and moral nausea. What a biographer says about Marx also applies to Trotsky: "that he wanted to declare himself a non-Jew before all the world." Trotsky systematically omitted from his autobiography all references to his Jewish background. Others behaved in a similar way; the more radical in outlook, the more they wanted to dissociate themselves from Judaism and from their fellow-Jews.

Léon Blum (1872–1950), French socialist and briefly premier of France in the 1930s. He attempted to reform agriculture, banking, and industry. Photo by Robert Capa.

Betty Friedan (1921–   ). Her book, *The Feminine Mystique*, and her founding of the National Organization for Women (NOW) initiated the Women's Liberation Movement. Photo by Sherry Suris.

Aesthetically it has not been a pleasing phenomenon, but whether these Jewish revolutionaries should be charged with moral cowardice and treason is a different matter altogether. The problem is, as with anything so complex, that there is no clear, cut-and-dried answer. A man like Marx was already far removed from the Jewish tradition, and what he knew of it did not in the least appeal to him. There was no reason to expect from him, and others like him, any solidarity or even special compassion for his fellow-Jews. As far as he was concerned, he was no more a Jew than a Patagonian; he was—as he saw himself—totally emancipated not only in the legal sense but free of any specific Jewish features. If he published from time to time offensive comments about individual Jews and the Jewish community, basically the whole issue was of no interest to him. Others, however, thought of Marx as a Jew however much he would disclaim it. M. A. Bakunin, commenting on Marx and his other enemies on the left, wrote that "they are all Jews. By tradition and instinct they belong to this restless, intriguing, and exploitative bourgeois nationality." Bakunin was certainly even more restless and intriguing than Marx, and he was also an anti-Semite. But the Jewish revolutionaries who claimed not to be Jews constituted something of a problem even for those of their Aryan comrades who were not anti-Semites. Engelbert Pernerstorfer, a leading Austrian socialist, related the story of a party comrade, an intellectual of the radical left, who when asked to what nation he belonged answered proudly: "To no one." "A wonderful answer for a logician," Pernerstorfer commented, "but everyone comes from some people or other. This man does not want to be a German, nor does he want to admit that he is a Jew." He was a "mixed subject," as Pernerstorfer put it, and "mixed subjects" have seldom inspired confidence.

But is it justified to put the blame mainly on the Jewish heretics for their estrangement from the Jewish community? This raises a wider question—namely, the uneasy relationship between the Jewish intellectual and a community with whose *parnasim* (leaders), their values and policies he has little, if anything, in common. A recent newspaper article by a Jewish writer on the occasion of a European conference of the World Jewish Congress singles the following out "for making a contribution to the enrichment of British and European life: the Rothschilds, the Wolfsons, the Berlins, the Markses, the Sieffs, the Birks, the Josephs . . ." (London *Times,* January 13, 1973). These are well-known names; their bearers, with a few exceptions, have risen to eminence for having made a great deal of money. They have been generous supporters of various worthy causes, Jewish and non-Jewish. But to single them out and not the great thinkers, the argonauts of science, the artists of genius (even if they were not knighted), betrays a set of values of success and achievement which are not the ones of the Jewish intellectual. With this establishment the Jewish revolutionary of 1890 did not feel much affinity, nor do his grandchildren.

Much has been said about the self-hate of Jewish revolutionaries, but again the issue is more complicated than it might appear at first sight. The comments of Marx and Lassalle on Judaism and their fellow-Jews have to be considered in the context of their time—that is, before anti-Semitism appeared as a mass movement on the European scene. The most extreme forms of Jewish self-hatred, moreover, were found not so much among the left as on the right. The Jewish revolutionaries who dissociated themselves from their community cannot fairly be called "traitors to their people"; one cannot betray something one has publicly repudiated. The non-Jewish Jewish revolutionaries had made it abundantly clear that they did no longer belong to the Jewish community, that they did not believe in the existence of a Jewish people, let alone a national revival. But there were Zionist writers equally bitter about the degradation of Jewish existence. It may be worth while to recall that underlying the idea of a Jewish national revival was not the desire to preserve the spirit of the ghetto but to break with it once and for all. What Lassalle wrote as a young man about the liquidation of the Jewish question reminds one of Theodor Herzl's ideas before he came to write the *Judenstaat.* To note these facts is not to embellish the apostasy of successive generations of Jewish revolutionaries but merely to point to obvious facts that cannot be judged in the light of Auschwitz. The non-Jewish Jews assumed that Jewish history had come to an end, or was about to end, an assumption they shared with most nineteenth-century liberals. The difference between them and the Zionists was that the latter believed that, however miserable the lot of the Jewish masses, all hope for a national revival was not lost. Furthermore, the Zionists argued that while it was not impossible that one day all mankind would live in brotherly love, equals in one world state, the Jews could not wait that long—they were in danger of extermination. The Jewish revolutionaries thought that under communism the Jewish question would be solved more or less automatically. The Zionists assumed that national passions would persist for a long time under any foreseeable political and social system. Events have shown that these fears were not unjustified.

So much about the non-Jewish Jew of the Old Left. The non-Jewish Jewish revolutionaries of the New Left and the Trotskyite "groupuscles" have received a fair share of publicity in recent years but their heyday seems already over. It is difficult to write about them with much sympathy for they combine most of the negative features of past generations of Jewish revolutionaries with few, if any, of the achievements of their predecessors. If aggressiveness, intolerance, invective, and chutzpah would have been all there was to Marx, Lassalle, and Trotsky, they would hardly be remembered today. To mention Mark Rudd, Abbie Hoffmann, Jerry Rubin, or Alan Geismar, Alain Krivine and Daniel Cohn-Bendit in one breath with Marx or Lassalle, Trotsky or Rosa Luxemburg, is to invite ridicule. Ernest Mandel, the chief ideologist of Trotskyism, is at best a talented epigone, not someone who has made a major, original contribution to socialist thought.

But it is not just the fact that nature has denied to Cohn-Bendit the intellect of Karl Marx. To be a revolutionary in nineteenth-century Europe, and even after the turn of the century, involved personal hardship and sacrifices, exile, prison, and occasionally death. To be a revolutionary in present-day America, in France or West Germany, implies on the whole no greater risk than corruption by the mass media and the whole climate of radical chic. To be a revolutionary is the fashionable thing; there is no danger to life, safety, property—or future prospects. At the universities it is the new conformism; not to belong to it is not to be with it. Among the left-wing revolutionaries there were, as in other political movements, adventurists and self-seekers, but no one in his right mind would have questioned their dedication and serious purpose. The New Left, with some notable exceptions, lacks seriousness; it seems a repeat performance by hams of a well-known play, bearing out Marx's dictum about great events happening twice, the second time as a farce.

This is not to say that there is no idealism among them, but there is at least an equal measure of boredom underlying their militancy. The offspring of child-centered left-wing families, who grew up intolerant of rules and restrictions, have come to choose, as one observer has put it, revolutionary activity as the Jewish equivalent of juvenile delinquency. Their negative attitude to the Jewish community and their hostility to Israel are not surprising for, like a previous generation of revolutionaries, they think that Jewish history has come to an end, with Auschwitz as an unfortunate accident of history for which capitalism is to be made responsible; and with the state of Israel as an embarrassment to all quasi-progressives. Their attitude seems attuned to the *Zeitgeist*. There is a new internationalism in the air; gentile society has lost its moorings; it has been Judaized, for, like the Jew, it is becoming rootless. Perhaps one should not be too harsh with the Red Diaper Babies, for they grew up in a climate not exactly conducive to the emergence of great thinkers and the steeling of revolutionary heroes. One should not be too harsh for yet another reason. The image of a generation is usually shaped by a few people who for a variety of reasons attract all the limelight. The contemporary Jewish revolutionary has the misfortune to find himself personified in Jerry Rubin and Daniel Cohn-Bendit. There are of course others less flamboyant who have attracted less attention simply because their militancy has been tempered with critical reflection, with learning from past experience, perhaps even with a dose of skepticism about the limits of revolutionary action. But, for all that, they have not become advocates of the *status quo*, and it may well be that the future belongs to them. To assume that the Messianic hope for a better world, the dedication to the struggle against injustice, which inspired successive generations of Jewish revolutionaries, was bound to culminate in Abbie Hoffman and Jerry Rubin is to regard human history as something akin to the theater of the absurd. It is a view of history both profoundly un-Jewish and running against the human grain.

OVERLEAF: Photo by Marc Riboud.

Court Jews

Maksim Litvinov (1876–1951) served as people's commissar for foreign affairs and as Russian ambassador to the United States. He is seen here in November 1933, arriving in New York to negotiate for American recognition of the U.S.S.R.

Bernard Baruch (1870–1965), adviser to Wilson and to Roosevelt in the two world wars, was also a close friend of Winston Churchill.

Clockwise from bottom left

Henry Morgenthau, Jr. (1891–1967), Roosevelt's Hyde Park neighbor, was his Secretary of the Treasury for eleven years. His father had been ambassador to Turkey and to Mexico; his son became a prominent government attorney. (Also pictured, Treasury Under Secretary Daniel Bell.)

Samuel I. Rosenman (1896–1973) served as special counsel to FDR and later to Harry Truman, who in 1946 awarded him a medal for exceptional services. During both administrations his advice was regularly sought.

Arthur J. Goldberg (1908–   ) became President Kennedy's Secretary of Labor, a justice of the Supreme Court, and later, at President Johnson's request, the ambassador to the United Nations. He sought elective office but was defeated in his attempt to become governor of New York State.

Abe Fortas (1910–   ), an able lawyer and intimate of Lyndon B. Johnson, was appointed to the Supreme Court to succeed Arthur Goldberg. Financial indiscretions led to his resignation.

RIGHT: Pierre Mendès-France (1907–   ) achieved the post of premier of France for a brief time, but his political role has been primarily that of a critic. Imprisoned by the Vichy government during World War II, he escaped and joined the Free French Army. Photo by Cartier-Bresson.

BELOW: Arnold Abraham Goodman (1913–   ), at right, was used by both Conservative and Liberal Prime Ministers Edward Heath and Harold Wilson in positions varying from chairmanship of the Arts Council to negotiator with Ian Smith of Rhodesia. Photo by Colin Davey.

OPPOSITE: Henry Kissinger (1923–   ), driven from Germany by the Nazis, became an adviser on foreign affairs to the Rockefeller family and then to President Nixon. His talents earned him the post of Secretary of State to both President Nixon and President Ford, and he shared the 1973 Nobel Peace Prize.

The Vital Choice

Arthur Koestler

When the state of Israel was resurrected after two thousand years, Jews all over the world rejoiced, then carried on business as usual. Their private lives were not affected. They did not realize that this historic event confronted them with a historic decision: either to become citizens of the Jewish state or to abandon the claim to be members of a distinctive Jewish nation, a claim that is the foundation stone of the Mosaic religion.

The dilemma is not of my making; it is implied in the "Proclamation of Independence of the State of Israel," of May 14, 1948, which states:

> Exiled from the land of Israel, the Jewish people remained faithful to it in all the countries of their dispersion, never ceasing to pray and hope for their return and the restoration of national freedom.

Note the terms "exiled," "dispersion," and "national freedom." Do they refer to factual conditions in the life of a "dispersed nation" (the collective equivalent of a "displaced person"), or are they merely part of a religious phraseology? The trouble is that the two meanings are inextricably mixed up. Christianity, Islam, and Buddhism propound doctrines and ethical rules that make no distinction between the believer's nationality and race; the Jewish faith implies membership of a historical nation. "Blessed be the Lord, our God, who led our fathers out of the bondage of Egypt"—every person who repeats that prayer professes to belong to an ancestral race, which automatically sets him apart from the racial and historic past of the people in whose midst he lives. Unlike Christian festivals, which celebrate mystical or mythological events, Jews commemorate landmarks in national history: the exodus from Egypt, the Maccabean revolt, the death of the oppressor Haman, the destruction of the Temple. The Old Testament is first and foremost the narrative of a nation's history; every prayer and ritual observance thus reinforces the Jew's awareness of his national identity.

At the end of the Passover meal, for the last two thousand years, Jews all over the world have drunk a sacred toast to "next year in Jerusalem." *If* a Jew is faithful to his religion he is compelled to regard himself as a person not only with a national past but also with a national future different from that of the gentiles among whom he lives. This refers not only to Zionists but to any member of the Jewish community, whatever his attitude to Zionism, *if* he takes his religion seriously. The fact that he is naïvely unaware, or only half aware in a muddled way, of the secular and racial implications of his creed, and that he indignantly rejects "racial discrimination" if it comes from the other camp, makes the Jewish tradition only the more paradoxical.

Let us face it, racial discrimination works both ways. Even among liberal and enlightened Jews who do not claim to belong to a "chosen race," there is a strong tendency to keep themselves to themselves in marriage, business, and social life. This is only partly due to the pressure of hostile surroundings; an equally important bond is tradition with an ethnic and racial tinge. It is reflected in the discriminatory character of the Jewish attitude to the gentile. That twenty centuries of persecution must leave their marks of suspicion and defensive hostility one takes for granted. But the Jewish attitude to the Stranger in Israel carries an element of rejection that is older than the ghettos; it dates back to the tribal exclusiveness of the Mosaic religion. The Hebrew word *goy* for non-Jews does not merely signify "pagan" or "unbeliever"; it corresponds rather to the Greeks' "barbarian," to our "natives" and "aborigines." It refers not to a religious but to a racial and ethnic distinction. In spite of occasional, and somewhat halfhearted, injunctions to be kind to the Stranger in Israel, the *goy* is treated in the Old Testament with a mixture of hostility, contempt, and pity. Later on, the word lost some of its tribal emotionalism, but it has never entirely lost its derogatory echo.

The point I wish to make is that we are faced with a vicious circle: that a religion with the secular claim of racial exclusiveness must needs create secular repercussions. The Jew's religion sets him apart and invites his being set apart. The archaic, tribal element in it engenders anti-Semitism on the same archaic level. No amount of enlightenment and tolerance, of indignant protests and pious exhortations, can break this vicious circle.

"Anti-Semitism is a disease that spreads apparently according to its own laws: I believe the only fundamental cause of anti-Semitism—it may seem tautological—is that the Jew exists. We seem to carry anti-Semitism in our knapsacks wherever we go." This was said by Chaim Weizmann in summing up the calvary of twenty long centuries. To expect that it will come to a spontaneous end in the twenty-first is to go against historic and psychological evidence. It can only be brought to an end by Jewry itself. But neither Weizmann nor any of the Jewish leaders of our time have had the courage to face this fact and to speak out openly.

The general distinguishing mark of the Jew, what makes him a Jew on his documents and in the eyes of his fellow-citizens, is his religion; and the Jewish religion, unlike any other, is racially discriminatory, nationally segregative, socially tension-creating. When this basic fact—supported by the evidence of the Old Testament and two thousand years of history—is firmly and uncontroversially established in our minds, and the unconscious resistances against accepting it are overcome, then the first step toward solving the problem will have been made.

The operative phrase is "unconscious resistances." Twenty years ago I wrote an essay, "Judah at the Crossroads," in which I set out the foregoing considerations. It was the only essay of mine that the magazine *Encounter* ever refused to print. (It appeared in a collection of essays, *The Trail of the Dinosaur* in 1955.) *Encounter* was at the time edited by my good friend Irving Kristol. He was embarrassed and never explained the reasons for his refusal. Though neither religious nor particularly involved in the Jewish question, he is, I suppose, what is called a good Jew. In other words, his unconscious resistance made the subject taboo, and this attitude seems to me symbolic.

I cannot see any reason to change the view I held at the time, which was shortly after the state of Israel had come into being. I may perhaps mention here that I was not a stranger to the developments leading up to that event. At the age of eighteen, as a student in Vienna, I joined a Zionist dueling fraternity and became one of the cofounders of Vladimir Jabotinsky's Revisionist party in Austria. Three years later, in 1926, I emigrated to Palestine, worked for a while as a *challutz*, a pioneer, in a kibbutz, then as a foreign correspondent and foreign editor of Jabotinsky's daily *Doar Hayom*. In 1929 I returned to

Europe for professional reasons but went back to Palestine for protracted periods during the times of trouble in 1938 and 1945 and during the War of Independence in 1948. The literary by-products of this involvement were a novel, *Thieves in the Night*, and *Promise and Fulfillment*, a history of Palestine from 1917 to 1948. It was while writing this later book that I came to the conclusion that the establishment of the state of Israel created a fundamentally new situation, confronting every Jew with a momentous choice.

Having thus briefly presented my credentials, let me continue with the argument.

We may distinguish between three categories of Jews: the minority of orthodox believers; the larger group of the adherents of a liberalized and diluted version of the Mosaic religion; the largest group of agnostics, who, for reasons of tradition or pride, persist in calling themselves and their children "Jews."

The orthodox believers outside Israel are a small and dwindling minority, and as a social group the remnants of orthodox Jewry no longer carry much weight. But their position is symbolical. Since the destruction of the Temple they have never ceased to pray for the restoration of the Jewish state. On May 14, 1948, their prayer was fulfilled. The logical consequence of the fulfillment of a prayer is that one ceases to repeat it. But if prayers of this kind are no longer repeated, if the mystic yearning for the return to Palestine is eliminated from the Jewish faith, then the very foundation and essence of that faith will have gone. No obstacle prevents any longer the orthodox Jew from obtaining a visa at the Israeli consulate and booking a passage on an Israeli airline. The choice before him is either to be "next year in Jerusalem" or to cease repeating a vow that has become mere lip-service. He can no longer refer to himself with the ritual phrase as living "in exile"—unless he means a self-imposed exile based on economic considerations, which have nothing to do with his religion.

The orthodox position typifies in an extreme form the dilemma that is inherent in any liberalized and reformed version of Judaism. Any attempted reform, however enlightened, that aims at eliminating the essentially racial and national character of Judaism would eliminate its very essence. Take this away—and all that would remain would be a set of archaic dietary prescriptions and tribal laws. It would not be the reform of a religion but its complete emaciation.

Let us now consider the position of that vast majority of contemporary Jewry who display an enlightened or skeptical attitude toward the faith of their ancestors, yet for a number of complex motives persist in confirming their children in that faith and impose on them the "separateness" that it entails. Paradoxically, it is this type of "nondescript" Jew, unable to define his Jewishness in either racial or religious terms, who perpetuates the "Jewish question."

In discussing this central problem, I shall quote from Isaiah Berlin's series of articles, "Jewish Slavery and Emancipation" (*Jewish Chronicle*, June 1950), which has come to be regarded as a classic treatment of the subject. Berlin starts by agreeing that "there is no possible argument against those truly religious Jews to whom the preservation of Judaism as a faith is an absolute obligation to which everything, including life itself, must without hesitation be sacrificed"; and later on he endorses the view that for these "full-blooded" Jews, as it were, the only logical solution is emigration to Israel. He then turns to the "nondescript" category and says:

> But it is not so clear that those who believe in the preservation and transmission of "Jewish values" (which are usually something less than a complete religious faith, but rather an amalgam of attitudes, cultural outlook, racial memories and feelings, personal and social habits) are justified in assuming without question that this form of life is obviously worth saving, even at the unbelievable cost in blood and tears which has made the history of the Jews for two thousand years a dreadful martyrology. Once . . . unreasoning faith is diluted into loyalty to traditional forms of life, even though it be sanctified by history and the suffering and faith of heroes and martyrs in every generation, alternative possibilities can no longer be dismissed out of hand.

Obviously, the "alternative possibility" for the nondescript majority who have outgrown Jewish nationalism and the Jewish religion is to renounce both and to allow themselves to be socially and culturally absorbed by their environment. Yet the psychological resistance against this is enormous. It is rooted in the general human tendency to avoid a painful choice. But equally important emotional factors are spiritual pride, civic courage, the apprehension of being accused of hypocrisy or cowardice, the scars of wounds inflicted in the past, and the reluctance to abandon a mystic destiny, a specifically Jewish mission.

Let me concede at once that psychologically there is every excuse for Jews to be emotional, illogical, and touchy on the question of renunciation, even if they are unable to say what exactly they are reluctant to renounce. But let it also be understood that, while every man has a right to act irrationally and against his own interests, he has no right to act in this way where the future of his children is concerned. I would like to make it clear at this point that my whole line of argument, and the practical conclusions derived from it, are aimed not at the present, but at the next generation, at the decisions men and women must take regarding the future of their children. Once this point is clearly established, a number of objections against the process of assimilation will be automatically removed.

I shall now consider some typical objections that have been raised since I first proposed my solution. They are well summarized in the questions put to me by an interviewer, Mr. Maurice Carr, from the London *Jewish Chronicle* after the publication of *Promise and Fulfillment.*

Question: *When you say categorically that the Wandering Jew must decide either to become an Israeli or to renounce utterly his Jewishness, are you thinking in ultimate or immediate terms?*

Answer: I think that the choice must be made here and now, for the next generation's sake. The time has come for every Jew to ask himself: Do I really consider myself a member of a chosen race destined to return from exile to the Promised Land? . . . If not, what right have I to go on calling myself a Jew and thereby inflicting on my children the stigma of otherliness?

Is your haste in proclaiming the choice between Israel and total abandonment of Jewishness attributable to the fear of new Belsens and Auschwitzes?

Anti-Semitism is growing. Even the British, for all their traditional tolerance, have been affected. . . . But, to my mind, it is not so much the danger of pogroms as the fundamental evil of abnormal environmental pressures from which the Wandering Jew must save himself and the coming generations.

Does it not occur to you that in seeking the will-o'-the-wisp of "normality" and security, runaway Jewry will be sacrificing the distinctive Jewish genius . . . ?

It is undoubtedly true that the stimulus of environmental pressure has produced a greater proportion of intellectuals among Jews than among their host nations. . . . We also know that most great men in literature, art, or politics had an unhappy childhood, were lonely and misunderstood, and that their creative achievements were partly due to their reactions to these pressure-stimuli. But would you recommend parents to give their children deliberately an unhappy childhood in the hope of breeding an Einstein, a Freud, or a Heine? . . . I reject as wholly indefensible the vague Jewish sentiment: "We must go on being persecuted in order to produce geniuses."

Of all the Jews persecuted by Hitler, none suffered such terrible despair as those who had thought to cast off all traces of their own or their father's or their grandmother's Jewishness. In one form or another, might not a similarly cruel fate—far worse than that which can ever befall a real Jew—overtake the would-be ex-Jews?

Whatever one does in life, there is always the chance that something will go wrong. But I am certain that by and large the gentile world will welcome wholehearted Jewish assimilation. . . .

Do you not feel that there is something abject, humiliating, in such a conformist surrender by the minority to the majority? . . . The [ex-Jew] is to bury alive his own traditions and memories, and these memories, unfortunately, include bitter persecution at the hands of those whose ranks he is now joining uninvited. Is that not asking altogether too much?

. . . Surely you do not suggest that resentment should be kept rankling and old hatreds perpetuated? It is, of course, never an easy thing to break with the past, to cast off traditions and memories. But millions of American immigrants have done just that without great effort. And if we accept the fact that anti-Semitism is not a transient phenomenon, then this sacrifice imposes itself to a much higher degree in the case of the Jews than, say, in the case of Italian emigrants to the United States. While the Italians are fleeing from poverty, the Jews must get away from the specter of extermination. It is imperative that the Jews should face up to their responsibilities to their children, whatever the wrench to their own feelings.

Do you believe that Israel . . . is now so "firmly established" that it can get along without further aid from the Diaspora? . . .

In view of the magnitude of the problem Israel is facing in the absorption of immigrants, I would suggest that for a limited period . . . world Jewry should be encouraged to help finance the settlement of those Jews who desire, or are obliged, to migrate to Israel. After this transition period, there should no longer be any Zionist organization . . . .

Do you still regard yourself as a Jew? Do you wish others to consider you as being no longer a Jew?

Insofar as religion is concerned, I consider the Ten Commandments and the Sermon on the Mount as inseparable as the root and the flower. . . . Hence, to give a precise answer to your question: I regard myself, first, as a member of the European community; secondly, as a naturalized British citizen of uncertain and mixed racial origin, who accepts the ethical values and rejects the dogmas of our Helleno-Judaeo-Christian tradition. Into what pigeonhole others put me is their affair. . . .

The publication of this interview aroused general indignation among the *Jewish Chronicle*'s readers. But the controversy served a useful purpose by letting the cat of fierce racial pride out of the religious bag and revealing the tragic contradiction of Jewish existence. For how is the world to reconcile the claim that an Englishman of Jewish faith is like other Englishmen, with the statement, printed in the same issue of the paper: "To be a Jew means that you believe that the past of Jewry is your past, its present your present, its future your future . . ."?

I shall now elaborate some of the points raised in the controversy and shall at the same time try to progress from abstract argument to the field of practical measures. It will be simplest to resort to the form of imaginary dialogue.

Question: *All previous attempts of Jewish communities to become completely assimilated to their host nation have ended in failure—Germany, for instance. Why should it be different this time?*

Answer: The reason for past failures and tragedies is that so far all attempts at assimilation were halfhearted, based on the faulty assumption that Jews could become full-blooded members of their host nations while retaining their religion and remaining the chosen race. *Ethnic assimilation is impossible while maintaining the Mosaic faith; and the Mosaic faith becomes untenable with ethnic assimilation.* The Jewish religion perpetuates national separateness—there is no way around that fact.

Your arguments are based on the assumption that the only, or at least the principal, distinguishing mark of the Jew is his religion. What about race, physical features, and those peculiarities of Jewish character and behavior which are difficult to define and yet easy to sense?

Racial anthropology is a controversial and muddy field, but there is a kind of minimum agreement among anthropologists on at least these two points: that the Biblical tribe belonged to the Mediterranean branch of the Caucasian race; and that the motley mass of individuals spread all over the world and designated as "Jews" are from the racial point of view an extremely mixed group who have only a remote connection, and in many cases no connection at all, with that tribe. The contrast between the short, wiry, dark-skinned Yemenite Jew who looks like an Arab, and his Scandinavian coreligionist is obvious. Less

102

well known is the fact that even Jews from geographically close neighborhoods—for example, Russian and Polish Jews—differ markedly in physical type. Certain Italian and Spanish physiognomies are pronouncedly Semitic in appearance, and some Spanish families have probably a higher percentage of Semitic genes than those groups of European Jews whose ancestors got into the way of the Crusaders and other marauding hordes. But the most puzzling racial paradox of all is the quite un-Jewish appearance and mentality of the new native generation in Israel.

When the fallacies of racialism have been discarded, all that survives of the Biblical race is probably a statistically very small "hard core" of genes, which, in segregated, intermarrying Jewish communities keeps "Mendling out," as the biologist says, in curved noses and wistful irises. But even regarding such facial features it is difficult to distinguish between true heredity and environmental influence.

Turning from physical appearance to the mental habits and peculiarities of Jews, these vary so widely from country to country that we can only regard them as the product of social, not biological, inheritance. The typical Jewish abhorrence of drunkenness, for instance, is the unconscious residue of living for centuries under precarious conditions, which made it dangerous to lower one's guard; the Jew with the yellow star on his back had to remain cautious and sober and watch with amused or frightened contempt the antics of the drunken *goy*.

Jewish casuistry, hair-splitting, and logic-chopping can be traced back to the Talmudic exercises, which until recent times dominated the Jewish child's curriculum in school; as Leopold Schwarzschild, a brilliant biographer of Marx, pointed out in *The Red Prussian* 1948, the dialectic owes as much to Hegel as to Marx's rabbinical background. The financial and forensic genius of the Jew is obviously a consequence of the fact that until the end of the eighteenth century, and in some countries well into the nineteenth, Jews were debarred from most normal professions.

We thus have a small and somewhat hypothetical "hard core" of Jewish characteristics in the sense of biological heredity, and a vast complex of physical and mental characteristics that are of environmental origin and transmitted through social inheritance. Both the biological and social features are too complex and diffuse to identify the Jew as a Jew with anything approaching certainty; the decisive test and official identification mark remains his religion.

Your arguments may be logical, but it is nevertheless inhuman to ask people to discard, in the name of expediency, a centuries-old tradition as if it were a worthless garment.

Let us try to define what exactly we mean by "Jewish tradition." Do we mean the concept of monotheism, the enthronement of the one and invisible God, the ethos of the Hebrew prophets, the wisdom of Solomon, the Book of Job? They are all in the King James version of the Bible and have become the common property of the Western world. *Whatever came after the Bible is either not specifically Jewish or not part of a living tradition.* The only specifically Jewish intellectual activity of the post-Biblical centuries was theological. But Talmud and Kabbala and the endless volumes of rabbinical exegesis are unknown to 99 per cent of the general Jewish public and are no longer part of a living tradition. Yet they were the *only* product of a specifically "Jewish tradition"—if that expression is to be given concrete meaning—during the last two thousand years.

In other words: since the first century the Jews have had no language, literature, and culture of their own. Their philosophical, scientific, and artistic achievements consist in contributions to the culture of their host nations; they do not constitute a common cultural inheritance or autonomous body of traditions.

To sum up: the Jews of our day have no cultural tradition in common, merely certain habits and behavior patterns derived from a religion whose commandments they reject, and from the unhealthy environmental pressures on a segregated minority. The sooner all this is discarded, together with segregation and minority status, the better for all concerned.

Even if all your arguments were granted, there would still remain a deep-felt reluctance, a spiritual and aesthetic revulsion in Jewish parents against the idea of bringing up their children in a faith in which they themselves do not believe.

My plea is addressed to parents who do not believe in the Jewish religion either, to that vast majority of agnostics and near-agnostics who accept the ethical values of our Judaeo-Christian heritage and reject all rigid doctrine. The proper thing for them is to say: "If my child must be brought up in a definite religion, then let it be the same in which his playmates are brought up, and not one which sets him apart by its racial doctrine, marks him out as a scapegoat, and gives him mental complexes. Which particular doctrine he is taught does not matter very much, as with maturity he will make his own spiritual decisions anyway; what matters is that he should not start under a handicap."

Your arguments betray a utilitarian approach to religious questions that seems to me cynical and improper.

Only because you suffer from the guilt complex of the agnostic who is unable to hold a dogmatic belief but wishes that he could. That, I suspect, goes for all of us, children of the post-materialistic era, filled with transcendental yearnings; once more conscious of a higher, extrasensory order of reality, and yet intellectually too honest to accept any dogmatic version of it as authentic. If you belong to this category, then surely you too regard the historical accounts of the lives of Buddha, Moses, Jesus, and Mohammed as eternal symbols, as archetypes of man's transcendental experience and spiritual aspirations, and it makes little difference which set of symbols will be taught to your child according to the hazards of its birth. I believe that it is essential for the moral development of the child to start with some form of belief in a divine order, whose framework he will at first take for gospel truth until the spiritual content matures into symbolic interpretation. From this point of view—which is the basis of our discussion since my argument is expressly *not* directed at the orthodox believer—it is quite irrelevant whether the child's imagination is centered on Moses bringing water forth from the rock or on water turned into wine at Cana.

Allow me to reverse the charge: I find it cynical on your part to turn your child into a potential victim by teaching him to believe in the miracle of the rock but to reject the miracle of Cana, or by celebrating the Sabbath on Saturday instead of Sunday. Do you realize that this futile calendrical dispute, the Jew closing his shop on Saturday and working on Sunday, has been a major irritant and cause of martyrdom for centuries? Do you call it cynical if one deplores the holocausts of Jewish victims burned, raped, robbed, chased, and gassed in the name of a Lilliputian fanaticism regarding the question on which end to break the spiritual egg?

Let us turn to the practical side of the problem. You advocate that nondoctrinaire Jews should bring up their children as members of the congregation of their neighbors; what about "restricted" residential districts and schools and similar obstacles, handicaps, and embarrassments?

No doubt in the first generation there will be plenty of all that, plenty of bitterness, disappointment, and failure in individual cases. But in the second generation there will be less of it, and in the third, with the disappearance of all self-segregatory motives, the "Jewish question" will gradually taper off and fade away. The obvious example of this process is the cultural and social homogeneity of third-generation Americans of heterogeneous origin.

I shall now have to deal with one last objection, which carries more psychological weight than all the others because it is based not on logic but on the denial of logic as a guide in human affairs. Isaiah Berlin has expressed this attitude with much insight and eloquence. After explaining that he was to a large extent in agreement with my position, he continued with a "but":

> But there are . . . many individuals in the world who do not choose to see life in
> the form of radical choices between one course and another, and whom we do not condemn for
> this reason. "Out of the crooked timber of humanity," said a great philosopher, "no straight

thing was ever made." Fearful thinkers, with minds seeking salvation in religious or political dogma, souls filled with terror, may wish to eliminate such ambiguous elements in favor of a more clear-cut structure, and they are, in this respect, true children of the new age which with its totalitarian systems has tried to institute just such an order among human beings, and sort them out neatly each to his own category. . . . To protest about a section of the population merely because it is felt to be an uncosy element in society, to order it to alter its outlook or get out . . . is . . . a kind of petty tyranny, and derives ultimately from the conviction that human beings have no right to behave foolishly or inconsistently or vulgarly, and that society has the right to try and rid itself by humane means, but rid itself nevertheless, of such persons although they are neither criminals nor lunatics nor in any sense a danger to the lives or liberties of their fellows. This attitude, which is sometimes found to colour the views of otherwise civilised and sensitive thinkers, is a bad attitude because it is clearly not compatible with the survival of the sort of reasonable, humane, "open," social texture in which human beings can enjoy those freedoms and those personal relationships upon which all tolerable life depends.

Isaiah Berlin is as skeptical as I am regarding the possibility of normalizing the social status of Jews so long as they insist on calling themselves and being called Jews. He also agrees that the rebirth of Israel puts every individual Jew in a dilemma. His argument is simply that you should neither expect nor encourage people to act logically, and that unreason, however irritating or maddening, must be tolerated.

I fully agree that nothing could be more unreasonable than to expect people to behave reasonably. But if you argue that Jews have a right to be guided by irrational emotion and to behave "foolishly or inconsistently or vulgarly," you must grant the same right to their adversaries, and I need not enlarge upon the result. It seems to me that if you have a voice and a pen, it is incumbent on you to advocate that course of action which you believe to be in the public interest, and thereby to influence the precarious balance between reason and passion in people's minds. It also seems to me, as I said before, that people have an inalienable right to mess up their own lives, but no right to mess up the lives of their children.

The pressure of totalitarian forces from outside and inside our Western civilization has led to a tendency among liberals to call any attitude of non-complacency "totalitarian." A certain amount of administrative and ideological muddle and a margin of tolerated confusion are indeed as essential to the functioning of a democratic society as lubricants and safety valves are to a machine. But the harsh, inhuman precision of totalitarian ideologies makes the liberal mind inclined to believe that the oily lubricants are all that matter, whereas pistons, pressure, and energy are totalitarian as such. Words like "blueprint," "planning," and even "order" have acquired a derogatory meaning ever since various forms of a "new order" were looming on the horizon. The understandable human weakness for evading painful decisions and responsibilities has come to be regarded as a virtue and the essence of democracy. The liberal in retreat does not ask for freedom of choice, but for freedom from choice.

If my saying that we must decide whether we belong to the chosen race or to the nation whose citizen we are, and if the revolutionary discovery that we can't eat our cake and have it, are figments of a totalitarian mind, then I must confess to a totalitarian mind. If "out of the crooked timber of humanity no straight thing was ever made," I still think it more honorable to try to straighten the timber than to make it more crooked for sweet crookedness' sake. Or shall we rather fall back on the ancient adage:

When in danger or in doubt,
Turn in circles, scream or shout?

I am acutely aware that Israel is once more endangered by hostile forces—as acutely aware as any person with a living conscience, gentile or Jew. My essay is concerned with the long-term solution of the Jewish problem, and its conclusions seem to me as valid as before. This does not affect the moral obligation of any right-minded person to support Israel's right of existence within secure frontiers.

Excerpt from a letter from Sir Isaiah Berlin to the editor, dated July 11, 1973

Arthur Koestler does not do justice to my argument. It is not, to use his words, "that unreason, however irritating or maddening, must be tolerated" or that Jews or anyone else "have a right to be guided by irrational emotion." My thesis was and is that to demand social and ideological homogeneity, to wish to get rid of minorities because they are tiresome or behave "foolishly or inconsistently or vulgarly" (these are indeed my words), is illiberal and coercive and neither rational nor humane. This is the position that, in very different forms, I attributed to Plato, to T. S. Eliot and to Arthur Koestler: it forms the heart of that "integralist" national-ism in Europe in the last century and a half, and now almost everywhere, which tells men to assimilate to the prevailing *ethos* inwardly, not merely in outward observance of the prevailing laws and customs; or else get out, or, at best, acquiesce in the treatment accorded to not very desirable outsiders, what Charles Maurras and his followers used to call *métèques*. The notion that differences should not (or cannot) be tolerated, and should therefore be ironed out, and so obliterated, is what, in my view, distinguishes barbarian from civilised societies.

Mr. Koestler, if I interpret him rightly, thinks that the mere existence of unassimilated minorities, especially those which are unclear about the nature of their identity, is bound to cause friction, and that it is therefore rational for them, in their own interest as well as those of the majority, to see to it that at any rate their grandchildren come to form part of that majority; whereas I hold the view that this is neither desirable, since variety is not an evil but a good, and the disappearance of any peaceful human species with a rich past is a gratuitous loss to mankind; and moreover, however feasible for individuals, evidently not practicable for the mass: even if we do not revert again to the terrible fate of the German Jews, the experience of Jews in the Soviet Union—the grandchildren, in many cases, of men and women who be-lieved in and practised assimilation with enthusiastic fervour—seems to indicate that the process does not work on the (pathetically) hoped for scale: the grandparents may force themselves to eat sour grapes, but the teeth of the grandchildren are set on edge. I do not, of course, expect my admired friend Arthur Koestler to accept this view: nor, I feel sure, does he expect me to accept his. But whereas I think we are none the poorer for such differences, he probably thinks that this, too, is a symptom of a lack of serious respect for logic and the belief in the final solubility by a collective act of radical choice, of important social problems. On this, too, we must continue to disagree: I shall continue to tolerate and, indeed, respect his view, even if he does not consent to tolerate mine.

Judaism, the Mid-Century, and Me

Michael Horovitz

Four excerpts from a much longer memoir in progress

*   *   *   *   *   *

During my 1940s and 1950s schooldays, the evening sun always seemed to go down earlier, and more firmly, on Fridays; for every Friday I was constrained—a shamefully reluctant groom—to go help usher in 'Our Lady of the Weekend' at the most orthodox local synagogue, the *shul*. The ritual worked, insofar as those celebrations shine out in retrospect like stars in the night: the exact *nigunim* of the *semiroth* (the melodies of the hymns); the arcane conviviality and impassioned arguments—often about religion—at dinner; evenings veritably spread out against the sky like T. S. Eliot's "patient etherized upon a table." Or indeed like a kind of safety curtain dropped, it seemed to me, against "the outside world," in order to shelter the private theater-piece of our Jewish Sabbath from the dreaded infections germane to any contact with "real life," as represented by the brash, unholy ambience of the non-Jews surrounding our precious *shechinah* (—a sort of hot line to the Divine Spirit).

Night fell extra early in midwinter, of course, licensing the handful of practicing (or sons of practicing) Jews at my grammar school to miss out on the whole afternoon's classes. I reveled in the privilege on "secular" grounds—at that age free time was a rarity—and fell to dreaming on the deserted midday tube-trains and dawdling along the sleepy suburban byways of Hampstead; or got happily lost probing the secrets of those fortuitous adventure-playgrounds, the bombsites. When I finally got home it would be—

"Hurry up, boy—bar mitzvah next month and still always last . . . Will you ever be a Man? —So, don't just stand there—tug off that weekday gear and into the *Shabbas* suit. Come *on* . . ." (—nervous fingers flurry, splash over face, slick down hair, tie the hated tie—) "We're going *now* . . . won't have you creeping in at the back for last Kaddish to show us up again, trying to pretend you've been there the entire service through. Nu—*Goy*, where's your hat?"

Must wear a hat to *shul*. At last, hanky-pinned-inside-jacket-pocket, strenuously prepared for The Day of Rest . . .

My four diligent brothers and white-bearded father truly sojourn this oasis of time, a time out of street-time and world-value—sure, but how weird—thinking Good, here we are, the only exalted people in the road of a Friday evening: the faithful few—fit to meet, hip to greet, the radiant Bride of Sabbath—every "outward and visible sign" in place . . .   —What about things like "the outward ceremony is anti-Christ"? Okay, so these ceremonies are avowedly anti-Christ. But when you think about it, really, what use our prayers and invocations? It's raining like hell . . . Just as well, that about hats . . . —not allowed to carry umbrellas: carrying anything on *Shabbas* Verboten, strictly taboo, gotta cast away

all weekday-workaday glue, let go like the Lord did when He'd made the world new . . . But the 'real' reason, They say, is that you should always have something separating yourself from God. *God?!* —Isn't He everywhere, not just an invisible power in Heaven? What god . . . And is heaven only in the sky? — Will I dare ask the family these things?

I would have thought the purpose of religion was to get you *closer* to whatever whoever God is: but the Jewish God is "jealous"!—Jealous of what, for god's sake? —Well, since He insists on being the only One, I guess He's bound to get lonely. No wonder He's jealous; but why must we, in turn, each be bound to His *no*-wonderland? —God knows! And that's just It, it really is: people want some mentality to believe in, accept what God knows when they don't, because they need to feel somebody knows. Well, I don't believe He can know so much if He's so busy being jealous. "God only knows"—:—nothing figures

. . . except—hand does like it in Father's greatcoat pocket, the special deep-pocketed coat he only wears for *shul*—till, Oh Jesus, "Report on the week's work": yes yes, I got good marks—don't tell about the panic punishment in the showers. . . Mmm, slither and slide down glistening Oakhill Avenue of squelchy leaves to the grass dip flanked by high hedges at the bottom. I like peering in at the tennis court there, puddledrenched tonight. Good to have a routine, walk the same path every week, develop a consistent way of seeing things—a "sense of reality," perhaps? —I dunno, no: the people in *that* house don't go out when it's raining. . . What good is Good anyway? How heavy weighs the drippinghat— feels much more like work than a brolly would!

—Darker. Out in the rain I don't want to bow to it with the creaking yet impacted families of trees, the moralizing priests, no—in defiance let me flee with the heathens, children unencumbered with this burden, this ancient lumber, this deliberately and incontrovertibly obscure mythology. Rather let me run riot with my heterodox coevals—students of the whole of life—free to make our own new ways in a brave new world. . . .

*   *   *   *   *   *

I'm youngest of the ten children of pretty fanatically Jewish parents, who were violently uprooted from a settled corner both *their* sets of parents had helped to establish in Frankfurt: a super-fastidiously enclosed, inbred, elitist community, founded by guardians of the sacred flame who'd forgathered across Germany from other parts of (Eastern) Europe during the nineteenth century. My father's father had come from Hungary, a direct descendant of golden oldies of Hasidic fame, to become a chief rabbi of this sanctuary; which seems to have attempted to absorb and assimilate the cream of the Teutonic high culture without forsaking the essentials of Judaic law and lore.

Being a young bud from such carefully cultivated roots, so suddenly transplanted, exposed me to all sorts of "alien" influences I should never have encountered had it not been for the enforced flight to England—where all of us were categorically aliens. The older family members spoke barely a word of English, whereas I, still the babe-in-arms when we emigrated, was actually able to brush up their accents and vocabulary as I grew more articulate. And being the youngest of so many, in the state of constantly varied evacuation extorted by the war years, my "formative" years, also made it easier for me to implement the alienation from Judaism I felt building up inside me; from those aspects, at least, which struck me as no more than the pious mumbo jumbo and obsolete rigmarole of observances and pensa and outlandish activities my parents and their refugee relatives and friends preserved with such apparently constitutional devotion. Some of my brothers and sisters, less distanced from it all, had a quite different reaction; indeed, Father's interpretation of the Torah was not fundamentalist *enough* for the next-youngest son, who's now a religious leader in Jerusalem (—by all accounts a saintly one); and those siblings who shared my skepticism were, by dint of being older, grounded under closer surveillance than I.

And yet, looking back on my childhood, I can see that the language of Judaism was—and to some extent still is, even for me—a living language and symbology. In boyhood and adolescence I gradually

109

quested farther afield, for meanings that would last, authority I could follow; but it was probably the Talmudic, scholarly, kosher-home-life disciplines that made me *want* to know, to be a disciple and value the time of asking questions until I'd have the answers under my skin. The patriarchal system was fairly solidly instilled—certainly up till the death of *Aba*, mine own Papa (who was still in full swing, as a "character," pillar amid the Diaspora, and adept lawyer who specialized in rehabilitating victims of Nazism), in his seventies—when I was just about to leave home anyway, for my first term at Oxford. His brand of European-Jewish paternalism doubtless implanted the notion that there *are* answers to every question, to be unearthed through study, history, and adherence to the Word of the God of our Fathers. Only much later did I find out—albeit from William Blake—"I must create my own system, or be enslaved by another man's"; and that "All Deities reside in the Human Breast."

The faith of parents which had weathered the Gestapo was unshakable by contrast to that of us children of the blitz. I remember one night of nonstop bombardment late on in that war, I was screaming my head off in agonized terror: then Father carried me up from the air-raid shelter and shook his fist at the throbbing flame-tailed bird, not a mile away in the sky. Although my heart was ready to burst its drum, the warming consolation of his sturdy arms about me on the moonlit lawn stilled my hysteria, into wonderment and peace. He made me steadily watch the demented "doodlebug" hover over our heads—and sputter on and away, till it was no more than a dusky speck, the vermilion blaze shimmered into small dot like a Guy-Fawkes'-Night rocket; till we could just barely see the flying-bomb drop anchor, a kind of remote-controlled bumble-bazooka, release its sting, diving to wipe out anonymous flaring homes, unaccountable buzzing brains, somewhere else—but still somewhere—in the neighboring borough. I had to relax and rejoice at his conviction, though—and to this day can't regret such unquestioning trust in the power of his strong hand and outstretched arm, in face of those inscrutably mechanized demonic forces.

So my daddy 'stood in' for God, and is surely rewarded in the heavenly kingdom. But when he died of a stroke ten years later, the concept of a "world to come" was no more consolation—to me—than that of an "angel of death." Later still it occurred to me (apropos Marlowe's Mephisto):—Why, This is Heaven, as well as Hell: is it not equally into *this* world the spirit departs—at birth: don't we create ourselves, each moment?   —Yet how strange, how pitiful and alarming, to have been Abraham Horovitz, raised on the Germanic virtues, on Beethoven and Nietzsche, awarded an Iron Cross for heroic soldiering in the trenches—and then. . .   After the 'Great' War he might have agreed with Ernst Toller, that—

> The words "I am proud to be a German" or "I am proud to be a Jew" sound ineffably stupid to me. . .   As well say "I am proud to have brown eyes." Must I then join the ranks of the bigoted and glorify my Jewish blood now, not my German? Pride and love are not the same thing, and if I were asked where I belonged I should answer that a Jewish mother had borne me, that Germany had nourished me, Europe had formed me, my home was the earth, and the world my fatherland. . . .

Yet for all that they'd done to realize that dream, the nurse responded by bitching Toller and my father alike. The valiant cavalry lieutenant, the fulsome host, respected *Rechtsanwalt*-lawyer and world citizen, had to fly by night, to the mercies of the country he'd fought against—reduced and perhaps at the same time (like King Lear) elevated to his common humanity; having to stand up again now, and fight the common enemy—the very nation-state he'd risked his life for in his prime.

Mornings after the bombings he'd walk me to the primary school, timing our arrival to coincide with the aftermath of Christian prayers. We often caught a glimpse of the surface wreckage, the devastated innards of walls and chimneys and basements, ripped out and gaping—the murmuring crowd agape at the still smoldering crater roped away—where four "new-built" semi-detached houses had been six hours before. . .   Home Guard and wardens picked through the rubble—one dragging out a motionless survivor, swiftly bundled into the dinning ambulance, whilst children sniveled and careened with abandoned pets, or huddled over hastily salvaged treasures in an up-ended shelter. . . How we swelled with relief and patriotic triumph on V-E Day, and again on V-J Day soon after. I didn't realize then the cost of these long-looked-for victories in terms of even more wasteful barbarism—the destruction of Dresden and Berlin; and the atomic plagues on Hiroshima and Nagasaki, which were designed (rumor had it) chiefly to keep the Russians out of Japan.

Throughout these horrendous public traumas, the family went on attending or conducting prayer services thrice daily, intoning fifteen-minute grace after each meal, and pursuing the time-honored "purified" Jewish way of life; blind, or at least blinkered, polemical regurgitations—which seemed to me to approach the very mistake Hitler's legions had perpetrated in seeking to become "the master race." I didn't want exclusivism, and the idea of revenge was absurd; only more violence could stem from counter-violence, whose justification could never redeem its futility. I hadn't wanted bombs any more than my elders had wanted the camps and massacres, and it was no satisfaction that a few cruel tyrants had gone under alongside the innocent millions. There was only one "good fight" worth fighting, which I tried to express in the following section of a poem *For Modern Man* (to end his nearly million-year-old war against his own kind flesh):

> —You're a Jerry, they said at school, and
> —You're a Jew, you go to *shul*—
>
> "Hardpunch Horofist" I became and fought
> for that same different me
> not for jolly Germany, not the chosen race
> for daily face to face I saw—each one of us
> chosen for the human race
> —its myriad individuality
>
> Why fight! —If fight, fight for that—for you
> and me and her and he
> fight for *all* humanity—

Without global unity, a truly united nations, this transcendental battle has hardly even begun: glumly I watched "the nuclear deterrent" plugged by friendly-government agents with the same brain-washing sales techniques as hucksters were using for the latest "new clear detergent" . . . The rationale was that both were indispensable, lest the economic and political balance would collapse; and a good thing too, cried the Aldermaston ban-the-bomb marchers. And yet no working synthesis has been devised to reconcile the lethal contradictions of our nationalist power blocs—the series of more or less pyramid structures, which literally suppress the large mass of people for the ease of a few towering bullies and tycoons. Only a tiny minority of minority groups has been setting up its own atomized alternatives. The military-industrial millennium has given up the human experiment—pronounces it, in effect, as moribund a failure as the dinosaur experiment.

Bernard Malamud blithely coined the epigram, "Nowadays every man is a Jew." I'd propose the converse, that every Jew today ought to wake up to his universal manhood; must, perforce, be a *mensch* (if not a humanist), stripped of the trappings of Old-World exile—sere and weary wandering in "the wilderness"—to emerge from 'flat-earth thinking' into what Karl Popper has characterized as "the open society." It is to such a society modern man must clearly adapt, here and now, or miserably perish.

* * * * * *

If we do inhabit a global village—or conceive of planet Earth as a spaceship manned by beings possessed of a sense of continuity into the future, as well as inborn race-memory—we're willfully courting extinction to go on charting our course according to bestial primitive superstitions from antiquity. This was the instinct I held in common with my sisters all along, and we simply refused to join in when the hearty family services took a vindictive turn, as in the passage at Seder where the door is opened and God is implored to exert the full weight of his scorn upon the enemies of Israel. The retributive "eye-for-an-eye" scale of justice seemed childishly unworthy of anyone aspiring to carry a torch for any kind of civilization, even though the subculture to which we'd accidentally been born had suffered so profoundly. Our libertarian antennae bristled at the way uncles and mentors trampled their feet at every mention of Haman's name throughout the Megillah (the Biblical story of Esther). When they retorted that Haman was the same as Hitler and the recurrent nightmare line of baiters and murderers of Jewry, we put it to them that the atmosphere of relish about these institutionalized reminders suggests a tribal paranoia, which might actually feed on persecution.

I came to assume the role of outspoken mouthpiece for the idealism of my sisters, and this may have sown some of the seeds which bore fruit years after, when I started dropping out from my post-graduate career in academe, in favor of fulfilling the implications of the kind of poetry I'd been writing —and performing it with my peers. We mounted a multi-medic nonconformist arts circus, which traveled all over Britain from 1959 to 1965. Reviving the word-of-mouth genre indubitably appealed to the part of me that had been steeped in another style of "underground" oral convention throughout my Jewish upbringing. The public poet-spokesman and the cantor-rabbi stand in a somewhat parallel relation to their following. Allen Ginsberg has declared that "Poet is Priest," invoking Blake's Old Testament–prophetic "voice of the Bard/ Who present, past, and future sees." And the basis of spoken poetry remains what Langston Hughes, the black American jazz-poet, described as "the common loneliness of the folk song that binds one heart to all the others—and all the others to the one who sings the song." The wheel is coming full circle today, bringing the word in its various manifestations closer to its origins in law-making, religion, and musical-dramatic configurations. The classic pattern of call and response joints the bonds of Reader and Congregation—although the resultant dialogues and activities are liable to cut right across the prevalent civic and clerical canons.

Responding to my fellow poets, singers, and musicians, and eliciting a voluble response myself from audiences that sprang up around us as spontaneously as we ourselves had sprung, I recalled how years before, in *dovening* (congregational praying), I'd sometimes caught more than a whiff of authentic catharsis, the tribal pull—toward the experience of being "members of one another." And for all that it was a harking back, I came to recognize positive aspects of primitive forms, such as communal incantation, or even the selfsame foot-stomping against Haman I'd shied away from in my rationalist teens—they functioned, for example, in the manner of wild Afric tomtoms, to exorcise demons—purging the shared emotion of fear; if not of pity.

Quite often, in the midst of supra-national poetry events, I find myself involuntarily imagining *yom tov* (a Jewish festival/holiday—literally "good day"), in the ghettos of Sholom Aleichem and Marc Chagall, or sensing that vaunted continuum that links forefathers and descendants—celebrants all, consigned to harmonize, preach, teach, sing, dance, clap hands, and achieve a genuinely popular yet ecstatic union. The large-scale happenings and recitals, festivals, and "be-ins" at places like Albert Hall, People's Park in Berkeley, Woodstock, and the Isle of Wight have in fact seemed positively Biblic to some—and more reminiscent of the fall of the Roman Empire to others! As far as most of the poets are concerned, we hold with Blake that "poetry is religion; religion is politics, politics is brotherhood"; and, with Adrian Mitchell, that we "want poetry to bust down the walls of its museum-tomb and learn to survive in the corrosive real world. The walls are thick but a hundred Joshuas are on the job."

The voice of prophecy doesn't necessarily provide traditionalist directives or endorse conventional morality. When I'd managed to split way out from the chrysalis in which "the Lord is One" was wound

113

round my brain and arm several times a day, to spread my butterfly wings and discover the diversity of religious myths, I was at first almost stupefied by the rich stores of nourishment available. But traditional Judaism continued to inform the imagery that burgeoned from the apparently infinite plantations of reference interpollinating. Even now my head reels daily with rhythms and tunes that ran through it in my youth: the echoes of ancestral lamentations, from fast days and evening prayers and Kabbalistic ravings; of signal variables of the liturgy—the portions of the Books of Moses, the Psalms, and the Apocrypha that kept Jews in touch from every outpost of exile through the ages; of the light-fantastical trips and melancholy of perennial pipes and timbrels and viol woof; of chutzpah and Chelm, the laughter inseparable from tears in Yiddish humor and play; of exalted Hebraic dirges, chants, and benedictions (*duchening*), tracking back from Bialik to Yehuda Halevi to the Piyyuth and Ecclesiastes and the marvelous world of primeval surreal-real praises in which the mountains skip like rams, and the hills like young sheep. . . .

*   *   *   *   *   *

Yet this tradition, even in "David," heavy with nostalgia to be reunited with some vast unity, the historic destiny which sustained our archetypes, was always qualified for me by presupposing a god who was in competition with other gods—cognate with the idols of yore. In "By the waters of Babylon" (another standing type of the heartless slayer of Judah) the singer insures the endless continuance of the degenerate war game: "O daughter of Babylon/ Foul destroyer—to be destroyed!/ Happy who pays thee back in kind/ as thou hast rewarded us./ Happy who snatcheth up thy little ones/ and teareth their bodies/ against the rocks . . ." (though this is friendly, even in my free translation, compared to the long-drawn-out ferocity of the revenge supplicated in Psalm 109 and other articles of the Pharisaic faith.) The main consequence seems to be that today we'd be hard put to it to sing the real songs of Zion if we wanted to—much as in these Psalms the Temple is hardly remembered, only our predecessors remembering it. The Divine Temple is not going to be rebuilt in Jerusalem today (of necessity a militantly chauvinistic state) any more than the Jerusalemic state of mind, "the spiritual Israel," is in England. This in spite of every Christian schoolchild's frequent singing of Blake's hope that it *will* be—whilst assimilated Jewish neighbors regularly (and paradoxically) repeat—"*Next* year in Jerusalem. . . ."

The memorial rites generally seem to act as little more than sentimental way-markers, as it were, of their own fossilization in the Philistine desert. Whoever really feels he is losing by his assimilation or individuation is free to create, to think, to unite a truer state of Israel—of Being—as Eckhart, Blake, Schweitzer, Buber have glimpsed it: a community of love, within which many Biblically sanctioned judgments were best left to historians, the backwash of an unenlightened past. Our recherché but authoritarian sense of religious origins is divorced, in the 1970s, from functional or constructively social ends. It's the sacramental tradition of Israel's tents understood as art and poetry that survives with the power to release our children from the yoke of Mammon, the inhuman pitch of exploitation and oppression exerted for the sake of ephemeral political advantages—a few scraps more wealth or dominion for this or that "power." The rebirth from materialism is well illustrated by Blake's engraving of Elijah (or God) alighting from the fiery chariot—the prophet who gives his cloak of inspiration to Elisha (or Adam), symbolizing the poet who grasps the eternal truth of the imagination, the divine presence in man, reveals it, and hands it on.

Jerusalem-builders on both sides of the Atlantic are rejecting the mores of an unknowable God of superhuman energy—in favor of something closer to Blake's visions, than to Orwell's "fallen" state of *1984*. Of course police states even more heinous than that fictitious one already operate, but there is also a radical underground or grass-roots growth over against them—plus a pearl necklace of small communities well away from them, decentralized pockets of resistance and independence—loosely knit, it's true, but growing all the time. And the seminal influence of the Movement (in America, since the 1950s, known as *The* Movement—that is, the anti-war Movement) comes from young men and women who, dedicated to peace and love, beauty and truth, must needs cut themselves off from allegiance to family, nationality, and religion. This is particularly evident amongst the architects of the new generation—the revulsion and revolution of the soul against mid-century suicide, "dark Satanic mills" of commerce scraping and polluting "the charter'd sky" over every city. In their capacity as heralds and awakeners, the musicians, artists, poets, find themselves, as James Joyce did, "forging in the smithy of his soul the uncreated conscience of his race"—which entailed a complete renovation of the equipment his Irish-Catholic heritage had imposed.

It is sometimes argued that apostasy usually reflects a long-rooted allegiance to the values sloughed off, and that sooner or later the lapsed psyche will rebound to its source; the current almost reactionary Zionistic family-man image of Bob Dylan may be a case in point. Nonetheless, in spite of inheriting the mantle of spiritual responsibility, "God's spies" today tend to thrive as relatively "*un-acknowledged* legislators"; and though poet and priest do move in the same areas, the poet's stance of vulnerability to experience and contradiction bespeaks a sharp divergence of vocations. I know many Jewish poets, but know of none who goes through the official motions of Judaism. Controlling compulsive intuitions with shaping intelligence, they can't pay lip-service to the outworn orders of totem and taboo; nor would they preach to the converted, let alone become converted to, another single set of formulas. The prescribed historicism of socio-politically organized religiosity would corrupt the poetry and program its insights.

Rabbis by definition do not set out to stretch feelers above and beyond the surface of their immediate, congenital environs; poets probe deeper to their foundations, having no constantly prepossessing "official business" to do. After the stridently protective rigidity of my home education, the discovery of the unmentionable Jesus to have been an original poet-priest came as a tremendous revelation to me— as it must to many who haven't been reared on the sententious dilutions of his message and hackneyed iconography of his legend (that is, authorized Christianity, and what Shaw called "Crosstianity"). Most shattering of all was the realization that billions of non-Jews were variously circling the same earth I'd been tromping around for a decade, virtually oblivious to their existence. . . .

*   *   *   *   *   *

Jewish Weddings

In New York. Photo by Cornell Capa.

In Israel. Photos by Elliott Erwitt (LEFT),
and Marvin E. Newman (RIGHT).

A glass cup from a burial society (Bohemia or Hungary, 1692). The enameled inscription reads, "This glass belongs to the Holy Burial Society of the Congregation of Polin. A gift from Moses, son of Jacob Polin, Hanukkah 1692." Collection The Jewish Museum, New York.

A circumcision knife (German, 1733) with a steel blade, porcelain handle, and carnelian stone on the end. It is inscribed with the date, name of the owner, and the words from Genesis, "And Abraham circumcised his son Isaac." Collection The Jewish Museum, New York.

A manuscript written in Amsterdam (1734). The illustration depicts grace after meals. Collection The Jewish Museum, London.

OPPOSITE: A Torah Ark made of pine wood, carved, painted, and gilded (Weilheim, Germany, c. 1720). Collection The Jewish Museum, New York.

The Schnorrer: Piety and Paradox

Leo Rosten

When I was a child in Chicago it often happened, during a walk with my mother and/or father, that we would be accosted by a man who would step up to us gravely and hold forth an open hand. The man would say *"Sholem aleichem"* and nothing more, waiting, with considerable dignity, until my parent fumbled in pocket or purse, then placed pennies in the mendicant palm.

"Aleichem sholem," my mother or father would respond, and upon the stranger's grave nod we would walk on.

Now, the beggar was not skinny or ill dressed, blind or tattered or lame. Nor did he wheedle or whine. Nor did he respond to benefaction with the slightest sign of gratitude. He just accepted the donation with a nod, a signal that a ritual had been completed: a proper transaction between equals.

The first time this happened I asked, "Who is that man?"

"He is our schnorrer" was the answer. Not "a" but "our" (sometimes, "the") schnorrer.

"Is he very poor?" I asked.

My father gave a wry "maybe, maybe not," shrug.

"Is he hungry?" I asked.

"I doubt it."

"But if he isn't poor or hungry or sick, why does he—"

"That's the way he earns his living."

And with the natural compliance of the very young I questioned no further. Schnorrers were people who accosted you, without a plea or confession of need, whom you automatically gave a handout. They were conducting their business; you were fulfilling your obligation.

When my father said "our schnorrer" he meant the man who patrolled our neighborhood as if he had been given the territory by royal fiat. And when, on occasion, a strange schnorrer appeared before us, my mother would say, "Our schnorrer must be sick," to which my father would add ironically, "More likely he's taking his vacation." And this too elicited neither question nor protest from me: after all, every workingman was entitled to a holiday. (My parents were socialists.)

Not that they approved of beggars or begging—except during times of great unemployment. "Better be a slave than beg," my mother once warned me. (I did not know then that this was from the Talmud.)

There was a vast difference, I sensed, between a scrounger and a schnorrer. Not until much later did I learn what the difference was. I heard my father and his friends tell jokes about schnorrers that expressed their ambivalence, and extended my perplexity. For instance:

> A schnorrer awakened a rich man very early one morning and asked for a dole.
>
> "You rogue!" cried the rich man. "How dare you wake me up at this time of the morning?"
>
> "Listen," retorted the schorrer, "I don't tell you how to run your business, so don't tell me how to run mine."

Or this one:

> A schnorrer accosted an "alrightnik," who snapped, "I don't hand out money on the street!"
>
> "So"—the schnorrer glowered—"you expect me to open an office?"

And another I never forget:

A schnorrer came to Mrs. Bloom's door on his biweekly round.

"I haven't a penny in the house," said Mrs. Bloom, blushing, "so please come back tomorrow."

The schnorrer frowned. "Lady, don't let it happen again. A man can lose a fortune extending credit."

Sarcasm and pedagogy were linked in these japeries.

I am not unaware that to many Jews the word "schnorrer" reeks of contempt. Schnorrers were often odious figures—grubby, unshaven, smelly, poorly shod, sleeves frayed—who spewed out hoarse, maudlin argosies of disaster. ". . . five children . . . shivering with cold . . . no food in the house . . . wife in hospital . . . who can work with broken ribs, a fractured spine?" These self-pitying deceits were designed to melt the most obsidian heart. But one never believed such a recitation of *tsouris* (troubles), for it came too fast, was too practiced, and usually betrayed its hypocrisy by the moocher's eyes, already unlocked from yours, darting about for another victim in the vicinity.

As time went on, as is its métier, I grew up and went to different places and encountered far different schnorrers from those I knew on Chicago's West Side. In my travels—to New York, Paris, Warsaw, Rome—I did indeed meet schnorrers who whined and schnorrers who demanded, schnorrers too sweet and schnorrers too sour, schnorrers apologetic and schnorrers arrogant, schnorrers who were filthy and schnorrers who were detestable. The tactics of their importunings were as varied as so narrow a field of enterprise permits. But I never met a schnorrer who was a fool (some were simpletons) or a bore. Many a schnorrer was clever, quick-witted, well versed in Talmud, expert in swimming through the vast sea of rabbinical literature.

Since schnorrers plied a craft that made their time their own, and were a pious lot, they spent hours in the synagogue; and there, between prayings, they engaged in the customary informal seminars—on God, man, the world, the hereafter, temptation, sin and guilt, connubial duties and familial bonds, ethics, truth, good and evil, the angels of light and the demons of darkness—a colloquium that Jews have conducted with zest for three thousand years.

The professional schnorrer expected recognition of the honorable *function* he performed, as we shall soon see. He expected monetary recognition of his status—if not praises for his character. He expected donations without interrogation, reluctance, or disdain. When a donor did accompany a benefaction with a sarcastic remark, the schnorrer could jettison his benign manner and launch into a tirade of abuse: "You call yourself a Jew! May your intestines churn like a music box! May all your teeth fall out—except one!" (So that you may be cursed with a permanent toothache.) The supplicants of Jewry were masters of moral outrage and theological maledictions.

Now, why were schnorrers this way? Where did they get their self-righteousness? Their sense of equality? Their cloak of professionalism?

We must begin by noting that there is no word for "charity" in either Hebrew or Yiddish. The closest is *tsedakah*, which means "righteousness." And righteousness is a *duty*, a religious duty, to be kind, compassionate, sensitive to the needs of others, forever helpful to the indigent or the unfortunate.

The Torah rests on three mighty pillars: "Law, Worship, Loving-kindness." The golden rule, "Thou shalt love thy neighbor as thyself," crowns the book of Leviticus (19:18). In Deuteronomy (15:11), Israel was told that the poor "shall never cease to be with us," and the Lord commands Israel to "open thine hand wide unto thy brother." The prophets castigated the early Hebrews for their indifference to the poor and hammered home the startling moral message that life without charity is not worthy of men.

After the pagan, licentious days before Moses, the Hebrews felt themselves chosen by God to shoulder the never-ending duties of *tsedakah*—to all their fellow-men, gentiles included. Leviticus ordered the Hebrews to tithe "out of the seeds of the earth"—more exactly, to leave for the poor the four corners of their fields (one-sixtieth) and all the gleanings of grain dropped in the reaping. (The priesthood received a fiftieth of the crops.)

So it was that worshipers in the Temple regularly helped "the worthy poor" with money put into boxes; and two alms-collectors passed the *kupha* around each Sabbath eve. From these funds, food was purchased or money donated to any in need. Under the Commonwealth (517 B.C.–A.D. 70), the legal fines paid by violators of certain laws were set aside as a special fund for the improvident. And those Hebrews who refused to contribute to the hungry, the ailing, the fatherless, the widows, were punished by the highest ecclesiastical court: the Sanhedrin.

Every Jewish community in the Diaspora contained a free hostel, often attached to the synagogue, for itinerants, wayfarers, the handicapped, the refugee. Every Jewish holy day included, as it still does, philanthropic fulfillments of the sacred obligations of *tsedakah*.

The rabbis carried obligatory handouts to an extreme: "We should be grateful for the presence of rogues among the poor; for if not for them, we would sin each time we ignored an appeal for alms" (Talmud: Kethuboth, 68a). The same passage goes on to say that to shut one's eyes to the duty to give alms is tantamount to worshiping idols. And when one rabbi saw a Hebrew give the equivalent of a farthing to a beggar, he exclaimed, "It would have been better had you given nothing—and not shamed this poor man in public" (Talmud: Hagigah, 5a).

And please note that to be a true *mitzvah* (good deed), the giving had to be accompanied by respect for the taker—and *gratitude* for the chance to be able to perform one of God's commandments! Even beggars were required to give to other beggars. Joseph Karo, in his monumental compendium of Jewish religious and civil law, the *Shulhan Aruk* (1567), executed a dialectical *tour de force* by ruling that *beggars* could fulfill their obligations to give by exchanging alms!

So the idea spread through Israel that the poor are the means through which the rich can gain salvation. Not only were the descendants of Moses required to demonstrate their piety whenever a mendicant stretched out his hand; they were required to be pleased about it. An old folk saying runs: "A man gives little if he gives much with a frown; he gives much if he gives little with a smile."

Against this jeweled backdrop of kindness, mercy, and love-for-your-fellow-man, there now enters the peculiar, self-assured, haughty or cunning figure of the professional mendicant. He does not beg: he claims. He does not thank: he acknowledges. He is as much your benefactor as you are his, for he is performing a holy (well, quasi-holy) task. He is a tithe-collector for the Lord, a priest-surrogate, metaphorically sprinkling holy water on your pocketbook to lighten its unspiritual load.

I think it fair to say that both the Christian and Moslem conception of the religious obligation to give alms rests upon the remarkable emphasis that Judaism gave charitable deeds executed with a willing and cheerful heart. This was something new in the history of the West.

Saul (Paul) of Tarsus, for all his hostility to certain aspects of Judaism, exalted what he had been taught: "faith, hope, and charity." And "the greatest of these is charity" (I Corinthians 13:13). Peter was echoing the Old Testament in the New when he declared: "Charity shall cover the multitude of sins." The Book of Common Prayer is entirely Hebraic in teaching: "All our doings without charity are nothing worth."

In Islam, philanthropy was (and is) a testimonial to, and a manifestation of, the mercy of Allah. To Buddhists, charity was man's way of doing the will of the compassionate Buddha. All manner of Hindu holy men held out their little cups in gestures of reminder, *not* beseechment; and the cups were filled with rice or coins.

Christian monks and nuns, similarly, considered mendicancy a God-appointed role. St. Chrysostom exhorted the Catholic world to remember that the poor are the benefactors of the rich: "If there were no poor, the greater part of your sins would not be removed. They are the healers of your wounds." St. Augustine quite rabbinically speaks of penance as consisting of prayer, fasting—and the giving of alms.

In Confucian, African, Polynesian, and many other cultures, alms-giving is a virtue, or a passport to reincarnation in not-diminished form, or a propitiation of deities, or a claim upon resurrection or life eternal. The Eskimos who offered both shelter and wife to the visitor (not, as is erroneously assumed, to any stranger), or the Burmese worthies who did likewise—all acted along their traditional religious code.

123

I have excluded the Greeks and Romans from this catalogue, please notice. The idea of compassion was ludicrous to them. To the Greeks, goodness was not merciful but rational. Acts of kindness bettered the self: for reason is the "ruling part" of the soul. To the Romans—well, Seneca somewhere says he "recoiled in horror" before the poor. Virgil praises one of his heroes for feeling no sympathy for the starving. Roman nobles thought it cruel to feed the hungry, because to do so only prolonged lives of misery.

In the civilization of the West, it was the Hebrews who gave respectability and status to the poor and the peculiar, the sick or the disabled, the old and the orphaned, the widowed, the blind, the variegated victims of fate.

Historically, Oriental holy men and gurus who begged for their livelihood were, in a sense, predecessors of the schnorerr—but in a narrow sense, for the schnorrer did not pretend to be either holy or transcendental. He was the self-appointed agent of the Lord, the enforcer of the noble requirements of *mitzvah*, the greaser-of-the-rails to redemption.

That is why the hallmark of the schnorrer was a certain cool presumption. Schnorrers were a sort of caste, *sub rosa*, but a caste. Unswerving self-righteousness distinguished the respectable schnorrer from the odious moocher. The schnorrer donned dignity with ease and cloaked his beggary with an ancient sanction and a quasi-noble patent.

In some villages in Eastern Europe the official census of Jews, maintained by the synagogue, read: "4 bakers, 3 butchers, 2 cobblers, and 1 schnorrer." Such occupational status is not to be ignored.

And so, early in life, every Jewish child was taught the sacred burden of "charity." In the most humble village of Eastern Europe, a poor or fatherless Jewish maiden took her marriage vows in a decent gown and possessed a trousseau and dowry—all provided by the community. In Jewish communities throughout the world, paupers received free burials.

The majestic Maimonides (who influenced Luther and the whole intellectual energy of the Reformation) analyzed the various forms of *tsedakah*, ranking them in order of nobility: the highest form is to help someone to help himself (by giving him work, or teaching him a skill, or financing his apprenticeship, or underwriting an enterprise); the second form, only a shade lower down than the first, is to help a man secretly, without revealing your identity, so that others do not know of the good deed and the recipient does not know who his benefactor is, and the givers do not either elicit or receive thanks or enjoy (however modestly) the warming acknowledgment of their goodness. *Tsedakah* is its own reward, not to be defiled by either praises or pride.

Very pious Jews would go through a poor quarter and toss little sacks of coins into open doorways. The more obsessive Samaritans would toss their contributions over their shoulder, so as not to risk knowing whom they had helped—not risk, that is, the vanity of philanthropy. The Talmud instructed Jews: "He who gives alms in secret is greater than Moses" (Baba Bathra, 9b).

I am far from faulting a Francis of Assissi for his ornithological compassions, or the Stylites for their sufferings on desert pillars, or the legions of holy men in India or Persia or Anatolia for their refusal to harm an insect, an aphid, or a tapeworm. I am only reporting how and why the sons of Abraham sought to ameliorate the sufferings and protect the self-respect of those whom fate does not favor. "He who gives, lives," is a Jewish saying. "He who does not give, does not live."

Even the Jews' passion for learning and their veneration of scholars and sages were subordinated to the primary, sacred duties of *tsedakah*: "It is better to help a cripple than a scholar."

It takes meager prescience to predict that in a society where charity is a *privilege*, crafty souls will seize the chance to provide the pious good with a large enough supply of the pious indigent. For if it is a *mitzvah* to give, there is a *duty* (on the part of those clever enough to see it) to make sure that *mitzvahs* are not strangled through lack of opportunity. Good men should not be cheated out of the chance to add an entry in the Book of Deeds that the angels keep up-to-date in paradise. Why, the pious will be denied their heavenly reward if denied opportunities to perform those acts which will win eternal reward!

To the sanctified ranks of the begging monks and friars of Christendom, and of the saintly acolytes of Shiva or Buddha or Allah, was added an unsanctified, unholy, unmeek apostle of salvation-via-alms:

the schnorrer. He was less sanctified than sanctimonious. He was an exploiter and magician of virtue, for he split benefaction into two parts so as to create double credit. He was your partner in *mitzvah*.

Polonius croaked that "neither a borrower nor a lender be"; but to the schnorrers of Jewry this was naïve *mishegoss*—utterly crazy. *Who's* talking about "borrowing"? What nonsense is this "lending"? Schnorrers do not borrow: they accept. They are not debtors but benefactors. And lucky are you, O sons of Moses, that someone is around to provide you with expert help in receiving what you must (remember Deuteronomy) give.

Few professions in history have rested on so soothing a self-image, so watertight a rationale, or so self-righteous a barnacling on the spiritual hulls of the pious.

Hieratic discriminations distinguished some schnorrers from others within the sociological "in-group." Israel Zangwill, a much-neglected author, wrote his *King of the Schnorrers* in 1893; and his description of London's Jewish mendicants contains this marvelous passage:

> . . . none exposed sores like the lazars of Italy, or contortions like the cripples of Constantinople. Such crude methods are eschewed in the fine art of schnorring. A green shade might denote weakness of sight, but the stone-blind man bore no braggart placard—his infirmity was an old established concern, well known to the public, conferring upon the proprietor a definite status in the community. He was no anonymous atom, such as drifts blindly through Christendom, vagrant and apologetic. Rarest of all sights, in this pageantry of Jewish pauperdom, was the hollow trouser-leg or the empty sleeve, or the wooden limb fulfilling either and pushing out a proclamatory peg.

The schnorrers of Eastern Europe were not so drenched in probity—to wit:

> A blind Jew stood at the corner, jiggling his tin cup. A woman stopped and dropped a quarter into the cup. The blind man said, "God bless you. I knew you had a kind heart the minute I laid eyes on you!"

You may ask, "But the schnorrer's role as an agent of Elijah, and the automatic acceptance of that role by Jews—surely both are old customs, now dying or gone forever."

There is much truth in this. The decline of orthodoxy among Jews (as among Catholics or Anglicans or Methodists, which all public-opinion polls reveal) and the proliferation of the welfare state have greatly altered our tolerance of the moocher. Beggars *can* be choosers today. The workman who pays heavy taxes surely resents handouts to those who do not. We dislike and despise the scrounger, and when we fall victim to his wheedling it is begrudgingly.

So it is a long time, I confess, since I have been accosted by a schnorrer. Winos or vagrants still panhandle, as they always will. And today young, healthy hippies, male and female, ask me for money— and when I inquire, "Why?" they smile and say, "For love."

The erosion of our patience with those who neither toil nor spin yet have the chutzpah to shill is reflected in new jokes:

> A schnorrer knocked on Mrs. Goldstein's door. "Lady, I'm starving. So do a *mitzvah*— give me a bite to eat."
>
> "Oh, dear," Mrs. Goldstein sighed. "I happen to have little food in the house. Tell me, Mr. Schnorrer, would you like some of last night's *kugel?*"
>
> "I'd love it!"
>
> "So come back tomorrow."

It is hard to believe that the golden days of schnorring will return, for there are so many Mrs. Goldsteins in our cynical world.

The Businessman

Stephen Aris

To describe the characteristics of the Jewish businessman and to speculate about the reasons for his remarkable success is to ask for trouble. The Jews have suffered so long and so much for their reputation as businessmen that any account, no matter how dispassionate, of their economic activities is bound to attract criticism on the grounds that the stereotype is being perpetuated. When, some years ago, I published a book called *The Jews in Business*, many Jews asked me, "Why us? Why not the Protestants or the Sikhs in Business?" It is a good question, and one that deserves a careful answer.

First, it is necessary to put the whole emotive subject in proper perspective. Contrary to popular belief, Jews have traditionally played a comparatively minor and narrow part in the economic life of the countries in which they have settled. This is particularly true of America, where the great wave of Jewish immigrants, which began to arrive in 1881, came too late and too poorly endowed to participate in the great industrial and economic boom that burst in the post–Civil War years and during which the foundations of modern American capitalism were laid. Among the "robber barons"—the Rockefellers, the Morgans, the Goulds, the Carnegies, and the Vanderbilts—there is scarcely a Jewish name. The men who built America's railroads, who developed her oil and steel industries, and who pioneered the mail-order revolution may have been as enterprising as any Jew but were in fact gentiles, almost to a man. Even Wall Street, with the notable exception of the Warburgs, the Schiffs, and the Lehmanns—German-Jewish refugees of an early generation—was very largely a gentile creation.

When in 1936 *Fortune* magazine, prompted by the rise of anti-Semitism in the 1930s, examined the extent of Jewish wealth and influence in America, it discovered, much to many people's surprise, that apart from the late-Victorian merchant-banking legacy, there were only three areas of American economic life in which the Jews had played a significant part: clothing manufacture, department stores, and the movie industry. But as shopping and film-going touch people's daily lives more nearly than, say, steel-making, this was enough to preserve the popular illusion, when combined with the mythic reputation of such families as the Rothschilds, of all-embracing Jewish economic power.

The pattern in England was very similar, although, being a smaller and less commercially developed country, both the opportunities and the impact were greater than in America. The mass-market tailoring business, which for the first time brought the price of men's clothing down to a level the working classes could afford, was very largely a Jewish creation; as was the modern supermarket and chain store. Though it was F. W. Woolworth who pioneered the dime-store concept, it was Jewish businessmen, led by Simon (later Lord) Marks and Israel (later Lord) Sieff, who developed and refined it to the point where Marks and Spencer became part of the fabric of Britain's social history. Very often the Jews were not the

Diamond merchants on a New York street in the 1950s. Photo by Cartier-Bresson.

first in the field. But again and again in the early years of the twentieth century the sons of the Russian immigrants seized opportunities that their rivals lacked either the energy or the imagination to develop.

The original base was a narrow one. In 1900 a full 60 per cent of all Jews in America were in the garment business, with another 15 per cent in merchant trade of one kind or another. But over the last three decades both American and British Jews have moved rapidly away from their tailoring and shop-keeping base, so that today the profile of Jewish economic man has become blurred and indistinct. This is particularly noticeable in America, where, for reasons I shall discuss later, there has been a massive shift away from business and into the professions—teaching (50 per cent of New York's teachers are, it is estimated, Jewish), medicine, dentistry, and the law. But even so there are, on both sides of the Atlantic, some economic activities that remain preponderantly Jewish. The great office boom of the 1950s and 1960s that has transformed both London and Manhattan is, for reasons that are both interesting and complex, very largely the work of Jewish developers.

None of this goes in any way to substantiate the claim of their critics that the Jews enjoy or exercise substantial economic power. But at the same time I think it is difficult for any honest observer to deny that the Jews have displayed a remarkable aptitude for business. The Jews may not have produced many business titans—though in his early years Marcus Samuel of Shell gave John D. Rockefeller a good run for his money—but they have undoubtedly generated more than their fair share of enterprising business-men. As Nathan Glazer, the American sociologist, has pointed out, the economic characteristics of the Jews are one of the factors that define them as a group.

Though Jews have been praised or blamed for their business acumen for almost as long as there have been Jews in the world, their present reputation largely derives from the activities of the two million refugees who fled from Eastern Europe between 1881 and World War I. It is they and their sons who are the latest exemplars of the classic rags-to-riches story of Jewish mythology: the entrepreneurs of the Western world whose fortunes were built on a mixture of enterprise, ambition, and chutzpah.

It is, of course, quite possible to explain their success entirely in terms of historical accident. The Jews of Eastern Europe happened to emerge from their medieval ghettos at the very beginning of the biggest consumer boom the world has ever seen. The techniques for feeding, clothing, and entertaining the burgeoning working classes had barely evolved. And as the Jews, anxious to find outlets for their tailoring and shopkeeping skills, had already been heavily involved in these areas in their native Russia, it was only to be expected that they should seize this opportunity. This argument is a persuasive one on a number of grounds. Not only does it fit the facts, but it conveniently allows one to avoid a difficult and awkward dis-cussion on the Jewishness of Jewish business. The disadvantage, however, of the historical accident theory, is that it still does not answer the question: If the opportunities were there, why was it that the Jews were among the first to spot and seize them? Nor does it satisfactorily explain why, after the original immigrants successfully established themselves, albeit for the most part in a modest way, their sons should have gone on to build often very substantial enterprises that were quite frequently unconnected with the original business. It is only in the third generation that this entrepreneurial drive appears to have slackened.

The answer, I think, is rooted in Jewish history and Jewish attitudes. As I have said elsewhere, I do not subscribe to the idea that the Jews are *inherently* better businessmen; that built into the Jewish character is a talent for business that has somehow been denied to others. Nor, as any student of economic history will confirm, do the Jews have any monopoly on enterprise. In their time the Quakers in Britain and the Scottish Presbyterians in America have been as entrepreneurial as any Jew. What I do believe is that the Jews, by reason of their history and culture, have inherited a whole system of values that, when combined with the environment in which they have found themselves, has led them to behave in quite specific and identifiable ways. And the more hostile and unfriendly the environment, the more marked this characteristic behavior becomes.

It is often forgotten that the Jews of the Russian Pale of Settlement were businessmen long before their expulsion from the rest of the Russian empire by Czar Alexander III. Unlike the West Indian immigrants to Britain or the blacks of the American South, who have displayed none of their entrepreneurial flair, the Jews were already an urban people accustomed to living in towns and used to handling money. Indeed, they had few other options. Forbidden to hold land or enter any of the professions, the Jews of the Russian and Polish ghettos were forced to eke out a precarious existence on the margins of the economy of the Russian empire.

They supplied many of the small but basic services of the town. They were traders, liquor salesmen, drapers, and shopkeepers—what economists call "marginal men." And to be a merchant, a trader, or a self-employed artisan had over the years become part of the Jewish tradition; a set of skills or, perhaps more precisely, attitudes that were handed down from generation to generation.

The immigrants moved first into the garment business and later into property and the film industry, not so much because they had a special knowledge of the techniques of these trades but because they were new forms of enterprise that demanded very little initial capital and presented, as a result of the economic climate of the time, great opportunities.

The Jews' great advantage was that they entered these trades encumbered by none of the traditional attitudes. As they had no preconceived idea of how things had been done in the past, they did not hesitate to try out new methods of financing and organization. The garment business is a case in point. When the Jews arrived in the early 1880s most of the great technological breakthroughs that were to transform the industry from a custom-made basis into a mass-market enterprise had already been achieved. The sewing machine, invented by Isaac Merrit Singer in 1851, had already been in use for over thirty years, and the band-saw, which replaced the tailor's scissors and opened the way to the mass production of men's suits, came only eight years later.

And yet these inventions had had comparatively little impact on the organization of the trade. British tailors continued to make suits just as they had for centuries. As the manager of one British firm explained: "The English tailor seems quite unable to take to the system of subdivision of labor; he likes to make an article throughout; but even were this system possible in our business it would be impossible to find more than an infinitesimal number of English tailors trained or capable of being trained to it. The ready-made trade, as we term it now, is entirely the work of foreign Jews. . . . The English tailor would take one hour to put in a pocket and the Jew tailor, with subdivision, puts in four in twenty minutes."

What the Jews recognized and what their British competitors failed to grasp was that a new industry like the mass-market garment business demanded new methods of working. Subdivision was the key to success. And the rewards went to those who were willing to parcel the work amongst themselves. It was an activity that involved all the members of the family. The cohesiveness of the Jewish family as a factor in their business success is a subject I shall return to later, but it is worth nothing here that without the willingness of all members of the family to help each other out, many of these infant businesses would never have survived.

The involvement of the Jews in the great postwar property boom is another example. The property empires built in the 1950s and 1960s are the work of the second generation, who in many respects are very different men from their fathers, but here again an ability to rethink the underlying principles and to cast aside traditional attitudes is a factor in their success and goes a long way to explaining why property development has come to be regarded as a prototypical Jewish business.

With the benefit of hindsight it can be seen that one of the attractions of property development is the speed at which very small sums can mushroom into sizable fortunes. But at the time this was not at all obvious. To see the latent profit in some run-down, bomb-shattered office block required not only a good deal of imagination but also a willingness to take risks. There were plenty of people in London in the late 1950s who were in an excellent position to cash in on the property boom. The insurance-fund managers, the solicitors, and the real-estate agents who owned these properties or represented those that did should have realized that they were sitting on a gold mine. That, in most cases, they failed to do so is, I think, the result of an attitude of mind. They regarded these buildings not as a commodity that could be bought and sold and whose value fluctuated according to market conditions but as a fixed investment whose sole purpose was to produce a safe and steady return.

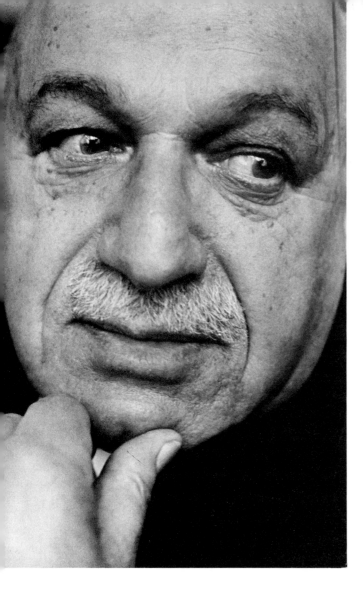

Marks and Spencer Ltd., the English chain store known for its low prices and high quality, continues to prosper under the direction of Joseph Edward Sieff, who joined the firm more than forty years ago. Photo by Chris Smith.

The Sassoons are a distinguished family of English bankers. Until recently Siegfried, the poet, had achieved the widest fame. However, now the family's reputation has spread even further through the work of hair stylist Vidal.

Historically the Jews had never owned land and therefore their attitude to property was much less sentimental: it was a commodity that could be bought and sold, just like any other. Over the centuries the Jews as dealers and traders had developed of necessity a very keen eye for market values, and this they applied to property. "We have been forced to work on tiny margins," one property developer once said to me. "And this has sharpened our skills as valuers. We have had to work to the last penny; to calculate how much an object is worth and how much it can be sold for. We are the best valuers. We are not so interested in how it is made, but we are very interested in how much it is worth, how much it can be sold for."

There is obviously a good deal of truth in this. But what must never be ignored is that the conditions under which the immigrants lived and worked were in themselves a spur to achievement.

Life in the East End of London may not have been as intolerable as it was in Poland, where the Cossack's form of anti-Semitism was a good deal more unpleasant than London's dockers; but even so the Whitechapel Road in the 1890s was not a particularly comfortable place. The housing was poor, the pay was miserable, and the hours inhumanly long. Toward the end of the week, as the Jewish tailors struggled to meet a Monday deadline, they frequently worked thirty-six or forty-eight hours at a stretch. To survive, let alone make enough money to send back to a wife who had often been left behind with the children in Russia, required a good deal of energy, stamina, and self-reliance. An ability to fend for himself is a characteristic of many a self-made man. Thus, in a sense, the ghettos of the cities not only provided shelter and the comfort of mutual assistance for the new arrivals: they also proved to be ideal business nurseries for the budding entrepreneur. It was on the streets of Whitechapel that many of today's Jewish tycoons first learned the basic elements of their trade.

To this must be added an atmosphere of optimism. Though life in the newly established ghetto was not easy, it was not, as it had been in Russia, clouded by a feeling of hopelessness and futility: a sense

that no matter how hard one tried, one's life would remain essentially unchanged. For all their latent (and often overt) anti-Semitism, both Britain and America were fundamentally open societies that rewarded enterprise and initiative. If the newcomers doubted this, they had before them the example of the previous wave of Jewish immigrants—the bankers and other City folk who had not only accumulated splendid fortunes but with their racehorses and country houses had acquired the style, the manners, and the influence of the upper classes. Not everybody aspired to become a Rothschild, but at least his success indicated the possibilities.

The Jewish immigrants who became successful businessmen fit J. A. Schumpeter's classic definition of the entrepreneur. In his *Capitalism, Socialism and Democracy*, the great economist wrote:

> To undertake new things is difficult and constitutes a distinct economic function, first because they lie outside the routine tasks which everybody understands and, secondly, because the environment resists in many ways that vary, according to social conditions, from simple refusal either to finance or buy a new thing, to physical attack on the man who tries to produce it. To act with confidence beyond the range of familiar beacons and overcome that resistance requires aptitudes that are present in only a small fraction of the population and that define the entrepreneurial function. This function does not necessarily consist in inventing anything or otherwise creating the conditions which the enterprise exploits. It consists in getting things done.

The second generation was even more enterprising than their fathers had been. The family tailoring business had performed its function: it had provided the basic necessities. But the work was hard and the rewards were meager. Driven by the need for wealth and the status that money brings, many of the children of the original immigrants turned their backs on their fathers' businesses and cast around for more

131

lucrative opportunities, either as shopkeepers, market traders, or later, as property developers. In a capitalist society there are many ways of accumulating capital: the conventional route is to build up a business to the point where it is sufficiently sound and long established for the shares to be floated to the public, thus putting an external value on the business and giving the founder, assuming he has kept his stake, a sizable capital sum. But even for the most successful the road to public status is long and hazardous. Many of the second generation, better educated and more confident than their fathers, were not prepared to wait that long.

This pattern of behavior is not, of course, peculiar to the Jews. To start at the bottom of the ladder is the customary fate of many immigrant groups. And very similar stimuli propelled the Quakers in mid-eighteenth-century England and the Irish in mid-nineteenth-century New England. But what is remarkable about the Jews is the speed and vigor with which they made the ascent. They may have started off by virtue of economic necessity as members of the proletariat, but unlike their native fellow-workers their instincts were fundamentally middle class. First and foremost, they were individualists who believed passionately in the virtues of education, self-improvement, and self-help. And to my mind the fact that they were Jews goes a long way to explain this phenomenon.

One of the most striking things about the immigrants was the extraordinary determination they displayed to rise above their misfortunes and to become masters of their own fate. This ambition, this dynamism, was something that struck nearly all contemporary observers most forcibly. "The English workers," a Jewish trade-union leader who had spent forty years attempting to organize the tailors of the East End once told me, "went along very slowly: he had to have his pint of beer and his fish and chips. The Jewish worker was an immigrant. He had to be ambitious to survive, and he had to fight for himself. The top workers, the ones who had been in the workshop the longest and were the most skilled, engaged the under-workers. The ambition of an under-worker was to become a top worker; that of a top worker to become a master; and that of a master to become a manufacturer." An obscure immigrant, giving evidence to a British Royal Commission on Alien Immigration at the turn of the century, spoke for a whole generation when he said, "I neither smoke nor drink and believe in everything that will make me better off."

This burning desire for independence and the prosperity that such independence often brings has been one of the most characteristic of Jewish traits. Virtually every study of Jewish economic activity has shown that historically the Jews are individualists who prefer to work for themselves rather than other people. It is not difficult to see why.

In the first place it is, as the trade-union leader I quoted earlier suggested, a function of their immigrant status. It must have been obvious even to the dullest that it was far better to be one's own master than to be a humble employee. But there is much more to it than this. The Jews, like the Quakers and other dissenters before them, were often barred both from the professions and much of big business and therefore had no alternative but to make their own way as best they could. Also, besides the reality of anti-Semitism, there was, perhaps even more important, the *fear* of anti-Semitism. The Jews have been persecuted for so long and been forced to move from place to place so frequently that they have, I would argue, constructed their own survival kit. A sense of identity, a feeling that if things go wrong there will always be other Jews to turn to for assistance, is an important part of this package. But the desire for financial independence is also, I think, an important ingredient. As one British self-made millionaire said to me, "At the back of my mind there is always the fear that one day we might have to take up our bundle and run." In such circumstances the knowledge that one's "bundle" is of a sufficient size to act as a cushion against the world's misfortunes is very comforting. And though today these fears have receded somewhat, a tradition of independence has become established. Quite simply, many Jews now prefer, as a matter of individual taste, not to work for large corporations.

Jewish success in business cannot, however, be completely explained by the external pressures pushing them forward—the harshness of the ghetto environment, the fear and the reality of anti-Semitism, the desire for independence and the security independence was seen to bring. To these must be added the pressures generated inside the Jewish community itself.

Social work was too limited a career for Bernard Cornfeld. His migration, to avoid government regulation and taxation of business, was from Brooklyn to Geneva, where his I.O.S. made fortunes for a few and lost them for many. Photo by Tony Prime.

Like other immigrants before them, the Jews, isolated in a hostile world, turned to one another for help and support. The atmosphere of the ghetto may have been charged with a spirit of cutthroat competition, but it was tempered by a certain charity: the willingness of one Jew to help another.

There is nothing untoward in the preference of Jews to do business with other Jews; nothing is more natural. They speak the same language, come from the same background, and share the same assumptions. Just as Old Etonians or Ivy Leaguers have their old boy nets, so Jews have theirs.

To this must be added the traditional strength of Jewish family life. Though the bonds may have weakened as the Jews prospered in such open societies as America or Britain, the natural cohesiveness and loyalty of Jewish family life would seem to be an undoubted asset when it comes to doing business.

One of the many explanations for the success of the international Jewish bankers, such as the Rothschilds and the Sassoons, has been the fact that they were, in every sense, true family businesses. Not only were all the partners related, but the firm's representatives were also often members of the family. In an era before the development of modern communications and when business was an altogether more personal affair, such an arrangement was distinctly helpful. It smoothed the transference of capital and helped to create the necessary atmosphere of trust and mutual understanding.

The bankers have not been the only Jewish businessmen to turn the family into a powerful secret weapon. Perhaps the most remarkable example of the Jewish family in business is provided by the British catering chain, J. Lyons & Co., the creation of two much intermarried families, the Salmons and the Glucksteins. It is not for nothing that the Gluckstein family motto is *"Union fait la force."* Right from the beginning, J. Lyons was run as a joint enterprise: not only were the responsibilities for running the firm equally shared between the Salmons and the Glucksteins, but the decision was made that all the

Hermione Gingold (1897–   ) promotes the products of the leisure industry. Photo by Arnold Newman.

Madame Helena Rubinstein (1871?–1965) emigrated from Krakow, Poland, to Australia in 1902 and there opened a beauty shop. Leaving the shop in the care of her sister, she directed the opening of salons throughout Europe and the Americas, and eventually developed a line of cosmetics that were marketed worldwide. Photo by Alfred Eisenstaedt.

proceeds should be equally divided. This principle extended far beyond the shares each member of the family had in the company itself. Houses, cars, and even jewelry were distributed on the same equitable basis. The family was the firm and the firm the family. Board meetings and family councils became practically indistinguishable. There are, of course, disadvantages to this approach as well as advantages, but it does illustrate how potent the Jewish family method can be.

Over and above Jewish family feeling lies Jewish attitude to wealth. Like everything else in Jewish society, this is changing as circumstances ease and alter. The findings of modern sociologists indicate that the desire for wealth, so marked in first- and second-generation immigrants, is weakening fast. But there is no doubt that in the status-conscious, hierarchical society of the ghetto, whose culture and mores fashioned the attitudes of the first-generation immigrants, wealth was regarded almost as highly as learning. Wealth in the ghetto was valued and sought after not so much for the material comforts it brought but for the respect and prestige that was attached to it—particularly if it was used for the service of the community. To be a servant of the community, to give one's wealth for the benefit of others, was, and still is, a religious obligation, a mark of one's quality as a Jew.

Powerful though this pressure was, it would perhaps be unduly naïve to regard this as the sole motive force behind the young entrepreneur's search for wealth. Money was not only the open-sesame to status and acceptance in the Jewish world: it opened many doors to gentile society as well. As the first- and second-generation immigrants recognized very clearly, with money they could buy the two things they desired above all: security and respect. Having money helped to reinforce a somewhat shaky sense of identity.

This need for wealth is often thought to be a permanent feature of the Jewish condition, but the events of the last twenty-five years would seem to prove otherwise. As the memories of the ghetto fade and the members of the third generation become increasingly assimilated into their host societies, the stereotype of the self-made, restless, acquisitive Jewish businessman is beginning to look increasingly old-fashioned. He was the product of a very special period in Jewish history, and for all his achievements he still moves in a small, Jewish world which his better-educated and better-endowed children find too narrow and too constricting. They have not completely forgotten their past. They are still wary of the large corporations with their armies of "Wasps" and often prefer to make their own way as self-employed professionals—as doctors, dentists, and lawyers. They are still interested in success, but it is status—that classic middle-class preoccupation—not money that is the yardstick now.

134

Trades learned in the Old Country provided the means of survival.

New York Business

Harry Golden

The Jews of America are, in the main, the single proprietary class. The only salaried Jew in most communities is the rabbi. Only in New York, Los Angeles, Chicago, and Philadelphia is there a Jewish proletariat. (Interestingly enough, from this proletariat come two-thirds of the taxi-drivers in these cities.) The rest are merchants, salesmen, peddlers, and professionals.

When the cotton mills of New England began to move to the South in the first decade of the twentieth century, Jewish merchants, principally immigrants from Eastern Europe, followed them. It was not long before there was a "Jew store" in every city and town, dealing in ready-to-wear, soft goods, and jewelry. Meanwhile Jewish peddlers were doing business in rural areas. First came the pack peddler—cloth, needles, notions; later came the clothing peddlers and the soft-goods peddlers; and finally the jewelry peddlers. There was a fellow in each state who handled mattresses. He called himself the "matritz man," and thousands of black sharecroppers used the same Yiddish pronunciation.

It may come as a surprise to many people who do not associate Jews with the grocery business to know that around 1905 there were hundreds of Jewish grocerymen in the South, taking advantage of the fact that the white gentile grocer was not yet interested in the black trade.

The term "Jew peddler" appeared in public print in the early part of this century; later came the term "Jew store," which is still widely used among the rural white and black populations of the South, although it is never intended as an insult. Customers upon entering an establishment often ask, "Is this a Jew store?"—their interest prompted by a widespread legend that a Jewish merchant will make every possible concession or sacrifice to chalk up the first sale of the day, accepting any offer rather than lose his first customer. The farmers and sharecroppers vie with one another to be the first one in the store to get the "bargain."

136

This tradition is old and comes from that Jewish concern for *parnoseh*, for a livelihood. I remember, as a boy on the Lower East Side of New York, that peddlers would shout, "Women, women, I need a 'first!'" I often accompanied my mother on her shopping expeditions to help her carry the heavy bags (we were a family of seven, plus three boarders). In those days many of the peddlers kept stalls under the Williamsburg Bridge. When we were ready to go home my mother would stop and say, "Go see if anyone hasn't had a 'first' yet." If I pointed to one of the stalls, my mother would make some token purchase for a penny or two so that the man could have his "first."

The Jew's desire to be self-employed dictated his choice of occupation. For one thing, orthodox Jews couldn't work on the Sabbath or on at least a dozen religious holidays; as self-employed, they could quit on Friday at noon and celebrate the Sabbath and stay away from work on all the holidays. This of course was only one of the reasons for being self-employed. Another reason was the desire to be individual-istic or "your own boss." It was the dream of every Jewish boy.

Furthermore, the Jew realized that he could not compete in the employment market. He talked with a heavy accent, and his clothes and habits were different. He would hardly be hired by R. H. Macy and Company or any other store. So he decided to present his merchandise to R. H. Macy instead. And thus he became an "employee" of R. H. Macy through the back door.

Wedged between Times Square and Herald Square, and bordered by Seventh Avenue on the one side and Broadway on the other, but spilling over east and west, is the most temperamental one-tenth of a square mile in the world, otherwise known as the Garment District. Easily the most colorful part of the needle trades is the women's clothing industry, which has its headquarters in the neighborhood. On Seventh Avenue the people who work at it, for it, and in it call it the rag game.

Much of the success of this business depends upon fluctuating emotions in the American home. The wife looks in the closet one day and gets a deprived feeling. She turns to her husband and says, "Do you

New skills were quickly acquired. David Sarnoff (1891–1971), born in Minsk and emigrating to America at nine years of age, became the fastest telegraphic operator in his new land. At thirty-nine, he became president of RCA. Photo at right by Alfred Eisenstaedt.

know, Sam, I haven't a thing to wear." That Saturday she comes home with a bulge in her shopping bag. "What's in the bag?" says Sam. "Oh, just a little nothing," she says.

Each year the American husband spends billions of dollars on these little nothings. What the housewife calls a little nothing the manufacturer calls a rag. Rags are made everywhere, but more of them are made and sold in New York City than anywhere else in the world.

Before the coming of the unions, the garment industry was a jungle. It was based on a subcontractor's system of the sweatshop. Work was done in the home. In one of the rooms four men would sit, one or two women, a couple of young girls, aged anywhere from nine to fourteen, and perhaps an eleven-year-old boy working after school; and they were all working on knickerbockers, or "knee pants," as everybody called them in the tenements and in the trade.

It was all piecework. The rate of pay a worker earned was based on the quality of the knee pants. The cheaper the grade of knee pants, the cheaper the rate of pay. The average was about seventy-five cents a dozen for the complete operation. This complete operation included everything from the cloth to the finished garment. This would leave a family of, say, five about fifteen dollars a week. Payment was at the rate of two cents a pair for the presser; thus the hot irons were kept on the stove in the heat of the summer (the season) so that the presser (usually the father) always had an iron available. The children would handle piles of knee pants after the mother got through with the sewing and pile them up for the finisher. The finisher, a young girl, received ten cents a dozen. These young girls (and often the wife) were all considered "learners," which enabled the contractor to pay them whatever wages he chose and also enabled everybody to circumvent whatever labor laws were on the books.

The sweatshop, with its trinity of evils—low wages, long hours, and female and child labor—remained the essential economic problem of the Jewish population of New York City until the workers organized and the unions became strong enough to act.

The International Ladies' Garment Workers' Union (ILGWU) was founded in 1900, followed by the Cap Makers' Union in 1901, the Fur Workers' Union in 1904, and the Amalgamated Clothing Workers' Union (ACWU) in 1914. The first general strike in the needle trades began on November 22, 1909, when twenty thousand Jewish factory girls, makers of blouses and skirts, walked out on their jobs. Upper- and middle-class women joined the picket lines after mounted police tried routing the strikers. For the first time uptown gentile clergymen and churchwomen from all over the city picketed with the shopgirls.

The following year the entire garment industry was paralyzed by the city's biggest strike when sixty thousand cloakmakers put down their tools. Dismayed by the bitterness of the struggle between Jewish workers and Jewish employers, and by the use of Jewish thugs to assault strikers, the uptown Jewish community helped bring about a settlement. Louis Marshall and Jacob Schiff with the aid of Louis D. Brandeis, who came down from Boston to serve as chairman of the mediation board, drafted "the protocol of peace" that marked a milestone in the history of industrial relations. The settlement sounded the death knell of the sweatshop by abolishing piecework in the home and contractors' shops. It also gave the workers shorter hours, higher wages, and decent working conditions, and set a precedent for peaceful resolution of labor conflicts in other industries by creating a permanent arbitration machinery.

The Jewish unions wielded important political influence in New York. As the backbone of the Socialist party, they elected Meyer London to the House of Representatives, seated several Socialists in the state legislature, and enabled Morris Hillquit to make a remarkable showing in the 1907 mayoralty election.

David Dubinsky and his aides, including his successor Louis Stulberg, built the ILGWU into a union that today has 450,000 members with millions of dollars in its reserves and welfare fund. It provides pensions, college scholarships, homes for the aged, low-cost housing in the city, and vacation grounds in the country. Not long ago Dubinsky made money available to the Rockefellers for a housing project in Puerto Rico.

David Schwartz is the largest manufacturer in the garment industry. He operates fifty-six industries in New York, New Jersey, and the South. His company is Jonathan Logan, the giant of the women's-wear business. It makes dresses not by the dozen but by the thousands—and this enterprise was built up by one

138

An active union member in Poland, where he was born in 1892, David Dubinsky survived his Siberian exile and reached New York in 1911, where he rose to the presidency of the International Ladies Garment Workers Union—a position he held for thirty-three years. Photo by Alfred Eisenstaedt.

man, David Schwartz, who is still in charge of it all. He has bought up company after company until he now controls the biggest dress empire in the country.

Complementing the garment trades is the fur industry, which is almost wholly in the hands of the Jews, who brought the manufacture of furs from Eastern Europe.

One of New York's great institutions, R. H. Macy's, accommodates every citizen in the city. The store, billed for many years as "The World's Largest," employs some fourteen hundred clerks, many of whom are bilingual; as a group they speak forty-two languages, which is probably enough to take care of a customer who wants a bedspread or a pair of socks for her nephew. During the Christmas season Macy's cash registers ring up three million dollars on a single Saturday. Their policy of service, we can assume, has paid dividends.

Rowland Hussey Macy was a Quaker from Nantucket, a square-built man who had been schooled, like Herman Melville, in the whaling fleet. After two or three poor starts in Massachusetts, opening small shops which did not prosper, Macy opened a dry-goods store on Fourteenth Street and Sixth Avenue. The year was 1858. One of his commercial weapons was using a healthy proportion of his profits for advertising, most of which he wrote himself. Another was the Nantucketer's sense of adventure: he experimented with different sales items; he branched out. Soon he had what would soon become known as a "department store." During his first year Macy pulled ninety thousand dollars in volume sales; by 1876 sales had risen to over one and a half million.

At Macy's death the store passed into the hands of two junior partners, Abiel La Forge and Robert Macy Valentine. La Forge died shortly thereafter, and Valentine brought into management a Macy relative and employee, Charles B. Webster. This gentleman, in turn, brought in his brother-in-law, Jerome B. Wheeler. After a number of disagreements Webster broke off with Wheeler and bought him and his stock out in 1887.

What has all this to do with the Jews of New York City?

Well, hang in there.

When Webster found himself standing alone in that huge store, with all that merchandise and all those customers, he went looking around for some new blood that might help him revitalize the whole operation. And that's what he found in the family of Lazarus Straus.

Straus was a Jewish grain merchant from Bavaria who had come to America in 1848. With four sons he opened a little store in Talbotton, Georgia. After the Civil War, in which he supported the Confederate cause, he moved to Philadelphia and then to New York, where he started a wholesale chinaware importing firm known as L. Straus & Sons. The company had done business with Macy's since 1874; Straus leased departments in the store to sell china, glassware, and silver. Eventually the Strauses became partners and ultimately bought Webster out.

Isidore was sensitive, nervous, and a worrier. Nathan, his younger brother, was popular, enthusiastic, outgoing, and a natty dresser. Together they built Macy's revenues from five million in 1888 to ten million in 1902, which was the year the store moved uptown to Thirty-fourth Street. In 1922 Macy's stock was offered to the public with the Straus family retaining control. During the succeeding decades of the century, the Strauses expanded by buying interests in various stores in the Midwest and California, as well as opening branches in many outlying areas of New York.

A block from Macy's is another department store, which had quite a different origin. Gimbel Brothers was founded in 1842, in the then frontier town of Vincennes, Indiana, by Adam Gimbel, an immigrant Jewish peddler from Bavaria. The first of the modern Gimbel stores opened in Milwaukee in 1887. A Philadelphia store, since grown to many acres of space, was opened in 1894. New York was invaded in 1909. The Saks Company (which once stood between Macy's and Gimbels and is now Korvettes) was absorbed by Gimbels in 1923, Saks Fifth Avenue was opened the next year, and the Kaufmann and Baer Company of Pittsburgh was purchased in 1925. Under dynamic Bernard F. Gimbel, one of the

William Zeckendorf's real estate ventures changed the landscape of several cities. His landmark will be the site which he assembled and then persuaded John D. Rockefeller, Jr., to purchase and give to the United Nations for its New York headquarters. Photo by Dennis Stock.

founder's grandsons, who became president in 1927 and board chairman in 1953, the firm developed unusually forceful advertising and promotion. Expansion carried it to Chicago, Detroit, Beverly Hills, Miami Beach, San Francisco, and elsewhere. Bruce Alva Gimbel, of the fourth generation, succeeded his father as president.

Another type of merchandising was promoted by Nathan Ohrbach, who came to America at the age of two from Vienna. By the time he was twenty-eight he had already spent eighteen years in retailing. With the profits from his small clothing shops he went into business with Max Wiesen, a dress manufacturer, and opened a large retailing operation on Fourteenth Street, across the square from S. Klein's. What Ohrbach's offered was high-style ladies' wear at low cost. Its policy was "a business in millions, a profit in pennies."

On opening day Ohrbach's was not only a success, it was a near riot: customers overwhelmed the store clerks, overturned tables, and left a score of persons bruised and battered. Police were called in. Merchandise was rushed to the store to refurbish the bare tables and racks. This was to be a repeated ritual on "sale days" at Ohrbach's.

In 1954 Ohrbach's made the bold move of relocating on Thirty-fourth Street, thus coming into competition with Macy's and Gimbels, not to mention the more exclusive department stores on Fifth Avenue. Ohrbach's not only made a go of it in the new location, they astounded their competitors. One hundred thousand customers crowded into their new store and spent half a million dollars on opening day. Macy's advertised: "If you live through this, you are ready for Macy's."

In the 1960s Nathan Ohrbach and his son Jerome merged interests in Ohrbach's with the Brenninkmayer family, which had built a mercantile empire in Europe, with a home base in Holland. Nathan and Jerome then quietly slipped into the background, and the exact stock ownership in the company, as regards the Ohrbachs and the Brenninkmayers, still remains unknown.

Other Jewish-owned department stores have included Lord & Taylor, Arnold Constable, and Bloomingdale's.

Between Fifth and Sixth Avenues from the lower Forties to lower Fifties, with headquarters on Forty-seventh Street, is the most amazing diamond market in the world. It was built up by Jewish refugees from Antwerp who moved their businesses to New York in the wake of Hitler's conquests.

Shop windows filled with diamonds ranging in price from fifty dollars to twenty thousand line both sides of Forty-seventh Street, which teems with uniformed policemen, private detectives, customers, buyers and cutters, polishers and setters. The ground floors of the buildings are lined by booths populated by dealers, appraisers, salesmen. On the floors above are the offices of diamond-cutting firms, equipment suppliers, and diamond brokers.

The entire diamond business runs on credit and memoranda. A nod of the head, a handshake, buyer and seller each repeating *mazel 'n brocha*—a benediction for good luck—are enough to seal a hundred-thousand-dollar deal in uncut stones. On any given day there is literally over a billion dollars' worth of diamonds along this street, mostly in the pocket wallets of the individual buyers and sellers, who attach their wallets to an iron chain, which in turn attaches to a leather belt wrapped around the body.

Rarely is there a disagreement or a mistake in this business. Many of these men belong to the Diamond Dealers Club of America, whose charter demands that no member ever initiate legal proceedings against another. When there is a disagreement, the Diamond Dealers Club sets up an arbitration board whose findings bind both parties. Its word is law, and a member who breaches that law is drummed out of the industry—and almost immediately the word reaches London, Antwerp, Milan, Buenos Aires, Tel Aviv, and Johannesburg.

The Diamond Dealers Club, which resembles a guild more than a club, controls the industry. Its membership is almost all Jewish. Jack Sigmon, its president, told me with a sad sigh: "We used to have four gentiles as members, but one died last year; now there are only three."

A significant number of Hasidim are dealers; many others are technicians. A Hasid-dealer will pause momentarily in a crowded street doorway, open his black wallet, and extract a small square of tissue paper; inside of this may be precious gems worth many thousands of dollars. He passes a gem over to a buyer, utters the *mazel 'n brocha*, and proceeds to another doorway—a man from an earlier century perfectly adept in the twentieth.

At seven every morning, most of the Hasidim arrive in Manhattan in buses which have transported them over forty miles from their ultra-orthodox enclave at New Square, New York. These pious Jews have literally created a Jewish shtetl in Rockland County. New Square is entirely new and entirely Hasidic. The women, who also work in the diamond trade, travel in a segregated section of the bus. The bus always carries the Torah and the Eternal Light, which shines on the Torah for the morning and evening services.

Each of the organizations on Forty-seventh Street has a central room with lockers, tables, telephones, kosher cafeterias, bullet-proof windows, and walls studded with burglar alarms. Above the headquarters of the Diamond Dealers Club is a small synagogue, where the dealers can attend the late-afternoon *mincha* service.

At night the street is barren, the windows stripped of stone and ring. And all over the city and suburbs there are hundreds of worried diamond dealers—"Did I close that safe? Did I pull it tight?" Invariably they did, but as one dealer told me, "We never stop worrying. Never."

A complement of Jews, indeed a large complement, transformed the needle trades of New York into the garment industry and built up the fur industry. Another complement of Jews, indeed a minuscule complement, established the movie industry in California. The National Broadcasting Corporation, which helped change America's listening habits, was founded by one Jew, David Sarnoff, in 1926.

The Jewish immigrant responded enthusiastically to the American dream of "from rags to riches." Indeed it was partly this that brought him to America in the first place to try his luck.

America has given the Jews freedom of religion, free education, and economic opportunity. The Jews have repaid America with industry, science, medicine, art, and entertainment. There has never been a more even trade.

Brooklyn-born William Jaird Levitt founded a construction company that was to build cities named after him. Between 1947 and 1951 he converted a Long Island potato field into a village of some 17,500 one-family houses which sold for less than eight thousand dollars each.

OVERLEAF: After a hard year's work . . . Miami Beach—or Tel Aviv. Photos by Charles E. Rotkin and Cartier-Bresson.

The Rothschilds

Nicholas Faith

The House of Rothschild was founded in Frankfort by Meyer Amschel Rothschild (1743–1812), and his five sons provided its international diversity and unity. The young Meyer Amschel (1793–1855) remained in Frankfort, while Salomon (1774–1855) moved to Vienna, Nathan Meyer (1777–1836) to London, Karl (1788–1855) to Naples, and James (1792–1868) to Paris. Photo by Arnold Newman.

In 1969 aficionados of the European financial scene were intrigued by a breach between the French and the British branches of the great house of Rothschild. In France, where the bank had re-established itself fully and glamorously since World War II, Baron Guy de Rothschild allied himself publicly with an outsider—Bernie Cornfeld and his Investors Overseas Services—to sell investments to the wider French public through a joint venture, Rothschild-Expansion. The British house refused, quietly but firmly, to have anything to do with Cornfeld at a time when most of the European financial world was falling at his feet. Within a couple of years it had become painfully obvious that the French house had committed a dreadful mistake, unique in Rothschild history, that of allying itself publicly with a financial trickster, whose methods of selling, accounting, and investing hovered at or over the boundaries of fraud.

The division between the two "cousins' " banks, which had been drawing together during the previous seven years, was bitter and personal. Jacob Rothschild, the driving force behind the success of the English branch in the 1960s, had told Guy of his suspicions of Cornfeld's business methods. But Guy had curtly told Jacob that he had forty years of banking experience against Jacob's mere forty months. The remark was unfair and only partly true, but it was characteristic; and so was the arrogant, truly Rothschildian way the then thirty-three-year-old Jacob led his much less important branch of the bank in a direction opposite to that of the French.

146

Jacob's self-confidence and his bluntness are not the only two qualities he shares with his fabled ancestor, Nathan Meyer Rothschild, the founder of the London house. Although Jacob's face is long, horsy, English, it shares with his pudgy ancestor's a heavy-lipped, lowering-lidded, give-nothing-away look. (This is no pose; I remember, during the height of a financial battle, seeing Jacob confronted by a secret and embarrassing document that had accidentally fallen into the hands of my newspaper: not a muscle moved; and he refused to allow the existence of the letter to alter his attitude in the subsequent discussion.)

Jacob needed all his ancestor's qualities, for the bank he entered at the beginning of the 1960s was very far from the usual picture of the shrewd, all-knowing, immensely rich house of Rothschild. It was badly run-down; its professional reputation was that of a virtually extinct volcano; it was, probably, not even very rich. What is more, Jacob was not the dominant shareholder, even though he is the eldest son of the present Lord Rothschild, the head of the family.

The bank had been slumbering, with a few brilliant exceptions, for over eighty years. Ironically the decline, unnoticeable at first, started soon after its most publicized triumph, when Lionel Rothschild lent 4 million pounds to the British government to enable it to buy the Egyptian government's shares in the Suez Canal in 1875.

Four years later Lionel died. His three sons—"Natty" (the first Lord Rothschild), Alfred, and Leopold, collectively famous as the Magnificent Rothschilds, the royal, almost the holy family of Judaism— deliberately renounced the commercial aggression which, together with the wealth, makes up the Rothschild inheritance.

Natty once revealed that he had turned down the chance to issue the shares in the Guinness Brewery, one of the soundest businesses in Britain. The introduction would have provided the house with a million pounds—a sum that, a journalist remarked, even the Rothschilds would have thought worth putting in their pockets. "I don't quite look at it that way," said Natty. "I go to the house every morning, and when I say no to every scheme and enterprise submitted to me I return home at night carefree and contented. But when I agree to any proposal I am immediately filled with anxiety. To say yes is like putting your finger in a machine—the whirring wheels may drag your whole body in after the finger."

Natty was not speaking the whole truth: it was Rothschild money that proved decisive in Cecil Rhodes' titanic battle with Woolf Barnato to control De Beers, the world diamond monopoly. The Rothschild-controlled oilfields in Baku, in Russia's Caucasus, and the Rothschild-supported Shell company were the major independent threats to John D. Rockefeller's Standard Oil in the early years of the century.

In addition the family could point to the problems of their great rivals, the Barings, who had to be salvaged from bankruptcy in 1890 because of their over-aggressiveness in Rothschild's traditional area, international loans. There was, wrote the late Cecil Roth, the collective biographer of the magnificent three, "an increasing tendency, more pronounced in England than on the Continent, to turn the banking house into mere administrative offices for the investment of the capital accumulated over the previous lucrative decades." Even a decade before World War I an (admittedly unfriendly) witness, the German ambassador, noted that "even if the Rothschilds were willing they would not be competent to float a foreign loan."

Business life for the three seems to have had all the lack of tension Natty could have desired. "Leopold arrived first about 11," recalls Ronald Palin in his charming memoirs of life in that gentlemanly backwater, "lunched at 1:30 and left at about 5. Alfred did not turn up until two o'clock or later, lunched between 3:30 and 4, and after his brother's departure often fell asleep on a leather-covered sofa." It was not that the three were lazy: it was simply that in their scale of priorities the bank came well after the social life centered in their London mansions on Rothschild Row, in Piccadilly, or on the country estates sprawling all over the Chiltern Hills—after, also, the manifold charitable and political problems imposed by their leadership of Britain's, and Europe's, Jewish community.

During World War I all three brothers died: Alfred, the bachelor, and probably the richest of the three, bequeathed much of his wealth to an outsider, the Countess of Carnavon. The legacy helped to finance

147

The Rothschild coat of arms. The five arrows symbolize the five sons. Photo by Patrick Ward.

the expedition that discovered the grave of Tutankhamen. The money, like that paid in death duties, was lost to the bank, and in the next generation there was no new impetus to replace it.

Leopold's two sons, Lionel and Anthony, were the only two of their generation interested in the bank, and they kept the old ways going. From all accounts, the bank they ran, while by no means sharp on business, had an enormous appeal. The staff numbered under a hundred—all known by name to the partners —and even in the grim days of the 1930s, when a lot of the work consisted in the renegotiation and refunding of loans on which countries like Brazil or Chile could no longer pay interest, there was never any question of anyone's being sacked, no idea of reducing salaries. Young gentlemen were still recruited straight from the best schools as clerks. They lived in the poky, overcrowded, old-fashioned Victorian offices on the site in New Court, near the Mansion House, where Nathan Meyer had settled after the Napoleonic Wars; they were a happy, relaxed, unbankerly family, lost in awe and admiration of the benevolent, headmasterly figures of Lionel and Anthony.

The creative energies of the family were employed elsewhere, largely in the world of scientific research. Once, when an interviewer implied that the family merely dabbled in scientific research, Victor,

148

the present Lord Rothschild, replied, "My father was a scientist and made an important contribution to our knowledge of how plague is transmitted. My uncle was a scientist and a fellow of the Royal Society; my Austrian cousin Louis was a competent scientist. My French cousin Edward founded the Paris Institute of Biophysics, the subject upon which I work. Finally, my sister and I are both scientists"—his sister, in fact, is one of the world's leading authorities on fleas.

Victor was a different kind of Rothschild. He tried the bank for a couple of months and found it dull. "Victor," according to one friend, "is an aristocrat. He is a socialist because he thinks socialists are nicer people. For a Jew of his generation, remember, Tories were noticeable for their lack of opposition to fascism."

As a young man in the 1930s, he "threw himself with all his driving energies into the work of rescuing Jews in Germany"; during World War II he gained the George Medal—given for bravery—for his work on bomb disposal. For twelve years after the war he was in charge of research for the Shell Oil group;

The House of Rothschild financed the construction of the Suez Canal. In recent years this engineering triumph has been one of the causes of the enmity between Israel and Egypt.

MONEY'S WORTH FOR THE MONEY.

"Egyptian Government sold to English Government Suez Canal shares for £4,000,000 sterling. Minister is authorised to draw on ROTHSCHILD at sight."—*Friday's Telegram.*

S our Indian door-key we mean to hold fast,
    BRITANNIA's will she has now found a way for;
On our shop-keeping instincts contempt let them cast,
    But who'll take what we've forked out four millions to pay for?

Such a sum if it suit JOHN BULL's int'rest to pay,
    It is clear it suits Egypt's 'cute Chief to receive.
Now KHEDIVE upon ROTHSCHILD may draw any day,
    We must take care that nobody draws on KHEDIVE.

Lord Rothschild in the study of his home at Cambridge. Photo by Arnold Newman.

Gathered in the board room of Rothschild Frères, Paris, are Baron Guy de Rothschild (foreground) and his cousins, the brothers Baron Elie, Baron Alain. Photo by Arnold Newman.

recently he has created in the "Central Policy Review Staff," popularly known as his "think tank," the first instrument a British prime minister and his cabinet have possessed that is capable of ruthless, impartial assessments of government policies, independent of the official Whitehall machine. But his greatest triumph —which required all his faculties, those of the arrogant aristocrat as much as those of the research scientist— has been to increase (over the dead bodies, metaphorically at least, of virtually the whole British scientific establishment) the degree of departmental control over the money spent by the British government in supporting scientific research.

Victor Rothschild, charming though he might be, was far from an ideal father. Jacob, awkward, slow to develop, was unhappy at home. At Eton he suffered from an unappetizing blend of anti-Semitism and envy peculiar to the well-born British young. To increase the humiliation he had the greatest difficulty in getting a commision when he did his two years of national service in the Royal Horse Guards. Possibly the worst experience came when he went to Oxford. As a Rothschild he was invited to read a passage of the Scriptures at one of the regular tea parties given by Cecil Roth, then the university's Reader in Jewish Studies, and had, blushingly, to admit that he could read no Hebrew. Even today, he greatly regrets his lack of a proper Jewish upbringing—and he married, in a Registry office, a Canadian heiress, Serena Dunn, the first time a Rothschild had married a girl richer than himself; she remains a Catholic.

At Oxford, however, for the first time he found friends of his own age and started to realize his abilities, gaining a first-class degree in history. On graduation he was unsettled: he realized that (despite his degree) he was not an able enough historian to become an academic. During his Oxford years he had been uninterested in banking (indeed was puzzled by the interest displayed in finances by contemporary

150

The partners' room of N. M. Rothschild and Sons, London, is the center of operations for Mr. Edmund Rothschild, his brother Leopold, at his right, and his cousin Evelyn. Photo by Arnold Newman.

The Honorable Jacob Rothschild.
Photo by Patrick Ward.

scions of other banking families). He had (and has) an interest in the arts—his parents had been divorced; his mother (the daughter of an English lawyer who had embraced Judaism on her marriage) had remarried an author, Rex Warner, and lived in an artistic environment in the country. Ten years later a Rothschild Trust bought shares in the Sotheby's and Park-Bernet auction business, and Jacob personally bought Colnaghis, a well-known London art dealer. But neither art nor academic life was really ever a serious possibility as a lifetime career.

When Jacob went into the bank in the early 1960s, after a period of training in other financial businesses (which taught him what modern investment banking was all about) the bank was already stirring. After the war Anthony, who had survived his brother, had continued as though nothing had changed. He sat in the Partners' Room, his only company a career banker, David Colville, vaguely connected to the family by marriage, and not himself a full partner, merely "an assistant to the partners." Anthony, according to Palin, "scorned to cultivate men he did not particularly like for the sake of possibly valuable contacts. He did not travel himself and did not sit on the boards of the numerous public companies which would have been delighted to have him. 'They know where we live,' he would say of potential clients, 'and if they want to do business with us, let them come and talk to us.' And when they did come, if he did not like their faces or their manners he showed them the door without hesitation, no matter how profitable the proposed transaction might be."

This attitude, indeed the whole bank, changed inevitably and completely with Anthony's death (partly caused by the strain of carrying on the business singlehanded) in the late 1950s. It was not all Jacob's doing; Anthony's son Evelyn, sallow, mercurial, and his cousins Eddie and Leo had already started the process that transformed the bank in a decade from a unique, paternalist Victorian institution into a

151

successful but somehow soulless merchant bank, resembling far more others of its kind, in Paris, London, or New York, than the charming anachronism it had remained until a few years before. Inevitably, too, the old hideout was replaced by a handsome modern building, noted for the tapestries in the hall, the bust of the founder, the traditional Rothschild courtyard, but otherwise just an anonymous office block. The rebuilding was Evelyn's initiative, but most of the business drive came from Jacob, a young man in a hurry to prove himself.

The desire to succeed is obsessive: Jacob will play tennis on and on with someone who is a better player until he wins at least one set. He never seems to forgive when he loses out in one of the take-over battles that are such a feature of life in the City of London. Other bankers may treat these contests like a game: he seems to retain a personal animosity against the men with whom he has fought unsuccessful battles.

Ironically, his chances were improved when the pre-Jacob bank lost a battle in 1961 when it was defending Odhams, a magazine publisher, in a take-over battle and was humiliatingly defeated. The jeering in the financial press at the bank's amateurishness brought to the fore Jacob's obsessional energies. He created a corporate finance department, which chased after clients as professionally as Anthony had turned them away. He recruited not clerks straight from school, who could be trained as pliable deferential retainers, but brilliant contemporaries, some already friends from Oxford, others former journalists, but virtually none of Jewish blood. The changes were not bloodless; his cousins welcomed his energies (and indeed the much underrated Evelyn has more and more important directorships in businesses outside the bank than Jacob), but Philip Shelbourne, a brilliant tax lawyer recruited before Jacob's time, left in 1970, realizing that there was no room for two top men in the bank. More constructively, in a throwback to Nathan Meyer, Jacob pioneered a major instrument of international finance. It was the London Rothschild bank that, together with Warburgs and White, Weld and Company, invented the international Euro-bond market, to enable governments, public corporations, and companies alike to borrow long-term vast sums of money in an international, freely negotiated currency. What Nathan Meyer did with sterling loans in the first half of the nineteenth century, his descendants did with dollars a hundred and fifty years later.

Yet, for all the changes, the London house has remained truer to itself and its inheritance than the grander, richer, Paris Rothschilds. When their general manager, Georges Pompidou, went off to run France as De Gaulle's prime minister in 1962, they seemingly lost their way. His successor induced them to go into retail banking and into the disastrous partnership with Cornfeld. The record of their holding company, the Compagnie du Nord (also the name of the railway system the family had financed so successfully a century earlier), ranged from the mediocre to the downright discreditable. And even though they retained their social glory as leaders of society, of *le tout* Paris, this was in a city which, increasingly through the 1960s, appeared to outsiders a trifle provincial.

But, as in London, rescue may be on the way. Another Rothschild, David, has just started work in the glass-and-marble headquarters in the Rue Laffitte with its incomparable view over Paris; and David has been properly trained—at École Polytechnique and the Harvard Business School. As so often in the past, it is only when their rivals have comprehensively written off this amazing family that they fight back most effectively.

The renowned vineyards of Château Mouton-Rothschild provide the background for Baron Philippe de Rothschild and his wife Pauline. Photo by Arnold Newman.

OVERLEAF, LEFT: In the main hall of their château at Ferrières are Baron Guy de Rothschild, his wife Marie Helene, and their son Edouard. Photo by Arnold Newman.

OVERLEAF, RIGHT: The eighteenth-century Paris town house of Baron Elie de Rothschild holds masterpieces of art from earlier and later centuries. With the Baron are his wife Liliane, his son Michel, and his daughters Nelly and Elizabeth. Photo by Arnold Newman.

Laurence Harvey (Laruska Mischa Skikne, of Joniskis, Lithuania) found there was Room at the Top in London and New York. Ringo Starr and Peter Sellers do not need binoculars to enjoy his acting. Harvey's unexpected death in 1973 ended a brilliant movie and stage career. Photo by Arnold Newman.

The Show-Business Entrepreneur

Philip French

On Sunday, January 7, 1973, the International Ballroom of Hollywood's Beverly Hilton Hotel was the setting for one of the most singular and spectacular events in the history of show busines. The guest list read like a roll call of film stars and movie executives past and present. Greetings from the President of the United States and effusive messages from around the world were read. Six cameras filmed the proceedings for posterity. While the illustrious guests ate the dinner for which they had paid one hundred and twenty-five dollars a plate, watched special films and an elaborate floor show, and listened to endless speeches, the guest of honor—a diminutive, wizened figure in a wheel chair—was resting in a nearby suite. He had a lot to think about, many memories to play back through his still active mind. One hundred years before to the day he had been born in Ricse, a small Hungarian town, where his father was an impoverished Jewish store-keeper. Orphaned as a child, he was raised by relatives before emigrating to America at the age of sixteen. He arrived in New York in 1889 with a few dollars sewn inside his shabby vest and scarcely able to manage a word of English.

His name was Adolph Zukor, president emeritus of Paramount Pictures, the company that he had created sixty years before and that was now experiencing one of its greatest periods of prosperity, having recently released *The Godfather*, a film that in less than six months had proved to be the most profitable movie ever made—a picture that dealt in a way with another approach to the American Dream. Zukor had outlived his partners, rivals, and enemies; he had survived at the top of an industry renowned for its ruthlessness, its sudden and cruel fluctuations of fortune.

When Zukor was wheeled onto the stage he received a standing ovation. The hundred candles on the massive birthday cake were sold for charity at a thousand dollars apiece. He was presented with President Nixon's Certificate of Distinguished Achievement "in recognition of his outstanding contribution to the American Motion Picture Industry." "The creative vision and ingenuity of Adolph Zukor," the citation read, "have inspired the growth of an art form that entertains, informs, and enriches the lives of millions around the world."

Zukor might have wondered about that, though his response was, "God bless the President of the United States and every move he makes." He might have wondered too at the possible ambiguity in the claim made by Jack Valenti, president of the Motion Picture Association, that he was "the motion-picture world's living proof that there is a connection between us and our past." No doubt the ancient patriarch was amused when Bob Hope, whose career was shaped by Zukor's company, looked at another former Paramount star and quipped, "Mr. Zukor knew some of the people personally that Charlton Heston is now playing."

Though born for the leading roles in *Disraeli* (as pictured) and *The House of Rothschild*, George Arliss (1868–1946) achieved stage fame in *The Second Mrs. Tanqueray* and film fame as the portrayer of historical characters of other faiths, from *Alexander Hamilton* (1913) to *Cardinal Richelieu* (1935).

The Shubert brothers, Sam (above) and Lee (right), followed Edgar and Arch Selwyn as Broadway's leading producers in the 1920s and 1930s. An alleyway surrounded by theaters now carries their name.

OPPOSITE: An illegitimate and delicate child who wanted to be a nun, Sarah Bernhardt was dispatched to the Conservatoire by her mother's current lover, the Duc de Morny. The world was her audience; a star of the Paris stage, she visited London regularly, came to the United States eight times, toured Australia and South America. She died in 1923, aged seventy-nine, still acting.

Ehrich Weiss, the son of a rabbi, escaped Appleton, Wisconsin, to become a trapeze performer and then continued to escape the rest of his life under the name of Harry Houdini. Shackled hand and foot, he is about to be encased and lowered into New York harbor (1914). He escaped.

For many, Twentieth Century and William Fox are inseparable.

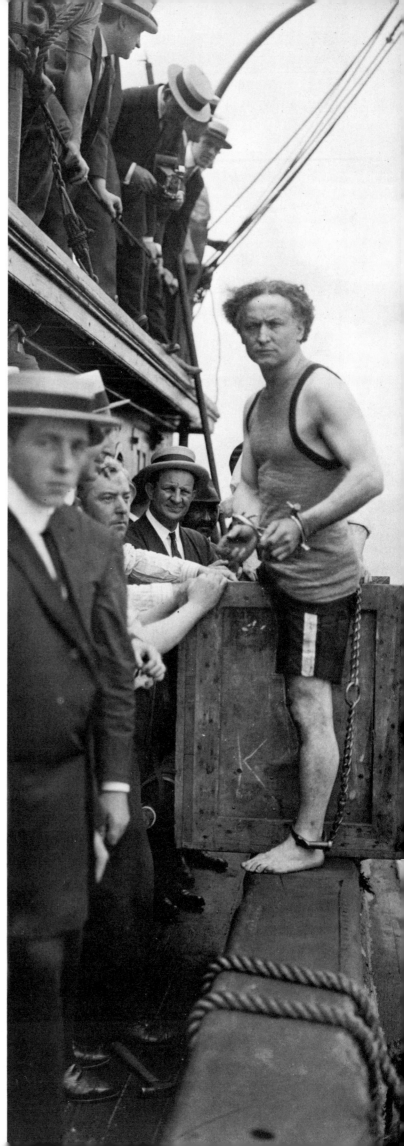

Jack Warner breaks ground for Warner Bros. studio on Sunset Boulevard, Hollywood (1919). Fifty-five years later, Warner Bros., an international entertainment complex, spent $4.5 million to persuade Pelé to join its soccer team, the New York Cosmos.

Adolf Zukor and Marcus Loew saw a 30-second movie at a New York penny arcade and saw their future. At first partners in establishing arcades, they separated —Zukor (right) to found Paramount Pictures, and Loew (below, with stars Ramon Navarro and Alice Terry) to build movie theaters and a fortune.

The films *Potemkin*, *Alexander Nevsky*, and *Ivan the Terrible* are undisputed classics created and directed by Sergei Eisenstein (born in Riga, Latvia, in 1898, died in Moscow in 1948), the great Soviet movie-maker. He is shown here with Upton Sinclair during a visit to Hollywood. Photo by Dr. Erich Salomon.

Max Goldmann (stage name Reinhardt) produced *A Midsummer Night's Dream* in Berlin in 1905. It brought him instant fame and started a career that included *The Miracle* (1911), the premiere of *Der Rosenkavalier* in the same year, and the founding of the Salzburg Festival (1920) with the staging of *Everyman* in the city's cathedral. He died in New York in 1943, having left Germany ten years earlier on Hitler's assumption of power. Photo by Alfred Eisenstaedt.

For twenty-three of his sixty-four years, Flo Ziegfeld's *Follies* dominated Broadway. The catchiest lines, the wittiest skits, the handsomest sets, the funniest comedians (Fanny Brice shown with Bobby Clark, among them), and the smallest costumes on the prettiest girls in town. His wife from 1913 until his death in 1932 was Glinda the Good Witch, Billie Burke.

The Chicago newspaper days of Ben Hecht (1894–1964) provided the background for *The Front Page*. In 1937 a contract with Sam Goldwyn paid him $6000 a week for such screenplays as *Scarface* and *Wuthering Heights*.

From Budapest, to Vienna, to Hollywood, to London, Alexander Korda (center) traveled, producing and/or directing films varying in social background from *The Private Lives of Henry VIII* (1933) to *The Thief of Bagdad* (1940). His 112 films also included *The Scarlet Pimpernel* (1935), *The Third Man* (1950), and *Richard III* (1955). Photo by Howard Coster.

A child of the stage—his parents were strolling ghetto performers—Muni Wiesenfeld arrived in New York in 1902 and by 1926 arrived on Broadway via the Yiddish Art Theatre. There, and in Hollywood until his death in 1967, he was recognized as *Louis Pasteur, Emile Zola, Juarez,* or Clarence Darrow, rather than as Paul Muni.

Probably the tribute Zukor found most touching came from the then president of Paramount, Frank Yablans, who said he was thankful for three things, "that Mr. Zukor caught the boat, that my father caught the boat, and that Charles Bluhdorn [chairman of the vast Gulf and Western conglomerate that now owns Paramount] caught the boat." For Zukor always saw his career as the fulfillment of the Jewish immigrant's dream. Back in 1926, at the opening of the palatial Paramount Theatre in New York, which marked the establishment of the mightiest combination of movie production, distribution, and exhibition ever known in one single organization, Zukor said, "I do not think that this is any monument to me, as you gentlemen have suggested, but rather a monument dedicated to America. To think that a country could give a chance to a boy like me to be connected with an institution like this."

Broadly speaking, before the latter part of the nineteenth century, professional entertainers—while frequently at the mercy of private patrons—organized their own performances. Most people devised their own recreation, as individuals or groups, according to their needs and resources. As leisure time gradually increased and a huge public eager for distraction and diversion grew up in the burgeoning urban centers, an entertainment industry developed, first slowly, then, with the coming of mass communications media like the cinema, phonograph, radio, and finally television, very rapidly. To exploit the new media on an international scale required capital investment, organizational ability, and a firm grasp of the demands of the

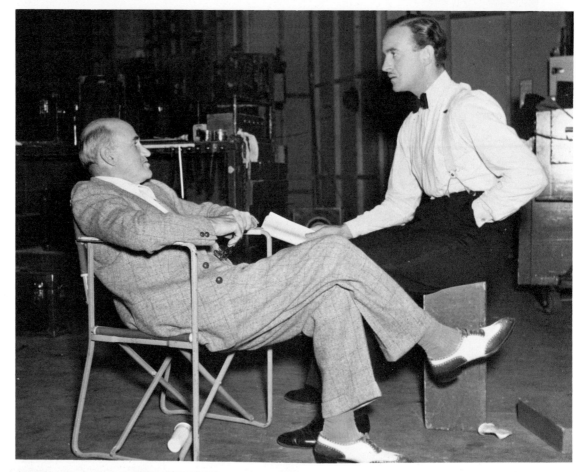

Sam Goldfish, orphaned at thirteen, left Warsaw, Poland, and reached Gloversville, New York, two years later. At twenty he was one of the best glove salesmen in the world; at twenty-nine he directed *The Squaw*, the first full-length film made in the United States; at thirty-five he made his first million and formed Goldwyn Pictures with the Selwyns. He changed his name to that of the company, and at his death at the age of ninety-two he had produced and/or directed some seventy films, including *All Quiet on the Western Front, Wuthering Heights,* and *The Best Years of Our Lives.* He is shown here with David Niven.

In Hebrew Tuvin means holiday, and Judith Tuvin (1922–1965) translated her last name and joined Adolph Green and Betty Comden to form a night-club group—"The Revuers." Garson Kanin's play *Born Yesterday* brought her stardom on Broadway and later in Hollywood. In *Bells Are Ringing* her disguise does not fool Sidney Chaplin.

vast amorphous audience whose tastes were to be met and molded. And this demanded a new breed of men prepared to take risks, not too concerned with personal reputation or existing notions of propriety. As the most advanced industrial nation with the most polyglot audience, America became the capital of international show business. The term itself is a twentieth-century coinage—and an indication of the quick rise of show business is the fact that by the 1920s the definite article had been dropped, whereas some fifty years later the "the" still attaches to most older businesses. For a variety of reasons—some obvious, some arguable, and some highly questionable—the creators and continuing administrators of this business have been largely Jewish—men like, or with similar backgrounds to, Adolph Zukor.

To remain for the moment with the film business, of the eight major Hollywood companies that came to dominate the world movie industry, six (MGM, Universal, Paramount, Columbia, 20th Century–Fox, Warner Brothers) were founded by Jews and the other two (United Artists, RKO) were managed by Jews. The Warner brothers, Louis B. Mayer, Samuel Goldwyn, Joseph and Nicholas Schenck, Harry and Jack Cohn, William Fox, Carl Laemmle, Marcus Loew, Lewis Selznick (father of Myron, the talent agent, and David, the independent producer who made *Gone with the Wind*) were, like Zukor, Jewish immigrants from Central and Eastern Europe or the sons of immigrants. They also had other features

At twenty-five, Leslie Stainer decided that banking was not his métier. Twenty-five years later Leslie Howard died in World War II, but in those years such movies as *The Scarlet Pimpernel, The Petrified Forest, Of Human Bondage,* and *Gone with the Wind* glowed with his talent.

In his forty-nine years Mike Todd (Avrom Hirsch Goldbogen of Minneapolis) traveled faster than Phileas Fogg of *Around the World in 80 Days*. He built sound stages, wrote radio skits, staged shows at the Chicago and New York World's Fairs, had four Broadway productions running at one time, introduced a wide-screen system named after him, and married Elizabeth Taylor.

With George S. Kaufman, he wrote *You Can't Take It With You* and *The Man Who Came to Dinner*. With Kurt Weill and Ira Gershwin, *Lady in the Dark*. He wrote the screenplay for *Gentleman's Agreement*. He directed the Broadway musicals *My Fair Lady* and *Camelot*. The best-selling autobiography of Moss Hart's early years, *Act One*, detailed the struggles of his Bronx boyhood and the joys of his first theatrical success. Mrs. Hart, Kitty Carlisle, starred in Hollywood and continues to Tell the Truth on television. Photo by Alfred Eisenstaedt.

ABOVE: In the 1960s Broadway's most successful producer was David Merrick (born Margulois in St. Louis, Missouri, in 1912). He earned his law degree at St. Louis University and practiced law for nine years in New York City before switching to the theater. His first investment was in *The Male Animal*, and later came *The Matchmaker*, *Look Back in Anger*, *Gypsy*. Phil Silvers (see page 233) is on his left, and also with him are Betty Comden and Adolph Green, writers of book and lyrics for such shows as *On the Town*, *Billion Dollar Baby*, *Bells Are Ringing*, and *Applause*, and such movies as *Good News*, *Band Wagon*, *Singin' in the Rain*, and *Auntie Mame*.

A penniless eighteen-year-old immigrant to America from Poland in 1906, Sol Hurok later brought to America Chaliapin, Pavlova, Schnabel, Emlyn Williams, Margot Fonteyn, the Azuma Kabuki dancers, the Bolshoi Ballet, the Moiseyev Folk Ballet. He was impresario to the greatest dancers, singers, and musicians from 1925 to his death in 1974. Photo by Arnold Newman.

Molly Picon was six years old when she played her first role at fifty cents a performance on the Yiddish stage. Thirty-four years later she played her first English-speaking dramatic role on Broadway in the 1940 production of *Morning Star*, and in 1961 all eyes turned to her in *Milk and Honey*, a musical set in Israel.

Richard Rodgers, Oscar Hammerstein, Alan Jay Lerner, and Frederick Loewe serenaded Broadway and the world.

OPPOSITE, ABOVE: The opening scene of Rodgers and Hammerstein's *Carousel* (1945).

OPPOSITE, BELOW: Mary Martin teaches "Do, Re, Mi" to the Trapp family in Rodgers' *The Sound of Music* (1959).

RIGHT: Rex Harrison dances with Julie Andrews in Lerner and Loewe's *My Fair Lady* (1956).

BELOW: Richard Burton and Julie Andrews receive homage in Lerner and Loewe's *Camelot* (1960).

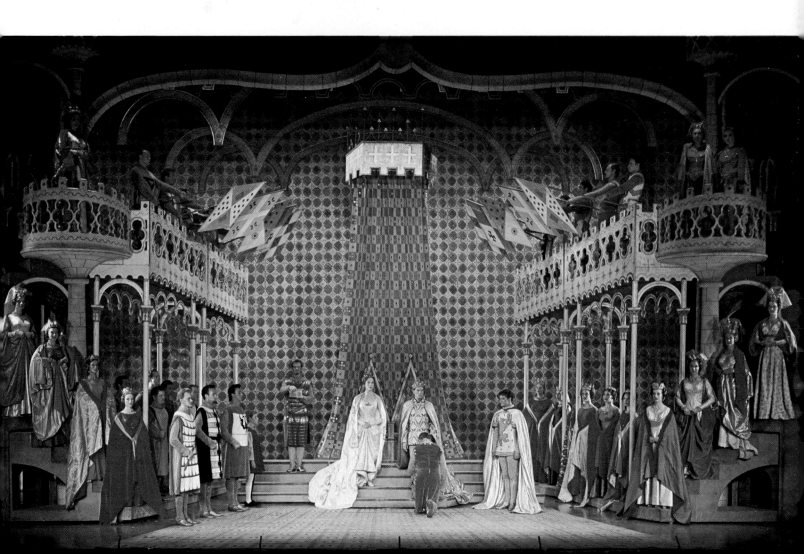

Fiddler on the Roof, a musical of the *shtetl* and *pogrom*, won the Antoinette Perry ("Tony") Award for Sheldon Harnick in 1964 and brought world recognition to the Israeli actor Topol, at left, for his role in the movie. Photo by Mary Ellen Mark.

Lewis Selznick's venture into the film business in Pittsburgh collapsed in 1923, but his son David (1902–1965) was not discouraged. Moving to Hollywood, David, with MGM and with his independent companies, produced many hits, including *A Star Is Born, Intermezzo, Rebecca, Duel in the Sun,* and the unforgettable *Gone with the Wind.* Photo by Alfred Eisenstaedt.

Three-year-old Louis B. Mayer (1885–1957) migrated from Minsk, Russia, to St. John, New Brunswick, in 1888. In 1907 for six hundred dollars he purchased a run-down theater near Boston. In 1918 he moved to Los Angeles and six years later joined Marcus Loew and Sam Goldwyn to found MGM. By 1943 he had for five successive years been the highest-paid American. Photo by Elliott Erwitt.

in common: most were short, aggressive children from extremely poor homes, born into large families, with strong mothers and weak, unsuccessful fathers, and received little formal education. Their desire to succeed was overbearingly powerful, and in a society that erected barriers if not unsurpassable obstacles to their progress they were forced to innovate. Most of them tried various jobs, usually involving some form of intensely competitive salesmanship, before drifting into the new motion-picture industry. Sam Warner sold ice cream, Harry Warner meat, and Albert Warner soap until they got together with brother Jack in the bicycle-repairing business, which they dropped in 1904 as soon as they acquired their first secondhand movie projector, with which they toured Midwestern fairgrounds. Zukor and his friend Marcus Loew (MGM) were both furriers. Carl Laemmle (Universal) was a storekeeper. Sam Goldwyn sold gloves until a lowering of tariffs on imported leather made him look elsewhere. "Those of us who became film producers," said Zukor, looking back over his life, "hailed from all sorts of occupations—furriers, magicians, butchers, boilermakers—and for this reason highbrows have sometimes poked fun at us. Yet one thing is certain—every man who succeeded was a born showman. And once in show business he was never happy out of it."

What is true is that most of those movie moguls who entered show business as entertainers were pretty second-rate artists. William Fox and Harry Cohn, for example, were failures as song-and-dance men. The British entertainment tycoons Sir Lew Grade and his brother Bernard Delfont (born Winogradsky in Tokmak, Russia, early in the century and reared in poverty in London's East End) have never concealed from themselves or the public that had they remained music-hall performers they would never have reached the top of the bill, let alone attained the positions of awe and respect that they occupy as pinnacles of the greatest interlocking entertainment empire Great Britain has ever known—comprising television companies, talent agencies, cinemas, restaurants, theaters, and movie studios. "I knew I wasn't going to get anywhere as a performer," Bernard Delfont has frankly admitted, "though I couldn't have been so bad— I played the Palladium once. First turn, of course." This is a little different from presenting fourteen consecutive royal variety shows there.

Historically, then, the infant cinema industry was one in which an aggressive immigrant Jew could find room for his abilities, despite the fact that the earliest pioneers were bent on excluding him through a phony patent-pooling cartel formed in 1908. To him, cinema was a business, and his ideas often did not mesh with those of the actual movie-makers, who naïvely expected to be left alone to make pictures of their own choice and to develop an infant art form. What chance had they against the diamond salesman Lewis Selznick, a man with such chutzpah that he could walk into Universal's New York headquarters in 1912, when the company was torn by internecine feuding, select an office, give himself an executive job, and learn the business before anyone discovered he didn't officially belong there? And what chance did the buccaneering Selznick have when coldly calculating Adolph Zukor and other tycoons decided to drive this irresponsible showman out of the industry in the 1920s?

The very conditions that made it possible for so many Jews to go into the movies also helped to make the industry peculiarly vulnerable to outside criticism. Resentment of Jewish dominance led to widespread anti-Semitic attacks on the business in America in the years immediately following World War I, with demands that it should be subjected to stern public control. Typical of what was appearing in newspapers at the time is this item from 1920: "The lobby of the International Reform Bureau, Dr. Wilbur Crafts presiding, voted tonight to rescue the motion pictures from the hands of the Devil and five hundred un-Christian Jews." For self-protection, the tycoons formed the Motion Picture Producers and Distributors Association of America, under the guidance of the four-square, middle-American, Presbyterian Will H. Hays, the jug-eared postmaster-general in the cabinet of Republican President Warren Harding. This anti-Semitism has never let up and has contributed, along with natural business caution and rigid censorship (whether from the outside or self-imposed) to making the movies so timid and so responsive to prevailing orthodox opinion. In the 1930s, a writer as sensitive as Graham Greene was capable of saying in one of his critical columns in *The Spectator:* "How the financial crisis has improved English films! They have lost their tasteless Semitic opulence and are becoming—English."

178

Evacuated from London during the blitz, twelve-year-old Anthony Newley found lodgings in Brighton with a retired music-hall performer who inspired a show-business career consisting not only of acting but of writing the book, lyrics, and music for *Stop the World—I Want to Get Off* (1961) and *The Roar of the Greasepaint—the Smell of the Crowd.*

Marcel Marceau is known as the world's greatest mime. Born in Strasbourg, France, he survived the Nazi occupation—his father was taken hostage and executed—joining the French Underground and later the French army. He studied in Paris, where in 1947 he created the white-faced character Bip—a role he continues to adopt for his one-man shows.

More recently, Truman Capote, in a magazine interview (*Rolling Stone*, April 12, 1973), revived and extended an argument that in the past has been a staple of, among others, backwoods preachers, Nazis, and the House Un-American Activities Committee in its witch-hunting days:

> The truth of the matter about it is, the entire cultural press, publishing . . . criticism, television . . . theater . . . film industry . . . is almost 90 per cent Jewish-oriented. I mean, I can't count on one hand five people of importance—of real importance—in the media who aren't Jewish. I can't. If these people could have done me in, they would have done me in. But they couldn't do me in, because not only wasn't I Jewish and wasn't I in the Jewish clique, but I *talked* about not being part of it.

Confronting this familiar argument (if argument in the word's more elevated sense it can be called), one must make several initial observations. First, Capote has never had any difficulty in getting published and has been consistently supported by Jewish editors. Second, David Selznick, with no personal interest at stake, sought to advance the diminutive Southern novelist's career in the cinema by pressing John Huston to have him taken on as a scriptwriter on *Beat the Devil* in 1953. And Capote composed one of the eulogies spoken (by director George Cukor) at Selznick's funeral in 1965. Nevertheless, one must acknowledge that there is a certain factual basis to his charge.

ABOVE: The life of John Garfield (born Julius Garfinkle) on New York's Lower East Side provided the background needed for his starring roles in *Golden Boy, Body and Soul, The Postman Always Rings Twice*, and *Gentleman's Agreement*. He was thirty-nine when he died in 1952. Photo by Arnold Newman.

His film *Rosemary's Baby* horrified many, but Roman Polanski's childhood was more horrible. His Polish parents were interned in a Nazi concentration camp—his mother died in a gas chamber—and he was shuttled from family to family. In 1954, twenty-one years old and for ten years a child actor, he was accepted in the director's school of the Polish National Film Academy. *Knife in the Water* (1962) was the first of his successes. Photo by Per Helmer.

OPPOSITE: Dustin Hoffman—Benjamin of *The Graduate*, Ratso Rizzo of *Midnight Cowboy*, and *Lenny*. He left Los Angeles for seven hungry New York years, until he won an Obie Award in 1966 as best Off-Broadway actor. Photo by Marvin Lichtner.

The Jews have indeed played a large part in everything that has to do with entertainment. The great builders of movie-houses, like Syd Grauman (of Grauman's Chinese on Hollywood Boulevard) and Samuel Rothafel, whose nickname "Roxy" has entered the language, were mostly Jewish. The fabulous Shubert brothers—Sam, Lee, and Jake—the impresarios who dominated the American theater for the first half of this century, were the sons of a poor Jewish peddler from Lithuania, named David Szemanski, whose family followed him to America in the 1880s. (Like Sam Goldwyn and Lewis Selznick, Szemanski sojourned in Britain for a while en route to the United States; one wonders what might have happened to the British entertainment world had they settled here.) The Broadway musical was the creation of Florenz Ziegfeld, son of a German-Jewish immigrant who founded the Chicago College of Music, and the tradition was carried on after his death by Billy Rose. Rose, the world's fastest shorthand writer, served as a secretary to financier Bernard Baruch during World War I, then became a popular songwriter and later a stage producer. Jules Stein, the son of an immigrant Jewish storekeeper in Indiana, abandoned his promising career as an ophthalmologist to become a pop music impresario, controlling bands throughout America, and eventually created through his Music Corporation of America the largest and most influential talent agency ever known. The list is endless, and so too are the stories—both amusing and hair-raising—of the ways in which many of these figures (most notoriously the Shuberts) used and abused their power.

Two matters, however, must be examined. First, did they ever employ their influence in pursuit of any specific ethnic cause or to advance the careers of Jews? Second, is there any evidence to support the charge that they ever functioned together in any conspiratorial fashion other than in the preservation of strictly business interests?

An emphatic no must be the answer to each of these questions. They were in business to make money for themselves and their investors. That is a simple fact—or, more correctly, a very complicated fact. Most of them contributed generously to Jewish charities, though not all. Columbia Pictures' outrageous

The Theater of the Absurd is partly the creation of London-born Harold Pinter. The plays and screenplays he wrote include *The Caretaker*, *The Homecoming*, *The Pumpkin Eater*. His direction of Simon Gray's *Butley* and *Otherwise Engaged* have further enhanced his reputation. Sketch by David Levine.

Broadway's most successful playwright of recent years is Neil "Doc" Simon. He left the Warner Bros. mail-room to write plays, among them *Barefoot in the Park* (1964), *The Odd Couple* (1965), *Sweet Charity* (1966), *Plaza Suite* (1969), *The Sunshine Boys* (1972). Photo by Jill Krementz.

founder, Harry Cohn, after reluctantly contributing to the Jewish Relief Fund, once exploded, "Relief for the Jews! Somebody should start a fund for relief *from* the Jews. All the trouble in the world has been caused by Jews and Irishmen." Most of them eventually came around to supporting Zionism, albeit rather reluctantly. Hollywood's leading Zionist, the ace-screenwriter Ben Hecht, received at best sporadic en-couragement; when he was blacklisted in the late 1940s by British film distributors for his admittedly intemperate anti-British outbursts over the handling of the Palestine situation, no one stood by him; eventually the ban on films bearing his name was lifted as a result of the intervention of 20th Century–Fox's boss, Spyros Skouras, a one-time Greek shepherd boy.

It is interesting to note that the second marriages of most Jewish movie tycoons and show-biz entrepreneurs were to gentile wives. Also, they were often reluctant to admit their racial identity. When ex-cornet player turned movie impresario Jesse Lasky (a founder of Paramount with his one-time brother-in-law Sam Goldwyn and Adolph Zukor) was rushed to the hospital with a heart attack, he replied "American" to the question of race. "Jewish? Oh, yes, yes, Jewish," he eventually conceded to the persistent entreaties of his coreligionist behind the admittance desk. David Selznick, too, insisted that he was an American and not a Jew. Ben Hecht allegedly took him up on it and won a sizable sum for the Zionist cause by phoning three people and asking them whether they looked upon Selznick as being foremost Jewish or American.

The movie tycoons and the show-business entrepreneurs generally were committed to a vague ecumenical Americanism. They believed—wrongly, as it happened—that they and everyone else would emerge from the melting pot as 100-per-cent Americans, solid citizens molded on the white-Anglo-

Issur Danielovitch, born in Amsterdam, New York, Americanized his name to Isadore Demsky after high-school graduation. At St. Lawrence College he was Senior Class President and an intercollegiate wrestling champion. By 1945 he had reached Broadway, and in 1949 he was Kirk Douglas, *The Champion*.

Bernard Berensen's appreciation of beauty came to life in his grand niece, Marisa, who first claimed public notice in the film *Cabaret* and achieved stardom in Stanley Kubrick's *Barry Lyndon*. Photo by Peter Sellers.

Joseph E. Levine of Boston, Massachusetts, and Paramount Pictures has been listed as the producer of *The Sky Above, the Mud Below*; *Two Women*; *Divorce—Italian Style*; *The Graduate*; and *The Lion in Winter*. Photo by Eve Arnold.

A graduate of the University of Chicago, Rush Medical College, with postgraduate work at the Eye Clinic of the University of Vienna, Jules Stein left ophthalmology in 1923 to found MCA (Music Corporation of America), of which he was president and chairman from 1924 to 1973. In 1928 that agency acquired Guy Lombardo as a client and gradually acquired more clients and more business. By 1965 net revenues had reached $200 million.

Saxon-Protestant pattern. Most of them anglicized their names and insisted upon the majority of their stars adopting good "Wasp" names that divested them of all trace of ethnic diversity. In their lives and their works they were dedicated to giving no offense to anyone—except, perhaps, to their employees, which is another matter. Florenz Ziegfeld scarcely considered himself a Jew at all. He did, however, make a superb, if largely unconscious, gesture on behalf of the succeeding generation of Jewish immigrants by purchasing—much to the annoyance of his wife—the dinner service of the Russian Imperial Court, at a price of some thirty-eight thousand dollars. "Where do you suggest stacking it?" his wife, the British comedienne Billie Burke, asked. "In Madison Square Garden?" And then she added, with more perception than she knew, "For the first time I understand what the Russian Revolution was all about."

The tycoons played the politicians each way. (Jack Warner had separate sets of autographed photographs of Republican and Democratic leaders ready to be placed on his office walls depending on who happened to be in town.) Their performance before the House Un-American Activities Committee in the late 1940s and early 1950s was lamentable, especially since the anti-Semitic attitudes of several committee members were making Hollywood's Jewish artists special targets.

If the tycoons employed a great many relatives—thus giving rise to the traditional industrial jokes such as "the son-in-law also rises" and "the only thing a producer produces is relatives"—that was just simple nepotism and practiced the world over. Nobody got a job because he was Jewish. Moreover, specifically Jewish themes and characters were rare during Hollywood's Golden Age.

If, as I have mentioned earlier, there is an historical explanation for the initial entry of Jews into show business, how does one explain the continuing involvement and dominance of Jews in this field? The American critic Alfred Kazin has persuasively suggested that American Jews played a significant part not just in creating but in shaping the character of mass entertainment through their urban immigrant exuberance, "the Jew's averageness and typicality," in the early part of this century:

> In this country the very poverty and cultural rawness of the Jewish immigrant masses, the self-assertive egalitarianism of the general temper, the naturalness with which different people could identify with each other in the unique half-way house that was New York (without New York it would no doubt have all been different, but without New York there would have been no immigrant epic, no America), gave individual performers the privilege of representing the popular mind.

Is it this quality—Al Jolson in blackface, Chico Marx impersonating a comic Italian, and so on—coupled with a now-established tradition of such employment that explains the situation? Have Jews some faculty, derived from an experience stretching back over two thousand years, of giving dramatic or comic form to the dilemmas and identity crises of twentieth-century man? In the title of what is the most probing of all novels about show business, the Jewish writer Budd Schulberg—son of the onetime Hollywood tycoon Ben Schulberg—posed the question, *What Makes Sammy Run?* The book's hero, Sammy Glick, ran literally and metaphorically from his New York Jewish ghetto of the 1920s, through the offices of a Manhattan newspaper, to Hollywood, trampling over and casting aside anyone who stood in his way. Many years after the novel's publication in 1941, Schulberg found that his alma mater, Dartmouth College, had chosen the novel as a text for a sociology course; the end-of-term paper challenged students to answer the question: "What *did* make Sammy run?" One suspects that Schulberg might have had difficulty answering that question.

So let us go on to an equally difficult question. What are the shared characteristics that link two of the most important phenomena of postwar Britain—the films produced by Ealing Studios and the launching of the Beatles pop group?

He made his acting debut in Max Reinhardt's *A Midsummer Night's Dream*, and at twenty-two was a producer-director, but the political climate in Vienna caused Otto Preminger to seek refuge in the United States. There he directed and played the lead role in Broadway's *Margin for Error* (1939), made the films *Laura* (1944), *Forever Amber* (1947), *The Man With the Golden Arm* (1955), *Porgy and Bess* (1959), *Exodus* (1960), *Advise and Consent* (1961), *Hurry Sundown* (1967). Photo by Burt Glinn.

Ealing movies, which captured in both serious and comic fashion the aspirations and anxieties of the British people during the 1940s and 1950s, were essentially the expression, through a team of talented artists, of the personality of Sir Michael Balcon, a quietly determined, middle-class, moderately left-wing Jew born in Birmingham in 1893, the son of a charming, feckless wanderer. Balcon was the greatest single figure in film production that the British cinema has known, far greater than the remote J. Arthur Rank. Despite the fact that his background was not wholly different from that of his Hollywood contemporaries, Balcon recognized a great difference between his sensibility and theirs when in the late 1930s he was hired by Metro–Goldwyn–Mayer to produce three prestigious, supposedly archetypal British pictures— *A Yank at Oxford, The Citadel,* and *Good-bye Mr. Chips.* After supervising these, he went on to take over Ealing and produced a string of superbly honest, eccentric, idiosyncratic movies. Wartime films like *The Foreman Went to France* and *San Demetrio, London,* postwar comedies as diverse as *Kind Hearts and Coronets, Whisky Galore,* and *Passport to Pimlico,* dramas like *The Blue Lamp* and *The Divided Heart,* to name but a few, were totally indigenous British movies that made no concession to the international market.

The Beatles—John Lennon, Paul McCartney, George Harrison, and Ringo Starr—simple, white Anglo-Saxon working-class lads before fame and prosperity made them gurus and devotees of complex Oriental religious disciplines, were discovered and tenderly nursed, until his premature death in 1967, by Brian Epstein, the retiring, middle-class entrepreneur from Liverpool. A provincial Jew like Balcon, Epstein was born in 1934, the grandson of a turn-of-the-century refugee from Poland who had established the family furniture and music-store business. Brian enjoyed a childhood as privileged as those of Balcon and the Hollywood moguls were impoverished, but until entering the family business and running the record department in one of its Merseyside stores his career was a succession of pathetic failures: he was dismissed from several schools, was released prematurely from the army for emotional instability, dropped out from the Royal Academy of Dramatic Art. But his life was redeemed, given permanent significance, through his disinterested commitment to the Beatles. The adjective "disinterested" is precisely used, for money was merely a symbolic token of his achievement. From the first he recognized their musical talent and saw that their brash vitality expressed in a uniquely potent form the new mood of their postwar generation in Britain and around the world.

Whatever the underlying explanation, the entertainment industry of the Western world continues very extensively to attract Jewish entrepreneurial and artistic talent, though the business is more Jewish in its personnel and in the character of its rhetoric than in its product. By no means everyone involved is Jewish, far from it, and one would be hard pressed to distinguish between the behavior and character of Jews and non-Jews in this industry. A good many of the latter—Darryl F. Zanuck and Cecil B. DeMille, to name two notable instances—have erroneously been taken to be Jews by members of the public at large and even by many of their associates.

Show business has now become, in its scope and size, one of the prominent industries of our time, and in some ways the most pre-eminent and influential one, affecting the way we talk, communicate with each other, conduct our politics. The world itself has become a branch of show biz through the dominance of mass communications. If critical observers denounced the "schmaltz" in Richard Nixon's 1973 Watergate speech, while recognizing that it appealed to many of his admirers, they were merely acknowledging the power of the entertainment industry, even to accepting its descriptive terminology of Yiddish origin.

Thirty-odd years ago the Russian-born, New York Jewish composer Irving Berlin, in his musical *Annie Get Your Gun,* provided the industry with its international anthem, a confident mixture of assertion, aspiration, and schmaltz called, "There's No Business Like Show Business," a claim that nowadays is difficult to deny. British cinemas have given up playing "God Save the Queen" at the end of performances of films and plays because their patrons head for the door when they hear the first bar, but Berlin's song can get whole audiences on their feet, often with tears rolling down their cheeks.

Bobby Fischer of Brooklyn won the United States Chess Championship in 1958 when he was fourteen and became the youngest international grand master in history. His antics and idiosyncrasies have created international furor while publicizing chess and earning Fischer a fortune. Photo by Philippe Halsman.

The Jew in Sports

He won the world's heavyweight championship in 1934 by K.O.ing Primo Canero, and he lost the title one year later to James J. Braddock. Maximilian Adelbert Baer of Omaha, Nebraska (1909–1959), boxed from 1929 to 1941, winning sixty-five of seventy-nine fights. His brother Jacob (a.k.a. Buddy) twice lost challenge fights to Joe Louis. Their father is the middle pedaler.

One perfect game, 3 other no-hitters, 2396 strikeouts in 2324 innings, 382 strikeouts in 1965, in his last season, 1966, 27 wins with a 1.73 e.r.a., Sandy Koufax was a Brooklyn boy who pitched for the Dodgers in his home town and in Los Angeles, compiling a lifetime record of 165 wins and 87 losses. Photo by Flip Schulke.

Dropping out of New York University into baseball, Hank Greenberg became a Detroit Tiger and twice the American League's Most Valuable Player (1935, 1939). His career interrupted for four years by military service, he celebrated his return with a bases-loaded home run on the last day of the season and brought the Tigers the pennant in 1945.

The most successful coach in basketball history, Arnold "Red" Auerbach of Brooklyn led the Washington Capitols to victory in the first year of the Basketball Association of America (forerunner of the NBA), and, coaching the Boston Celtics from 1950 to 1966, won the championship nine times. His record as the Celtic's general manager has been equally spectacular.

Another Brooklyn boy, Sid Luckman, carrying the ball, went from Columbia University to the Chicago Bears, quarterbacking them to four National Football League championships (1940, 1941, 1943, 1946) and becoming the League's Most Valuable Player in 1943.

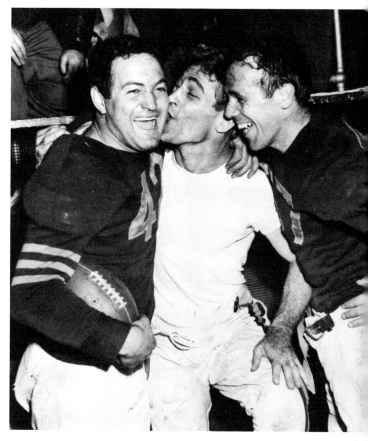

The Wimbledon and Australian titles fell to Dick Savitt (Bayonne, New Jersey; El Paso, Texas; and Cornell University) in 1952, but the Forest Hills title continued to elude him. He was a dominant figure, along with Vic Scixas, in the tennis world of the 1950s.

OVERLEAF, LEFT: Actor Tony Curtis (Bernard Schwartz) keeps youthful through exercise. Born in New York City in 1925, he has been under contract to Universal Pictures since his twenty-third birthday, starring in many movies, including *Some Like It Hot*, *Spartacus*, and *The Boston Strangler*. Photo by Dennis Stock.

OVERLEAF, RIGHT: The 1972 Olympic games will be remembered for the massacre of the Israeli team and the seven gold medals won by the California swimmer Mark Spitz. By 1972 Spitz had broken world records twenty-three times (he set four more in the Olympics) and U.S. records thirty-five times, and in 1971 he won the Sullivan award as the outstanding amateur athlete in the United States. Photo by Burt Stern.

PAGES 194–95: The *Weatherly*, skippered by Emil "Bus" Mosbacher, Jr., is on its way to victory in the 1962 America's Cup Races. He was educated at Choate School and Dartmouth and became Chief of Protocol, U.S. State Department. Photo by Stanley Rosenfeld.

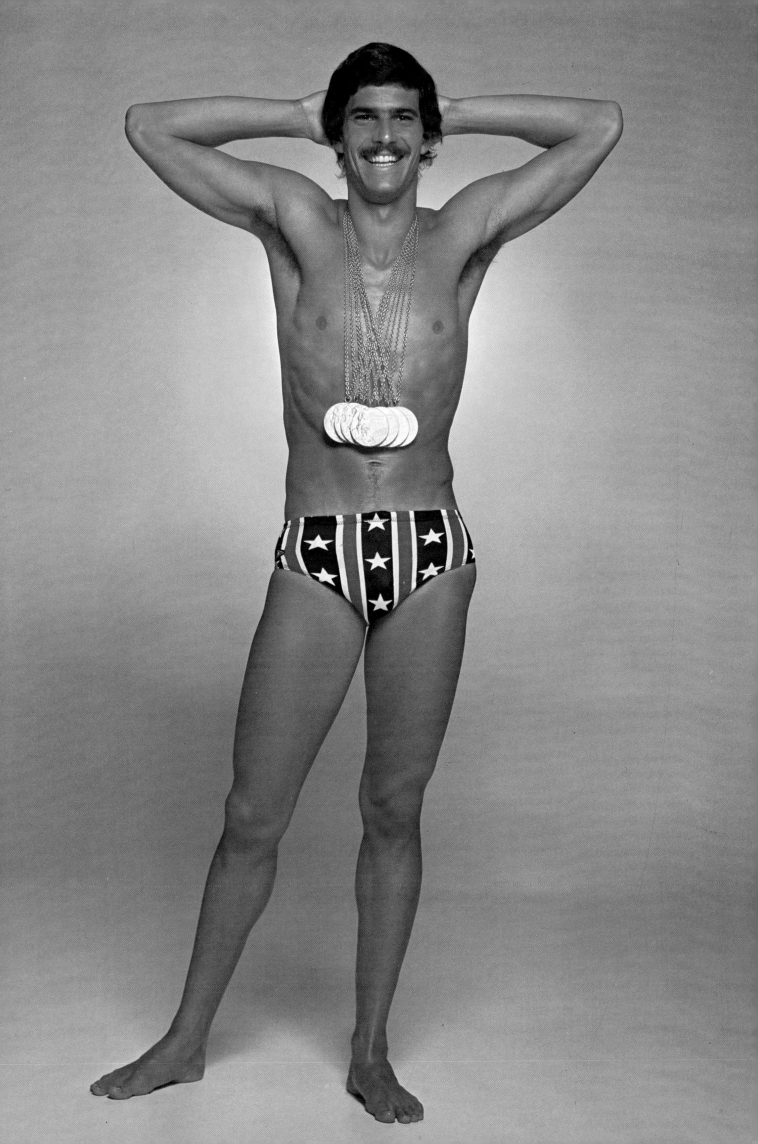

Robert Zimmerman ran away from his Minnesota home seven times before he was eighteen, hit the road for good in 1960, changed his name to Dylan after his favorite poet, and revolutionized the popular song with "The Times They Are A-Changin'," "Blowin' in the Wind," "Masters of War," "A Hard Rain's A-Gonna Fall." Photo by Elliott Landy.

The American Popular Song

Ronald Sanders

The Al Jolson movie *The Jazz Singer* is said to have initiated the era of the talkies, but this is not its only significance in American popular culture. It also tells an archetypal story: a cantor's son, inheritor of his father's musical gifts, leaves the fold and becomes successful in the gentile world as a singer of popular songs. It is a version of Jolson's own life, which in some ways resembles the old Yiddish tale "Dos Vilner Balabessl"—made into a movie a few years later with the celebrated cantorial singer Moishe Oysher in the lead role. This is another archetypal singing story, Old Country version: here the young prodigy goes to Warsaw and becomes a great opera star, but his personal life becomes a series of setbacks, and in the end, mortally ill, he returns to the little synagogue in Vilna on the Day of Atonement, sings the Kol Nidre, and dies. In the Jolson variation, the jazz singer also goes back to the little synagogue on the Lower East Side to sing the Kol Nidre, but it is the father who is dying, and one knows that the young renegade, who postpones the opening night of his big Broadway show to perform this final act of piety, will go on to greater and greater worldly triumphs. And it should be noted that if the quality of schmaltz in Jolson's intonation of the Jewish prayer seems not at all different from that with which he sings "Mammy" in blackface elsewhere in the film, this is no accident: indeed, the true essence of the story lies here.

Intimations of a kind of Jewish musical fulfillment in blackface appear even more forcefully when one moves on from the realm of performance to that of composition. Harold Arlen, for example, perhaps the foremost white composer of blues-type songs ("Stormy Weather," "Blues in the Night"), is the son of a cantor, as is one of the greatest pop songwriters of them all, Irving Berlin (whose father eked out a living doing various odd jobs, which included part-time cantorial singing). Irving Berlin's case is especially significant, for his is one of the great Jewish-American success stories—from Russian pogroms and Lower East Side squalor to wealth, fame, and the composition of what has often been thought of as an alternate national anthem, "God Bless America"—and it was with a blackface song that he made his first success. In many ways Berlin's rough New York boyhood—he was born Israel Baline in Russia in 1888 and brought over four years later—was a white, Northern, urban equivalent of that of some of the great black musicians of the twentieth century: newspaperboy, street-gang fighter, singing waiter, he struggled like them toward the realization of his great raw talent. And it was precisely the new currents arising from black music in Berlin's youth that brought him to fruition and fame as a songwriter: for "Alexander's Ragtime Band," which was composed in 1911 and helped to bring about a revolution in the Tin Pan Alley style, was a spin-off from black ragtime and emphatically proclaimed itself to be such in its lyric.

197

This song and the career of its composer up to that time in many respects represent a twofold strain in the history of American popular culture—that of ethnic pastiche in general, and of black pastiche in particular. From their earliest days, Anglo-Americans have had a strong inclination to entertain themselves with imitations of minority groups. The Indians were the first out-group to be so honored, and redface drama was a favorite American form down at least to the time when James Fenimore Cooper began imitating it in fiction. Then the Negro replaced the Indian as the favorite subject of dusky caricature, and minstrelsy, that pre-eminent breeding ground of American entertainment conventions, ran its course throughout the nineteenth century. But the nineteenth century also saw the rise of white ethnic caricatures: "Dutchmen" (meaning anything from the native Rip Van Winkle to the latest immigrant arrivals from German-speaking Central Europe), Irishmen, Italians, Jews, to name only the most outstanding stage favorites. Sometimes the actor was of the ethnic background he was portraying and sometimes he was not, but in either case the technique was caricature: even blacks did minstrel-style pastiche, and Jews did "Yiddisha" pastiche. In the case of popular song composition, the ethnic mantle was changed even more easily than on the stage, and a skilled composer could wear several. The young Irving Berlin composed both Italian and Yiddisha pastiche, as well as what were then unblushingly called "coon" songs. George M. Cohan tended to restrict himself to his emphatically Irish identity in his songs as well as on the stage, but he wrote some coon songs too: blackface composition had become irresistible to popular songwriters by the first decade of this century.

It seems to be a peculiar trait of American culture that ridicule and caricature also often contain an element of tribute. It has often been pointed out that the black has traditionally played the role of America's libido, and the history of the minstrel show is a demonstration that this vicarious function also manifested itself through the use of blackface. Playing black gave white comedians a freedom they would not otherwise have enjoyed (was this the only way Al Jolson could have gotten his intense Jewish schmaltz across to general audiences?), and gave license for theatergoing to puritanical elements who would otherwise have stayed home. The element of longing admiration was always present. And since music in particular was the area in which the vibrations of the Negro soul made themselves most vividly felt and were most vigorously imitated, it is not surprising that some of the best songs written by white Americans in the nineteenth century were black pastiche: Dan Emmett's "Dixie" (for most of his early career Emmett was a blackface minstrel), Stephen Foster's "Swanee River," "Camptown Races," and others.

But the best American songs of the nineteenth century were the works of blacks themselves, and these began coming across directly to general audiences, along with actual black performers, with growing frequency in the decades that followed the Civil War. The first important breakthrough was made by the Fiske University singers in the 1870s, when they toured America and then Europe, performing those transcendent creations of American black folk, the spirituals. It was also in the 1870s that James A. Bland, a black man from Flushing, New York, began writing "darky" pastiche songs in the manner of Stephen Foster, and perhaps went him one better with such works as "Carry Me Back to Old Virginny," "In the Evening by the Moonlight," and "Oh! Dem Golden Slippers."

With the fuller emergence of black music on the general American scene that took place in the 1890s, there was a return to the libidinous tradition that had become obscured during the era of Reconstruction, when the tutelage of New England had been a major factor in American-Negro culture. Indeed, puritans were offended and ministers spoke out scathingly from their pulpits when ragtime and the cakewalk began achieving popularity among white middle-class Americans. Something more startling than the old minstrelsy was going on, as was manifested above all in the fact that, for a moment at least, blackface in composition and performance was being replaced by real black composers and performers. The elevated tones of the Fiske singers and James A. Bland had opened the way for the authentic "lowdown" sounds of a Scott Joplin.

But white middle-class America was still not ready to swallow large quantities of black music unadulterated—one of the great Negro rag musicians, Ben Harney, a composer and singer, made his career by passing for white—and by about 1910 there was a return to blackface pastiche as a popular fashion. With Tin Pan Alley now in full swing and ever eager to grab hold of any attractive mode and imitate it for commercial use, the coon songs came out in streams, written occasionally by black men but more often by white would-be Stephen Fosters and Dan Emmetts in updated rhythms. Irving Berlin was virtually writing a Tin Pan Alley manifesto when, in "Alexander's Ragtime Band," he echoed a few strains of "Swanee River" and described it as now "being played in ragtime," as was the young George Gershwin eight years later, when he wrote of "Swanee" and "the folks in D-I-X-I-E." In both cases the outstanding nineteenth-century models of blackface songwriting were being commemorated.

This brings us to a remarkable fact. Not only were Irving Berlin and George Gershwin, the two young men who, in 1911 and in 1919, respectively, proclaimed themselves the descendants of Stephen Foster and Dan Emmett, both Jews, but so also were such eminent blackface performers of that era as Al Jolson, Eddie Cantor, and Sophie Tucker. Indeed, it would not be farfetched to say that, during the time of its twentieth-century revival, blackface music virtually became a Jewish monopoly. We have come back to the world of *The Jazz Singer*, approached this time from the general direction of the plantation rather than that of the synagogue, and rediscovered an ethnic convergence that no longer seems accidental.

It would be well to begin by pointing out that this special relationship between Negro and Jew is something that has manifested itself from time to time throughout American history, but with special force since about 1890, and in other areas besides music. A history of American literature in the twentieth century, for example, if drawn carefully along sociological lines, would readily show the significance of the Negro-Jewish relationship in this field. In politics too—in the left-wing alliance of the thirties and forties, in the history of the civil-rights movement from the founding of the NAACP in 1909 to the marches on Washington and Selma in the early sixties, in the interplay of the respective ethnic nationalisms, even in the family quarrel that broke out in the late sixties—a vital relationship has consistently been evident. On one level, this can be seen as a coming-together in the modern American city—for this has occurred during the era in which blacks have become increasingly urban—on the part of two peoples who have perceived in each other the most significant mirror of their own histories of collective suffering. Much of the relationship is a cultural and political exchange based on this mutual recognition.

But it would be wrong to stop there and not observe that there do seem to be deeper-lying resonances in their relationship, especially in the field of music. Isaac Goldberg, who was George Gershwin's Boswell, heard resemblances between Negro music and certain strains of Jewish folk melody, especially the songs of the Hasidim. In *George Gershwin: a Study in American Music*, suggesting that the blue note shared by these two musical traditions is the common intonation of long-suffering peoples, Goldberg says startlingly: "I leave it to the musical anthropologists to determine how much of this resemblance may go back to a common Oriental ancestry in both Negro and Jew." Racial mysticism aside, however, he makes a good case for the importance of the Jewish element in the music of Gershwin, with whom he clearly had discussed this point. The song "My One and Only," from *Funny Face*, Goldberg writes, "begins Yiddish and ends up black." Its main theme certainly is, to my ears, as Jewish-sounding a melody as Gershwin ever wrote. As a matter of fact, at the time Goldberg wrote his book (1931), the opera Gershwin was planning to write was to be based on Ansky's *The Dybbuk*; subsequently, after reading DuBose Heyward's *Porgy*, he returned to the idea for a black opera—an idea foreshadowed in 1922 with his one-act piece about Harlem, *Blue Monday Blues* (later retitled *135th Street*). This certainly was a case of beginning Yiddish and ending up black!

One can detect a similar line of development in the early Irving Berlin. Although he had done both Italian pastiche and coon songs in the years just preceding "Alexander's Ragtime Band," Berlin seems to have established himself in that period as a specialist in Yiddisha songs. In 1909 he published "Sadie Salome Go Home," for which he wrote the lyric to Edgar Leslie's tune, and "Yiddle on Your Fiddle, Play Some Ragtime," for which he wrote both words and music, as he was to do throughout his subsequent

199

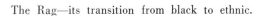

The Rag—its transition from black to ethnic.

The Jazz Singer went from the Yiddish stage (page 57) to Hollywood as the first talking picture (1927) and in a way was the story of its star, the Russian-born Asa Yoelsen, whose ambition to be a cantor was transformed to a compulsion to be an entertainer. As Al Jolson (1866–1950) he frequently appeared in blackface and kept alive the tradition of the minstrel show.

career. These two songs, especially the latter, might be described as Yiddish rags and represent a characteristic Tin Pan Alley (and American) idea of yoking together disparate strains as if by violence, especially ethnic ones. What is striking about Irving Berlin's synthesis of Jewish and ragtime is that, especially in the song for which he himself wrote the music, it manages to sound authentically Yiddish and Negro at the same time. This is the kind of musical discovery George Gershwin was to make eighteen years later with "My One and Only."

There is an extra-musical aspect to both these Berlin songs that is also of significance. Their lyrics are vivid examples of the tradition of ethnic ridicule, which was so essential an aspect of the coon song that even black practitioners felt compelled to use it, as Ernest Hogan did in "All Coons Look Alike to Me."

200

In 1919 Al Jolson sang "Swanee" by George Gershwin (Jacob Gershvin, 1898–1937, born in Brooklyn, original family name Gershowitz) in *Sinbad*, and that hit was the first of a steady stream of Gershwin songs ("Fascinating Rhythm," "The Man I Love," "Someone to Watch Over Me") to sweep Broadway and America. Gershwin's folk opera, *Porgy and Bess*, his *Rhapsody in Blue*, *An American in Paris*, and Piano Concerto in F became part of the classic repertoire after his death. He is shown with his older brother, Ira (right), an accomplished lyricist for many songwriters, and Guy Bolton (middle), who collaborated with the Gershwins on the show *Lady, Be Good!*

One widely used technique was to place bumbling or rag-talking darkies in conventional situations typical of white middle-class experience, so that if the black was being made fun of, the experience was being parodied at the same time. Joe E. Howard's 1899 coon song "Hello, Ma Baby," for example, was a delightful ragging (read: "razzing") of the very popular telephone-song convention which, in response to the new great American toy, had by this time literally been done to death with Charles K. Harris's "Hello Central, Give Me Heaven."

Berlin's two 1909 songs are direct offspring of coon-song conventions in both lyrics and music. "Sadie Salome Go Home"—the title clearly echoes that of the celebrated 1902 coon song, "Bill Bailey, Won't You Please Come Home"—is, quite simply, about a Jewish girl doing things that only gentile girls do: Sadie Cohen leaves her nice family, becomes an actress, and does a striptease act as Salome. All this is described in the verse; the refrain consists of the outcry of her boyfriend Mose—(a name that is both Yiddisha and coon—indeed, it is more the latter), who has come to the theater and discovered for the first time what her act is. This is where the song's title comes in, as well as four "oy's," which, being spondaic, help produce a ragtime effect. There are various minor Yiddishisms, either explicit, as in some inversions of phrase, or implied, as when "glasses" is made to rhyme with "dresses." Greater possibilities of Yiddish intonation were left to the performer, and these were fully exploited by Fanny Brice, who made this song something of a trademark, as she did a subsequent Yiddisha song by Irving Berlin, "Good-bye, Becky Cohen."

It is in Berlin's other 1909 Yiddisha song lyric that something truly remarkable happens. For if the standard coon song made fun of blacks playing white and "Sadie Salome" made fun of Jews playing gentile, the humor of "Yiddle on Your Fiddle" lies in Jews playing black! The scene is a Jewish wedding, vividly described both musically and verbally, at which Yiddle the fiddler starts playing ragtime to the delight of at least one guest, Sadie, who eggs him on with the chorus, which contains the title phrase. The subtle touches suggesting coon-song conventions here and there in the lyric reach a verbal climax when Sadie calls him "mine choc'late baby." It is a case of full circle again, the cultural history that runs from Dan Emmett to Al Jolson retold as a Jewish joke.

Pastiche is a gift of peoples who live in culturally ambivalent situations, as white Americans have in general throughout their history—which is ever poised somewhere between a European past and a New World present—and as Jews have throughout their much longer history. It is therefore not surprising that Jews have always had a special talent for pastiche. (The outstanding example in the area of classical music was Felix Mendelssohn, who alone among the great German composers successfully imitated alien motifs—Scottish, Italian, Shakespearean, and so on.) In this vein Jewish and American culture came together with a resonance that is still being heard and will be for years to come.

American-Jewish pastiche and musical blackface greatly influenced the development of the musical theater on Broadway in the two decades between World Wars I and II. Gershwin's *Porgy and Bess* (1935) was the outstanding masterpiece of this genre, but this "folk opera" was not simply an offspring of the kind of Tin Pan Alley blackface that both Gershwin and Berlin had been doing in the decade preceding 1920. By this time another strain of pastiche had entered the American popular-song tradition, the strain from which the Broadway musical arose in the first place, and which combined with blackface to produce the synthesis from which *Porgy and Bess* emerged. Here Jewish composers have also played a crucial role. If the blackface strain has been, for the most part, brassy and "lowdown," an earthy defiance of American bourgeois conventions, this other strain is mellow and often conscientiously genteel. If the first is the offspring of Negro ragtime and jazz, the second is the offspring of European operetta; and if Irving Berlin was in effect the founder of a new era for the one strain, his equivalent for the other was Jerome Kern.

Oscar Hammerstein II, who was Jerome Kern's lyricist for *Show Boat* and other works, described an interesting scene, in his introduction to the *The Jerome Kern Song Book* (1955):

Jerome Kern and I were at one time contemplating writing a musical version of Donn Byrne's *Messer Marco Polo*. Discussing the general problems of adaptation, I confronted Jerry with what I considered to be a serious question about the score. I said, "Here is a story laid in China about an Italian and told by an Irishman. What kind of music are you going to write?" Jerry answered, "It'll be good Jewish music."

The remark was only a jest, but I think that Kern touched here, however lightly, and perhaps even unconsciously, upon a root of his artistic sensibility: it was as though he were announcing the principle that made possible this startling variety of cultural pastiche.

Although Kern was celebrated above all for a score resonant with themes from the American South and was, indeed, the first Broadway composer to develop what Alec Wilder, both a composer and a writer, calls a genuinely "American sound," it is significant that he made this remark with reference to a combination of non-American motifs. Kern never completely freed himself from the ambivalence resulting from bicultural influences, hanging irresolutely, but often with a creativity all the greater for the uncertainty, between Europe and America. This is an ambivalence that often besets American writers and artists and characterizes American-Jewish culture in particular. It can be said of Kern that, even though his music pioneered the way to a truly American school of song—and both George Gershwin and Richard Rodgers were to acknowledge him as their master in this respect—his aspirations always included that of creating an American version of operetta.

Kern's origins and formative years are in significant contrast with those of Irving Berlin, who was only three years his junior. Kern was born in New York in 1885 at the peak of what can properly be called the German era of American-Jewish history. Until just a few years earlier, the bulk of the Jewish immigrants to the United States had come from German-speaking Central Europe, displacing the old Sephardic community as the predominant element in American-Jewish life and imparting their own particular character to it as well as to aspects of American life in general. By the time of Kern's birth these German Jews were on the whole thoroughly established, fully American, and solidly bourgeois, like Kern's parents. When he showed signs of having inherited the musical gifts of his mother—who had considered a career as a concert pianist before her marriage—he was given a solid musical education, first with private tutors, then at the New York College of Music, later (in spite of some opposition from his practical-minded father) in Europe. His aim was a career in classical music, either as a pianist or as a composer, but in Heidelberg Kern discovered that Brahms' vein was not his after all. This might have been the beginning of the end of music for him altogether, except for a fortunate sojourn in London that followed. This city—rather more in tune than Heidelberg with Kern's sensibility—became a second home for him in body and spirit. Here is where he found a job writing incidental music for the theater; here is where he met the young man who was to be his lyricist in years to come, P. G. Wodehouse, and here is where he met the girl who was to become his wife. Even after his return to the United States in 1904, he was to spend his first professional years as a kind of musical link between London and New York, composing songs that were interpolated into imported British musicals—a common practice at the time.

The difference between Kern's early years and those of Irving Berlin exemplifies the difference between the German era in American-Jewish history and the East European era that displaced it. On the whole, the contrast between the German Jew and his East European coreligionist was like that in their respective languages: the Yiddish-speaking Jews were more earthy and indecorous, filled with a brash vitality that at first startled and even dismayed the German-American Jews but eventually engulfed them. The people who had started out as sober schoolmasters in relation to the new arrivals often ended up rolling back their shirtsleeves and taking lessons from their former pupils. Something like this happened to Jerome Kern. There is a striking difference between Kern's first really big hit show, *Sally*, which, though written in 1920, still had a somewhat British sound to it, and the utterly American *Show Boat* of 1927, and an important reason for this was the appearance of Gershwin in the interval. By this time Gershwin had shown

His famous book collection was auctioned in 1928 for $1,729,462, but Jerome Kern (1885–1945) was better known for his musicals *Sunny, The Cat and the Fiddle, Music in the Air, Show Boat.* His father, president of the Street Sprinklers' Association, had the concession for watering Manhattan. The composer of "Ol' Man River" is seen here with screen star Jean Harlow.

"The Last of the Red Hot Mommas," Sophie Tucker started singing in the Abuza family's restaurant in Hartford, Connecticut. (Her father had changed his name from Kalish to Abuza when he emigrated from Russia three months after Sophie's birth.) In 1909, twenty-three years old, she landed a part in the Ziegfeld *Follies* and two years later adopted "Some of These Days" as her theme song. London's Palladium and New York's Palace were high spots in her many travels.

"September Song" and "Mack the Knife" are the most popular of the songs of Kurt Weill (1900–1950), but his haunting music was the best on Broadway in the fifteen years following his flight from the Nazis. Lotte Lenya, whom he married in 1926, an actress and singer of great artistic stature, continues to be the finest singer of Weill's songs. *Knickerbocker Holiday* (1938), *Lady in the Dark* (1941), *One Touch of Venus* (1943), and *Lost in the Stars* (1949) are part of his musical legacy.

not only that lowdown contemporary American blues sounds and jazz rhythms could be used for quality musical theater, but also that these could be turned into concert music. *Show Boat* was certainly, in part, a response to this. Gershwin, on his part, had been inspired by Kern's music, from the very beginning of his precocious career, to write more serious songs than the standard Tin Pan Alley variety.

Indeed, it can be said that this interplay between Kern and Gershwin was what led the way in the evolution of a truly "American sound" in the Broadway musical theater during the 1920s. Yet these composers had learned their craft in the act of imitation, and they continued to derive a part of their inspiration from it. Their most outstanding respective works, *Show Boat* and *Porgy and Bess*, were both returns to their early inclination to pastiche, but now on a far higher level, and in the case of Gershwin's *Porgy and Bess* on a

transcendent level. Their very choice of material was significant. Kern and Hammerstein, after they had done *Show Boat*, were quite interested in DuBose Heyward's novel *Porgy* as the basis for a musical show and might have beaten Gershwin in the bidding for it, but eventually the project was abandoned by them. This was probably a wise move, for one can hardly imagine Kern functioning in the abrasive atmosphere of Catfish Row, whereas the sentimental nineteenth-century Americana of Edna Ferber—another offspring of genteel German-American Jewry—perfectly suited his temperament. Essentially, *Show Boat* was an operetta, a perfect fusion of that form dear to Kern's heart with the American sounds he had been absorbing in recent years, and consequently it has been the most truly American operetta ever written.

Kern was not to return to the grandiose, nineteenth-century Americana vein he had opened up in *Show Boat* until his last years in Hollywood in the forties. In the very next years after *Show Boat* he found his line of development not in the direction *Porgy* suggested, but in a return to fairly traditional operetta in a new kind of American dress. *Sweet Adeline*, in 1929, was a nostalgic pastiche of the Gay Nineties. *The Cat and the Fiddle*, in 1931, was closer to traditional operetta in its themes and setting: it dealt with a romance, set in Europe, between a Rumanian composer of operas and an American girl who loves popular music—in effect, a confrontation between Kern's two musical identities. *Music in the Air*, in 1932, was almost wholly a traditional operetta: the story of a love affair in a picturesque Bavarian town. By this time Kern's artistic identity was so firmly established that he could do his own distinctive type of song even when working with old-fashioned material like this; nevertheless, he did not do his best work in this period.

It was in 1933, with *Roberta*, that Kern found his most fruitful vein outside of the nineteenth-century Americana of *Show Boat* and his last movies. Working with a story about Americans in Paris, he was at last able to evolve a truly contemporary American style for himself. Its mood of gay if slightly world-weary cocktail sophistication, American-international expressed one aspect of himself. In this show were "Smoke Gets in Your Eyes" and "Yesterdays," two of his finest songs. As a result of this show he went to Hollywood, where he settled down both physically and professionally, and where he acquired a splendid interpreter for whom he was to write some of his best songs. Fred Astaire is universally recognized as a great dancer, but relatively few people know that, despite his thin, rather matter-of-fact-sounding voice he was a very good singer, charged with musicality, rhythm, and wit. Indeed, he was so good an interpreter that not only Kern but other popular American composers, including Gershwin and Berlin, wrote some of their best songs for him. Astaire, who had not been in *Roberta* on Broadway, appeared in the film version, and for him Kern interpolated a song he had written for a London show the previous year, "I Won't Dance," and it was transmuted. From then on a distinct Kern-Astaire style came into being. The year after the film *Roberta*, Kern wrote one of his most delightful scores for the Astaire-Rogers movie *Swing Time*, which included "The Way You Look Tonight" and "A Fine Romance."

It was Fred Astaire who lured George and Ira Gershwin back to Hollywood—to which they had thought they would never return after a brief stint there in 1931—to do his next film, *Shall We Dance?* This score and two more for the movies—including that for Astaire's *Damsel in Distress*—were the last things Gershwin wrote, for he died in Hollywood of a brain tumor in 1937, at the age of thirty-eight.

In this final period of his life Gershwin wrote some of his loveliest ballads of the traditional show type—such as "A Foggy Day," "Love Walked In," and "Our Love Is Here to Stay." But this was a return to an old vein, and did not really represent the direction in which he had been going for much of the previous, ten years. For if we saw in Jerome Kern the case of a man with a classical, European-oriented training who worked his way back to American popular song, we have in Gershwin a case of movement in the opposite direction, from the popular song tradition to some kind of classical style, a synthesis of the American and the European.

Gershwin's boyhood resembles Irving Berlin's more than Jerome Kern's. He was born in Brooklyn in 1898, the son of Russian-Jewish immigrants. He grew up in the rough and tumble of the streets of New York, came to music on his own, and embarked upon his musical career at sixteen as a Tin Pan Alley song plugger and composer. Unlike Irving Berlin, he had managed to obtain some solid private musical training before going out to work, and he was recognized as a child prodigy by his teachers. He came to Tin Pan Alley an accomplished musician and seems to have had more grandiose ambitions from the start. As we have seen, he was inspired by Kern's music early in his career to write popular songs of high quality, but it did not take long before his restless ambition reached beyond this goal. To *George White's Scandals of 1922* he contributed not only "Stairway to Paradise," which established him in the front rank of theater song composers, but also his first essay in "opera," *Blue Monday Blues*. For the next few years it was the same story: new shows alternating with new concert pieces: 1924 was the year of *Lady Be Good* and of the *Rhapsody in Blue*; 1925 the year of *Tip-Toes* and of the Piano *Concerto in F*. By 1927, when he wrote *Funny Face*, he had also composed the "Three Preludes for Piano" and *An American in Paris*.

Although Gershwin and his brother Ira, his lyricist, continued writing shows in the lighthearted vein they had helped create and establish as the typical Broadway style—indeed, they came up with their best work in that vein in 1930, with *Girl Crazy*—they began in 1927 to develop a new type of musical theater. *Strike Up the Band* that year, *Of Thee I Sing* in 1931, and its sequel *Let 'Em Eat Cake* in 1932 had much in common with the mordant social and political satire then being done in Berlin by Kurt Weill and Bertolt Brecht. With the exception of a song like "Who Cares?" in *Of Thee I Sing*, the old carefree mood was gone. In Hollywood, Gershwin showed that he could still write wonderfully in the earlier vein, but clearly the stage was becoming for him a more serious medium. *Porgy and Bess* was waiting in the wings; this synthesis of popular and classical music brought out his greatest gifts.

Gershwin's early death ended in mid-flight the career of an authentic American genius—a distinctly American-Jewish one at that. By "American" genius I mean one that is raw, unruly, characterized by an eagerness to try everything and a propensity to scatter its shots too far and wide, which comes from a combination of untutoredness and boundless energy: it is the roughneck genius of a Walt Whitman. And by "American-Jewish" I mean a persistent Europeanness combined with an almost overeager, because slightly alienated, Americanism, a relentless intellectuality that transcends mere education or the lack thereof and is endlessly plummeting after insights which are never less brilliant for being occasionally crude. From all the accounts written about George Gershwin, one gets the picture of a man who was in constant flight, buzzing after new ideas night and day with either his tongue or his fingers. Conversation, in which he was also quite gifted, evidently was a great pleasure to him, but it was as nothing alongside his passion to ad lib at the piano, to create, for example, endless jazz variations on his own compositions (a few of which got written down, to the good fortune of posterity) for the delectation of friends, guests, or fellow-guests at parties. And in his later years (a relative term!), when music did not take up quite enough of his overbrimming energies, he tried painting and showed great skill at it. Had he lived long enough, he probably would have written a book or two as well. The fuse of his energies perhaps burned too brightly and furiously to last into middle age.

With Gershwin's death and Kern's departure for Hollywood—as well as Cole Porter's riding accident in 1937, which greatly curbed his creativity (*Kiss Me Kate* in 1948 was his one return to top form)—Broadway musical tradition rested primarily in the hands of the fourth of the major Jewish songwriters of that epoch, Richard Rodgers. (Kurt Weill had arrived by then and was doing interesting work, but he was still just developing an American idiom for himself.) And it was Rodgers' work at the end of the thirties and the beginning of the forties that bridged two epochs in the Broadway musical theater and became the chief influence in the formation of a new style. These two epochs in Rodgers' career were formed in relationship with two lyricists successively, Lorenz Hart and Oscar Hammerstein II.

It is relevant to note that Rodgers, Hart, and Hammerstein all came from German-Jewish backgrounds rather than from the East European–Jewish background of Berlin and Gershwin. They belonged, though each in a somewhat different way, to the more genteel tradition represented by the old German-American Jewish life-style. Like Gershwin, Rodgers fell in love with Kern's music at an early age (he was born in 1902), but, unlike Gershwin, he never departed from the mellow, romantic vein that Kern had opened up to him, even though he produced a style very much his own. He alone among the Americans is Kern's equal as a pure melodist (in a way that Gershwin, oddly, is not), and perhaps he even surpassed him. Yet these very qualities had their pitfalls. He did not have Gershwin's talent for forms of composition more ambitious than what the framework of the Broadway musical provided, but within that framework he did have somewhat elevated ambitions from time to time: a relatively early manifestation of this is the "Slaughter on Tenth Avenue" ballet in his 1936 show *On Your Toes*, which, though rather colorless and simplistic as musical composition, is nevertheless enchanting because of its melodies. The excesses evident in this piece did not really begin to get free rein until the forties, with such numbers as the "Soliloquy" in *Carousel* (1945). It is hard to avoid the conclusion that the change manifested here was intimately related to the change in collaborators that had taken place in the meantime.

Lorenz Hart claimed to be a lateral descendant of Heinrich Heine, and this claim is appealing, not only because Hart was one of the finest lyricists in the American musical theater, but because his writing is full of a mordant vulnerability that is very much in the Heinesque vein. This is a quality often found among Jewish artists of nineteenth- and early twentieth-century Germany (Kurt Weill had it in abundance), but it was rare among the old-stock German-American Jews; the liberal optimism that had brought them to America in the first place precluded it as a trait in their personality. Hart was a delightful exception. "His lyrics knew," Rodgers wrote in his introduction to *The Rodgers and Hart Song Book* (1951), "that love was not especially devised for boy and girl idiots of fourteen." Hart's worldly wit held Rodgers' broad romantic lyricism in check without constricting it; indeed, he inspired it in the direction of a uniquely poised and highly poetic loveliness in songs like "There's a Small Hotel" from *On Your Toes* and "My Funny Valentine" from *Babes in Arms* (1937). On the other hand, as Alec Wilder has observed, there is sometimes an odd but appealing tension between melody and lyric.

This tension finally caused a break. One hears much about this in purely personal terms—Hart's stormy, unhappy personality, his increasingly wild life-style and undisciplined work habits contrasting

ABOVE: Joseph J. Lerner founded Lerner Stores, Inc., a nationwide chain of women's clothing stores, and fathered Alan Jay (right). Edmund Loewe, a Viennese operetta tenor who was the original star of *The Chocolate Soldier* and *The Merry Widow*, fathered Frederick (left). The sons met at the Lambs Club in 1942 and fathered *Brigadoon* (1947), *Paint Your Wagon* (1951), *My Fair Lady* (1956), *Gigi* (1959), *Camelot* (1960). Music by Loewe, words by Lerner.

FROM LEFT TO RIGHT: Richard Rodgers found his first lyricist at Columbia University, teaming with Lorenz Hart for the 1920 Varsity Show, and continued the partnership until Larry's death in 1943. The result, *On Your Toes, Babes in Arms, The Boys from Syracuse, Pal Joey.*

Oklahoma! paired Rodgers with Oscar Hammerstein II (1895–1960), whose grandfather owned and operated the Manhattan Opera House and whose father was also a theatrical manager. A graduate of Columbia Law School, Hammerstein had already supplied books and lyrics for *Desert Song, Music in the Air,* and *Show Boat,* and with Rodgers was responsible for *Carousel, South Pacific, The King and I,* and *The Sound of Music.*

An apprentice for Rodgers and Hammerstein while at Williams College, and a lyricist for Rodgers' *Do I Hear a Waltz?* and Leonard Bernstein's *West Side Story,* Stephen Sondheim wrote both music and lyrics for *Gypsy, Company, Follies,* and *A Little Night Music.* Arthur Laurents, pictured between Rodgers and Sondheim, was playwright for many shows, including *West Side Story* and *Do I Hear a Waltz?*

sharply with the ways of Rodgers, the sober, hard-working family man—but it was above all the intolerable strain that developed in their work itself that pulled them in opposite directions. When one considers that it was only three years between the bitter ribaldry of *Pal Joey*, Rodgers' next-to-last work with Hart, and the super-wholesomeness of *Oklahoma!* (1943), his first with Hammerstein, one finds it difficult to imagine how the collaboration could have gone on even under better personal conditions. It was Rodgers who was eager to take up the Theatre Guild's suggestion that he do a musical of Lynn Riggs' play *Green Grow the Lilacs*; Hart simply was not interested. Hart died shortly after that, although he lived long enough to see the opening night performance of *Oklahoma!*, which heralded the new team—and the new era—of Rodgers and Hammerstein.

Of all the representatives of the genteel German-American Jewish tradition Oscar Hammerstein II is by far the truest to form. The scion of a great theatrical producing family and the grandson of a producer of grand opera (after whom he was named), Hammerstein was as determined as the Gershwins to find more elevated forms for the musical theater than those of the early twenties, but since he lacked their intellectuality and sense of irony as well as their gifts, his tendency was ever in the direction of a kind of middlebrow schmaltz. This tendency was clearly present in *Show Boat*, as well as in the pure operettas he was doing during that time with Rudolf Friml and Sigmund Romberg. When elevatedness fell out of fashion on Broadway in the thirties (even *Porgy and Bess* was a flop the first time around), so also did Hammerstein. He was virtually out of work when Rodgers approached him to collaborate on the project that became *Oklahoma!*

By 1943 a new spirit had entered into the Broadway theater and into American culture in general. The world-weary, fun-seeking sophistication of the twenties and the bitterness and irreverence of the thirties were being replaced by a new mood of pietism induced by World War II. This included a passionate embracing of good old American values in various forms and a folklore revival that ranged from the highly authentic through good pastiche to the wholly synthetic. In the popular arts the predominant vein was a pure white, front-porch Americana, a way of life that had reached its peak at about the turn of the century, the era most often focused upon. This was the vein of *Oklahoma!* and its successor *Carousel*, as well as of such outstanding Hollywood musicals as *Meet Me in Saint Louis*, *The Harvey Girls* (both with Judy Garland), and Jerome Kern's two last scores, *Can't Help Singing* and *Centennial Summer*. It was the vein of Harold Arlen's Broadway show *Bloomer Girl*, where the composer was, in spite of the *Oklahoma!* conventions it was founded upon, at his best in black pastiche, with songs like "Evelina" and "The Eagle and Me." It was the vein in which Irving Berlin, returning to Broadway after a number of years in Hollywood, wrote the best over-all score of his career, *Annie Get Your Gun*. And, finally, it was the vein in which Kurt Weill was making his most radical American explorations, with his unique experiment in "folk opera," *Down in the Valley*, with *Love Life*, a 1948 collaboration with Alan Jay Lerner, and with the score for a musical version of *Huckleberry Finn*, to Maxwell Anderson's book and lyrics, which he was writing at the time of his death in 1950.

For nearly two decades, starting with *Oklahoma!* and ending with Hammerstein's death in 1960, Rodgers and Hammerstein were to be the ruling duumvirate of the American musical theater, and during this time they largely set its tone. What they proclaimed was a new synthesis of the Broadway musical tradition with the conventions of serious drama. And for a time Rodgers plucked some of his finest melodies out of Hammerstein's cornfields, but their collaboration tended on the whole to decline into the kind of ponderous middlebrowism that reached its nadir in *The Sound of Music*.

On the other hand, Harold Arlen, Frank Loesser, and the team of Frederick Loewe and Alan Jay Lerner all demonstrated the best possibilities of the new seriousness; but most important in its progress was the American work of Kurt Weill. Next to Gershwin (to whom he was, of course, far superior on a technical level), Weill was the greatest composer ever to devote himself to the Broadway musical theater,

Three years as an accompanist for Marlene Dietrich polished Burt Bacharach's talents, and the following year Dionne Warwick sang his intricate rhythms and melodies to success. With his longtime lyricist, Hal David, Burt wrote songs for the Broadway hit *Promises, Promises* (book by Neil Simon), and many others, including "Raindrops Are Falling on My Head," "What the World Needs Now," "The Look of Love." Born in 1929 in Kansas City, Missouri, and raised in Forest Hills, New York, Bacharach has become a television performer and entertainer.

and his premature death at fifty was a great blow because he was then just beginning to find himself at home in an American idiom.

The Gershwins and Weill became good friends after the latter's emigration to the United States in 1935. Ira Gershwin was to be Weill's most felicitous lyricist. In a sense, the meeting of George Gershwin and Kurt Weill, both physically and artistically, was like a crossing of paths on their opposite musical journeys: Weill from Europe to America, from German composition to Broadway melody, and Gershwin from America to Europe, from the sounds of Tin Pan Alley and Harlem to those of the Paris *conservatoire*. Though Weill's Berlin collaborator, Bertolt Brecht, also sought refuge in the United States during the Hitler period, Weill alone became an American in his art and his personal commitment. After the war Brecht went back to Europe, from which he had spiritually never departed. Both leaned heavily on Americanisms in their work, and both pursued an ideal of democratic theater; but Brecht wanted to develop a communist-intellectual version of the ideal, and Weill restructured his art on an American base. Of the two, Weill's is the utterly Jewish history, and so it hardly seems an accident that his finest achievement in the American musical form was a work of black pastiche.

Lost in the Stars, which opened in October 1949, a few months before his death, was in a way a completion of Weill's relationship with George Gershwin. As splendid and independent a work as it is, it clearly would not have been written had there never been a *Porgy and Bess,* which it resembles in many ways—including its aspiration to be not just a Broadway show but a Broadway opera. It is interesting to note that its leading role was played by Todd Duncan, who had been Gershwin's original Porgy fifteen years before.

Beginning about 1950, the stress in Broadway musicals shifted rather consistently in the direction of book at the expense of music and of production numbers at the expense of songs. While staging became more lavish and choreography more complex, there seemed to be fewer and fewer tunes that one was either inclined or able to hum upon leaving the theater. The best work of the newly emerging Jewish composers and lyricists—and the field continued to be dominated by Jews—proved to be in the mordant vein that both Weill and Gershwin had abandoned rather than in the straightforwardly serious one they had taken up. These younger writers, largely college-educated in an era when the bright, college-humor style was becoming a significant phenomenon in American, and above all in American-Jewish culture, sought to rise above the general trend toward banality (*South Pacific*) and bathos (*The Sound of Music*) through satire and irony. Indeed, one can scarcely find an important musical by a composer-lyricist team who came into their own after World War II that did not have a strongly ironic stance.

This vein had been foreshadowed as far back as 1937 with Harold Rome's delightful satirical review, *Pins and Needles,* staged by the International Ladies' Garment Workers' Union, but its true era began precisely in 1950 with the opening of perhaps the wittiest musical ever written, Frank Loesser's *Guys and Dolls.* (Both Rome and Loesser wrote their own lyrics at a time when that had become quite rare; Loesser, in fact, began his career as a lyricist.) In a sense, *Guys and Dolls* is a continuation of the Rodgers and Hammerstein and *Show Boat* tradition of the serious book musical (Abe Burrows wrote its book). Like *Show Boat,* it is based on a literary source—indeed, one has every reason to take Damon Runyon's work more seriously as literature than Edna Ferber's. But its literary source is all satire and irony, and the result, while a healthy harking back to some of the gaiety of old, is hardly the fluff Guy Bolton wrote for the early Kern and Gershwin musicals. Here is a new sensibility on the Broadway musical stage, and if the old melody is not there in all its gloriousness, it has not been completely lost, while something else not at all extraneous to the entertainment has compensated for the slight diminution of musical values. The show forms a unique whole which stands among the very best.

This new type of musical made a vigorous return to the use of pastiche, that old American-Jewish specialty; but the new context of self-conscious irony in which it was applied, utterly different from the naïve commercialism of "Alexander's Ragtime Band" and "Swanee" or from the primitive sentimentality of an Al Jolson, heralded a new era. Indeed, this was a foreshadowing of the pop music revival of the sixties, in which pastiche was an all-important element, not only in the work of the Beatles but in that of those latter-day American-Jewish masters of folk pastiche, Bob Dylan and Simon and Garfunkel.

My Fair Lady, which opened in 1956, was the product of a felicitous blend of the new elements; a serious book, irony, and pastiche. Loewe and Lerner had done pleasant but undistinguished work before this and had shown themselves to be astute practitioners of national pastiche in their pseudo-Scottish *Brigadoon* (1947). Indeed, they seem to have had all the qualifications for writing good musicals in the new era except genuine wit; and they finally got George Bernard Shaw to take care of that for them. Working with a text that brought out the scintillating talent and innate cosmopolitanism of Loewe (who was born and raised in Vienna and who has never achieved an "American sound" in his music), they came up with a new, highly verbose patter song, urbanely delivered by Rex Harrison, which caught the spirit of Shaw. A scattering of cockney pastiche—sung in delightful music-hall style by Stanley Holloway—added color to the palette, and the result was one of the better musicals ever written, certainly one of the most famous, even though there was not one truly distinguished song in it.

Leonard Bernstein, who has been something of an American-born version of Kurt Weill as a composer, has made the most of the new uses of wit and irony in his Broadway musicals. *On the Town* (1944), his first show, was really something between a robust American-style ballet in the Aaron Copland tradition and a parody of a Broadway musical. But the history of the arts is filled with instances in which parody, in gifted hands, has become at least as good as the thing being parodied, and *On the Town* is a case in point; even the romantic ballads, though they really are parody ballads, are good, and the quartet "Some Other Time " strikes a felicitous balance between wit and sentiment to become a song of great tenderness. Bernstein's next show, *Wonderful Town* (1953), however, was bogged down by its college-humor smartness, and it took a classic work of literary wit to bring his ironic intelligence back on the beam: *Candide* (1956) is a very fine work and is really not so much a musical as a unique kind of operetta.

Bernstein became a truly popular Broadway composer with *West Side Story* (1960), which was a new twist on the ironic style of the fifties. The show is a burlesque, in the classic sense of the word, of *Romeo and Juliet*; it contains much Latin-American pastiche and makes use of the language and vocal mannerisms of Puerto Rican and other slum kids in New York. The latter element in particular brings the witty vein introduced by Frank Loesser, who also parodied New York lower-class speech, from the fifties into the incipient atmosphere of the sixties, when a revival of high seriousness, primarily colored by a social consciousness, imposed itself upon the entertainment arts. In *West Side Story* one has difficulty perceiving the line that distinguishes a wit directed against its subject matter from one directed against society, a spirit that is merely pleasure-seeking from one that is morally earnest.

This infusion of social consciousness into the ironic style continued to mark the sixties. *Fiddler on the Roof* (1964), one of the rare Broadway musicals ever devoted wholly to Jewish subject matter, was a product of this synthesis. Its authors, Jerome Bock and Sheldon Harnick, had shown themselves to be true representatives of the college-humor generation in their early work, and their leaning toward social consciousness had been evident in their 1959 musical *Fiorello!*, a witty and affectionate tribute to a great liberal whose career was a living burlesque of the politician. In Sholom Aleichem's stories about Tevya—as adapted for the stage some years earlier by Arnold Perl—they found material that was funny and deeply serious at the same time, that played with wit and irony on the highest level but also dealt with the sufferings of poverty. They found something even more important: a source of inspiration for a pastiche of their own all-but-lost heritage of Yiddish song. Performance values—another significant aspect of the post-1950 musical—also played a crucial role in the evolution of the score: Jerome Robbins, the director and choreographer, created for many of the songs the dramatic situation that gave them their special resonance (and that, in many cases, caused them to be born in the first place), and Zero Mostel, the original Tevya, a

Art Garfunkel teaches school in Litchfield, Connecticut, while Paul Simon continues to record and tour, but for several years together these collegiates captured America's heart by writing and singing "The Sounds of Silence," "Bridge Over Troubled Waters," "Mrs. Robinson," and "Homeward Bound."

A Canadian who stole the show at the Newport Folk Festival of 1967, Leonard Cohen has written two novels, has published six collections of poetry, and has recorded three best-selling albums. Photo by Shepard Sherbell.

In vaudeville since his fourth birthday, Sammy Davis, Jr., dances, sings, acts, and impersonates. In 1946 Will Mastin and his father formed a trio with the twenty-year-old Sammy which began to attract attention. They reached Broadway ten years later in *Mr. Wonderful*, and since then Sammy's life has been a succession of movies, night-club acts, and TV specials. His autobiography, *Yes I Can*, was a best seller. Photo by Burt Glinn.

Jewish comic genius, served as virtually a third composer in evolving the unique, folklike structure of many of the songs, such as "If I Were a Rich Man," with its rhythmic patter.

The result is something approaching a genuine folk musical, and if the original English-language version of the show had a slightly synthetic Broadway ring to it, the version done a few years later by an Israeli company in Yiddish sounds truly authentic. In a brilliant translation by Shraga Friedman, in which "Tradition, Tradition" becomes "Die Toyreh, Die Toyreh (The Torah, The Torah)" and "If I Were a Rich Man" becomes "Ven Ich Bin a Rotshild" (the title, with only the addition of an "a" for rhythm, of a non-Tevya story by Sholom Aleichem), and a performance by the Russian-born Israeli actor Shmuel Rudensky so true it seems to be Tevya himself speaking and singing, it becomes a genuine return to sources. With it the great American-Jewish popular music tradition seems to come full circle.

Recognized as a brilliant comedienne in her first Broadway role (Miss Marmelstein in *I Can Get It for You Wholesale*, 1962), Barbra Streisand struck gold with her first record, which became the top-selling album on its release the following year. Her Broadway and film success in *Funny Girl* (1964) led inexorably to the movie *Funny Lady* (1975). Her films also include *Hello, Dolly!*, *The Owl and the Pussy Cat*, and *The Way We Were*. Photo by Alan Pappé.

Laughtermakers

Albert Goldman

"Jewish" and "comic" are words that slot together like "Irish" and "cop," "Chinese" and "laundry," "Italian" and "tenor." From the earliest years of vaudeville—Weber and Fields, Dutch jokes, slapstick, to silent movies, Ben Blue, Charlie Chaplin, to early radio, Ed Wynn the Fire Chief, Eddie Cantor, Jack Benny, to talkies, the Brothers Marx and Ritz; to burlesque, Phil Silvers, Red Buttons, to Broadway revues, Bert Lahr, Willie Howard, Phil Silvers, Zero Mostel; to night clubs, Joe E. Lewis, Henny Youngman, Buddy Hackett; to the great days of television, Milton Berle, Sid Caesar; to the cabaret theater, Nichols and May, to the sick comics, Lenny Bruce, Mort Sahl, Shelley Berman, Woody Allen—they've all been Jews.

Yet until the 1950s there was never any Jewish humor in the American media. So many Jewish comics and never a Jewish joke! Far from exploiting their identity as Jews, most comics did everything in their power to disguise the fact that they were Jewish. They changed their names from David Kaminski to Danny Kaye, from Joey Gottlieb to Joey Bishop, from Jerome Levitch to Jerry Lewis, from Murray Janofsky to Jan Murray. They tacked cute little pigtails on their names: Joe-y, Dan-ny, Sand-y, Len-ny, Hen-ny. They studied radio announcer's diction so they shouldn't nasalize, dentalize, glottal stop, and fall into the yeshiva-student singsong. Nose jobs they got because people wanted to see a nice gentile face—no more beaks and popeyes. Quiet, "tasty" clothes; cigarettes instead of cigars; flat-finished tuxedos instead of shiny mohairs —why, some of those Jewish comics studied so hard to be *goyim*, rubbed out so many Jewish features from their faces, cosmeticized their voices and speech so drastically, they wound up looking as if they had been molded in the same factory that makes Barbie dolls. "Ladies and gentlemen, the networks are proud to present Bob Blank! He isn't Jewish—but then he isn't human either."

Some comics might let down and do some Jewish material at a meeting of the Friars or Lambs (show-biz organizations) or at a big B'nai B'rith dinner or UJA banquet—not much, just enough to say, *"Ich bin ech a Yid"*—"I'm a Jew too." Of if they were working the "mountains," the Catskill resort area outside New York, they would adjust to audiences most comfortable in Yiddish. Apart from such old-fashioned ethnic enclaves, there was no room in America for Jewish humor, which was regarded as a dangerous and embarrassing commodity; something the *goyim* could never understand; something the Jews themselves—the successful, highly assimilated Jews—would be embarrassed to acknowledge. So your typical Jewish comedian, like Jack Benny, would pretend to be a typical American, a small-town skinflint from Waukegan, Illinois. Just in case you missed the point, he would bring on a caricatured old Jew out of

220

A collection of comics. Gracie Ethel Cecile Rosalie Allen (1906–1964), daughter of a song-and-dance man, had quit the stage for secretarial school when in 1923 she met Latin dancer George Burns (Nathan Birnbaum, 1896–   ). They married three years later and their act—a scatterbrained wife and exasperated husband—was successful in vaudeville, radio, movies, and television. Eddie Cantor (Edward Israel Iskowitz) (1892–1965), orphaned at two, took to the stage at sixteen, married his childhood sweetheart Ida at twenty-two, became a comedian for Ziegfeld at twenty-four, made his first movie at thirty-four, was the highest-paid star on radio at forty-four. With them, George Jessel (see page 57) and Janet Reade.

vaudeville—a Schlepperman or Meester Kitzel—to play opposite him and bleach his already immaculate face a whiter shade of pale.

Jack Benny's comedy—and that of most of his radio contemporaries—was emasculated comedy, comedy that insisted on being beyond reproach: a humor that would shock nobody, offend nobody, challenge nobody's tastes or prejudices. Perhaps it was radio, the first mass medium, or perhaps it was the Great Depression, that forced American humor in the thirties to enter a phase of white-on-white neutrality, that made it impossible for a Jewish comedian—or, for that matter, any comedian—to stand forth and speak his mind with the force and clarity of comic genius.

Back in the days when Chaplin ruled the screen, American comedy had been the unfettered expression of the comic artist. Chaplin was an English Jew who was at pains always to deny or minimize his Jewish origins. At the same time his comedy was an abstract of Jewish humor, with the essential Jewish properties operating in their traditional Jewish manner, the only difference being that the Yiddish tags were removed so as to achieve a "universal" effect. The Little Fellow was the apotheosis of the schlemiel. His vulnerability and helplessness, his quick wit and ingenuity in self-preservation, his absurd affectation of dandyism, his infatuation with blond-haired, fair-skinned, voluptuously innocent maidens, whom he courted with eyes brimming with Jewish soul and sentiment, were the classic notes and signs of the Jewish comic hero.

Charles Chaplin—born in the London slums in 1889—motion picture actor, writer, director, and producer. Mack Sennett's "little tramp" made *The Kid, The Gold Rush, City Lights, Modern Times, The Great Dictator, Limelight.* He married Oona O'Neill, Eugene O'Neill's daughter, in 1943, and they have seven children.

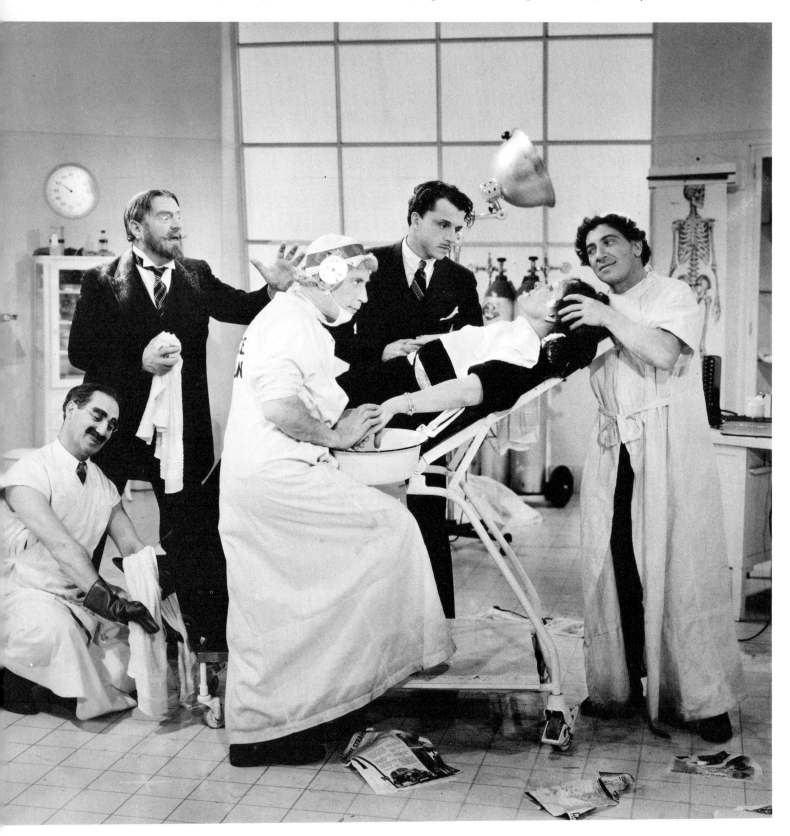

The doctors in white are the Marx Brothers—Julius polishing shoes, Arthur holding hands, and Leonard stroking hair. Their father was a tailor nicknamed "Misfit Sam"; they inherited the stage through their mother, Minna Schoenberg, whose brother Al was the Shean of the vaudeville team Gallagher and Shean. From vaudeville they went to Broadway, to Hollywood and *The Cocoanuts, Animal Crackers, Horse Feathers, A Night at the Opera, A Day at the Races.* Groucho continues to entertain, but Harpo died in 1964 and Chico in 1961, both in their seventies.

The comedy of the Marx Brothers was also Jewish farce *manqué*. If Chaplin distilled the self-pitying comedy of the schlemiel, the Marx Brothers brought to intense focus the other great mode of Jewish humor: the anarchic mockery of conventions and values, which crumble to dust at the touch of a rudely irreverent jest. "Subversive" was the word for the Marx Brothers, as it has been the word often since employed both as condemnation of and tribute to the work of Jewish humorists who refuse to be trammeled by the conventional pieties, delighting instead in demonstrating the fragility and preposterousness of much that passes as social law and order. (The Jew is not only exceptionally adroit at assimilating the values of other cultures but stubbornly skeptical about the value of many of these values.) So the essential dynamic or working power of Jewish comedy operated powerfully in America without declaring itself as such—until it was throttled by the age of the corporation-sponsored, family-entertainment gag. *Gag* indeed!

Meanwhile, in the American ghetto, pure, uncut Jewish humor continued to play the vital role it has always played in Jewish life wherever Jews have lived or however they have fared. Surely no other people in history has made greater use of humor to assuage its pain, assert its pride, exhibit its wit, con-

223

ABOVE: Mama Sarah Berlinger spoon-feeds her Milton Berle. A child actor in *The Perils of Pauline*, a nightclub and vaudeville star with two years as MC at the Palace on Broadway, he became America's first television star. Berle was forty years old when, in 1948, NBC chose him to be host of *The Texaco Star Theatre*, and his program, receiving higher ratings than any previous television or radio show, was responsible for the rapid increase in the number of home television sets.

LEFT: TV's second hit was *Your Show of Shows*, starring Sid Caesar. Born in Yonkers, New York, in 1922, the future comedian studied music at the Julliard School and played the saxophone in several bands, including Charlie Spivak's and Claude Thornhill's. His comic talents were uncovered while he served in the U.S. Coast Guard during World War II, and less than four years after he was discharged from service, he was enlisted in television.

RIGHT: The Cowardly Lion, Bert Lahr (Irving Lahrheim, 1895–1967), turned the role of vulgar clown into high art. His brilliant performance in Beckett's *Waiting for Godot* was the capstone to a stage career which began in vaudeville and burlesque, reached Broadway in 1927 and Hollywood in 1931; some shows: *The George White Scandals, Seven Lively Arts, DuBarry Was a Lady, Two on the Aisle*; some films: *Flying High, Burlesque, The Wizard of Oz*.

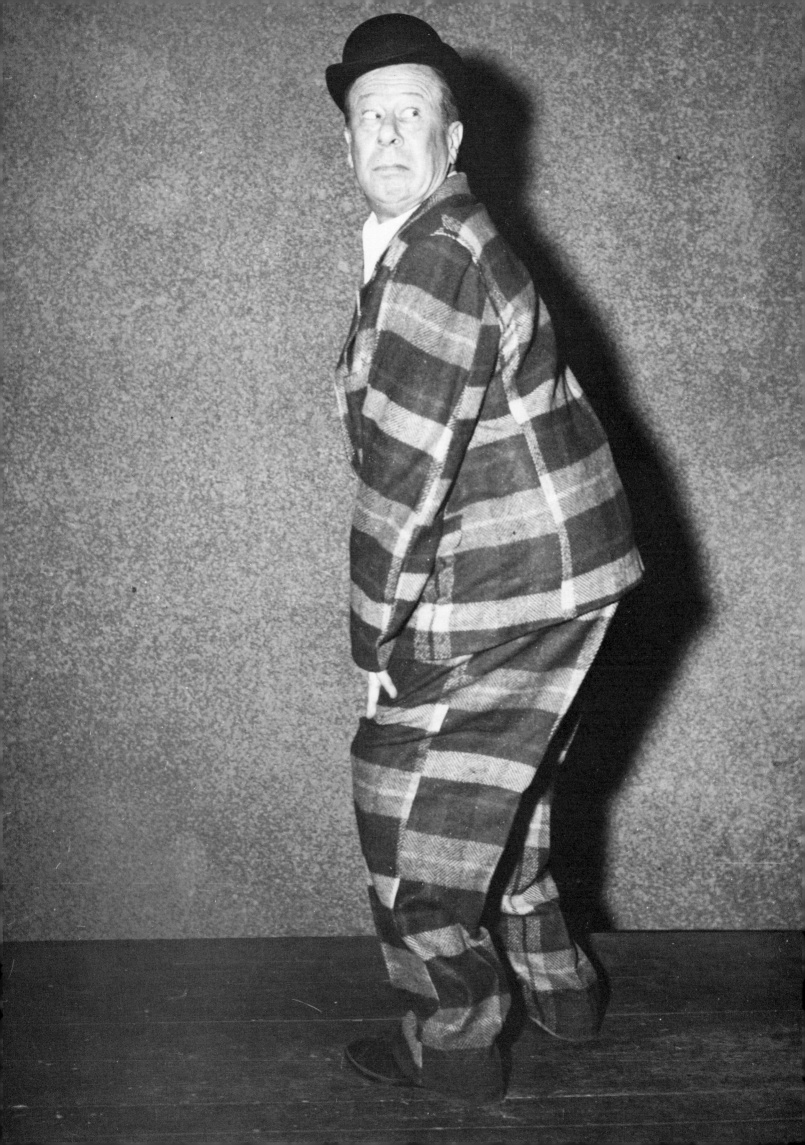

"The Perfect Fool," Isaiah Edwin Leopold (1886–1966; his stage name became Ed Wynn) was clever enough to be producer, show and skit writer, music and lyrics writer with more than a hundred published songs, newspaper columnist, giggling buffoon, and dramatic actor in his late years. He first drew laughs when he modeled the women's hats his father made and sold in Philadelphia; he ran away from home and the hat business, but ridiculous headgear became his stage trademark.

Joe Weber and Lew Fields were both born in 1867, and nine years later were in the same act on New York City's famous Bowery. The "Dutch" comedians toured the country in vaudeville, appeared in plays and movies, owned Weber and Fields Music Hall, and worked together for sixty-five years. Fields died in 1941 and Weber less than a year later.

Sketches by Al Hirshfeld.

solidate its sense of identity, buoy up its spirits, intensify its sexual attractiveness—even blaspheme against its god!—without taking any more responsibility than a man who makes an innocent joke! To tabulate all the ways in which humor functions in the Jewish community would be virtually the same as tabulating all the ways in which Jews are Jews.

When I first moved to Jewish Brooklyn in the early fifties (having been reared in a wholly gentile community in western Pennsylvania and consequently viewing Jewish society in the same way as a *goy* who has for some odd reason been accepted as a fellow-Jew), I was stunned by the audacity, the ferocity, the

The 1930s were bad times for artists, so Samuel Joel Mostel (Brooklyn, 1915–   ), a WPA art teacher at the Museum of Modern Art and the Frick, took to the stage to earn enough to buy paints. He still paints, and he has published a book of his photographic work, but his performances in *Ulysses in Nighttown*, *Rhinoceros*, *A Funny Thing Happened on the Way to the Forum*, and *Fiddler on the Roof* have won the critics' applause. In recognition of his scholastic achievement at P.S. 188 he was nicknamed Zero.

Melas Matuschanskayasky first deserted the Catholic priesthood and Mother Russia, then later deserted his Lithuanian-Jewish wife, Rose Berkowsky, his New York home, and his three-year-old son, Walter. Raised by his mother, Matthau (1920–   ) held a score of odd jobs, working as floor scrubber, file clerk, boxing instructor, axman, basketball coach, cement-bag hauler, and in World War II an Air Force radio operator and gunner, earning six battle stars. He played supporting roles (The Drama Critics Award, 1959, the Tony Award, 1962) for twenty years before starring on Broadway in *The Odd Couple*, 1965, and in films.

His father, a clarinetist with the Cleveland Orchestra, founded a dance band "Mickey Katz and His Kittens," toured the country for two decades with his *Borscht Capades*, and brought his *Hello, Solly!* to Broadway in 1967. Son Joel (1932–   ) had arrived a year earlier in *Cabaret*, a veteran of three years with his father's tour, five years in night clubs, and ten years as a Broadway understudy and replacement. His role as the sleaziest of all master of ceremonies won a Tony and in 1973 an Oscar. Joel (Katz to Kaye to Grey) continues to star on television, stage, and screen.

originality, the sheer abundance and ubiquity of humor among the young people of the neighborhood. Getting together in ritual staging sessions at the backs of candy stores, in parked cars or in some well-barred bedroom, they would perform for hours, much like professional stand-up comics but with vastly greater freedom in the use of obscene language and references, in Yiddish and English, pouring ridicule equally on the feared, admired, and despised *goyim* and on the Jewish family and society that surrounded them and infected them with the disgusting taint of Jewishness. The Jewishness of their humor lay precisely in its obsessional concern with the fact of Jewishness, a fact as ineluctable and irritating as the piece of grit inside the oyster, and just as productive of the pearl-like luster of gleaming wit.

What these laughtermakers were doing was exorcising the Jewish evil spirit, the *dybbuk*, from their souls by screaming out the curses of a particularly hysterical and obscene self-mockery. They were all schlemiels puffed up with a great sense of their own importance, but at the same time painfully deflated by the endless discovery of weaknesses, failures, and stupidities in themselves that militated against the cherished self-image. Eager to purge themselves before suffering another's criticism, they made endless verbal confessions of weakness, folly, and depravity, not only forestalling criticism but distancing their true "good" selves from the selfish, mean, stupid little beings they had been in the past. Theirs was the Jewish psychological predicament in America, the exaggerated demand upon the child by his parents that he attain some wonder of achievement, undermined at the same time by a rearing so fondly indulgent and devoid of frustration that the child never developed the discipline and self-control necessary for great accomplishments. Hence the solution provided by humor, that marvelous device of fantasy that enables us to fail and be forgiven, to attack and not be resented, to assert ourselves to the height of our bent and never have to deliver anything more substantial than a laugh to a receptive and sympathetic clique.

Jewish humor in mid-twentieth-century America, I soon discovered, was not a gentle, ironic, Sholom Aleichem folksiness; nor was it a sophisticated Heinesque intellectual wit; nor was it simply the one-two-three, laff! pattern of the professional joke huckster. It was the plaint of a people who were highly successful in countless ways, yet who still felt inferior, tainted, outcast; a people who needed some magic device of self-assertion and self-aggrandizement. Humor was for modern urban American Jews as basic and necessary as food and drink. It was their stimulant, their narcotic, their secret weapon. It was also the only channel through which their imaginative and creative energies seemed to flow with fable-like fluency in countless "bits" and "shticks" and uproariously funny narratives of the schlemiel and his endless discomfitures.

Inevitably, as the generation to which these young people belonged made their way into the entertainment industry, some of this potent, explosive but hitherto unacknowledged Jewish humor began to leak out through the media. One of the first manifestations was the comedy of Sid Caesar, the great television comic of the fifties. Caesar was a master of travesty, taking off from some typical Hollywood film type or some familiar social situation to soar into vastly exaggerated burlesques that substituted for the object of satire a grotesque satiric myth of the sort in which a cruder and half-illiterate Swift might have rejoiced. Caesar blew up the hoodlums and cowboys and ethnic stereotypes of American folk consciousness to monstrous dimensions and produced a cathartic laughter that was the comic counterpart to the catharsis of terror and violence triggered by his Hollywood originals. Though there was nothing decisively Jewish about his paranoid imaginings, there was often a sly insertion of Jewishness in his skits. The characters in his Japanese movies bore names like Takah Mishiggah or Prince Shmatah (literally, "Really Crazy," "Prince Rag"). The barrister in his British court scene would complain, "Your honor, the defendant *opened such a mouth to me!*" Sid himself bore plainly the stamp of the urban Jewish scene in his accent, gestures, and facial grimaces. He was the newly assimilated American Jew: no longer a shuffling, stoop-shouldered character epitomized by the Yiddish actor Menasha Skulnik, but a young man of prodigious size and power. Mel Brooks, Caesar's principal writer, quipped: "Sid was the strongest comic in history. He could punch a Buick in the grill—and kill it!" The last great Jewish comic of the old tradition, the tradition of infusing Jewish fantasy and soul into the universal forms of low comedy, Sid Caesar provided at the same time the direct inspiration for the first great Jewish comedian of the new style, the explicit comedy of the Jew as Everyman.

His talent with words was discovered in 1950 when he became a writer for *Your Show of Shows*. His voice was heard in 1960 when he recorded the 2000-Year-Old Man series. His face was revealed to the public in 1974 when he appeared in his movie *Blazing Saddles*. For half of his fifty years, Brooklyn-born Mel Brooks (Melvyn Kaminsky) has kept America laughing.

OPPOSITE: Jerry Lewis (Joseph Levitch) was born to show business—his father a night-club singer, his mother a radio pianist. By five he was singing in the borscht circuit; by fifteen he was in burlesque. In 1946, aged twenty, he joined singer Dean Martin and within eight months their salaries rose from $350 to $5000 per week. After ten years, sixteen movies, and endless night-club engagements they separated, Martin to become a TV star and Lewis to sign a ten-million-dollar seven-year cinema contract with Paramount. Jerry Lewis has also been National Chairman of the Muscular Dystrophy Associations of America, to which he has given and for which he has raised many millions of dollars.

Lenny Bruce was a comic genius who revolutionized his art by insisting that the tightly impacted humor of the New York ghetto be made the common property of the American people. Driven by the twin screws of talent and chutzpah, Lenny blasted into the open the golden veins of comedy that for many years had lain hidden behind tons of shame and self-consciousness and fear of self-assertion. Reared in a totally gentile environment on Long Island, Lenny discovered Jewishness when already a grown man. Fascinated by the difference between Jew and gentile, he was fond of ticking off—like God with a wet pencil stub in his mouth—the entire creation into Js and Gs:

All Drake's cakes are *goyish*. Instant potatoes are *goyish*, TV dinners are *goyish*. Fruit salad is Jewish. Black cherry soda's very Jewish. Macaroons are very, very Jewish! Lime jello is *goyish*. Lime soda is very *goyish*. Titties are Jewish. Trailer parks are so *goyish* that Jews won't even go near them. Chicks that iron your shirt for you are *goyish*. Body and fender men are *goyish*. Cat boxes are *goyish*. Ray Charles is Jewish. Al Jolson is Jewish. Eddie Cantor's *goyish*.

Lenny's obsession with Jewishness proved prophetic of the whole period of the sixties: the Jewish Decade. Overnight, the Jew was raised from his traditional role of underdog or invisible man to the glory of being the most fascinating minority in America. Benefiting from universal guilt over the murders by the Nazis, stiffening into fresh pride over the achievements of the State, Israel, reaping the harvest in America of generations of hard work and sacrifice for the sake of the "children," the Jews burst suddenly into prominence in a dozen different areas of national life. They became the new heroes of commerce, art, and intellect. They scaled the social heights. Characteristically, they celebrated their triumph in a rash of Jewish jokes that ran the gamut from advertising slogans to masterpieces of oral and written humor.

230

At the high point of the Jewish Decade, you could walk into a bookstore and find it stacked with such entertainments as: *How to Be a Jewish Mother, Kosher Kaptions, Oy Oy Seven*; Jewish novels in various shades of humor—sick, black, and blue—by Philip Roth, Bruce Jay Friedman, Wallace Markfield, and Norman Mailer; plus collections of Jewish jokes, humorous Yiddish expressions, absurd posters (a bearded Hasid wearing Superman's costume), and the collected works of such Jewish humorists as Jules Feiffer, David Levine, and the various comedians, headed by Lenny Bruce, whose paperback collection of bits and pieces was a best-seller in New York and on college campuses all over the country. What you couldn't find in the bookstore, the authentic oral intonations and accents and "timing" of Jewish humor, you could obtain in record stores, which displayed albums by Nichols and May, Shelley Berman, Mort Sahl, Mel Brooks, and Carl Reiner, to name just a few. Leaving the record store and descending into the subway, one stared at huge posters of a Chinese or a black proclaiming, "You don't have to be Jewish to love Levy's rye." Switching on the radio or TV, you were amused by the clever concoctions of the Jewish advertising writers eager to keep pace with their colleagues in show biz. Yiddish, once a dying language, received a shot of adrenalin as it was picked up and exploited by journalists. Even the kind of Jewish joke that was once confined to the garment district suddenly surfaced in the privileged purlieus of the Jet Set.

As the Jewish Mama and the Jewish Boy and the Jewish Princess and the Jewish Doctor became the familiar *dramatis personae* of American humor, lo and behold! a cultural miracle was wrought. For the first time in modern times the minute particulars of a little minority's life-style suddenly proved out as the "universals" of American culture. Far from regarding the jokes of the Jewish humorists as offensive or self-serving or unintelligibly parochial, Americans embraced Jewish humor and the Jewish schlemiel as a perfect rendering of themselves and their own problems. *Portnoy's Complaint*, the masterpiece of the genre, became one of the greatest best-sellers in the history of American publishing; and its author, after years of trying to write distinctly American fiction, was acclaimed as one of the greatest living American writers on the strength of his depiction of a hopelessly neurotic and hysterical Jewish boy.

Time has shown that this embrace of Jewishness was just the first in a series of minority-group identifications that has now expanded to include the Negro, the hillbilly, the American Indian, and other despised or proscribed groups. In making such identifications, Americans are motivated by a complex mixture of emotions ranging from profound feelings of guilt and penitence through their own sense of alienation, persecution, and self-hatred to the simple longing to belong to a group small enough and tight enough to provide its members with a true sense of personal identity. Being simply an American has not satisfied many souls; however, nobody is willing to be patronized as a member of a minority; hence the characteristic modern way of having your social-cultural cake and eating it too: the flight into ethnic masquerades via jokes, jargon, costume, and music.

Today the Jew is losing some of his prominence in American culture, his fad having worn itself out and his own identity showing signs of yet further transformations through the continuing process of assimilation. (Today's Portnoys typically marry their gentile sex goddesses instead of worshiping them from afar; the resulting offspring are not apt to suffer from having been reared by a Jewish mother.) Having scored heavily in all the cultural and social occupations to which they once aspired, American Jews are now eager to excel in pursuits that would have seemed startlingly alien to their ancestors. The most idealized Jewish hero of the early 1970s was neither a scientist, businessman, entertainer, or artist: he was Mark Spitz, a sensuously beautiful swimmer, the male equivalent of the traditional *shiksah* "cheese-cake"—what is now called "beefcake."

The golden age of modern humor has also come to an end as American culture enters upon a new utopian phase in which the sense of impotence and the baffled anger that breed great satire are supplanted by the philosophy of activism and social amelioration preached by countless ecologists, conservationists, consumer protectionists, women libbers, etc., etc. The role of the comedian or humorist in this new social order is obviously far less important than it was in the days of Eisenhower stagnation and apathy. The once-familiar figure of the night-club comedian has virtually vanished along with the clubs in which he entertained. The cabaret theater has also disappeared. The big TV comedy shows have given way to situation comedies with their neatly formulated plots and trivializing attitudes. Only in an occasional film by Woody Allen does one still see anything of the genius of Jewish comedy. Philip Roth has continued to extend the resources of black humor in books like *Our Gang*, the mordant satire on Richard Nixon, and *The Great American Novel*, a burlesque of American baseball myths and stereotypes; but Roth's finely honed satire of Jewish society—perfected in a long sequence of brilliant tales and novels, from *Goodbye, Columbus* to *Portnoy's Complaint*—seems to have finally worn itself out for lack of fresh material.

How far, how wide, how deep, the impact of the latest outburst of Jewish humor has reached in terms of the enduring structure of American culture is a matter on which it is still too early to pronounce. Nothing ages more rapidly than jokes; nothing is more ephemeral than a cultural fad. Yet there is no denying the basic fact that the current crop of Jewish comic geniuses has attained through the obsessive assertion of their own Jewishness precisely the same breadth of appeal and universality of interest that was achieved in previous generations by comics who didn't dare even to hint that theirs was the perspective of a special and persecuted minority. Everything that was once strictly taboo in the comedy business is now routine, accustomed, and almost positively enjoined. The determination to smash through the remaining barriers to a total expression of the once shamefully repressed fantasies of the modern urban Jew remains strong largely because it has been so strongly endorsed by the society as a whole.

This may be a good thing for the Jewish comic or writer, if he has anything left to say. It certainly is not a good sign for Americans. The word "paranoid" is on everyone's lips today. Precisely! What greater evidence of the paranoia of the average American could be found than the fact that he identifies so glibly with the Jew?

His grandmother produced the musical revue *Splash Me*, in which Peter Sellers (Southsea, Hampshire, 1925–   ) made his debut at age five; his parents and eight uncles were also in show business. Twenty-two years later the BBC produced the hit *Goon Show*, a radio program in which Sellers, along with Spike Mulligan and Harry Secombe, in a variety of voices poked fun at the British establishment. In the mid-1950s he turned to films—*The Mouse That Roared*, *I'm All Right, Jack*. In 1970 he married Miranda Quarry (right).

His soprano voice made such a hit at the local Brooklyn prizefight gym and movie hall that at thirteen Phil Silvers (Silversmith) was enlisted in *Gus Edwards' School Days Revue* at the Palace. It was twenty-two years later—1947 —after five years with Minsky's burlesque troupe and seven years in Hollywood, that Broadway greeted him as the star of *High Button Shoes* and, in 1951, *Top Banana*. On his left, Jack Benny (Benjamin Kubelsky, Chicago, 1894–1975), who actually reached the stage by playing the violin—first in the orchestra pit and later in an act, performing popular tunes. In 1927 he married a hosiery salesgirl, Sadye Marks, who as Mary Livingstone shared his vaudeville and, from 1932 on, his radio show.

Born in Chicago in 1926, Shelley Berman studied at Chicago's Goodman Theatre, joined Chicago's Compass Players, and made his night-club debut in the Windy City in 1957. Since then he has appeared in shows and movies, written situation comedies, published two books, and recorded his monologues, winning the Grammy Award for the best comedy record.

The beats and collegians that patronized San Francisco's hungry i were the first to pay attention to Mort Sahl with his sweater, open-collared shirt, and rolled-up newspaper. His improvised, satiric remarks on contemporary personalities, customs, and events made sense and brought laughter. Born in Montreal, raised in Los Angeles, Sahl served in the Army Air Force and earned a degree in city management at USC before finding his night-club and television audience.

His high-school afternoons were spent working for a public relations firm writing fifty jokes a day; two years and 25,000 jokes later the seventeen-year-old Heywood Allen was hired by NBC as a staff writer. In 1961 Woody faced his first audience, and in 1965 appeared in his first movie—*What's New Pussycat?* Since then more laughs, more movies, including *Play It Again, Sam,* and *Love and Death,* and three books—the latest *Without Feathers*—all before his fortieth birthday. Photo by Claus Meyer.

Acid-tongued Lenny Bruce, the moralist on stage ridiculing the prides and prejudices of American society, lived as an immoralist immersed in drugs, sex, and revenge. He despised his loving father, Mickey Schneider, but was devoted to his mother, Sadie Kitchenberg, who had deserted their Long Island home to become a dance-hall entertainer, a.k.a. Sally Marr or Boots Malloy. He married, hated, and loved a stripper, Hot Honey Harlow. His obscene monologues in night clubs and night courts became a crusade for free speech; his death in 1966, at the age of forty, of an overdose, became a martyrdom. Photo by Dennis Stock.

Walter Mitty and Hans Christian Andersen have in common Danny Kaye (David Daniel Kaminski, Brooklyn, 1913–   ), who portrayed both on the screen. Until 1940 when he arrived on Broadway in *Lady in the Dark*, he apprenticed at private parties, on the borscht circuit, in vaudeville, and on a two-year tour of the Orient, where, playing before non-English-speaking audiences, he learned the art of face-making and mime. Kaye has performed as a conductor at benefit concerts for symphony orchestras across the country. Photo by Eve Arnold.

GOLDEN NUGGET
GAMBLING HALL
1905
CASINO
LUCKY STRIKE
BINGO
SON SHOW
GOLDEN NUGGET
BINGO
GIRLS OF PARIS
SOUVENIR BINGO

OVERLEAF: *The Gambler* appropriately starred George Segal (center) and Elliott Gould (at his left). A transplanted New Yorker from a well-to-do family, Segal arrived by his twenty-fifth birthday in *Ship of Fools* and *Who's Afraid of Virginia Woolf?* and later starred in *The Owl and the Pussycat, The Hot Rock, The Terminal Man*, and a host of other pictures. Brooklyn-born Elliott Goldstein was renamed by his mother when he was ten and appeared on local TV shows, the start of a career in borscht belt hotels and chorus lines that eventually led to the lead role at twenty-six in David Merrick's Broadway musical *I Can Get It for You Wholesale*. He married a young newcomer in the cast—Barbra Streisand. Eclipsed by his wife's fame for seven lean years, in 1969 Gould became one of Hollywood's leading box-office attractions, with *Bob and Carol and Ted and Alice* and *M*A*S*H*.

The Jewish Vice

Chaim Bermant

In 1861, Henry Mayhew, an English journalist noted that gambling was the Jewish vice, and wrote:

The trades which the Jews most affect are those in which "there's a chance," that is, they prefer a trade in such a commodity as is not subject to a fixed price, so that there may be abundant scope for speculation, and something like a gambler's chance for profit and loss. . . . They gamble for money, either at their own homes or at public houses. The favourite games are tossing, dominoes and cards; . . . on a Saturday some gamble away the morning and the greater part of the afternoon. They meet in some secret place about ten, and begin playing for "one at a time" —that is, tossing up three halfpence and staking a shilling on the result. Other Jews and a few Christians will gather round and bet. Sometimes the bets laid by the Jew bystanders are as high as £2 each! and on more than one occasion the old-clothes men have wagered as much as £50. . . .

In 1861, £50 could mean a year's income to an old-clothes man.

In the last years of the nineteenth century over one hundred thousand Jews poured into Britain from Russia. There was some agitation against the influx, and newcomers were charged with every conceivable crime. A royal commission was appointed in 1903 to look into alien immigration, and, in giving evidence, Mr. Charles Emmanuel, secretary of the Board of Deputies for British Jews, showed that every charge was imaginary save one—gambling. "It is not an easy habit to break at once," he declared, "and undoubtedly it is the main failing of these foreign Jews."

It was not a habit that they ever shook off, and, indeed, the more anglicized they became the more they were addicted. If "betting and a passion for the turf are to be taken as the hallmarks of our nationality," wrote a social observer, "the young Jews of Whitechapel may be allowed to be British to the core."

Gambling is the one vice that the Briton has in common with the Jew, except that the Briton treats it with a certain amount of conviviality and surrounds it with gaiety and good humor.

To the Jew it is a deadly serious matter. His face becomes drawn, his brows frown, his eyes acquire a strange intensity, as if trying to peer into the beyond. Every sense is employed and every instinct tensed. There is, of course, the occasional Jewish dilettante in gambling as in everything else, but the normal Jewish gambler is a zealot, and whether his venue is the dog track, the racecourse, the casino, or the card room, he will approach it with almost religious dedication. "Sporting Life" and the racing editions of the evening papers become his liturgy; he debates "form" with the thumb-weaving erudition of a Talmudist; his card table is his altar; he watches the roulette wheel with the earnestness of a supplicant approaching the Day of Judgment.

Las Vegas, Nevada.

The casinos of Europe and Nevada generally have one thing in common, a fixture in some way akin to the figureheads that used to grace the masted schooners: elderly dowagers or divorcees, gray hairs piled high on their heads, their faces crumpled, weighed down with jewels and years, dead to the world about them, never smiling, never looking up, calling out orders to the croupier through one corner of their mouths, a cigarette smoldering in the other. The Yiddish a momma is having her fling.

There are many Jews who have forsaken every observance of Judaism but prefer their holidays in Jewish resorts, for wherever three or four Jews congregate there is always a chance of a card game.

Every large Jewish hotel will have a card room as naturally as every large synagogue has a beth hamidrash. The Sabbath in such places is a closed season for gaming. Gaze around the lounge on a Friday night and you will see the strained faces and fidgety hands of gamblers denied their game, looking a little like dipsomaniacs denied their drink, and not even allowed to smoke to steady their nerves.

In recent years Jewish hotels have sprouted another attraction, the one-armed bandit, situated by the doorway almost as a companion to the mezuzah on the door, and with a youngster at the handle serving his apprenticeship—one must begin young. Gambling is also the staff of old age. In Miami at a quiet hour one can hear nothing save the soft lapping of the sea and the shuffling of cards. Gambling does not keep the Jew young. It may, indeed, age him prematurely, but it keeps him going long after he might have been tempted to give up the ghost.

For a game of cards meals may remain uneaten, drinks undrunk, television unwatched, games unplayed. Visit a Jewish golf club and you may find more men around the green baize than on the greens.

There are Jewish social clubs in most communities of any size, and they have charity committees and cultural committees, and even pull in a rabbi from time to time to give them a touch of grace, but the activity in which 80 per cent of their members indulge for 80 per cent of their time is gambling. And even where they are involved in a game of skill, like billiards or bridge or even—so heaven help us!— chess, they will still place bets on the side. Winnings may go to charity, but that isn't the point: the game's in the gaming.

One rarely hears of Jews ruined by drink, though one often hears of them ruined by gambling, and where they are involved in crime it is often through their involvement in gambling.

The colorful brotherhood of criminals and touts who peopled Damon Runyon's Broadway tended, even when they were Irish and Italian, to be Jewish in their mannerisms, attitudes, and speech. There was a Yiddish tone to their English. They hovered over the fringes of show biz and no-biz, *luftmenschen* with earthy ways. There is, of course, no greater gamble than show business, and there is something of show business about gambling. It was perhaps inevitable that many of their expressions, like *shpieler* and *gunz*, should be borrowed from the Yiddish.

One could attempt to explain the Jewish passion for gambling in historical terms, and the afore-mentioned Mr. Emmanuel, when giving evidence before the royal commission, did. Most of the Jews, he said, came from Russia, and Russia was notorious for its gambling and gamblers. But the German Jews also gambled, so did the Dutch, as did Jews from wherever they came. Rabbis denounced it as a pernicious Greek influence before the time of Christ, but Jews were gamblers before the Greeks were even heard of.

The Mishnah, which was completed in the second century A.D. and was a compilation of oral laws passed on from generation to generation for centuries before that, referred to two forms of gambling prevalent among Jews, dice and pigeon-racing. It looked upon the gambler as a delinquent and idler whose testimony was not acceptable in a court of law. Some rabbis urged that gamblers be placed under an interdict and excluded from burial in Jewish cemeteries; others that they should get no help from charity. Later rabbis were somewhat less severe and suggested that such strictures applied only to full-time, professional gamblers. One sage suggested that the wives of compulsive gamblers should join them in their games, otherwise their marriage might come apart. There is a story dating back to the Middle Ages of a man who had forsworn gambling and promptly went mad, but it was noticed that he improved whenever watching a gambling game in progress. A rabbi thereupon absolved him from his vow, and he returned to the gaming house and to sanity. One famous rabbi of the sixteenth century ruled that compulsive gamblers should not make such vows, otherwise they would compound gambling with perjury.

Card-playing seems to have been carried to excess among Jews in medieval Italy; in Bologna, Cremona, and Forli edicts were passed prohibiting such games. Court tennis and chess, both popular among the Jews of sixteenth-century Italy, were attended by large crowds who wagered on the outcome. One doesn't know where the first Jewish bookies originated, but it may have been there. They have been numerous since and have given a new meaning to the expression "the people of the Book."

One of the most celebrated victims of gambling was an Italian Jew, the Venetian scholar and sage Rabbi Leon de Modena, who, at the age of sixty, entered upon a Jekyll-and-Hyde existence, absented himself from study in the deep hours of the night, and ruined himself at cards.

In those parts of Europe where Jewish communities had their own local autonomy, the harshest measures were taken to suppress gambling. The following edict dates from the Middle Ages:

> Nobody may play at cards or dice or any other game whatsoever that the mouth could speak or the heart think . . . and everybody whoever it may be, including boys and girls, manservants and maidservants, shall be punished if they should (God forbid) contravene and play; if the offender is prosperous, he shall pay for every occasion two silver coins . . . and if he is poor so that he cannot be punished by fine, he shall be punished by imprisonment and tortured by iron chains as befits such offenders. . . .

Why the addiction? It may be that a people exposed throughout the centuries to continual hazards cannot wholly adapt themselves to the security of a stable existence and therefore seek out the contrived hazards of gambling. But why only gambling? If it's hazards they're after, why not climb mountains, explore caves, go up in the air in a balloon, or cross the Atlantic singlehanded? Such excursions, the Jew may answer, are not hazards, they're crazy: in gambling one can at least win. If there is a national Jewish passion for risks, it mainly takes a monetary form.

Alternatively, one may argue that people condemned for centuries to confined lives and drab circumstances tried to brighten their existence by flirting with chance, very much as millions today dabble in football pools. But this overlooks the fact, which we have just demonstrated, that Jews always have been gamblers. The Jewish gambler predates the ghetto and probably predates Jewish exile.

It may be that the Jewish passion for chance is a by-product of the Jewish entrepreneurial instinct, except, of course, that gambling is the most un-enterprising form of investment imaginable—unless, that is, one can call the odds, which brings us back to our friend the bookie.

The Jew tends to go to extremes and is prepared to hazard his little to gain a lot even at the risk of being left with nothing. The schnorrer has a status in Jewish life, and so, of course, has the *gevir*, the man of means. The man who is merely comfortable is nobody.

In spite of the rabbinic sanctions against gambling, money carries its own merit, no matter how acquired. To gamble and to lose may be unforgivable, but winnings carry their own redemption. "As long as you make it and spread it around," a successful bookie once declared, "you're in with them all." One can, in fact, be "in with them all" without spreading it around, as long as there is an assurance that one has it in the first place. One need not be generous, one need only be rich, and to many people gambling carries the only hope of richness, and with it social eminence.

But at the bottom of it all may be the blind, incorrigible Jewish optimism that has unmade the Jew and sustained him, the unspoken conviction that God is there, hovering over the dice, loading the odds in one's favor. The fact that one may lose night after night, or year after year, merely confirms one in the belief that sooner or later one's fortunes must change, and provided one is prepared to wait long enough—say four thousand years—one may be proved right. The belief in Jewish luck may be totally without foundation, but it is ineradicable in the Jewish breast.

The Artist

Edward Lucie-Smith

"What is a Jew?" It seems impossible to answer this question to everyone's satisfaction. "What is a Jewish artist?" is a yet more difficult question. Are we to confine ourselves to artists who are not only Jewish by birth but who make use of Jewish themes? Or are we to speak of artists who are Jewish by birth, no matter what style they may adopt?

Despite the iconoclastic element so deeply rooted in Jewish culture and Jewish tradition, the visual arts have a long connection with Judaism, but it is a connection of a curiously ambiguous kind. To choose a famous and early example: there are the elaborate wall-paintings, dating from the third century A.D., which were found in a synagogue at Dura-Europos on the Euphrates, and which are now in the Damascus Museum. These murals cover a wide range of Old Testament themes. The style is an eclectic mixture of the influences that then prevailed in the eastern part of the Roman Empire: it does not fuse into anything we can now characterize as recognizably "Jewish." This lack of a recognizable stylistic flavor is something that can be discovered in many other works of art known to have been produced by Jews or containing Jewish iconography.

The most impressive statements to be made, artistically, about the Jewish culture of the seventeenth century are to be found in the paintings of Rembrandt. But, despite occasional assertions to the contrary, there is in fact no evidence that Rembrandt was a Jew or even that he had Jewish blood. Indeed, the specifically Jewish content of his work is much less than has been popularly supposed, since the Old Testament subjects that make up a substantial part of Rembrandt's total output were themes taken over by Christianity from Judaism and were likely to have been given a quite special emphasis in a Protestant nation such as Holland.

The Jewish artist, as we know him in modern times, is a product of the Age of Enlightenment. But even with the dawn of this new era Jewish art was a long time in finding the courage of its own Jewishness.

The first Jewish artists to make professional careers for themselves were cautious men indeed. Their whole aim seems to have been to demonstrate the degree to which they had assimilated the non-Judaic heritage. Perhaps the first Jewish artist to achieve universal fame in modern times was Anton Raphael Mengs (1728–1779), son of a Jewish painter who rose to be director of the Dresden Academy. Ishmael Israel Mengs took his gifted son to Rome in 1740 to complete his artistic education. There the younger Mengs fell completely under the spell of the classical past. After a return visit to his native Dresden, he settled in Rome, became a Catholic convert, and carved out a career for himself under papal patronage.

In 1755, in Rome, Mengs made the acquaintance of Johann Winckelmann and thus came into intimate contact with the burgeoning neoclassical movement. Winckelmann seems to have found in Mengs the perfect instrument: the means of giving concrete expression to his new theories of art.

As a revolutionary artist, Mengs is a paradox, because the revolution with which he was connected stressed above all things the power of convention, the need to conform. Another thing we notice about neoclassicism, when we compare it to the styles that preceded it, is the importance of abstract ideas. One can well understand how, to an ambitious and malleable outsider—which is precisely what Mengs was, in terms of the society of his time—it provided the solution to psychological as well as purely artistic problems.

In the nineteenth century the number of identifiably Jewish artists began to grow very rapidly, though at first the quality of their artistic contribution did not improve to anything like the same degree. Gradually, however, the disinclination for taking aesthetic risks began to be broken down, and Jewish painters became associated with most of the really vital currents in European art. As the Jew achieved a securer place in European society, and as that society itself became more liberal, the need to conform became less absolute.

Nevertheless, though we may admit that a man like Camille Pissarro (1830–1903) deserves the place that is always accorded to him as one of the founders of Impressionism, it is difficult to discover any aspect of his work that we can call specifically Jewish. The same might be said of many other leading Jewish artists of the second half of the nineteenth century, among them the Swede Ernst Josephson (1852–1906), the leading Russian landscape painter Isaac Levitan (1861–1906), and the German Impressionist Max Liebermann (1847–1935). Indeed, both Levitan and Liebermann are notable for their feeling of identification with the non-Jewish world. Levitan is the founder of a new school of landscape painting in Russia, with a fresh and accurate vision of the melancholy Russian countryside. Liebermann gives us a panoramic evocation of Germany under Kaiser Wilhelm. It is perhaps significant that Levitan's work was adored by Chekhov, who thought that it pierced through to a new truth about the Russian soul.

There are, of course, cases in this generation of the artist turning toward Jewish subject matter in an endeavor to find his own identity and his own roots. The best examples are the Dutch painter Joseph Israëls (1824–1911) and the Englishman William Rothenstein (1872–1945). It is significant that both came from societies where Jews did not have to struggle so hard to become assimilated. When Israëls tackles a specifically Jewish subject, such as the shopkeeper in the Amsterdam ghetto who appears in "The Son of an Ancient People," he approaches it not through his own personal experience but through his admiration for Rembrandt. His paintings of fisherfolk on the beach at Zandvoort, which are equally typical of his *oeuvre*, now seem much fresher in their response to observed fact. Similarly, Rothenstein's temperamental limitations are exposed very clearly in the few paintings he did of Jews in Whitechapel. The most familiar of these is the canvas significantly entitled "Aliens at Prayer." We see in it how great a gulf Rothenstein placed between himself, the middle-class Englishman, and these immigrants, newly emerged from Russian ghettos.

The Jews that Rothenstein painted were part of the great outsurge from the Pale of Settlement— that area of the Czarist Russian dominions where Jews were allowed to live—which had been going on since the pogroms of the early 1880s and which was intensified by another series of pogroms in the period 1903–1906. This outsurge carried Jews not only to England and the United States, but also to parts of Europe that seemed to promise more tolerable conditions. It represented the first stage in the break-up of an extraordinarily introverted, but also extraordinarily individual culture, whose final dissolution came with the holocaust of 1940–1945. To speak of Jewish art and of its place in the contemporary world as something recognizable and separable from other kinds of art is, it seems to me, rather strictly a question of this culture and of its effect upon those brought up in contact with it.

Camille Pissarro (1830–1903), born in St. Thomas, Virgin Islands, and educated in Paris, was twenty-five before he could convince his prosperous father that he preferred painting to retailing. He encouraged the younger impressionists—Monet, Renoir, Cézanne, Gauguin—although he had a constant financial struggle until 1892 when Durand-Ruel held a successful retrospective exhibit of his work. (*The Old Market at Rouen and the Rue de l'Epicerie*, at right). Courtesy of The Metropolitan Museum of Art, New York.

RIGHT: Appropriately, this founder of the New York school of Abstract Expressionism was born, educated, and a lifelong resident in Manhattan. Adolph Gottlieb (1903–1974) studied briefly at the Art Students League and the Parsons School of Design, but he was largely self-taught. He became a major influence on other artists. His "pictograph" style of the 1940s broadened in the 1950s into a new kind of spatial depth and culminated in his "Burst" series of red and black explosive oils. (*The Frozen Sands, Number 1*, 1951. Gift of Mr. and Mrs. Samuel M. Kootz, Whitney Museum of American Art)

ABOVE: Fame came after death to Amedeo Modigliani (born Leghorn, Italy, 1884–died Paris, France, 1920) for his stylized portraits and sculpture. His life was a struggle against delicate health, poverty, alcohol, and drugs. In the painting shown here, he portrays Léon Bakst (Lev Samoylovich Rosenberg, 1866–1924), the Russian artist who revolutionized theatrical costume and scenery design with his work in St. Petersburg and Paris. (*Léon Bakst*. Collection of the National Gallery of Art, Washington, D.C.)

ABOVE: Dean of the modern art movement in the United States, Max Weber (1881–1961) came to Brooklyn from Bialystok, Russia, at the age of ten. Three years of study in Europe introduced him to the French modernists, and he in turn introduced that style of painting to the United States. In the early 1920s he began to receive recognition, culminating in a retrospective show at the Museum of Modern Art in 1930. (*Chinese Restaurant, 1915*. Collection of the Whitney Museum of American Art)

RIGHT: Jules Pascin (Julius Pincas, 1885–1930) was born in Vidin, Bulgaria, worked in Austria and Germany, moved to Paris in 1905, and lived there for the balance of his life, except for five years of travel during World War I in Cuba and the United States, where he became a citizen. He committed suicide immediately before his most important one-man show. (*Salomé, 1914*. Collection Perls Galleries, New York)

LEFT: Emigrating to Paris when he was twenty years old, the Russian Chaim Soutine (1893–1943) developed an individual style closely linked to early twentieth-century expressionism. Agitated brushwork, compulsive rhythms, heavy layering of paint reveal the disturbing psychological content in his work. (*The Pastry Chef*. Collection of the National Gallery of Art, Washington, D.C.)

The Pale put great pressures upon its inhabitants, and these pressures were exercised in two directions. The first and most obvious was the pressure exercised by the Czarist authorities. The second came from within the Jewish community, the pressure of rabbinic orthodoxy. While these forces remained in play, Jews from the Pale could scarcely be expected to produce very sophisticated forms of visual art. They were too poor, too much oppressed, and too inhibited by religious convention. Later, as first the culture and then the accepted political structures of the area dissolved, the liveliest and most creative spirits emigrated. This dissolution and this diaspora were responsible for a great outburst of creative energy.

The Russian-Jewish world seems to have left—at least if we may judge from the artistic legacy—an indelible mark on every child brought up in it. The most obvious example, the artist everyone thinks of in this connection, is Marc Chagall, born in Vitebsk in 1887. Chagall's work looks back to, and re-creates, the childhood experience I am referring to with a directness and nostalgia that have made it immediately accessible. Chagall has become the very epitome of the modern Jewish artist.

But we must be careful not to oversimplify Chagall's career. Chagall studied in St. Petersburg, where he came in contact with Léon Bakst, the cosmopolitan associate of Diaghilev. Bakst was, like himself, Jewish. In 1910 Chagall made his way to Paris, but he returned to Russia in 1914 and was trapped there by the war. He sympathized at first with the aims of the October Revolution, and in 1917 he was made commissar for fine arts in Vitebsk and director of the Free Academy of Art, which had just been established there. But he soon came to realize that his own aims and those of the Bolshevik regime were bound to be at variance, and in the summer of 1922 he abandoned Russia and returned to the West.

Two experiences in particular had a profound effect on Chagall's development. The first was contact with Cubism, a movement that often seemed to have, for Jewish artists, the attraction that neo-classicism had exercised for Mengs—although, and this is perhaps significant too, few persisted with Cubism throughout their careers, the exceptions being minor figures such as Louis Marcoussis (1883–1941) and Henri Hayden (1883–1970).

The other experience, uncongenial as it was to prove, was the experience of the Russian Revolution. As commissar in Vitebsk, and later through his connection with the Moscow State Jewish Theater, Chagall found himself consciously trying to formulate a national Jewish style of art. In reaction to the oppressions of the Czarist regime, Jews in the early revolutionary period in Russia were being encouraged to develop modes of expression peculiar to themselves. But what were those modes to be? What roots were they to draw upon? Chagall's attempt to tackle the problems posed by this policy was one of the earliest attempts to discover the true nature of that paradoxical being, the Jewish artist.

As one might expect, Chagall was forced to draw upon all the resources available to him. Some of the things which influenced his work were not Jewish at all but specifically Russian. In his Petersburg years he had been very much impressed by icon painting. The circle frequented by Bakst and Diaghilev had been responsible for calling attention to the merits of icons, till then neglected. But, though made for a Christian purpose, icons were sympathetic to the traditional orientation of Jewish taste and Jewish thinking because they were symbolic. Their anti-realism was linked to the iconoclasm of Judaism. Indeed, the Byzantine iconoclasts had rejected even these images for a very Hebraic reason: what they feared was that these images of outer reality, however stylized, might weaken the consciousness of inner reality.

Where the Jewish tradition itself was concerned, the background Chagall came from was Hasidic. His parents, like most of the Jews of Vitebsk, were influenced by this cult, mystic rather than rational, founded in the eighteenth century by the Baal Shem Tov. Hasidism is hostile to precisely those qualities which have often been most valued in Western European civilization, at least in the centuries since the Renaissance. It puts no value on reserve, objectivity, or logical analysis. We soon notice that it is a

The twentieth-century painter who best combines the traditions of Judaism with the innovations of modern art is undoubtedly Marc Chagall (1887–   ). His birthplace was Vitebsk, Russia—his father a worker in a herring warehouse, his mother a shopkeeper. One of nine children, he studied in St. Petersburg before reaching Paris in 1910. Except for six years in Russia during and after World War I and for seven years in the United States during and after World War II, he has lived in France. Photo by Arnold Newman.

peculiarity of Chagall's art that he does not analyze his subject matter, even though, in an early period, under the influence of Cubism, he tries to analyze forms.

Cubism's real gift to Chagall is to be found in its new conception of space. The original Cubists arrived at the "shallow space" now considered typical of their work through necessities of logic and technique. If all aspects of an object were to be shown on a flat surface, then the conventions of Renaissance perspective could no longer be observed and a new convention had to be invented to take the place of the old. The fanning out and overlapping of planes practiced by Braque and Picasso in their Cubist phase produces the feeling that objects float just behind the picture plane, often in positions displaced from the true horizontal. Chagall takes this new convention and puts it to a different use, symbolic rather than logical. Franz Meyer, in his monumental biography of Chagall, speaks of the poetic freedom characteristic of his compositions: "Certain figures as well as objects—pairs of lovers, animals, a wall clock, flowers— appear in his pictures in what appears to be a free arrangement, emancipated from the customary visual context." What we find in Chagall's work is not Vitebsk itself but a metaphor for Vitebsk, a kind of collective dream. The metaphoric quality of his art can be traced in many details; we notice, for example, how, in his illustrations to Jewish literature, a strong link can be found between the forms used and Hebrew letter forms. The book is made of words and letters, and these letters magically "come to life" in the pictures that accompany the text.

There is also in Chagall's work a sense of failure and yearning. Chagall has always had a feeling of closeness to his contemporary Franz Kafka, and Kafka's nightmares can be regarded as the obverse of Chagall's dreams. Though Vitebsk is lovingly preserved in Chagall's depictions of it, the paintings never- theless seem to contain an admission, thanks to their nostalgic playfulness and capriciousness, that the traditional Judaic view of the world can no longer form the basis for any real order.

An artist whom critics have often linked to Chagall—and who belongs to precisely the same generation—is Chaim Soutine (1884–1943). But their differences seem to me to be almost as important as their similarities. Though both men were born in the Pale, Soutine's background seems to have been narrower and more orthodox. The milieu he knew as a child was entirely and traditionally Jewish. One story has it that he got the money to pay for his training at the Academy of Fine Arts in Vilna as payment of damages, after he had been badly beaten up by the son of a rabbi; Soutine's offense had been to ask permission to make a drawing of the rabbi. Unlike Chagall, Soutine never had the experience of artistic circles in St. Petersburg. After Vilna, he made his way to Paris; he arrived there in 1913. He was to remain in France for the rest of his life.

Soutine's work, unlike Chagall's, seems to show no direct influence from the experiments that were going on in Paris when he arrived there. The ability to resist the seductions of Cubism, just at the time when the Cubists were overturning the whole basis of art, seems to argue that Soutine was directed by particularly powerful obsessions and inner necessities. Is it possible to define what these were? One thing we can say is that Soutine never, at any point in his development, paints reminiscently. The presence of the motif is absolutely necessary to him, and this is true even when he is rephrasing the invention of another master, as he does in the picture influenced by Rembrandt's "Flayed Ox." But he does not analyze what he sees. The way in which he renders what is in front of him is entirely at the mercy of inner impulses, which cause him to distort the forms that he puts on the canvas. The spectator's experience of the picture ideally becomes as active as the painter's own experience of the motif. From the psychological viewpoint, one might hazard a guess that this method of experiencing reflects a pattern imposed by the claustrophobic society of the Pale, in Jewish towns and villages where the inhabitants were constantly under threat, constantly seeking new social and economic outlets, which were just as regularly denied to them.

Yet, though Soutine identifies so completely with the motif, to the point where the barriers between the self and the not-self are broken down, we are also aware of a movement of alienation. This applies particularly to the portraits. Andrew Forge has remarked that Soutine seems to look at those who sat for him "as if at freaks—as if appalled by the differentness of human beings." Perhaps this feeling of differentness may be thought of as a kind of birth trauma, the loneliness of a being cast out from one society and trying to inhabit a very different one.

The point at which, despite visible differences, Soutine's work seems to resemble Chagall's is in its total commitment to subjectivity; in the feeling it gives us that the artistic impulse is also an impulse to impose the inner on the outer, to wrench appearances to correspond to a truth that the artist already perceives within himself.

It is interesting to note that Soutine's status as a characteristically "Jewish" artist is never challenged by critics, even though he makes no use of identifiably Jewish subject matter. In this context it is worth contrasting Soutine with the Italian Jew Amedeo Modigliani (1884–1920), who befriended Soutine when he first came to Paris. At one stage the two artists shared a garret. Modigliani's Jewishness seems entirely irrelevant to his art. If we need a comparison to express the quality of his sensibility, we look not to anything in the Judaic tradition but to the great Japanese printmaker Utamaro.

A Jewish artist from the world of the Pale did not, however, have to follow in the footsteps of either Chagall or Soutine. El Lissitzky (1890–1941) pursued a very different path. He was born at Polshinok in Smolensk province and grew up, as Chagall did, in Vitebsk. After being rejected by the St. Petersburg Academy of Fine Arts (probably because of his religion), he went in 1909 to study architecture in Darmstadt. While in Western Europe he was able to travel extensively, visiting Paris in 1911, in the company of the sculptor Ossip Zadkine, and wandering through most of northern Italy in the following year. He returned to Russia on the outbreak of war. His first considerable artistic success was as an illustrator. Chagall influenced him at this time, and so did *lubki* (Russian popular prints). When Chagall was appointed to the Free Academy of Art in Vitebsk, he invited Lissitzky to join the staff as head of the applied arts department and professor of architecture. Lissitzky accepted the invitation, the more willingly because he had early identified himself with the aims of the revolution. But, just for this reason, he was not content to remain within Chagall's sphere of influence. Once arrived at the Vitebsk academy, he allied himself with Kasimir Malevich, who also became a member of the staff, and moved forward to Constructivism, the practical, abstract style which, its inventors hoped, was a true, because unsentimental, reflection of Marxist ideals.

Lissitzky is a figure of outstanding interest for several reasons. The first and most obvious is that he was a pioneer abstractionist, and abstraction at last abolishes age-old inhibitions, as far as Jews are concerned, about the compatibility of Judaism on the one hand and professional involvement with the visual arts on the other. It is relevant that Lissitzky himself evolved toward pure abstraction through work on books and posters. Students of Jewish culture have always stressed the traditional importance of the letter and the sign. The grandeur of the Hebrew alphabet surpasses that of any other. It is this source of creative strength that Lissitzky was able to tap, and other modern artists have followed in his footsteps.

We also see that Lissitzky's Constructivism, which was so intimately linked to his commitment to the revolution, may in the personal sense have been a way of dealing with the sudden release of pressure as the Jewish world he had grown up in started to collapse. As much as Chagall, he was concerned with a collective dream, but the dream was not nostalgic. "Lissitzky," his widow has written, "in his enthusiasm for art's great mission in the socialist state, pledged all his mental and physical forces to this cause. He was no longer the individualist, but the representative of a great idea, and this fact gave him a persuasive power in all his actions." Compared to the intense subjectivity of other Jewish artists from the same background, Lissitzky's Constructivism is simply the other face of the coin.

I have chosen to speak of these three artists in particular because I believe that they do in fact suggest that the task of defining Judaic characteristics in twentieth-century art is not entirely a hopeless one—that is, if we are prepared to add the qualification that Jewish art is not merely Jewish but springs

OPPOSITE: Ossip Zadkine (1890–1967) was sent to London from Smolensk by his father, a classics professor, to learn English, but he moved to Paris and studied at the Ecole des Beaux-Arts, where in 1911 he first exhibited his sculpture. Only flight from the Nazis interrupted his residency in Paris. He won the grand prize for sculpture at the 1950 Venice Biennale and the 1960 grand prize of the City of Paris.

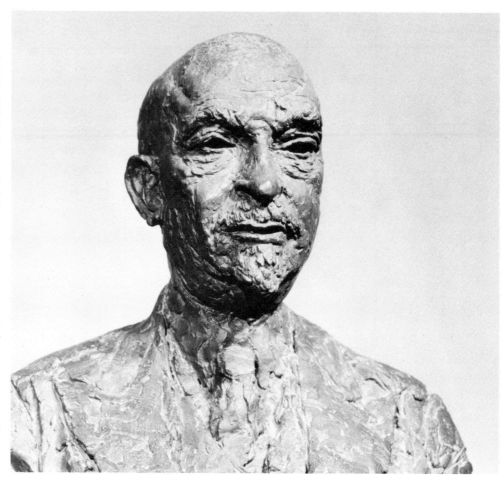

The English sculptor Sir Jacob Epstein (1880–1959) was born in New York but established his studio in London in 1905 and in a short time became well recognized for his portraits. A conservative in style, in an age of experimentation he became famous for his ability to depict character. At right is his bust of Israel's founder, Chaim Weizmann. Photo of sculptor by Peter Simon.

New York sculptor Louise Nevelson was born in Kiev, Russia, in 1900 to Isaac and Mina Berliawsky, who migrated with their four children to Rockland, Maine. Her marriage to Charles Nevelson brought her to the big city, where she taught and exhibited, battling for attention to her constructivist work, until she received major recognition in a retrospective one-woman show at the Whitney Museum of American Art in 1967. Photo by Arnold Newman.

LEFT: In 1975 a retrospective exhibition of Anthony Alfred Caro's work was presented at the Museum of Modern Art, New York; the Museum of Fine Arts, Boston; the Walker Art Museum, Minneapolis; and the Museum of Fine Arts, Houston—American homage to the fifty-one-year-old British sculptor. A graduate of Charterhouse School and Christ's College, Cambridge (M.A. in engineering), Caro continued his studies at the Royal Academy Schools and apprenticed for two years with Henry Moore. He was thirty-five years old when he broke away from his figurative style and began to construct his abstract, painted steel sculptures. Photo by Arnold Newman.

OPPOSITE, ABOVE: Judge Alfred Frankenthaler educated his daughter Helen (b. 1928) at the best New York City private schools and at Bennington College, where she edited the college newspaper. But painting was her field, and shortly after graduation she exhibited her work in the first of a series of annual shows at New York galleries, culminating in a retrospective exhibit at the Jewish Museum in 1960. She is now considered one of America's leading artists. Photo by Arnold Newman.

OPPOSITE, BELOW: Man Ray has never disclosed his real name or facts about his early life except that he was born in Philadelphia, Pennsylvania, in 1890. He began to paint in 1908, met Duchamp in 1915, became a Dadaist, moved to Paris in 1921, and joined the Surrealists. His art was supported by his fashion and portrait photography, and he was an innovator with the camera as well. He fled the Nazis, living for a while in Los Angeles, but returned to Paris after World War II. Photo by Arnold Newman.

specifically and identifiably from the world of the Russian Pale. It may perhaps seem farfetched to apply this notion to American painting as well as to European art, but I think one can demonstrate that the ideas put forward here apply so neatly to developments in the United States that this gives a kind of proof of their validity.

Of course, no one should be surprised to discover that Jews have made an important contribution to American painting, since Jewish immigrants have made so vast a contribution to the development of the American nation.

One of the most interesting of the pioneer American modernists is Max Weber (1881–1961). Not the least fascinating aspect of his career is the way in which it duplicates, though in a transatlantic context, a pattern already familiar among Jewish artists of European origin. Weber was in fact born in Europe, at Bialystok in Poland, and came to New York at the age of ten—too early, one would have thought, for the Judaism of Eastern Europe to have much impact on him. Like many American artists, he made the return pilgrimage to Europe, working in Paris from 1905 to 1909. He was for a time a pupil of Matisse. But his earliest allegiance as a mature painter was to a version of Cubism. Later his art becomes more inward-looking. Subject matter began to count for more, and much of this was drawn from memories of early childhood. Like Chagall, he commemorated the lost world of the shtetl in paintings where personal fantasy played a major role.

Other American-Jewish painters, especially during the bitter years of the Great Depression, when a socially committed art was in vogue, evolved styles in which Expressionism came to terms with the long-established strain of realism in American art. Prominent among them were Ben Shahn (1898–1969) and Jack Levine (born 1915). One may find it understandable that artists such as Weber, Shahn, and Levine, with their overtly Jewish references, should be the painters most commonly referred to when Americans speak of their tradition of Jewish painting. In fact they are, though gifted, artists whose importance is local rather than universal. The major contribution made by Jews in America to the development of the visual arts is to be found elsewhere, in the history of the Abstract Expressionist movement, the first art movement of world significance to emerge from the United States.

In the strictly historical sense, the Abstract Expressionists are the children of Surrealism—not a movement in which Jewish artists played a major part, despite the influence of Freud on Surrealist doctrine. But when the leaders of Surrealism fled *en bloc* to New York in 1940, they found themselves in a city whose culture had an even more important Jewish element than was to be found in Paris.

Abstract Expressionism, the new style that Americans have created on the ruins of the old European Surrealism, differs from its principal source in a number of important respects. It is, as the label implies, largely, though not entirely, non-figurative. In addition, there is a strong commitment to the idea that the canvas is a surface upon which something is written, a vehicle for the sign. Last, there is the open-endedness of the way in which Abstract Expressionist pictures are painted, the fact that they are not "finished" works in the old sense but reflections of the inner turmoil involved in painting a picture, mirrors of a creative act that remains in process instead of completing itself.

The Jewish artists who have adhered to Abstract Expressionism have been a strong contingent. Their work has certain characteristics that sets it apart from that of their non-Jewish colleagues. The most prominent of these characteristics are mysticism and radicalism. The Hasidic spirit emerges very clearly in some of the pronouncements made by these artists, and even more clearly in the work itself.

The three most interesting artists to examine in this connection are Mark Rothko (1903–1970), Adolph Gottlieb (born 1903), and Barnett Newman (1905–1970). Of the three, Rothko was the only one to be born in the Pale, at Dvinsk, and we may regard his work as a kind of fulcrum. In it the conflicting impulses of a Chagall and a Lissitzky are harmonized, and we are confronted with an abstract but purely subjective art, where all dreams can be reconciled.

Both Rothko and Gottlieb have been primarily myth-makers. Each of them progressively abandoned figuration, in the effort to make the personal myth more nearly universal. By 1947 Rothko had reached a position where he thought that references to existing art, or to nature, put unacceptable limitations on what he wanted to do, which was to communicate to the spectator the stirrings of an all-embracing "Spirit of Myth." By 1950 he had begun to paint the abstractions we now think of as typical—soft-edged color rectangles symmetrically placed, one above the other, on a slightly opaque ground. They have been described, significantly and aptly, as "icons for contemplation."

Gottlieb's independent development as a painter began in 1942, with a series of paintings he entitled "Pictographs." In these, the idea that the images are something written on the canvas emerges clearly. Later Gottlieb simplified his compositions, reducing the number of elements, enlarging the forms, and putting greater emphasis on symmetry. His later paintings, under the general title "Bursts," suggest the release of cosmic energies, but this release is not related to a specific place, person, or event.

Newman differs from the other two because he is, at first sight, more objective, less psychologically complex. His paintings usually consist of broad color fields animated by thin vertical stripes of contrasting color. But his intentions in making these works were nevertheless symbolic. In 1947 he was writing of "the idea-complex that makes contact with mystery." In another statement he says, "Man's first expression was a poetic outcry . . . of awe and anger at his tragic state, at his own self-awareness and helplessness before the void. . . . The purpose of man's first speech was to address the Unknowable." The Hasidic note sounds unmistakably in this.

Long contemplation of the work produced by Rothko, Gottlieb, and Newman tends to suggest that it is in their paintings, more so even than in the work of Chagall, that the spirit of the Pale of Settlement reaches its truest fulfillment. There is a tragic irony in the fact that the destruction of the Pale itself had only just been completed at the moment when they were produced. We can read these canvases as great elegies, in which the Jewish spirit reaches a peak of profound and noble expression, true to old traditions and yet at the same time profoundly original. Jewish art, if it is to be defined at all, is not to be discovered by the search for a recognizably Jewish style but by tracing attitudes of mind that reach expression through a variety of styles. These attitudes nevertheless always reveal the same fundamental preoccupations and the same kind of temperament.

Savant and Salesman

Edward Lucie-Smith

Anyone who attempts to write about the relationship between Bernard Berenson and Joseph Duveen (who eventually was to become Lord Duveen of Millbank) must recognize, from the very start, a fundamental difficulty. Berenson is a man who has left us ample information about his interior life, most notably in the published volume of his letters and in the *Sketch for a Self-Portrait*. We have no such information about Duveen, and indeed many people would doubt if the great dealer had an interior life at all, in the sense that Berenson understood the matter. S. N. Behrman's famous biography, *Duveen*, which has probably fixed Duveen's image for us for all time, depicts its subject essentially from the outside. What Behrman chronicles is Duveen's impact on other people, most notably on the self-made American millionaires who were his clients. Duveen moves through the world that his biographer shows us like a force of nature. If he had complexities, he kept them well hidden. To this extent, therefore, any description of the relationship between the two men must be weighted in Berenson's favor. And the latter's wish was, quite clearly, to mark the difference between himself and his associate—the man who provided the substantial resources that made the Berenson life-style possible.

Yet Berenson and Duveen had at least one important thing in common, in addition to the fact that they needed each other. Both were Jewish, and both were "typical" to the point where we immediately recognize in them two characteristic Jewish types: Duveen the salesman, with his irresistible chutzpah; Berenson the scholar, always in pursuit of the esoteric. This said, it must be admitted that their backgrounds were very different. Duveen belonged to a family of Dutch Jews, now settled in England. Antique and art dealing was already the family profession, and Duveen himself inherited not only a share of the family business but to some extent an established social position. His father achieved a knighthood. Berenson, on the other hand, was born at Butremanz in Lithuania, within the Pale of Settlement. His family emigrated to America when he was ten, and the place they chose as their new home was Boston. The family was not rich—Berenson's father earned his living as a peddler—but the boy's brilliance secured him a place, first at Boston Latin School, and later at the much more prestigious Harvard. It was Harvard and the men he met there that formed Berenson's mind and sensibility. At the same time, he discovered the writings of the English aesthete Walter Pater, and in particular Pater's *Studies in the History of the Renaissance*.

Despite the gulf that yawned between the two men, Berenson's scholarship was an important, indeed perhaps the most important, weapon in Duveen's armory, apart from his own formidable personality. Duveen was a dealer, and a dealer of the purest, most dedicated sort. Dealing in pictures was his obsession as well as his profession, and he tended to think of objects almost purely from this point of view.

A picture was a mere picture till it entered his own possession. After that it became, as Behrman tells us, "a Duveen," and a whole new range of financial possibilities opened up. If it was an Italian picture, Berenson played a key part in the process of transmutation. Berenson was interested, not in the price a work of art would fetch, but in its origins, the cultural nexus of which it formed a part, and above all in its authenticity. Was it genuine? Was it painted by a particular and recognizable hand? Berenson investigated these questions and made his conclusions available to Duveen. The virtual unchallengeability of a Berenson certificate enabled Duveen to advance on his chosen victim with his flanks and rear protected. In a way that none of his rivals could claim, Berenson made Duveen infallible—his attributions were papal pronouncements. And even when the work in question was—at least in theory—outside Berenson's professional province, when it was a question of a Velásquez or a Van Dyck, Duveen could still pick Berenson's brains; or, failing that, could allow his clients and his rivals to believe that he had picked them.

Duveen was quick to realize how useful a man like Berenson could be to him. They first met in 1906, after Lady Sassoon took Berenson to Duveen's gallery in London to inspect some pictures from the Hainauer Collection. Berenson had agreed to go only on condition that he and Duveen were not to be introduced. Among the pictures he saw at the gallery was one he wanted for his patron, Mrs. Jack Gardner. This woman was perhaps the most colorful figure in the Boston of Berenson's youth—energetic, dominating, a born show-off, and one of the earliest of the great generation of American art collectors. In 1898 she had started to build an extraordinary house in Boston, a mock-Venetian *palazzo* called Fenway Court, which is now one of America's most remarkable museums, still redolent of the personality of its founder. Mrs. Gardner had aided Berenson when he wanted to go to Europe to continue his studies, and in return he helped her to create her collection.

Duveen, who knew perfectly well who his visitor was—Berenson had been for some years a force in the art world—refused to come down to brass tacks about the picture. But he decided to buy Berenson. Soon afterward he sought him out and asked him to become his paid adviser—Berenson was to be given an annual retainer and a commission on sales. Berenson was tempted by the financial prospects thus revealed, and he agreed on condition that he was to have nothing to do with the selling of the merchandise.

Later Berenson was to experience feelings of poignant regret about having decided to become an expert. He recognized, of course, the material advantages that his decision had brought him: "Not only did it enable me to pay for assistance in any work, for comfort at home and abroad, and for expensive journeys, but it gave me the means to acquire the books and photographs that my study and research required." Yet at the same time he felt that he had sacrificed something very precious:

My only excuse is, if the comparison is not too blasphemous, that like Saint Paul with his tentmaking and Spinoza with his glass-polishing I too needed a means of livelihood. Mine did not take up more of my time but very much more of my energy. Those men of genius were not hampered in their careers by their trades. Mine took up what creative talent there was in me, with the result that my trade made my reputation and the rest of me scarcely counted. The spiritual loss was great and in consequence I have never regarded myself as other than a failure.

Duveen was not responsible for Berenson's fall from grace—the latter was already a good way along the path to perdition when the two first encountered each other. But the relationship with Duveen did become, for Berenson, the symbol of spiritual bondage, and he chafed at it—far more, indeed, than he chafed at his relationships with other dealers, such as the Steinmeyers in Lucerne and Contini Bonacossi and Luigi Grassi in Florence. Something of this emerges from the description of Duveen's personality that Berenson

OVERLEAF: The Florentine villa I Tatti, which housed the magnificent library and art collection of Bernard Berenson (1865–1959) was bequeathed to Harvard University, and it serves as a Center for Italian Renaissance culture. The taste and learning of the Lithuanian-born Harvard-educated Berenson teamed with the showmanship and salesmanship of Lord Joseph Duveen to bring to the United States and England many masterpieces of Renaissance art. His books also served to popularize previously little-recognized art and artists. Photo by David Seymour.

gave to Behrman. According to this, Duveen felt uneasy in the society of cultivated persons, such as those who made up the household at I Tatti, Berenson's villa outside Florence. He tried to compensate for this uneasiness by clowning. His paid expert found in him "a Chaplinesque quality," irresistible when Duveen was present, less attractive when he was gone. Nicky Mariano, Berenson's devoted friend and companion for forty years, remarked that B. B. was "half repelled and half fascinated" by the great dealer.

But Berenson often had reason to complain, not only about Duveen's personality, but about his conduct. Immediately after World War I, for example, Duveen tried very hard to get Berenson to endorse the attributions of a number of pictures that he had sold during the war without waiting for Berenson's seal of approval. Berenson refused. There were rows about money. Miss Mariano says that Berenson "suffered bitterly from having to wrangle with [Duveen] over payments due to him and not unfrequently retarded or contested." In fact, as the I Tatti archives show, Berenson more and more tried to avoid dealing directly with the firm of Duveen—most correspondence with them passed through the hands of his wife, Mary Berenson.

Berenson's wife—who came from Quaker, not from Jewish, stock—liked Duveen much more whole-heartedly than her husband did. She appreciated his boyish humor and his capacity for telling stories. In any assessment of the relationship between the two men, Mary's personality must be accounted an important factor. Nicky Mariano, for example, remarks on her attitude to money:

> Mary had an almost childish love of money, of the pleasure of handling it, of squandering it, of giving it away, one might say of throwing it out of the window. Everything seemed to her calculable in terms of money, every act of kindness or courtesy could in her opinion be repaid with a cheque. That in many cases one can only *payer de sa personne* was outside her range of vision.

All accounts of Mary Berenson leave one with the impression that there was in her character, mingled with much goodness and charm, a disconcerting vein of coarseness and insensitivity. This coarseness may have responded to a similar quality in Duveen. She also had the confidence of one who came from "good society" and who was correspondingly certain of herself.

In his *Sketch for a Self-Portrait*, Berenson has an interesting passage about his own attitude to social position. He says that he wasted too much of himself "in attempting to establish my position as a *monsieur*":

> Seeing that I had no roots in any of the countries I was living in, it was but natural, although neither noble nor even wise, to harbour such an ambition, and to resent any question as to my right to a place in society.
>
> Whence came the innate sense of that right? From the fact that my childhood was spent in an aristocratic republic and though under Russian rule all the more aristocratic for being Jewish.

The Jewishness, of course, was often enough the rub. Berenson had, as he confessed, a weakness for society women; he said that he found them "more receptive, more appreciative, and consequently more stimulating." Sometimes these fair companions sought him out, more especially in the early days of his reputation, because they had family pictures they wanted authenticated. When the scholar refused they were apt to remember his race—and this must have hurt the subject of their gossip, though he pretended to be amused by their hypocrisy. On the other hand, he never attempted to deny being what he was. But he did feel exasperated by the gentile habit of finding all Jews alike, and perhaps this was one of the underlying causes of his friction with Duveen. Duveen was not a man he wanted to be mistaken for.

The art dealer, too, had a taste for ladies in high society. Like Berenson, he enjoyed escorting them round picture galleries. But he was willing to extend his instruction to anyone who might be useful, and particularly to the rich who were his clients. Among his companions on these visits were Jules S. Bache, Andrew W. Mellon, Mrs. Horace E. Dodge, and Mrs. Arabella Huntington. He was also accompanied on occasion by Ramsay MacDonald, then an M.P. without particularly glittering prospects. Later, as prime

In 1931 twenty-four-year-old Norton Simon began to collect companies with the purchase for $7000 of a bankrupt orange juice bottling company. In ten years its sales had gone from $43,000 to $9,000,000. He began buying stock and control of Hunts Foods in 1941, and its sales in fifteen years went from $14,550,000 to $102,501,000. In 1954 Simon began collecting paintings; he is pictured here at Christie's in London (March 19, 1965) as he successfully fought off other bidders to purchase Rembrandt's *Titus* for $2,234,000.

minister, MacDonald was to reward Duveen with a peerage and a trusteeship of the National Gallery in London (he was dislodged from the latter post by another prime minister, Neville Chamberlain).

Duveen, long before his entry to the House of Lords, had evolved methods of dealing with members of the peerage. Sometimes he made genuine friends of them: an instance was his friendship with Lord D'Abernon, who was British ambassador to Germany during the early twenties. But his tactics for the most part combined total directness with endearing insolence. Invited by the Duke of Devonshire to spend the night at Chatsworth, he made a beeline (as Behrman relates) for a Riccio bronze he wanted and, putting his hand on it, evoked a vanished self: "Joe Duveen speakin', Your Grace! Sixty thousand pounds for this bronze! Joe Duveen's price, Your Grace. Going, going, gone!" The duke was by no means insulted, though he refused to part with the bronze. He gave instructions that in future Duveen should be given first refusal of anything he wanted to sell.

Berenson could not have behaved like this, because to do so would not only have violated his own temperament, it would also have meant an admission of social inferiority. Duveen did not care about such shades; and in any case he was not interested in gaining acceptance of the kind that Berenson valued. What interested Duveen was power. Art dealing was a way of imposing himself; controlling works of art was a way of controlling people. Aristocrats were his suppliers, and to that extent they interested him, but mingled with the interest was a certain contempt—both experience and instinct told him that their compliance could be bought. The American millionaires who were his clients were a tougher proposition, and, correspondingly, they fascinated him more. The Duke of Devonshire's sensibilities worried Duveen a good deal less than Mellon's impassivity.

This is perhaps the point to say something about Duveen's ability to get very high prices from his clients. He extracted £130,000 from the Huntingtons for Gainsborough's "Blue Boy," and got more than a million dollars from John D. Rockefeller for a group of Renaissance busts (the latter deal was an example of Duveen's penchant for wholesale trading). He also believed in paying highly, and he was careful to maintain the prices of any works of art purchased from him which once again came on the market during his own lifetime. He even managed to maintain the level of his own particular market after the crash of 1929. Indeed, the Duveen level of art prices has only recently been overtaken, in the art boom of the sixties and seventies, and even then it must be remembered that today's prices are paid in much devalued currency. There is, however, no valid comparison to be made between the Duveen art market and the one we know today. Duveen's clients were a small group, securely rich. They were not buying for investment or as a hedge against inflation. They were buying for immortality; their collections were destined for public institutions.

My analysis of Duveen's methods and attitudes must not be taken to mean that Berenson was totally without some of Duveen's own characteristic qualities. As one reads Berenson's correspondence, it is fascinating to see how he handled the temperamental Mrs. Jack Gardner, whom he continued to supply with paintings even after he had cemented his alliance with Duveen. In 1901, several years after the treaty was signed, we find him appealing to her to find him more clients:

> I could sell ten times as much as I do now if only I had a larger circle of friends. I know I can rely on you to help me enlarge this circle, can't I? I want America to have as many good pictures as possible. You have had the cream. Other collections will only enhance the merit of yours. . . .

Here, from 1906, is part of the sales pitch for a Velásquez:

> They assure me that Roger Fry who has recently seen it will move heaven and earth to get the Metropolitan Museum to buy it and that he suggested 600,000 [dollars] as a fair price. All that

On the road to becoming the foremost dealer in rare books, eleven-year-old Abraham Simon Wolf Rosenbach (1876–1952), with $10 in his pocket, made his first purchase at auction—an illustrated *Reynard the Fox*—with a bid of $24. In 1925 he paid $106,000 for a Gutenberg Bible, at that time the record price for a book at auction. He was instrumental in building, among others, the J. P. Morgan Library in New York and the Henry Huntington Library in California. A graduate and teacher in English at the University of Pennsylvania, where he obtained his Ph.D., he opened his first store at 1320 Walnut Street in his native Philadelphia, which remained his main office for forty years. A. S. W. Rosenbach is pictured in his branch outlet in New York.

OPPOSITE, ABOVE: In 1939 Sidney Janis (born in Buffalo, New York, in 1896) retired on his earnings from the M'Lord shirt business to devote the next nine years to writing and lecturing on art. The gallery he opened in 1948 was to represent exclusively in subsequent years Albers, Baziotes, de Kooning, Dine, Gorky, Gottlieb, Guston, Kline, Motherwell, Oldenburg, Pollock, Rothko, Segal—the best in American painting from Abstract Expressionism to Pop. Janis donated his personal collection to the Museum of Modern Art in 1967. *Andrus*, 1961 (courtesy of Sidney Janis Gallery, New York), shown here, is the work of Franz Kline (1910–1962), a leader of the New York School, born in Wilkes-Barre, Pennsylvania.

Edith Gregor Fivoosiovitch Halpert (born Odessa, Russia, 1900; died New York, 1970) opened the Down-town Gallery in Greenwich Village in 1926 and there displayed the talents of Stuart Davis, Yasuo Kuniyoshi, Charles Sheeler, Jack Levine, and Ben Shahn (1898–1969), who came from Kaunas, Russia, to the United States in 1906—the same year Mrs. Halpert arrived. Shahn's paintings, murals, and graphics, in a poetic but realistic fashion, espoused liberal, political, and social causes and emphasized the dignity and worth of mankind. (*Albert Einstein with Other Immigrants*, mural at the Community Center, Roosevelt, New Jersey)

OPPOSITE, BELOW: The Marlborough Gallery and its owner, Frank Lloyd, have been engaged in a bitterly contested legal battle with the children of Mark Rothko (born Marcus Rothkovitch, in Dvinsk, Russia, 1903). The Abstract Expressionist, whose pictures are characterized by large areas of melting colors floating in an indeterminate atmosphere, committed suicide in 1970. Frank Lloyd (born Franz Kurt Levai, in Vienna), whose parents died in a Nazi concentration camp, emigrated to France before World War II, later escaped to London, and eventually became the most important dealer in modern art in London and New York. His conflicting role as Rothko's exclusive dealer and executor has been seriously questioned. Shown here: *Number 10, 1950.* (Courtesy of The Museum of Modern Art, New York)

The Boucher room of the Frick Collection. This mansion, which stretches for one block on Fifth Avenue, was conceived and created for steel magnate Henry Clay Frick by Joseph Duveen (1869–1939) to house the works of art that Duveen had acquired and planned to acquire for his client. Joseph Joel Duveen, who moved the family art business from Holland to London in 1877, was knighted; his son, who added a wing to London's Tate Gallery, was also knighted in 1919, was made a baronet in 1926, and was elevated to the peerage in 1933—Lord Duveen of Milbank.

I cannot guarantee. But what I can tell you as a fact is that Mrs. Potter Palmer only awaits for my approval of the picture to purchase it.

There is no need to attribute base motivations to the author of these letters. The collection he built up for Mrs. Gardner has a magic that any visitor to Fenway Court will remember. On the other hand, Duveen must be given some credit too. He was responsible for immense benefactions in his own name and in his own lifetime, including gifts to the Tate Gallery and the gallery that houses the Elgin Marbles in the British Museum. But his real monument is to be found elsewhere, in the great public collections of the United States, most particularly in the National Gallery in Washington. The nucleus of this was formed by the Mellon Collection—those Mellon pictures that did not come directly from the Soviet government came from Duveen—and Duveen provided the impulse to build it. Mellon was sued for massive tax evasion, and it was Duveen's evidence that the pictures had been bought for charitable purposes and that the owner intended to provide a building in which they would be made available for public enjoyment that got Mellon off the hook.

In general, the American system, whereby gifts to galleries could be used to alleviate the burden of income tax, was skillfully exploited by Duveen and provided the basis for an American dominance of the art market that lasted for many decades and that has only just begun to be challenged. It was another Duveen client, Samuel Kress, who supplied most of the pictures that were needed to fill up the immense building that was constructed with Mellon's money. Duveen took the closest possible interest in its design, rather as he did with the design and furnishings of his other clients' houses. His taste put its stamp to an equal degree on what was then Henry C. Frick's private house and is now a public museum in New York.

Most of the Kress and Mellon pictures were bought from Duveen with the backing of Berenson's advice and the guarantee of his certificates. To this extent the National Gallery in Washington may be regarded as their joint monument. What impression does it make on the visitor that might make it seem different from other galleries of comparable importance? Anyone who knows the history of the gallery will, I think, be struck by the speed and certainty with which it seems to have been built up. As one walks through the various rooms, it is hard to believe that it is not the product of centuries of accretion, like the Prado in Madrid or the Kunsthistorisches Museum in Vienna. To this must be added the fact that it is, to my eyes at least, a collection of exceptional charm.

The charm must be attributed as much to Duveen himself as to his adviser. Duveen knew that his clients wanted pictures that were easy to look at and easy to like, with bright colors and attractive subjects. Berenson, on the other hand, wanted Duveen and his clients to have pictures that were absolutely authentic, superb examples of important masters—and correctly attributed. Duveen's wishes and Berenson's principles often came into conflict, but, until the final break, Duveen always had the good sense to give way—at least to the extent that he placed his trust in Berenson's approval, though he sometimes refused a work Berenson was enthusiastic about.

The final break between the two men came over a point of attribution, when Berenson refused to certify that the "Allendale" Adoration, which Duveen was about to sell to Mellon, was by Giorgione. Berenson stubbornly insisted that it was an early Titian. Because of this, Mellon did not buy, though the picture later arrived in the National Gallery in Washington as a gift from Kress. There is a further and ironic twist to the story: the picture now figures, in the most recent edition of Berenson's *Italian Pictures of the Renaissance: Venetian School*, as a work of Giorgione. Berenson's refusal to certify it as such was due, no doubt, as much to his own subconscious desire to escape from Duveen's clutches once and for all as to his intellectual convictions as an expert.

For it was not only that Duveen wanted to have control over the family firm (he drove nearly all his relations out of it), over pictures, over vendors, and over clients. He wanted to rule over Berenson as well. He was always offended when the latter bestowed his advice elsewhere, though he did not have an exclusive contract. More subtly, he put continual pressure on Berenson to conform to his own view of what art was about. I think it is evident that Duveen was far from being the Philistine he has sometimes been called. He

American antiques, particularly Rhode Island and Pennsylvania furniture of the eighteenth century, now command the attention and prices previously obtained only by the finest English and French pieces. In recent years at Parke-Bernet, a Newport Townsend-Goddard kneehole desk and small black front chest sold for $120,000 and $110,000, and a Philadelphia Chippendale card table for $90,000. The limited supply of fine examples, the increased museum interest, the re-emphasis on the American past arising from the Bicentennial combine to force prices higher even during the recession of the mid-1970s.

In 1901 Isaac M. Levy and John Ginsburg opened a shop in lower New York City dealing primarily in American antiques, and since that time Ginsburg & Levy has continued to offer the finest in American furniture. In 1974 Bernard Levy and his son, S. Dean Levy, the third generation in the firm, separated from that family business and opened their own emporium, which also deals in American painting of the eighteenth and nineteenth centuries. Their brightly illuminated and carefully arranged showroom (pictured above) differs markedly from the treasure-cluttered five-story narrow building still presided over by Benjamin Ginsburg.

In 1905 Israel Sack became a dealer in American antiques in Boston. His reputation grew, the firm moved to New York, and under the direction of his three sons, Harold (at left), Albert, and Robert, continued to prosper. The extensive illustrated catalogues issued by the family have become basic reference tools for study in the field and have been reissued in book form. The Introduction to the 1974 Israel Sack catalogue was, as in the past, signed by the three brothers, but the name of Donald Sack was added—the third generation had made its appearance.

These dealers make available to their favored clients, including now the Winterthur Museum, the Metropolitan Museum of Art, and the National Trust, examples of American furniture so expertly crafted and rare that they command prices well above those prevailing at Parke-Bernet.

Little Caesar's favorite empire was his collection of rare books and French Impressionist and Post-Impressionist art. Edward G. Robinson (Emanuel Goldenberg, 1893–1973) came from Bucharest to New York in 1903 and was graduated from Townsend Harris High School seven years later. He bought his first picture for two dollars in 1913, became a Broadway and Hollywood star, turned the badminton court of his Beverly Hills home into an art gallery open to the public, and before his death sold the bulk of his collection at auction. He is pictured holding a Tang figure (seventh century A.D.), standing before Renoir's *Girl with Red Plume*.

had the typical sensibility of the great dealer: working with an extraordinary and instinctive rapidity, and to all appearances quite apart from scholarly analysis. Not to credit Duveen with an "eye" is to fly in the face of the evidence.

Berenson was much more finely tuned, and also the inventor of an aesthetic system that he had elaborated through much thought. His intellectual achievement was more considerable than he would himself admit. He made accessible to a new generation the achievements of a great period of Italian art, mostly by teaching people to look at the old masters abstractly, for the relationships of form and color rather than for the subject matter. He also taught them to empathize, consciously rather than unconsciously, with what was going on in the painting; with the movement of the figures and the physical tension or relaxation of the way in which they were posed. His doctrine was summed up in the phrase "tactile values," which was to become the parrot-cry of his disciples. Duveen, I suspect, would have been happier if "tactile values" had never been invented. To him they must have represented yet another avenue of escape down which the elusive Berenson vanished as soon as the pressures Duveen put on him seemed to grow too great.

Basically the story of the savant and the salesman, of Berenson and Duveen, strikes me as a comedy, because, despite the Jewishness they held in common, they could never quite get on terms with each other, never quite meet. In fact, a comedy of a particular kind: a comedy of exasperation.

William Samuel Rosenberg—Billy Rose (1899–1966), at eighteen the fastest shorthand taker in the world. His songs (among 400), "Barney Google," "Without a Song," "That Old Gang of Mine," "Me and My Shadow." His shows included *Jumbo, Carmen Jones*, the *Aquacade* at the 1939–1940 New York World's Fair; his night clubs, Casino de Paree, the Diamond Horseshoe; his wives, Fanny Brice, Eleanor Holm; his art collection, the greatest of modern sculpture, given to the State of Israel, where it is now displayed at the Israel Museum, Jerusalem. Photo by Arnold Newman.

The Smithsonian Institution of Washington, D.C., opened a new building in 1975 to exhibit a small portion of the art collection of Joseph Hirshhorn. The eleventh of twelve children, he emigrated to the United States from Mitau, Latvia, in 1905 with his mother, who supported them on $12 a week earned in a purse factory. In 1916, seventeen years old, Joseph took his savings of $255 and became a broker on the curb market, earning $168,000 in his first year. In August 1929 he withdrew $4 million from the stock market; the crash was in October. In 1956 he exchanged his uranium investments for some $50 million. Ten years later President Johnson announced Hirshhorn's gift to the nation—an art collection which then had more than 5600 pieces. It has continued to grow. Photo by Arnold Newman.

The Solomon R. Guggenheim Museum, designed by Frank Lloyd Wright, displays on New York's Fifth Avenue to countless thousands of art lovers the best artists and art of the twentieth century. The Palazzo Venier dei Leoni displays on Venice's Grand Canal to her invited guests the personal collection of Peggy Guggenheim. Her grandfather and granduncle controlled the American Smelting and Refining Company, which dominated the mining industry for the first three decades of this century. An international bohemian on a grand scale, she briefly operated commercial art galleries in London (showing Cocteau, Tanguy, Kandinsky) and New York (showing Pollock, Motherwell, Rothko, Hofmann), briefly married Lawrence Vail and Max Ernst, but steadily, under the guidance of Samuel Beckett, Marcel Duchamp, Herbert Read, and after World War II on her own, established one of the finest collections of modern art in Europe. Photo by David Seymour.

Babel and Bellow

David Daiches

Grandma Lausch, a dominating matriarch who plays a significant part in the early chapters of Saul Bellow's novel *The Adventures of Augie March*, lived in a run-down area of Chicago but remembered her former glory as a member of a well-to-do Jewish family of Odessa. She was not religious. "But although she never went to the synagogue, ate bread on Passover, sent Mama to the pork butcher where meat was cheaper . . . she was not an atheist and free-thinker." She "burned a candle on the anniversary of Mr. Lausch's death, threw a lump of dough on the coals when she was baking, as a kind of offering, had incantations over baby teeth and stunts against the evil eye." She lived in a tiny Jewish enclave among a community of Catholic Poles, with their "swollen, bleeding hearts on every kitchen wall, the pictures of saints, baskets of death flowers tied at the door, communions, Easters, and Christmases." The Poles sometimes chased and beat up the Jewish boys in their midst.

Grandma Lausch is a transitional figure: an emancipated Russian Jewess, oriented at least as much toward Russian culture as toward Jewish, who late in life tries to come to terms with modern American city life in the light of standards derived from her upbringing in Odessa. If we read "post-revolutionary Russian society" instead of "modern American city life" we could apply this description with complete appropriateness to Isaac Babel. He too came from Odessa, son of a sales representative for a manufacturer of agricultural machinery. He was born in 1894 in the southwestern suburb of Moldavanka, largely inhabited by Jews of varying social and financial position: indeed, the whole of Odessa had a Jewish flavor, about 35 per cent of its population being Jewish in the years when Babel lived there. Most Odessan medical practitioners were Jewish, and Jews also played the dominant part in the grain exports that were so central in the port's economy. More than half of Odessa's lawyers were Jewish, and there was also a considerable number of Jewish engineers, architects, chemists, and members of other technical professions. About a third of the total Jewish population of Odessa could have been called members of the proletariat, ranging from industrial workers to unskilled manual laborers of the crudest kind. The Jews of Odessa were known before the Russian Revolution for the high degree to which they had assimilated Russian culture and for the relatively low standard of their Jewish learning. They were a lively, colorful, and varied lot, including gangsters as well as bankers; they moved between Jewish and Russian culture with an excited but precarious footing; they were subject to periodic persecution, as in the pogrom of 1905, which young Babel witnessed and which he wrote about in two of his Odessa stories, "The Story of My Dovecote" and "First Love"; above all, they were tenacious and seething with vitality.

In many respects prerevolutionary Odessa was rather like Chicago in the heyday of gangsterdom, and sometimes, reading those stories of Babel that are set in Odessa, one can easily imagine that one is

Why Isaac Babel (1894–1941) displeased the Soviet authorities remains a mystery. He was exiled to Siberia, where he died. His short stories of Odessa and of war (he served in the Cossacks) earned him Gorki's praise and official approval until the mid-1930s.

reading about Chicago. That extraordinary story, written in 1923, entitled "Kak eto delalos v Odesse" ("How it was done in Odessa"), has all the characteristics of a Chicago gangster tale: a leader organizing a protection racket, violent measures taken against those who refuse protection money, deaths by shooting, plush funerals of the murdered paid for by the gangsters. But these are *Jewish* gangsters: they are not the passive suffering Jews of the *shtetl* that we see so often in the pages of Sholom Aleichem, but characters—often eccentric, violent, unscrupulous, ingenious, flamboyant, cunning—who insist on being in charge of their own destiny. Benya Krik, the hero-villain of these stories, is both a Jewish gangster and a Jewish Robin Hood: he can behave with great savagery, but his good Jewish heart reveals itself oddly and unexpectedly in acts of compassion and moments of understanding. He uses traditional Jewish rituals and customs as means of giving color and social reality to his actions. The funerals of his victims are conducted by whole choirs of cantors chanting the traditional prayers. The story of how Benya deploys his forces and arranges flamboyant rituals in order to make himself in everybody's estimation *korol*, Benya the King, is told, partly in awe, partly in admiration, by an old man with a traditional Jewish name, Reb Arye-Leib.

Babel was primarily a writer of short stories, though he also wrote at least part of a novel, two plays, and some film scripts; Bellow is primarily a novelist; both are (among other things) interpreters of residuary Jewishness. Neither is concerned to document areas of Jewish life from within, as did Sholom Aleichem, Mendele Mocher Seforim, Isaac Bashevis Singer, and other Yiddish writers of the *shtetl*. Babel wrote in Russian; Bellow writes in American English. Bellow, son of Yiddish-speaking Russian-Jewish immigrants to Canada, born in Montreal in 1915 and raised there and in Chicago, sprang from the same culture as Babel and, in spite of being removed from it by his parents' immigration, was in some respects nearer to it than Babel, whose parents spoke Russian not Yiddish, though his grandparents spoke Yiddish and he himself knew the language. Again, Babel was a good linguist and was especially competent in French, in which language he first began to write stories at the age of fifteen: he spent some time in Paris in the 1930s.

275

Bellow's native city of Montreal was bilingual in English and French, and these two languages, together with Yiddish, were thus part of his early background. Bellow uses his Jewish knowledge sometimes as a means of exploring the transitional situation of American immigrant Jews and their sons and daughters, their intermixed and fragmented culture, their social and intellectual mobility, their response to the American social and economic scene (*The Adventures of Augie March* is his most important novel in this category), and sometimes as a means of projecting Jewish characters as symbolic of the alienation of sensitive man in modern Western civilization, so that Jewishness becomes, as in James Joyce's character Leopold Bloom, a means of exploring problems of identity and of social fragmentation that go far beyond the purely Jewish dimension (*Herzog* and *Mr. Sammler's Planet* are the two most significant of Bellow's novels in this category). The Jewish element in Babel's work is much less easy to classify. His Jews are certainly not symbols of modern alienated man. They weave in and out of his stories, sometimes occupying a fairly central place and sometimes appearing on the sidelines for an instant only, and for the most part his attitude toward them is one of studied coolness; only occasionally does he as writer claim kinship with his Jewish characters; more often they are there because they are there—part of the Russian scene he is describing.

But of course there is another dimension in Babel's work, as there is in that of every writer who lived and worked in Russia after the 1917 revolution. This dimension is the product of his response to the new Soviet state and of the new Soviet state's response to him. An enlightened supporter of social change, he at first welcomed the overthrow of the Czarist regime and then willed himself to see everything that made for social betterment in the new Soviet system. From the beginning, however, the human realities of the revolution made a searing impact on his writer's imagination, and some of the stories that appeared in his friend Maxim Gorki's journal *Novaya zhizn* (New Life) in 1918—including "Evacuees," "Premature Babies," and "The Palace of Motherhood"—were pretty grim documentaries of human misery and have been reprinted in the Soviet Union. Later, after his period of service with Budënny's First Cavalry during its 1920 campaign against the Poles, he wrote those extraordinary stories of life with a Cossack army, *Konarmiya* (translated as *Red Cavalry*). That a Jew should in any way identify himself with Cossacks, the Jews' traditional enemies and persecutors and epitome of everything counter to traditional Jewish values, cruel horsemen who hunted down Jews in pogroms, has been held to be a startling paradox, and it certainly requires some explanation. These stories were written in the early 1920s and much worked over before publication in book form in 1926. They attracted immediate attention and brought Babel fame as a great Soviet writer, in spite of the fact that Marshal Budënny himself (in an article in *Krasnaya gazeta* in October 1928) attacked the stories as "slinging dirt at our best Communist commanders" and failing to do justice to the simple heroism of the First Cavalry. Though Gorki replied to Budënny's article in *Pravda* the following month, defending Babel vigorously, the attack was symbolic of the precariousness of Babel's position with respect to the Soviet authorities. As Stalinism developed and the demand for a simplified glorification of the new Soviet society (under the guise of "socialist realism") constricted writers more and more, Babel fell into long periods of silence, which itself was regarded as suspicious. With the death of his friend and protector Gorki in 1936, Babel's position grew more dangerous, and in May 1939 he was arrested and disappeared from view forever, as did nearly all of his unpublished and unfinished work. He was officially rehabilitated in 1954, at which time his date of death was given as March 1941. L. Polyak's introduction to the collected edition (which of course did not include the works that disappeared on his arrest and even omitted some that had previously appeared in the Soviet Union), published subsequently in Moscow, says coolly that in May 1939 Babel was "*nezakonno repressirovan i pogib* (illegally repressed and perished)."

So we cannot ignore the Soviet dimension in Babel's life and work. At the same time we must remember that he was twenty-four at the time of the October Revolution, already determined to make his way as a writer and mature for his age. He had had a childhood and youth rich in knowledge and experience. His family spent some years at the Black Sea port of Nokolayev during his very early childhood,

ABOVE: "The incomparable Max" Beerbohm (1872–1956) lived his last years in Rapallo, Italy, where he charmed visitors with tales of Victorian and Edwardian England and wrote witty comments in the margins of books he read. In his first thirty-eight years, he was graduated from Oxford, published books of essays and caricatures, became a press agent and drama critic, and wrote the novel *Zuleika Dobson*.

RIGHT: Since his father was a famous Austrian throat specialist, Arthur Schnitzler (1862–1931) was introduced in boyhood to both his father's medical practice and his patients—the dramatic and operatic stars of Vienna. Arthur became a doctor and published in that field, but in 1891 his first play appeared, and four years later he deserted medicine for literature—with distinguished success.

and there he attended primary school and began his study of English, French, and German. His father was educationally ambitious for him and, though he was not especially orthodox in his Jewish belief or practices, insisted that his son learn Hebrew together with his other languages. Babel's earliest known story, which came to light in the Soviet Union some years ago and was published in 1965 in the Soviet series *Literaturnoye nasledstvo* (Literary Heritage), is headed simply "Detstvo. U Babushki" ("Childhood. At Grandmother's"): it tells how his grandmother, whose mother tongue was Yiddish and who spoke Russian badly, had a passionate belief in learning and would say to him, "Study! Study and you will have everything—wealth and fame! You must know *everything*." On his family's return to Odessa, Babel entered the Commercial School there. In 1911, unable to enter the University of Odessa because of the *numerus clausus* (restriction on the number of Jews allowed), he was sent to the Institute of Financial and Business Studies at Kiev; the institute was moved to Saratov at the beginning of World War I, and it was there that Babel graduated. It was at Kiev that he met Evgenia (Zhenya) Gronfein, daughter of a Jewish manufacturer and importer of agricultural machinery who had long been doing business with Babel's father: he married her in 1919. But before his marriage he spent some time in St. Petersburg (or Petrograd, as it now was), probably not leading the life of a starving bohemian writer that he describes in a number of quasi-autobiographical stories, for his father kept him in funds, but savoring the life of that beautiful city while striving to improve his craft as a writer. In an early sketch entitled simply "Odessa"—it was one of four such sketches that appeared in the winter of 1916–17 in the Petrograd daily *Zhurnal zhurnalov* (Journal of Journals)—he contrasts Petrograd and Odessa. Petrograd, St. Petersburg, is the city of mysterious fog, of stifling human passion, Dostoevskian gloom and frenzy, whereas Odessa, with its bright sunshine and colorful mixed population (half of whom, he says, are Jews), is a poetic and carefree city, if now in helpless decline. Russian literature, he concludes, needs revitalizing with the sun of Odessa, which will redeem it, as Gorki has redeemed it, from northern sadness.

In the 27 volumes of *Men of Good Will*, Jules Romains (1885–1972) attempted to re-create in fiction the spirit of French society from 1908 to 1933. He was elected to the Académie Française in 1946 after his return from the United States, where he took refuge during World War II.

OPPOSITE: The gift of Allegheny, Pennsylvania, to Paris, Gertrude Stein (1874–1946) left Johns Hopkins School of Medicine to establish a literary salon in 1903 with her brother Leo and later with her lifelong companion, Alice B. Toklas. Her personal influence on writers and artists may have been greater than the influence of her most famous works, *Three Lives*, *Four Saints in Three Acts*, and *The Autobiography of Alice B. Toklas*. Photo by Horst.

Emile Herzog (1885–1967) found appropriate names for the writers he depicted in narrative biographies—for Shelley, *Ariel* (1923) ; for Victor Hugo, *Olympio* (1954) ; for Balzac, *Prometheus* (1965). For his own pseudonym he chose André Maurois. He was elected to the Académie Française in 1938. Photo by Horst.

Driven from Vienna by the Nazis, Stefan Zweig fled from London to Rio de Janeiro, where he and his wife committed suicide in 1942. In his sixty-one years he wrote poetry, essays, stories, and plays, but his most notable works were biographies of imaginary and historical characters.

His plays of social protest, *Waiting for Lefty, Awake and Sing, Golden Boy*, stirred Broadway during the Depression 1930s. Later Clifford Odets (1906–1963) moved to Hollywood to become a successful director and screenwriter—*The Country Girl*, for example.

Dinner at Eight and *Stage Door* were among the successful collaborations of Edna Ferber (1887–1968) and George S. Kaufman (1889–1961), but her novels were even more successful. *So Big, Saratoga Trunk, Show Boat*, and *Giant* earned best-seller status at both bookstores and movie houses. Two plays Kaufman co-authored won the Pulitzer Prize—*Of Thee I Sing* (1931) and *You Can't Take It With You* (1936).

Her stinging wit displayed in *Vanity Fair* and *The New Yorker* won Dorothy Rothschild Parker (1893–1967) a place at the Algonquin Round Table. Her change of role from "smart woman about town" to supporter of left-wing causes lost her a place in Hollywood. She is pictured with her husband, Alan Campbell.

Samuel Josef Czaczkes (1888–1970) Hebrewized his name after settling in Palestine in 1907, and as Smuel Yosef Agnon shared the 1966 Nobel Prize for Literature. He was the first Israeli writer to receive worldwide recognition. Photo by Alfred Bernheim.

OPPOSITE: His mother was a pianist and his father an art professor and portraitist, but Boris Pasternak (1890–1960) preferred another form of art. The manuscript of his novel *Doctor Zhivago*, which helped him win the 1958 Nobel Prize, had to be smuggled out of Russia, and its publication led to abuse and persecution for the author in his homeland. He was also a poet and a professional translator. Photo by Cornell Capa.

ABOVE: Rumanian-born Eugene Ionesco has lived most of his life in Paris. In *The Bald Soprano* (1948) he portrayed the theme of self-estrangement and communication failure with the innovative wit and technique that characterize "the theater of the absurd." Photo by Jill Krementz.

RIGHT: His humorous sketches in *The New Yorker*, his many books and his screen plays (the Marx Brothers brought him to Hollywood) have entertained America since the early 1920s. Born in Providence, Rhode Island, S. J. Perelman considered his Bucks County, Pennsylvania, farm his home for forty years. His brother-in-law, Nathanael West, acquired posthumous fame with *Miss Lonelyhearts* and *The Day of the Locust*. Photo by Jill Krementz.

BELOW: Each of the Trillings, Lionel and Diana, has played an important role in American literary criticism. On the faculty of Columbia University for more than forty years, and visiting professor at Harvard and Oxford, Lionel Trilling was considered the dean of American critics. Diana Trilling's writings on a variety of literary and social subjects appear regularly. Photo by Jill Krementz.

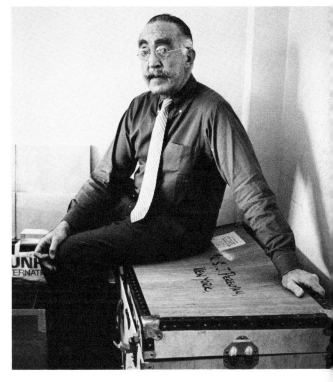

After the October Revolution, Babel (who had been exempted from military service in 1914) joined the army and served on the Rumanian front before being invalided out with malaria in 1918. He was back in Petrograd in 1919, and in 1920, with the civil war raging, in spite of being recently married, he rejoined the army to serve as correspondent for IUGROSTA, the southern branch of the national news service that was the predecessor of TASS. Under the name of Kiril Vassilevich Liutov (which presumably concealed his Jewish identity) he was assigned to Budënny's First Cavalry, the Red Army unit that during the summer of 1920 pushed back the Poles from the Ukraine and White Russia as far as Warsaw, where the Poles finally made a stand and forced the Red cavalry to retreat. Babel had a passion for horses and a deep curiosity about the mind of the Cossacks. His stories of his campaigning with them—although he was there as a journalist he shared their life and does seem to have been accepted eventually as one of them—reveal not so much the paradox of the Jew as Cossack, which has so intrigued some critics, but Babel's remarkable attempt as a writer to cultivate a new sort of objectivity about the inevitable violence that is the price of revolution. *Konarmiya* is about men caught up in this violence—those who have been brought up to practice it, those who have to learn to practice it, and those who are its victims. Conspicuous among these last are the Jewish communities of the little Polish towns overrun by the Cossack army.

These poor and shabby Jews were very different from the gay and lively and often aggressive Jews Babel had grown up with in Odessa: they were the true ghetto Jews of Eastern Europe, and Babel observed them with a carefully objective combination of irony and pity which, however, was occasionally broken into by the welling up of a sense of Jewish fellowship.

"The commander of the Sixth Division reported that Novograd-Volinsk was taken today at dawn." The stark opening of the first story in *Konarmiya*, "Crossing the Zbruch," sets the tone of bleakly objective narrative. The writer then places himself as observer, describing the countryside in which the "noisy rearguard baggage train" finds itself: fields crimson with poppies, the wind ruffling the fields of rye, the orange sunset, the blackened Zbruch with its bridges destroyed, the landscape dotted with square carts. They finally reach Novograd late at night. "I find a pregnant woman in the house where I am billeted, and two red-haired Jews with scraggy necks." Nothing in the tone suggests that the author is a fellow-Jew. He goes on to describe the behavior of the distraught Jews with sardonic brevity. They then all fall asleep—the two Jews, the pregnant Jewess, and the writer. The writer shouts in his sleep, is awakened by the Jewess, who points out that he is sleeping beside her dead father, murdered by the Poles. This very short story ends abruptly with the Jewess telling the narrator how her father had begged the Poles to kill him outside so that his daughter would not see, but they refused and killed him then and there. "*I teper ya khachu znat* (and now I want to know)," the woman suddenly said with frightful violence, "*gde eshchë na vsei zemle vui naidëte takogo otsa kak moi otetz* (wherever in the whole world you'd find another father like my father)." These are the last words of the story. There is no authorial comment. The horror and the tragedy emerge of themselves from the complete deadpan in the manner of telling.

That is one of Babel's methods in these stories. Sometimes the author suppresses himself completely, as in *Pismo* ("A Letter"), where he transcribes a letter written to his mother by a semi-literate peasant, which gives, all unconsciously, an appalling account of paternal tyranny and filial revenge as an explanation of the son's joining the Red Army; offhand anti-Semitic remarks made in the course of the letter are given no emphasis. After he has read the letter the narrator is given by its writer a broken photograph of his family.

In his account of Cossack officers and men Babel allows his coolly objective account of violence and endurance on their part and of the strange code of values by which they live to tell its own story, conveying a sort of admiration side by side with a sort of revulsion. In some stories, however, he attacks a Jewish theme directly, and the tone changes. In "Gedali" he describes himself in Zhitomir, haunted by memories of his grandfather stroking the volumes of Ibn Ezra and his grandmother lighting the Sabbath candles. He walks by the old synagogue and sees the ragged Jews with their prophets' beards and finally makes his way to Gedali's little shop. Gedali wants to believe in the revolution, but he also believes in the Sabbath. He wants to say yes to both but finds the revolution hiding from him. The revolution, Gedali tells the narrator, should mean joy, but it seems to bring death instead. The narrator tries to explain briefly that the revolution is eaten with gunpowder and flavored with best-quality blood, but he cannot keep up this tough Cossack pose. He suddenly breaks out, "Gedali, today is Friday, and evening is already here. Where can one get Jewish biscuits, a Jewish glass of tea, and a little of that retired God (*nemnozhko etogo otstavnogo boga*) in a glass of tea?" But none can be had, Gedali tells him; in the tavern next door people no longer eat, they weep. And Gedali goes off to welcome the Sabbath in the synagogue. "The Sabbath approaches. Gedali, founder of an impossible International, has gone to the synagogue to pray." And so the story ends.

Another Jewish story in the *Red Cavalry* collection is called simply "The Rabbi" and describes how the narrator goes with Gedali to Rabbi Motale's. The rabbi talks to the narrator as a fellow-Jew, but at the end the narrator leaves for the station and the new world to which he is committed: "There, at the station, in the propaganda train of the First Cavalry Army, there awaited me the brilliance of hundreds of lights, the magic brightness of the radio station, the continual running of the printing presses, and my unfinished article for the newspaper *Red Cavalryman*." A sequel to this story, entitled "The Rabbi's Son," appears later in the collection and tells of the death of the rabbi's son Elijah as a result of wounds received in a desperate action against the Whites. The scattered belongings of this Red Army man include portraits of both Lenin and Maimonides, pages of the Song of Songs and revolver cartridges. He had tried to bridge the old world of Jewish learning and the new world of the revolution, and he "died, the last of the princes, among his poetry, his phylacteries, and his foot-cloths." The story concludes (and here a literal translation is best): "We buried him in a forgotten station. And I, scarcely able to contain the tempests of my imagination in this old body of mine—I received the last breath of my brother." Here the identification of author and subject is, unusually, deliberate and emphatic.

Sometimes in these stories the narrator is neither the objective recorder nor the feeling Jew, but a troubled participant in strange scenes of violence who intermittently expresses his trouble and his sense of strangeness. Thus in "The Road to Brody," recording the elimination of bees in Volhynia with sulphur and gunpowder, he slips in a sentence saying how the chronicle of their daily offenses weighed on his heart and, after telling how he and his Cossack friend Afonka Bida had to flee from a Polish attack, concludes with an unexpected apostrophe to Brody with the mummies of its crushed passions and its chipped stone synagogues. And in his "Discourse on the *Tachanka*" (small cart) the narrator talks quietly of his pride in driving a *tachanka* and being in charge of the horses, to conclude suddenly with an account of the "lifeless little Jewish towns" huddled at the foot of Polish nobles' estates and contrasting these shabby Jews with their tragic yellow beards with the Jews of the Russian South. "The movements of the Jews of Volhynia and Galicia were uncontrolled, jerky and undignified, but the strength of their grief was full of a gloomy greatness and their secret contempt for the Polish gentry was boundless. Looking at them, I understood the bitter history of this district, the stories about Talmudists renting pot-houses, of rabbis practicing usury, of girls raped by Polish troopers and fought over with pistols by Polish magnates."

In yet other stories the narrator presents himself as trying hard to prove himself as worthy of acceptance by his comrades as a fellow-Cossack, but though he records with quiet pride those occasions when he achieves acceptance, there is always some degree of feeling of guilt or revulsion however obliquely expressed. In "The Death of Dolgushev" the narrator cannot bring himself to shoot a horribly wounded comrade and so put him out of his misery, and someone else has to do it; and so he loses the friendship of his comrade Alfonka. In "My First Goose" he shows how he wins acceptance by the Cossacks by being ruthless with the old woman in whose house they are quartered; at night, sleeping among his Cossack comrades, he dreams of women while his bloodstained heart brims over. In "After the Battle" he prays for "the simplest of abilities": "*umenye ubit cheloveka*"—"the ability to kill a fellow-creature." In short, these stories of the Red Cavalry in action reveal, when taken together (as Babel meant them to be), the inner tensions of a Jew who has thrown in his lot with the violence demanded of the revolution, together

ABOVE: Irving Stone paid his way through the University of California by playing the saxophone in a dance band and won a teaching fellowship in economics at USC, where he earned his M.A. Nine years later, in 1934, his life of Vincent Van Gogh, *Lust for Life*, became an immediate best seller. Other biographies include *Sailor on Horseback* (Jack London), *Clarence Darrow for the Defense*, *The President's Lady* (Rachel Jackson), *Love Is Eternal* (Mary Todd Lincoln), and *The Agony and the Ecstasy* (Michelangelo). Photo by Jill Krementz.

Her father, Maurice Wertheim, an international banker and philanthropist; her mother a member of the wealthy and distinguished Morgenthau family. A Radcliffe graduate, Barbara Tuchman was *The Nation*'s correspondent in Madrid during the Spanish Civil War, honing the writing and historical talents that produced the Pulitzer Prize winners *The Guns of August* and *Stillwell and the American Experience in China, 1911–1945*. Photo by Bruce Davidson.

For a number of years New York City's educational system included Townsend Harris High School, a school for gifted children, and among its distinguished graduates was Herman Wouk. Five years' apprenticeship as a writer for Fred Allen's radio show and four years' service in the U.S. Navy were prelude to *The Caine Mutiny*, which won the Pulitzer Prize for fiction in 1952, *Marjorie Morningstar*, and *The Winds of War*. Photo by Jill Krementz.

RIGHT: He was twenty-six when *Goodbye, Columbus* won the National Book Award with its understanding and evocative views on American Jewish life. Philip Roth's writing is now more biting as he reviews American sex and politics in *Portnoy's Complaint* (1969), *Our Gang* (1971), and *The Breast* (1972). Photo by Jill Krementz.

with the ambivalences of admiration and moral dubiety with which he approached the extrovert Cossacks and the alternation of historical dismissal (for they belonged to the unhappy past) and compassionate identification with which he regarded the unfortunate Jews encountered in the course of the campaign.

Sometimes, not in the *Red Cavalry* stories but in an Odessa story set after the revolution, Babel shows an open nostalgia for the colorful characters of the past, who have no place in the Soviet order. "Tell me as a revolutionary," say the Cheka officer Simën to his dismayed subordinate Borovoi after the picturesque gangster Froim Grach, who had come unarmed to plead for his boys, has been shot out of hand, "what sort of use could that man be to the society of the future?" "I don't know," Borovoi replies; "no use, I suppose." This is the end of the story "Froim Grach." In "Sunset" (a short story which he later made into a play), Babel returns to Benya Krik and shows how he deposed his tyrannical father Mendel: this is hardly the attack on "the stagnant petty-bourgeois ways of the Moldavanka" that the Soviet critic L. Livshits took it to be, but a depiction, both admiring and ironic, both brilliantly colorful and humanly sad, of the picturesque individualist violence of a departed age.

Babel's wife, mother, and sister settled in Paris and Brussels and would not return to Soviet Russia. In his numerous letters to his mother and sister written between 1925 and 1939 we see clearly how hard Babel fought to keep his art honest and at the same time, with increasing desperation, to believe in the new Soviet society. In these letters he is consistently ironic about his Jewish background, asking "the ex-God" to bless his correspondents, but he never lets a Passover go by without referring to it and to his eating matzo. He was able to make some visits to Paris and one to Italy, but it became increasingly difficult for him to get a passport. He could of course have stayed in Paris when he went on his final visit in 1935. But Babel was a Russian author and belonged to Russia. He regarded his Jewish background as part of his Russian-ness. He was determined to make his own authentic contribution to Russian literature, if it killed him. And it did.

For the most part, Babel's Jewish characters are left behind or destroyed by the new world represented by the Soviet Union. The heroic entrepreneurs of Odessa and the depressed Jewish masses of the Polish ghetto are presented in vividly observed detail to which is added occasionally a note of nostalgia or regret or compassion. Sometimes—notably in his unfinished work of the middle 1930s, *The Jewess*, never published in Russian but first published in English in America by his daughter Nathalie—he tries to chart the social and psychological problems of bridge-building between the old and the new worlds, and sometimes, as in "Shabos Nachamu," designed as part of an unwritten or lost cycle of stories revolving around a ghetto hero-trickster called Hershele Ostropoler, he reverts simply to a traditional Yiddish form of ironic humor. But whatever he does with his Jews, they are Jews of a given time and place, buffeted by history and responding as they do because they are what they are. They are not exalted into symbols of alienated modern man or of the liberal failure of nerve or of the problems faced by the educated humanist in the twentieth century. That symbolic dimension, however, is precisely what we do find in the novels of Saul Bellow. Bellow is much more of an intellectual writer of fiction than Babel is; his novels set out to probe and explore certain cultural dilemmas and their psychological implications, and the wealth of sheer reflectiveness in, say, *Herzog* (1964), is quite overpowering. At the same time, the social documentary element in Bellow is precise and convincing. It is the combination of persuasive social detail, continuous reflectiveness, and insistent symbolizing that is the mark of Bellow's fiction. His Jews are freed from the elemental struggle to survive by redefining their relation to their non-Jewish environment, a struggle that Babel's Jews become involved in after the revolution. Their process of adaptation to America's mixed culture is less desperate (though economically it can be desperate enough) and more relaxed. But most of all they enact in their lives and illustrate in the problems they face something that transcends their Jewish origins and concerns the modern world as such.

Better recognized as a Brooklyn street brawler than as a Harvard graduate in electrical engineering, Norman Mailer has written novels (*The Naked and the Dead, Deer Park*), books of personal reporting (*Miami and the Siege of Chicago, Armies of the Night*), biography (*Marilyn*), produced and directed three improvisational films, and lost a campaign for mayor of New York City. Photo by Jill Krementz.

It is interesting and significant that the novel which is in many ways Bellow's best, *Henderson the Rain King* (1959), has an American "Wasp" as hero and has no Jewish character in it at all. At the same time, Bellow takes his hero Henderson on a journey of self-discovery and self-healing to a purely symbolic Africa where he tests himself against a series of symbolic African characters, notably Dahfu, the brilliant and doomed king of the Wariri. Henderson's search for salvation, which is partly an attempt to break out of the prison of his own character, is essentially the same search that Bellow's Jewish characters are driven to engage in. Moses Herzog, the trapped, victimized, disturbed, self-analyzing, Jewish intellectual, and Mr. Sammler, the elderly survivor of the holocaust confronting today's America with his European and British memories, are varieties of Henderson, as Henderson is, as it were, a variety of Jew. It was the American critics who (following the clue laid by Joyce) first saw the possibilities of using the Jew in fiction as a symbol of modern alienated man, and so of presenting modern alienated man as symbolically Jewish. (This is precisely the theme of Bernard Malamud's 1957 novel *The Assistant*.) Norman Podhoretz has written of the excitement with which he and other Jewish students in New York heard that Lionel Trilling was writing an essay on Wordsworth and the rabbis, and in doing so he has pinpointed the moment when sophisticated critics of modern literature turned to Jewish themes as means of exploring and illuminating the larger world of their own time. Of course many—indeed, the larger majority—of those critics were themselves Jewish: besides Trilling, there were Philip Rahv, Alfred Kazin, Irving Howe, Leslie Fiedler, and many others. Jews presented themselves, and were accepted by others, as experts in alienation, the modern disease; the Jewish novel became the novel of alienation par excellence and the Jewish critic the specialist in demonstrating the presence of alienation in literature. It is because Bellow belongs to

Ilya Ehrenburg (1891–1967) and his wife entertained the American dramatist Arthur Miller (left). Much of Ehrenburg's early life was spent away from his native Russia, disapproving of both the Czar and the Bolsheviks, but by 1924 he was reconciled to Stalin and became both personally and through his writings one of the Soviet's most effective spokesmen. Arthur Miller, playwright (*Death of a Salesman*, *The Crucible*, *The Misfits*), as president of PEN, spoke for international freedom of thought and of the press, a position he also took before the House Un-American Activities Committee in 1956 when he refused to identify possible Communists. Photo by Inge Morath.

A New Orleans childhood, the New York City literary world, wartime Soviet Union, the relationship with Dashiell Hammett—all are movingly described in her autobiographical books *An Unfinished Woman* (1969) and *Pentimento* (1973). But thirty-five years earlier, twenty-seven-year-old Lillian Hellman won acclaim with her first play, *The Children's Hour* (1934), which was followed by such memorable dramas as *The Little Foxes* (1939), *Watch on the Rhine* (1941), *The Searching Wind* (1944), and *Toys in the Attic* (1960). Photo by Arnold Newman.

this movement that he, though his parents came from the same Russian-Jewish milieu that Babel came from and though he shares Babel's eye for the vivid social and psychological detail that places the Jew of a given time and place, belongs to a different literary world from Babel's. The sufferings of Herzog and Sammler, and to a lesser degree the bizarre adventures of Augie March, like the weird encounters of Henderson, are presented not as illuminations of Jewish life in a non-Jewish world but as ways of illuminating modern man in search of a soul.

It is perhaps because the Jewishness of his characters serves more often as a signal of the symbolic function of their fate than as an expression of the author's interest in Jewish life and problems as such that Bellow's Jewish characters have only a marginal relationship to their ancestral culture. Once Grandma Lausch's background is disposed of in *The Adventures of Augie March* (1953), there is little in the novel that exploits Bellow's very real knowledge of Jewish life in the Western Hemisphere. The Einhorns, who play an important part in the book, are also a Jewish family, but one could hardly tell, except for the infrequent introduction of some attenuated Jewish custom. Occasional references to bar mitzvahs and even rarer references to visits to the synagogue remind us of the Jewish background of many of the characters, but the really significant things that happen to Augie himself are not in any realistic way related to his being Jewish. The most bizarre episode of all, Augie's association with Thea Fenchel and her eagle, would not be out of place in *Henderson the Rain King*: it moves on a level of probability far more rarefied than that on which the rich Chicago social detail of much of the rest of the novel moves. In fact, Bellow has here taken off into more or less pure symbolism. There is another feature of this novel that removes it from any kind of Jewish documentary, and that is the fact of the hero's wide reading and his love of literary and historical references taken from a wide area of Western culture. This is part of Bellow's self-indulgence: he cannot restrain his own education, as it were, his own range of interest in European history and literature and languages, and he must have heroes who are able in greater or less degree to reveal this. In *Herzog* he goes much further and uses his disturbed and highly cultured hero as a cultural sponge, which he squeezes for the benefit of the reader after it has soaked up an impressive range of knowledge about European literature and philosophy. Although this is not presented as part of Moses Herzog's Jewishness (for the authors he refers to and quotes from might well have been read by any American academic of the time), it is nevertheless bound up with his being Jewish. For, as Leslie Fiedler put it in his essay "Negro and Jew: Encounter in America," the Jew "is the gateway into Europe for America; for he has carried with him, almost against his will, his own history, two thousand years of which is European." More than any other American-Jewish writer, Bellow is aware of this fact and deliberately exploits it in his novels.

He is doing something rather different, however, in *Mr. Sammler's Planet* (1970), though here the hero, a Polish-Jewish survivor of Hitler's concentration camps who comes to spend his last years in America, might well be expected to provide precisely that link with European culture that Fiedler sees it as the function of the Jew in American literature to provide. For Mr. Sammler is not an American Jew but an observer of the New York scene, who has arrived in America too late in life to see himself as more than an outsider there and whose experiences—notably his prewar years in London as a correspondent of a Polish newspaper and the friendship with H. G. Wells he formed during that time—equip him not with the exploratory mind of an Augie March, a Henderson, or a Herzog but with the sad and censorious wisdom of a liberated Jewish humanist of an earlier generation confronting the America of the 1960s. Further, his wisdom is not in any direct sense a Jewish wisdom, for he had emancipated himself from Jewish religion and traditional Jewish culture long before Hitler reminded him of his Jewishness; he now represents the secular enlightenment of the earlier part of the twentieth century trying wearily to come to terms with the facts of the second half of the century. In this he seems to speak in some respects for his creator, for the novel is more purely a novel of ideas, an on-going critique of modern America, than any other of Bellow's

Three-time winner of the National Book Award for fiction, Saul Bellow has created several of the most diverse and memorable characters in twentieth-century literature—Henderson the Rain King, Augie March, Herzog, Mr. Sammler. Born in Canada two years after his family had emigrated from St. Petersburg, Russia, he has lived most of his life in Chicago, where he is now chairman of the Committee on Social Thought at the University of Chicago. Photo by Alfred Eisenstaedt.

novels. The intellectual discussions that go on in Herzog's mind, his unposted letters to politicians and philosophers alive and dead, illustrate a dilemma rather than present a point of view, whereas Mr. Sammler's reflections, as well as the conversation he has with the Indian scientist Dr. Lal, present a point of view, and the book concludes with an emphatic assertion by Sammler that man knows the terms of the unwritten contract with God that determine the conditions of his existence: "The terms which, in his inmost heart, each man knows. As I know mine. As all know. For that is the truth of it—that we all know, God, that we know, that we know, we know, we know." This is an unusual ending for a Bellow novel, for the author here is not exploring the different sides of a dilemma, which is what most of Bellow's fiction does, but concluding a symbolic story with an emphatic assertion of its meaning.

Ihab Hassan observed in his book *Radical Innocence* that the hero of the modern American novel could assume the role of a scapegoat, where irony borders on tragedy; or of the self-mocker, where irony, hovering between comedy and tragedy, may border on romance; or of the picaresque rogue and mocker, where the form is unabashed comedy. Bellow's novels tend to combine the first two of these prescriptions, with sometimes a dash of the third. His very first novel, *Dangling Man* (1944), is the diary of a man suspended between worlds as he awaits his call-up to the army. The diarist is a Jew, but it is his position as a searcher for identity in the vacuum between the world of daily business and the as yet unknown world of military life, a searcher who discovers the difficulty of managing his freedom, that reveals him as acting out the role of the emancipated Jew in the modern world rather than any actual facts about his Jewish background. He is both a scapegoat and a self-mocker and, like so many of Bellow's heroes, most of all a searcher. *The Victim* (1947) comes more clearly into Hassan's second category: it is the story of Asa Leventhal, a moderately prosperous Jewish businessman, accosted and taken over by the failed anti-Semitic gentile Kirby Allbee, who preposterously sees Leventhal as the true author of his (Allbee's) misfortunes: the process forces on Leventhal a nightmare of reconsideration of problems of identity and relationship, conducted under the daily physical pressure of bruising daily life in New York City. The process is presented as educational both for him and for the reader. *Seize the Day* (1956) comes after *Augie March:* it is a short novella, presenting the reactions of Tommy Wilhelm to his failure, frustration, victimization, and humiliation on the marital, financial, and professional levels and the consequent processes of agonized reflection, to the climax where, by identifying himself in a funeral parlor with an unknown dead Jew, he achieves some kind of redemptive sorrow. (The structure, though not the details, of the novel has been compared to Philip Roth's short story "Eli the Fanatic," where an assimilated Jew in a wealthy suburb assuages the guilt he feels as a result of having repudiated the habits of traditional Jews by assuming the dress and bearing of an ultra-orthodox Jewish immigrant—and is then deemed mad by his fellow-citizens. But Roth's story hovers uneasily between documentary and parable, while Bellow's has a symbolic penetration of a deeper kind.) Henderson is both scapegoat, self-mocker, and picaresque adventurer, and again a seeker, while Mr. Sammler is the victim and survivor engaged in ironic redefinition of his ideas in the face of a new world.

The dimension of symbolic exploration, of continuous seeking for meaning, is characteristic of Bellow and differentiates his work sharply from that of Babel, in spite of important elements shared by both writers. Babel's early hero was Maupassant; Bellow's, it seems, was Kafka. Babel's intention was to present in as lucid, precise, sharply etched a manner as possible, in a Russian prose in which there was not a superfluous word and every phrase carried maximum weight, a documentation of situations he knew about, which became more than a documentation in virtue of the power of the style. Bellow, one might perhaps say, is primarily interested in recasting a character such as the K. of Kafka's novel *The Castle* in the rich social landscape of the America he knows (and, once only, in a symbolic African landscape) and in providing that character not only with a fully realized environment but also with an active and well-stocked mind that enables him to reflect continuously on the symbolic significance of his own destiny. It is a remarkably ambitious program, and the most remarkable thing of all is that he has carried it out so well.

Twentieth-Century Physics

Sir Rudolf Peierls

In any recent list of distinguished scientists, Jewish names are far more prominent than would correspond to the number of Jews in the general population. However, this trend shows striking variations with the subject, the period, and the country. In this article, which is concerned with physics, of which I have some knowledge, I shall not attempt to analyze this phenomenon, which poses an interesting challenge to the social scientist, and even less attempt to find the causes, but confine myself to describing some typical cases and to commenting on the variations.

The outstanding example is, of course, Albert Einstein (1879–1955), the most famous scientist of our century. His name is widely known among more or less educated people, who usually have not the least idea of the nature of his work. This has even proved very convenient to physicists like myself when asked in social contact to explain one's profession. The occasion usually does not warrant a dissertation on the nature of physics; the answer "Einstein was a theoretical physicist" generally satisfies, even if it does not enlighten, the questioner.

What is, then, in simple language, the basis for Einstein's fame?

The theory of relativity, which bears his name, was the first of two major revolutions in the basic concepts of our understanding of nature that helped the twentieth-century scientist to deal with questions his predecessors were unable to answer and sometimes were even unable to ask.

The difficulties that required the first revolution had arisen from the problem of the relation of light to moving bodies. The laws of motion had been settled since the work of Galileo and Newton in the seventeenth century, and in the nineteenth century the studies of Michael Faraday, James Clerk Maxwell, and others had led to a full description of electricity and magnetism and had shown that light consisted of electromagnetic waves. These were at first thought to propagate in a hypothetical medium, the "ether," and this suggested the possibility of finding out whether we were standing still in space or moving. If the earth was moving through the ether, so that the ether appeared to be streaming past, light would appear to travel a little faster "downstream," with the ether, than "upstream," against the ether flow. This possibility aroused much interest, because until then there was no way of telling a state of rest from that of steady motion. (In a fast plane, for example, in steady air, we are not aware of moving, and there is nothing to show us the high speed with which we are going around the axis of the earth and the earth around the sun.) This was a general feature of the laws of nature, except, it seemed, for light.

When the test of this possibility showed that the expected difference in the speed of light did not exist, and that nature seemed to have conspired here, too, to prevent our telling motion from rest, one

295

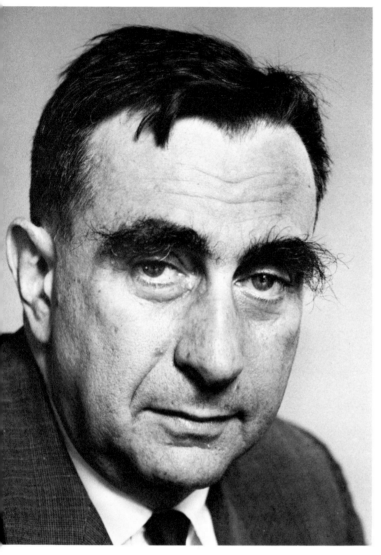

faced a contradiction. Other great thinkers, such as H. A. Lorentz in Holland and Henri Poincaré in France, came close to the answer. But it was Einstein who came to the conclusion that we had to revise our ideas about space and time, and that, in particular, it was not possible to say which of two events taking place a large distance from each other was earlier or later—the answer might depend on how fast the observer who was timing the events was moving. The possible ambiguity in time is very small, less than the time it takes light to get from the place of the one event to that of the other, and so for practical purposes this ambiguity can be ignored. No wonder, therefore, that our intuitive sense of time has not developed in a way that leaves room for this.

The new laws of motion that Einstein developed from this basic idea found immediate confirmation in new tests. For example, it was predicted that light should be deflected by the gravitational attraction of the sun, and that during an eclipse of the sun stars appearing very close to the darkened disk of the sun should appear to have shifted slightly from their normal positions, because the light from them had passed very close to the sun—and this prediction was confirmed.

Today these ideas of "relativity" firmly underlie all the physicist does. They matter particularly when motion at speeds close to that of light is involved. We can today accelerate electrons to speeds short of

Albert Einstein (1879–1955), born in Ulm, Germany, a Swiss citizen (1901) and a patent examiner in Berne for seven years. Ph.D., Zurich (1905), when he published five papers that revolutionized physics. Nobel Prize for physics in 1921. Escaped Hitler in 1933, abandoning a house given him by the grateful citizens of Germany. Became a U.S. citizen in 1940. Declined the Presidency of Israel in 1952. Throughout his life he developed and refined theories that were later proved to be fact. Photo by Alfred Eisenstaedt.

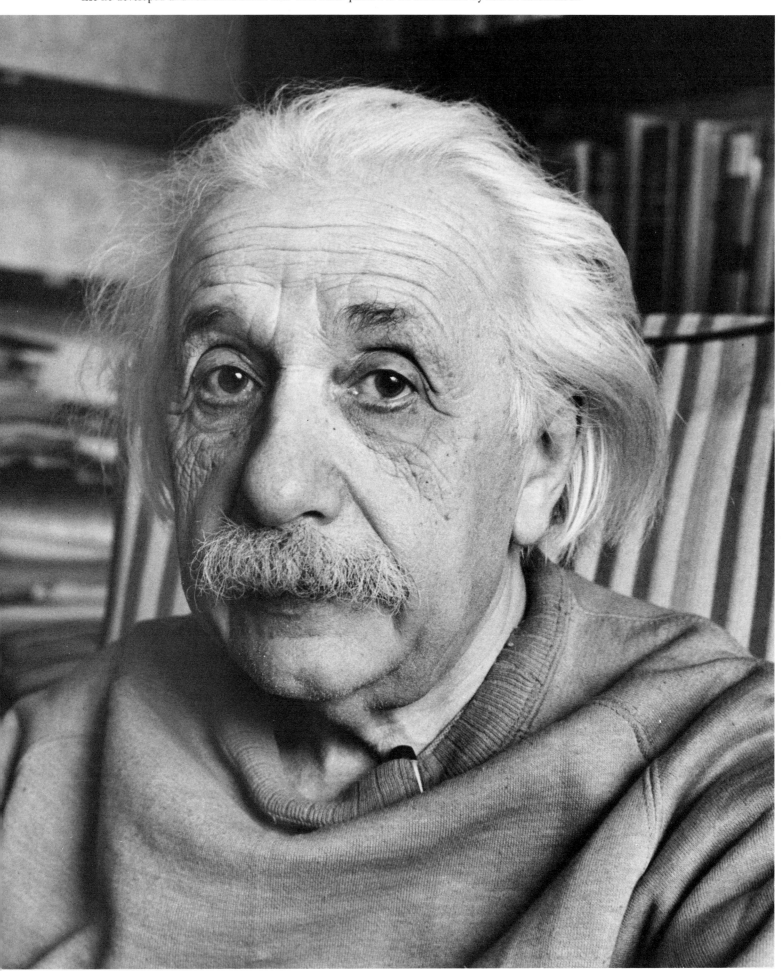

that of light by much less than one part in a million, and their behavior is then completely different from what it would be according to pre-Einstein ideas. There is, then, no room for doubt that Einstein was right.

What I have sketched is called the "special" theory of relativity as distinct from the "general" theory, which Einstein developed later and which deals with gravitation and with the possible structure of the universe. This is another great intellectual achievement, but its immediate consequences for the practical scientist are less important. Einstein also made important contributions to other areas of physics, including the second great revolution, to which I shall return.

It is not surprising that Albert Einstein is universally admired by scientists, but it is less easy to understand the extent of his fame among the general public. This may be due to a misunderstanding of the term "relativity," which may suggest an attitude of general skepticism or nihilism—"everything is relative." In fact, his contribution to science is the very opposite, in showing that the laws of nature have an absolute validity for observers in very different states of motion, provided the influence of their state of motion on their observation is duly taken into account.

Some philosophers objected to Einstein's theories because of this misunderstanding, and others because they felt they were the guardians of the basic ideas of space and time and could not allow a physicist to modify them. Nonetheless his fame was tremendous, and he was aware of this. He did not seek the publicity, but given that it existed, he felt it his duty to use the attention his words could command to support causes that seemed to him deserving.

Einstein was born in the small southern German town of Ulm in 1879 and grew up in Munich. His parents were not practicing Jews and did not observe any of the dietary or other restrictions. His interest in science was not stimulated by any parental influence or by school, where he resented the rigid discipline and was not an outstanding pupil. His first contact with mathematics and physics appears to have been through books chosen for him by a student who was a friend of the family. Even later he preferred his own reading to lectures and other instruction. His advice to others was often to study on their own. He never had any pupils in the usual sense, and few collaborators.

He was conscious of his dual background, as is evident in the famous answer he gave to a reporter who asked about his nationality. This was at the time of the first test of relativity during an eclipse. "If the test confirms my theory," he said, "the Germans will regard me as German, and the French as a Jew. If my theory is disproved, I shall be a Jew to the Germans, and a German to the French."

He was a convinced pacifist until the rise of Hitler and then changed his mind—fighting the evil of Nazism justified war. For this reason he agreed in 1939 to help persuade President Roosevelt to authorize research into the possibility of an atom bomb. It is sometimes said that the possibility of an atom bomb, of obtaining energy from nuclei, is a consequence of relativity, because of Einstein's conclusion that mass and energy are one and the same thing. This is misleading, since the loss of mass of the nuclei in the reaction is incidental.

If we ask how Einstein's work affects not only our intellectual heritage but our practical life, the answer must be found not in relativity but in his contributions to the quantum theory, which, by giving us a full understanding of the behavior of atoms, has led directly to many tangible products of technology, such as the transistor and the laser.

This brings us to the second revolution in physics. Relativity showed that our conventional concepts, based on our everyday experience, failed when we were dealing with very great speeds, up to the speed of light. The quantum theory, originally advanced by Max Planck, corrected a similar failure when dealing with very small objects, the size of atoms or less. This German theoretical physicist, in thinking about the behavior of radiation from hot bodies, which disagreed with what the laws of physics then said, was led to the unexpected idea that light, or other radiation, was not infinitely divisible but consisted of definite quanta. As the implications were studied, it became clear how profound a change this meant in our basic concepts, and Planck was reluctant to see such a drastic upheaval. He tried hard to minimize the consequences of his own idea. Einstein realized that the major upheaval could not be avoided and took the new ideas seriously. He drew conclusions that helped to show that the experiments of Arthur H. Compton in

298

America on the deflection of gamma rays in passing through matter gave further confirmation of the idea of light quanta.

It was the Danish physicist Niels Bohr (1885–1962) who took the next step in this development. Bohr was working in 1912 with Ernest (later Lord) Rutherford in Manchester. Rutherford had just discovered that the atom consisted of a positively charged nucleus surrounded by negatively charged electrons. Bohr succeeded in applying the new idea of quanta to the motion of the electrons, and this explained the spectral lines of atoms, in particular of hydrogen, which up to then had been mysteries.

In its original form Bohr's theory of the atom was, in spite of many successes, unsatisfactory in that it mixed old and new laws in a seemingly inconsistent and arbitrary manner. To some questions it gave manifestly wrong answers, and others it was unable to answer. Bohr realized all these difficulties clearly and worked hard to overcome them. The final step was taken in 1926–27, following two very different approaches: one started by Werner Heisenberg in Göttingen, the other by Erwin Schrödinger in Zurich, who used a brilliant but incomplete idea of Louis de Broglie, who was working in Paris. There was now a consistent set of laws, but their interpretation was not too clear.

Over the next few years Bohr took a strong lead in the discussion on the significance and interpretation of the new quantum mechanics. His Institute for Theoretical Physics in Copenhagen had become a center where the world's physicists came to learn and to expose their ideas to comments, particularly to those of Bohr. Unlike Einstein, Bohr tended to work with others, and his contribution to physics consisted in part of his influence on the thoughts of others. He was fluent in English and German as well as in Danish, but he used all these languages in a slightly personal way; one could always recognize that a colleague had spent a few months in Copenhagen by his having picked up some of Bohr's ways of speaking. Bohr's arguments and his papers were not easy to follow; as he himself explained, truth and clarity are complementary. He meant that if you want to speak clearly and simply you must oversimplify and what you say will not be quite correct. The closer you stick to the truth, the more complicated the statement that will emerge.

In this period he had many arguments with Einstein, who did not believe in the quantum theory, which he himself had helped to start, and always tried to disprove it. He believed that the right answer would ultimately be a "unified field theory," which for the rest of his life he attempted to construct, but in vain. Bohr enjoyed the challenge of Einstein's objections, and his refutations remain very instructive reading.

When in the mid-thirties it became possible to carry out experiments on the atomic nucleus, Bohr took a great interest in these problems and was responsible for understanding certain nuclear reactions whose explanation had been missed by everyone else. After the discovery of nuclear fission, he saw, working jointly with John Wheeler of Princeton, how to interpret this new phenomenon, and in a sense this paper paved the way for the work on the atom bomb.

After the Nazi occupation of Denmark, Bohr regarded it as his duty to remain and look after the members of his institute. But in 1943 the German command decided to arrest all Jews (this included Bohr, who was certainly a Jew in Hitler's definition, for his mother was Jewish; he was also known to be anti-Nazi). Fortunately the news leaked out, and all those to be arrested (except for a few bedridden people) fled to neutral Sweden. Bohr was flown to England and then joined the atomic-energy team in the United States. By then his main concern was the effect of atomic weapons on the postwar world, and he worked hard for an imaginative move toward an "Open World." He was able to talk to Roosevelt and Churchill; he did not have much effect on Roosevelt, and the interview with Churchill was an utter failure, because Bohr's way of expressing himself was quite incomprehensible to Churchill.

The distinction of Robert Oppenheimer (1904–1967) was of a rather different kind from that of Einstein and Bohr. He was born in New York City, where his father, who had immigrated from Germany, was a prosperous businessman. His parents were cultured people with a taste for art but no special interest in science. Though conscious of their Jewish background, they were not religious. Robert was a brilliant

BELOW: An international team of neurologists battled with limited success to save the mind of Lev Landau (1908–1968) after an automobile accident left him technically dead in 1962. In that same year he was awarded the Nobel Prize for his work on the behavior of helium at low temperatures. He was instrumental in the development of Russia's atomic bomb and of her earth satellites.

In exile from Germany for twenty years until his retirement in 1953, Max Born (1882–1970) shared the 1954 Nobel Prize for his fundamental research in quantum mechanics. Fourteen years after he received his doctorate at Göttingen, he was named head of its physics department, which, under his direction, rivaled that of Niels Bohr at Copenhagen. Elected to the Tait chair of natural philosophy at Edinburgh University, Born became a British subject in 1939. Photo by Ullstein.

After fleeing Nazi-occupied Denmark in a fishing boat, Niels Bohr (1885–1962) contributed much to the creation of the atomic bomb, begun at Columbia and Princeton before the war, but his contribution to twentieth-century physics centers in his development of the atomic theory for which he was awarded the Nobel Prize in 1922. His teaching and leadership at the University of Copenhagen influenced several generations of scientists.

A child prodigy, he earned his Ph.D. from Harvard at the age of eighteen. Norbert Wiener (1894–1964), of Columbia, Missouri, began a forty-year association with M.I.T. in 1919. His book *Cybernetics: or Control and Communication in the Animal and the Machine* (1948) reached both the scholarly and the lay audience and brought attention to this new field. During the war years he left his studies of Brownian movement and harmonic analysis to work on guided missiles and gunfire control. Photo by Alfred Eisenstaedt.

Biochemist Ernst Chain (1906–   ) shared the 1945 Nobel Prize for Physiology or Medicine for his work at Cambridge on isolating, purifying, and clinically testing penicillin. In 1948 he became scientific director of the International Research Center for Chemical Microbiology in Rome, but returned to England fifteen years later to direct the Laboratories of the Imperial College of Science and Technology at the University of London, which were established by Sir Isaac Wolfson. His mother and sister, who remained in Berlin after Chain's departure in 1933, died at the hands of the Nazis. Photo by Godfrey Argent.

OPPOSITE: The development in 1954 by Dr. Jonas Salk of an antipolio vaccine put an end to the epidemics of this disease that had for many years been a major crippler of children. Educated at New York's Townsend Harris High School, City College, and New York University Medical School, he became director of the Virus Research Laboratory of the University of Pittsburgh, where his major research took place. He is now married to Françoise Gilot, who has written about her life with Pablo Picasso.

student and completed the Harvard four-year course in three years, learning many subjects, including Sanskrit, besides his professional subject, theoretical physics. He spent his years of post-graduate study in Europe, where he took part in the work of consolidating the new quantum theory on the foundations laid by Heisenberg, Schrödinger, and others. On returning to America he settled in California. He divided his time between the University of California at Berkeley and the California Institute of Technology at Pasadena and continued actively in the front line of the development of theoretical physics. He attracted a large number of students and became one of the great teachers of the subject.

One of his great qualities was his quick understanding; in talking with him one hardly ever needed to complete a sentence, because halfway through he knew what you were saying and was ready with his comment. Another was his ability to find the right word, to sum up a scientific or a human situation perceptively and clearly. He was perhaps the most articulate of physicists.

At the beginning of the war, when many started speculating whether the newly discovered phenomenon of fission could be used to make an atom bomb, he was one of the first to appreciate clearly the essence of the problem. He was put in charge of the theoretical work on the way the bomb would function, and he later built up and directed the Los Alamos Laboratory, which was to design, make, and test the first bombs from the materials produced in the large plants built elsewhere. It was an unusual idea to put a theoretician—and a rather highbrow and seemingly impractical one at that—in charge of a laboratory that had to get results in a hurry, but he was outstanding as director. His quick mind and clear perception helped in that, and so did his capacity for finding the right word.

After the war he was much in demand as adviser on many military matters. In 1947 he became the director of the Institute for Advanced Study at Princeton, where he did no more active research himself but still had a profound influence on physics. He remained conscious of his responsibility for the atom bomb and for the death and destruction it had brought—he had been a member of a committee that in 1945 agreed to, or at least acquiesced in, the decision to drop the bomb on Japan.

When in 1949 it was proposed to start a crash program to develop a hydrogen bomb, Oppenheimer opposed this, partly for technical and partly for moral reasons. Soon he was accused of disloyalty—for having been sympathetic to communism in the 1930s. This became a *cause célèbre*, and he was judged unreliable and barred from access to secret information. This was in the witch-hunting days of Senator Joseph McCarthy in the 1950s. When by the early 1960s some sanity had returned, some amends were made. Oppenheimer was awarded one of the nation's highest honors, the Enrico Fermi Award.

Lev Davidovich Landau (1908–1968) was the greatest Russian theoretical physicist. He grew up in Baku, where his father was an engineer in the oil industry. His high ability in mathematics and science showed very early. He completed the undergraduate course in physics at the University of Leningrad in 1927 at the age of eighteen. This was the time of the rapid growth of the new quantum mechanics, and Landau was at once at home with it. His way of studying new material was to look at an important paper

briefly, to get a general idea of the author's aim and method, and then work out the results for himself. He rapidly developed a very deep understanding of all aspects of physics.

After finishing his research training under Yakov Illich Frenkel, a man of great versatility and originality, Landau spent two years abroad, working particularly with Wolfgang Pauli in Zurich and Bohr in Copenhagen. By this time he had already gained attention as a result of a number of papers, of which the most important was his explanation of the diamagnetism of metals, where he resolved very simply an old problem that had puzzled many. After his return to the Soviet Union he continued to tackle problems of fundamental importance, ranging from the internal structure of stars to collisions of atoms in gases, from cosmic radiation to the strange behavior of liquid helium at very low temperatures. His theory of the "superfluidity" of liquid helium was cited when he was awarded the Nobel Prize in 1962, but it must have been hard to choose from among his many important ideas the one to single out for this purpose.

He was a brilliant if demanding teacher, and most of the best theoretical physicists of the Soviet Union are his pupils. He was extremely critical of unsound or careless arguments, but he was guided more by physical intuition than by mathematical rigor. He could be very scathing to unfortunate colleagues who did not accept his intuitive insight and demanded proof. He had equally strong views, equally hotly defended, on many subjects outside physics, including poetry, ethics, and human relations. As a young man he had theories—developed quite as seriously as his physical theories—about what a satisfactory relation between man and woman should be, and he patiently but firmly explained to many acquaintances nearly twice his age that their particular marriage did not measure up to this standard and should they not get a divorce?

Politically he was for the revolution and regarded the capitalist society of the West as rather stupid, particularly the British monarchy. But he did get incensed at many features of the late Stalin era—he himself had to spend a year or so in jail. He was violently against religion, Jewish or any other.

In 1962 Landau was severely injured in a car accident, and in hospital he was several times pronounced clinically dead. He made a partial recovery as a result of intense efforts by medical teams supported and urged on by numerous pupils and colleagues who volunteered their services to run errands, solicit special drugs from friends abroad, and help in any other possible way. However, he never recovered his intellectual powers, and he remained an invalid until his death in 1968.

The four men sketched so far were all theoreticians, and it is probably true that the weight of Jewish contributions has been greater to theoretical than to experimental physics. But there were also great Jews on the experimental side. Heinrich Hertz, who was born in Hamburg in 1857 and died in 1894, was impressed by the ideas of Maxwell, who had succeeded in combining all known facts about electricity and magnetism into one consistent set of laws (the "Maxwell equations"). This predicted the existence of electromagnetic waves—today called radio waves.

While many physicists still had doubts about Maxwell's ideas, Hertz was convinced of their truth and set out to produce the predicted waves and to demonstrate their existence. He succeeded; he was able to transmit signals over a distance of some sixty feet. He used this discovery to study the nature of these waves, but it was left to others to develop this phenomenon into a means of communication. Thus the name of Maxwell, who predicted, and that of Hertz, who discovered, the waves, tend to be forgotten by the general public; one chiefly remembers Marconi, who pioneered the practical application.

Hertz would undoubtedly have received the Nobel Prize if it had existed in his time. The list of Nobel Laureates in physics includes James Franck (1882–1964), who was a professor at Göttingen until Hitler came to power. His greatest piece of work, done jointly with Gustav Hertz, was the discovery that, in collisions of electrons with atoms, the electrons lose energy only in definite amounts, equal to the amounts of energy the atom in question can receive according to the Bohr theory. At a time when the Bohr theory was still in an unsatisfactory state and physicists were groping for a more consistent description, this discovery was of great importance in demonstrating that some detailed parts of the theory were indeed right, and therefore helped to channel the further discussion along more definite paths.

In 1933 Franck left his chair in Göttingen, before he was dismissed (which undoubtedly he would have been), and settled at Johns Hopkins University. He later joined the atomic-energy project, of which he was a valuable member. He is remembered particularly for the "Franck report," a document written by scientists under his chairmanship that urged strongly that the atom bomb not be used. The effort failed, but it is characteristic of the spirit of Franck, who was not only a great physicist but a person who had won the affection of all who knew him.

We should remember Otto Stern (1888–1969), who won the Nobel Prize in 1943 for his invention of the atomic-beam technique, by which he and Walther Gerlach were able to follow the behavior of single atoms in magnetic fields. This again confirmed some predictions of the Bohr theory, and at the same time raised, as a challenge to the theoreticians, questions that the Bohr theory was not able to answer consistently.

This is a small sample of a long list of physicists of Jewish extraction. I have tried to detect common characteristics among them. Not of course in the substance of their physics—the idea of "Jewish physics" or "German physics" is safely buried in the ruins of the Nazi ideology—but there is a personal style in one's work—the kind of problems a scientist selects, the boldness with which he tries new ideas, the way he works with his colleagues or his pupils. In this the Jewish scientists seem to be all different; the range of styles seems to me to be as wide as among all physicists.

The interesting general point is that already mentioned at the beginning: the surprisingly large number of Jews among the leading physicists. A closer look shows that this strength is not uniform. There is little of it in the nineteenth century, where few examples come to mind apart from Heinrich Hertz and H. Rubens (1865–1922), who, in Berlin, did important work in optics. The other surprising observation is the enormous variation from country to country. The abundance of Jews among the physicists of Germany (before 1933), of Russia, and of the United States, particularly since the 1930s, is as clear from a casual glance at any list, as the relative scarcity in Britain, France, or Italy. Any such comparison should of course exclude immigrants, at least those who moved as mature and established scientists, since the exodus of refugees from Germany and Austria added numerous Jews to the ranks of scientists, particularly in Britain and the United States. To be sure, there are eminent Jewish physicists in England, including the latest Nobel Laureate, Brian Josephson, but their proportion among physicists is hardly greater than that of Jews in the general population.

What could be the reasons for the prominence of Jews in science, and in particular in physics? The suggestion has been made that the intricate arguments of modern physics have some resemblance to Talmudic studies, and that people who grow up in an environment in which such studies are traditional find this mode of thought natural. However, quite apart from the question of how real or deep is such a resemblance, one notices that a large proportion of twentieth-century Jewish physicists came from families in which religious customs have not been observed for generations. Perhaps this attitude was bred by a kind of natural selection, since it was for so many generations a cause of pride for a family if a daughter married a learned scholar. One could judge his hypothesis better if more were known about the genetic character of intellectual traits. It sounds just possible, but a little farfetched.

What could be reasons for the great differences between countries? It is not very likely that some subtle selection factor might be at work which would result in a different incidence of the ability needed to be good at science. It is more likely that the other requirements, motivation and opportunity, particularly educational opportunity, which do depend on the environment, might be responsible.

Getting to the right school or the right university can be an important condition for getting the right start in science (much less important for an Einstein than for lesser men), and in England and France the "pecking order" of schools and universities is strong and was even more pronounced one or two generations ago. The selection process for getting into the right channel could conceivably act against Jewish students, even in the absence of any actual discrimination.

But that is speculation without evidence. As a scientist I prefer to register the interesting phenomenon and to admit that I am unable to offer an explanation.

The Composer

Peter Stadlen

We shall probably never find out exactly what the music was like that David played for Saul, though its powers as an antidepressant with which to dispel the king's melancholy moods are firmly documented. It is, moreover, unlikely to have been more complex than, say, the chanting Aeschylus devised for his chorus, and what can one expect of a music—hours of it, punctuating Attic drama or religious services in Jerusalem—which a group of singers was able to memorize even though it had to be conveyed virtually without the help of script? This is not to make light of the fact that the seamless transition, via the synagogues, from Biblical to early Christian chant marks one of the two points in history when Jewish music was the sole begetter of fundamental developments in gentile music.

Sporadic discouragement by the rabbinical authorities of secular as well as sacred music-making —considered unseemly for a people who had suffered the loss of their Temple—may partly explain why medieval Jews played no part during the crucial stages in the evolution of musical notation: by the mid-thirteenth century the same symbol indicated both the duration and the pitch of a note—musical man's most formidable intellectual achievement and a condition for the emergence of controlled polyphony, and thus, in due course, of the discovery (no less) of tonality and key feeling. Not until 1343 do we find one Levi ben Gershom making a substantial contribution to the rhythmic innovations of Philippe de Vitry's *Ars Nova*, with a treatise "De Numeris Harmonicis," written at the invitation of that renowned bishop-composer.

As for active musical life in the Diaspora, Jewish communities throughout the Middle Ages tended to absorb features of their hosts' musical idioms, while prevailing hazards of hostility determined the extent of Jewish participation in Christian music-making—not easily ascertained where the Jewishness of a jongleur or a fiddler or minstrel has to be deduced from his name: a host of Eliases, Charlot le Juif, and Suesskind of Trimberg, recently doubted but happily restored to the fold by further research; and even so, one needs to consider the possibility of a conversion or, poignantly, the certainty of it in the case of Israel le Bienheureux.

It is worth noting that the most celebrated figure to have emerged from one of the later spells of localized liberalism, the Mantuan court composer Salomone Rossi (1570–1628), who called himself "Ebreo," wrote madrigals in a style that is indistinguishable from Marenzio's or Monteverdi's, as are the equally polyphonic settings of psalms, hymns, and prayers with which he tried, in vain, to replace the time-hallowed cantillations in the synagogue.

A general thaw that set in toward the late eighteenth century—Joseph II's Edict of Toleration of 1782 in Austria, the emancipation of Jews decreed by the French Revolution in 1790 and 1791, and, most relevant in the present context, the respect earned among Prussia's educated classes by the philosopher Moses Mendelssohn—created the conditions for the global fame achieved by two Jewish musicians, both born into cultured Berlin banking families and thus benefiting from first-rate training and a full participation in the age's awareness of a glorious past and of a present that included Rossini as well as Beethoven. As early as 1831, after the Paris première of *Robert le Diable*, no less a critic than François-Joseph Fétis proclaimed Giacomo Meyerbeer (1791–1864) to be the indisputable leader of German music—somewhat ironically in view of a fatherland that took careful note of the adherence to his ancient faith of this chief exponent of French grand opera. Felix Mendelssohn (1809–1847), acclaimed as the greatest musician of the century on the occasion of the première of his oratorio *Elijah* in 1846, was a profoundly committed Protestant—without any trace of the opportunism his father, Abraham, had professed on having his infant children baptized—except that one does perhaps sense a faint theological glee to be on to the best religion of all: in marked contrast to grandpa Moses' concept, revolutionary at the time and dramatized by his friend Lessing in the play *Nathan the Wise*, that all three religions represented equivalent variations on one true theme. Felix's unflinching loyalty to his Jewish origins, on the other hand, would prompt stern rebukes of his sister Fanny's sneers on encountering unassimilated Jews.

The legal and social setbacks suffered by emancipation on and off throughout the century are dwarfed by the philosophical stance adopted by Richard Wagner in an article published in 1850 under a pseudonym and entitled "Judaism in Music." It shows him as the true founding father of Nazism, with Hitler a mere epigone, and the same is true of his essays "Know Thyself" and "The Heroic and Christianity" of 1881 (so much for the attempts to shrug off the 1850 essay as merely due to a young composer's frustration after some harsh and unsuccessful years in Paris). In these he recommends deportation of the Jews ("Well done, Kiev!") and generally applauds, in the wake of Gobineau, the domination of inferior by superior races, an arrangement, we may add, that is symbolized by Siegfried's outrageous behavior toward the misshapen Mime, his benefactor for all he knows.

Wagner, taking for granted the people's agreement with his own crudely professed revulsion at the sight of all things Jewish, makes the more specifically musical point that the Jews, since they speak their hosts' language with a foreign accent, are necessarily affected with the same disability when trying their hand at musical composition. It does not appear to have occurred to him that in such a case *Figaro* and *Don Giovanni* may be marred by what must have been an atrocious Austrian accent when Mozart tried to speak Italian.

The syntactic and grammatical peculiarities that Wagner castigates—without of course being aware of research that has meanwhile established the characteristic restriction, in Yiddish, of the genitive to its function as a possessive, or the elimination of the accusative after prepositions—are too obviously incapable of being reflected in music. But the intonational resources of a sound system—known as *jüdeln* in German (there is no English equivalent)—where semantic distinctions may be conveyed by melodic modulation, have in fact been portrayed good-humoredly, and perhaps affectionately, by Musorgski in *Pictures at an Exhibition*. Yet who would care to try and trace either "Samuel Goldenberg" or "Schmuyle" in Mendelssohn where he is his post-classical self: the strictly copyright fairy forest of the Octet, the Piano Capriccios, the *Midsummer Night's Dream* Overture, or even in the Violin Concerto's romantic exuberance, which he shares with Schumann, with Weber, and indeed with the Wagner of at least the early opera *Die Feen*. In fact his music could not differ more drastically from that of Meyerbeer, which has a good deal in common not only with the spirited anti-pogrom opera *La Juive* (1834) by Jacques Halévy, also a Jew, but with their common ancestors in French and Italian grand opera. Yet both Mendelssohn and Meyerbeer are singled out for the charge of triviality and coldness, Jewish characteristics according to Wagner, who forgot to include in his *Collected Writings* the rave notice of *Le Prophète* he had sent from Paris in 1841 to the *Dresdener Abendzeitung*; Thomas Mann, on the other hand, attributed a touch of sensuality in Wagner's own music to his hero's Jewish blood, at a time when the Jewishness of Wagner's presumed natural father, Ludwig Geyer, had not yet been definitely disproved.

The shallowness of the music produced by freshly emancipated Jews is not to be wondered at, says the philosopher-critic Bryan Magee, who, notwithstanding his pronounced admiration for Jewish achievement, has recently spied a healthy babe in Wagner's foul bathwater. Given their rootlessness in the society they found themselves in, how could Jews be expected to articulate its past and present fantasies, aspirations, needs, and conflicts? Now the belief that mnemic engrams and other acquired characteristics are passed on is liable to be exploited not only by Nazis but, from different motives, by Communist regimes when they justify their insistence on simplist art by alleging the inability of the working-class to catch up in the course of one generation. As far as music is concerned, the myth is currently being exploded, not, admittedly, in the field of composition, which is by now far too internationally nondescript to qualify, but through the idiomatic purity of style shown by non-European newcomers to musical interpretation.

As for Wagner's seemingly more reasonable claim that a composer whose early habitat has been the synagogue with its cantillations is thereby cut off from the popular song and dance on which a nation's art music inevitably feeds, this is based on the still widespread fallacy that the classics' inclusion of an

BELOW: In his fifty-one years Gustav Mahler (1860–1911) composed ten symphonies, a number of song cycles, including *Das Lied von der Erde*, and much other music while serving as artistic director of the Vienna Court Opera for ten years, and as conductor of the Philharmonic Society of New York for three years. The torment in his music reflects the torments of his youth as a Jewish German-speaking Austrian living among the Czech population of Bohemia, one of eleven unhealthy children witnessing physical conflicts between his robust tavern-keeper father and delicate, socially superior mother.

ABOVE: Jakob Ludwig Felix Mendelssohn (1809–1847) added Bartholdy to his name on conversion to Christianity, an integration beyond that advocated and foreseen by his philosopher grandfather Moses. He died as a result of overwork shortly after the death of his sister Fanny, but in his thirty-eight years he performed as a concert pianist and conductor throughout Europe, served as a musical director in Düsseldorf, Leipzig, and Berlin, and wrote five symphonies, three concertos, a number of choral works, including two oratorios, and many other compositions.

310

His opera *Tales of Hoffmann* and his music for the ballet *Gaîté Parisienne*, along with the operettas *La Périchole* and *Orpheus in the Underworld*, continue to delight music lovers. Jacques (originally Jacob) Offenbach (1819–1880) was the son of Isaac Juda Eberst, a cantor at the Cologne Synagogue, who had been born at Offenbach am Main. Moving to Paris, Jacques studied the cello at the Conservatoire, became a conductor at the Théâtre Français, and at the age of thirty-six opened his own theater. He wrote more than a hundred works for the stage.

occasional minuet or waltz implies the relevance of folklore to the substance of their music. Moreover, while mindful of the important part played by the dance suite of the Baroque period in the evolution of large-scale instrumental forms, one would perhaps hesitate to say that Bach's allemandes are both better and more truly German than his gigues or sarabandes. National musical characteristics derive less than is commonly held from landscapes and genes than from the politically conditioned or merely chance accumulation of skills and styles that are available for study by the professionals of a given region. That Mendelssohn presumably never set foot in a synagogue, while Meyerbeer may well have done, is neither here nor there. What matters particularly in an art like music, which is not concerned with milieu, is that when they were boys they became at least as conversant with the classical heritage and with Italian and French opera as did little Wagner. If Mendelssohn, and even more so Meyerbeer, lacked profundity, this is a weakness that most Jews share with most gentiles.

Both sides would no doubt agree that there is such a thing as Jewish humor, however elusive may be the distinction between this particular brand and all others. But it is as well to realize that Jacques Offenbach's proverbial powers of satire reside exclusively in the link-up with the immortal feats of persiflage performed by his librettist Ludovic Halévy, nephew of the composer. Autonomously witty music is restricted to rare instances of self-persiflage: when the unwieldy double bass is made to compete with

311

ABOVE: A memorable trio of three Russian artists. The violinist, Nathan Milstein, first met the pianist, Vladimir Horowitz, in Kiev in 1917 when each was thirteen years old, and they became close friends, occasionally touring together. Gregor Piatigorsky, the cellist, joined them in the United States, where the three eventually settled, Piatigorsky having married the daughter of Baron Edouard de Rothschild and Horowitz the daughter of Arturo Toscanini. Photo by Alfred Eisenstaedt.

LEFT: Ruvin Heifetz unwillingly enrolled at the St. Petersburg Conservatory, for only as students were Jews permitted in the Czar's city. In fact, he was there to accompany his nine-year-old son Jascha, who, after studying at the Conservatory with Leopold Auer, made his first European tour in 1914, and two years later, at sixteen, made his famous New York debut. Considered since then the finest violinist in the world, he is pictured playing his first concert in Israel.

more agile instruments in Stravinsky's *Pulcinella,* or when shortwinded quotes from Schubert's "Marche Militaire" strike one as funny in Stravinsky's "Circus Polka," even without its dedication to a young elephant. The music of Offenbach (1819–1880), on its own, is merely gay and *vif,* as Verdi's would be without the sight of Falstaff's embonpoint, and not too dissimilar to the waltzes, polkas, and marches by Johann Strauss *père et fils,* those sons of the people. In fact, however, the Nazis' ultimate unconditional surrender has recently come to light in the form of evidence showing that the Reichssippenamt removed a page from the register of St. Stephen's Cathedral in Vienna in order to replace it with a photostat, where the entry of Strauss *grandpère's* baptism, at a ripe age, has been carefully covered up.

"To think that a comedian and a Jew-boy restored to the world the greatest Christian music": Mendelssohn's celebrated remark to his actor friend Edward Devrient while they were preparing the first performance since Bach's death of the *St. Matthew Passion*—considered on various grounds unperformable by Mendelssohn's teacher Zelter, Goethe's friend, who possessed the autograph—has been taken to stem from a wish to be *plus allemand que les allemands.* The towering stature of the work obviates such speculation; but these may not be altogether unfounded in the case of Gustav Mahler (1860–1911), who felt irresistibly drawn to German folk song—twenty-six settings out of sixty-four he acomplished are of poems taken from *Des Knaben Wunderhorn,* a severely doctored collection published by Arnim and Brentano in 1806, while a further five were written by the composer himself in the same artificial vein. But if the Romantic writers, in a period of national stress, had feigned primitivity in order to inject the fatherland with a new invigorating awareness of its past, now, three-quarters of a century later, a Jewish music student in his twenties, who had arrived in Vienna as a boy from a provincial town in Bohemia, may well have been driven by an instinctive desire to identify more closely with "the people." The price he was eager to pay

312

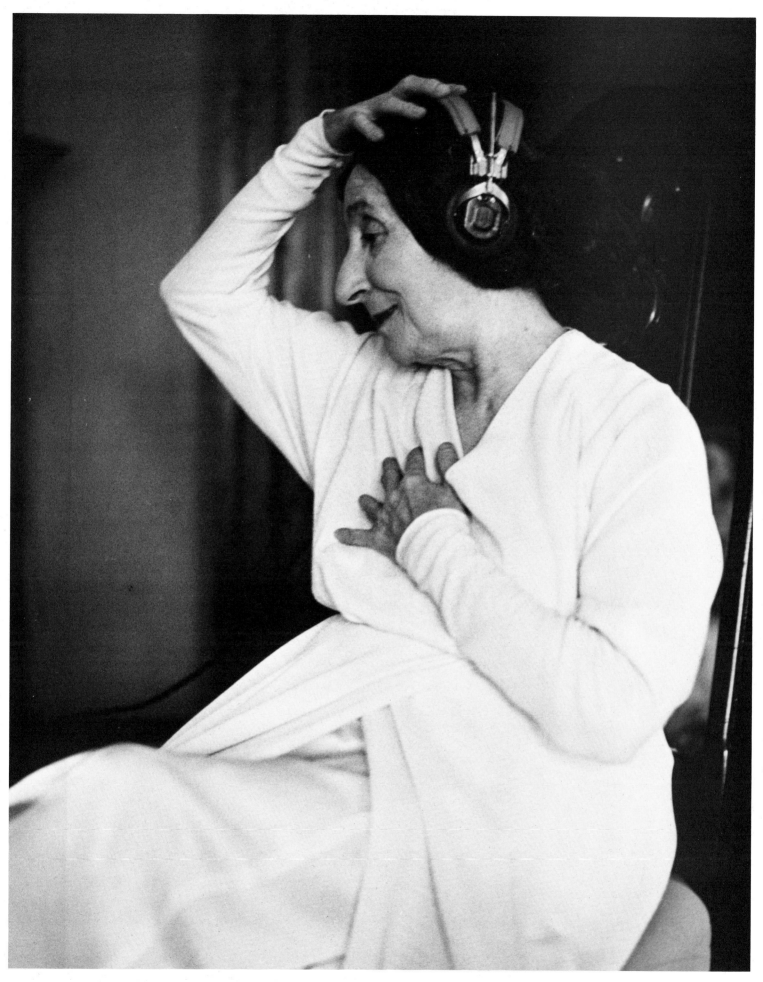

Interest in the harpsichord was reborn in 1912 when Wanda Landowska (1879–1959) commissioned Pleyel to build a reproduction of the eighteenth-century instrument. From then on, her concerts, her teaching in Berlin, in Paris, from which she fled in 1941, and in the United States, and her many records, including Bach's complete Well-Tempered Clavichord, led to the revival of interest in music of the past.

RUBINSTEIN
L'AMOUR
DE LA VIE

filmé par
François Reichenbach

filmé p

OPPOSITE: A connoisseur of life, Artur Rubinstein always seems to take as much pleasure from his audience as he gives. In his autobiography *My Young Years* he detailed his boyhood in Lodz, Poland, his training in Berlin, and his successes with the piano and with women. At the beginning of World War II he moved from France to Beverly Hills, California (his thirty-second home). Now in his eighties, Rubinstein continues to give concerts throughout the world, many of them for the benefit of charity.

The Austrian cellist Emanuel Feuermann developed from a child prodigy to one of the world's leading musicians. He settled in the United States and died in 1942 in his fortieth year, his legacy a relatively few magnificent recordings. He is pictured here with his daughter, Monica.

In 1933 the German authorities banned his concerts for threatening public order, so Bruno Walter (Schlesinger) devoted the remaining twenty-nine years of his life to conducting orchestras throughout the rest of the world, including the New York and Boston symphony orchestras and the Metropolitan Opera. Born in Berlin in 1876, son of a poor shopkeeper, he worked with Mahler for ten years at the Vienna Imperial Opera and for another ten years led the Munich Opera from which, as a result of pre-Hitler anti-Semitism, he was driven in 1923. Photo by Dennis Stock.

LEFT: Now a resident of England, Vladimir Ashkenazy was born in Gorki, U.S.S.R., in 1937; both his parents were pianists. In 1955 he placed second in the International Chopin Competition in Warsaw, the following year first in the Queen Elizabeth Competition in Belgium, and six years later shared first in the International Tchaikovsky Piano Competition in Moscow. He left Russia, for marital, not political, reasons—his wife a British-bred pianist whom he had met at the Tchaikovsky competition—and he continues to tour his homeland. Photo by Clive Barda.

BELOW: In 1937 he won international recognition and first prize in the Eugene Ysaye competition in Brussels; in 1942 he became a full professor at the Moscow Conservatory, joined the Communist Party, and won the Stalin Prize, the highest recognition of merit in the Soviet Union. David Oistrakh, born in Odessa in 1908, was one of the first Russian artists following World War II to tour Western Europe and the United States.

ABOVE: Trained on the clarinet at Chicago's Kehelah Jacob Synagogue, Benny Goodman became both a jazz and a classical musician. In the former role he developed a band that was the most popular in America in the late 1930s and the 1940s (alumni included Teddy Wilson, Harry James, Gene Krupa). In the latter role he was a soloist with major symphony orchestras (New York, Philadelphia, London) and chamber-music groups. He played in movies—*Big Broadcast of 1938, Stage Door Canteen, Make Mine Music*—and a movie was made of his life, *The Benny Goodman Story* (1956). Photo by Robin Douglas-Home.

was a descent from the intellectual ivory tower, and not only through his self-conscious flirting with German literary lore: if his near-contemporary Anton Dvořák would incorporate Slavonic musical heritage with such sophistication as he could muster, while Béla Bartók collected Hungarian folk songs like stamps or butterflies only to comment on these melodies with relentless twentieth-century acerbity, Mahler, in his settings as well as in many a coy instrumental piece, did not *quote* German folk songs but provided imitations. He *was* the folk, most charmingly so in the Fourth Symphony, but it is surely no coincidence that his miniature yet distinctive lyrical gifts found most memorable expression in the politically neutral selection from Hans Bethge's translation of ancient Chinese poetry in *Das Lied von der Erde*.

On the other hand, Mahler's reckless disregard, in his vast symphonic canvases, for the economics of aesthetics differs from Schubert's or Bruckner's being tempted by the magnitude of some strictly musical thought to undertake correspondingly large-scale forms that they lacked the skill to master, and differs equally from Mendelssohn's polishing to perfection large structures that are not vindicated by the needs of his material. When one considers Mahler's steep, transcendental aspirations in the Nietzsche settings of the Third Symphony or, in the Eighth, of the closing scene from Goethe's *Faust* and of the medieval hymn "Veni, Creator Spiritus" (revealing a complex attitude in one who professed to an inability to set the Credo of the mass), one may suspect an element of overcompensation for the catastrophically under-privileged position Mahler never ceased to be conscious of: even after his conversion to Roman Catholicism, a condition for his appointment to the directorship of the Vienna Court Opera (1897), he would liken the handicap of Jewishness to being born with a physical deformity, and he admitted that one needs to forget Wagner's writings before one can begin to admire his music.

As for Mahler's unbounded super-schemes, they would never have come into being without a measure of naïveté that enabled him to ride roughshod over the elemental need, in all art, for sublimation. If Beethoven (according to his factotum Schindler) likened the start of the Fifth Symphony to Fate knocking at the door, Mahler, in the score of his Sixth, prescribes three blows to be struck with an actual mammoth hammer. The slice-of-life operations, with offstage marching, post-horn calls, and alpine cowbells, constitute the composer's sole radiation into posterity: many a page in Shostakovich used to be mistaken for party poster music until the Soviet master revealed his allegiance to Mahler.

It was Alban Berg and Anton von Webern who achieved the total integration of such acoustical *objets trouvés* into the fabric of a work: the military band marching across the stage, led by the drum major, Wozzeck's superior and rival, or the low-toned bell-like sounds that intermingle with tam-tam and drum rolls to form a murmuring cushion throughout the fourth of Webern's Orchestral Pieces op. 6. And little wonder, for, unlike Mahler, who was virtually an autodidact, Berg and Webern, in their formative years, were subjected to the rigorous discipline of Arnold Schönberg (1873–1951).

No one musician has ever influenced the course of events to any comparable degree. Here, indeed, we are faced with the other instance—more crucial than the passing on of plain chant—where gentile music —or, as we may happily say now, Western music—was decisively influenced not so much by Jewish music as by the music of a Jew.

First, Schönberg's atonality—to be defined in the present context (as distinct from pre-tonality) as composition without consonance and without reference to key feeling: it would never have come to stay as a condition of twentieth-century radicalism but for Schönberg's professional prestige; no notice would have been taken of the amateurish attempts at such a breakthrough by the American Charles Ives or by the Austrian Josef Matthias Hauer. Yet Schönberg's authority did not ultimately derive from his search for theoretical vindications of a step that he himself described as "the violation of all boundaries of a bygone aesthetic." For all the mystique that surrounded his "Treatise of Harmony" at the time (1911), one is reminded of the facile epigram in vogue among the intellectuals, many of them Jews, frequenting Vienna's coffee houses, when Schönberg justifies the emancipation of the dissonance by denying any basic difference in kind between consonances and dissonances. These, he says, are merely located on a more distant point on a fundamental overtone series. This is not only factually incorrect—no one appears to have pointed out to him that the dissonant major second, overtone No. 9, and major seventh, No. 15, come before the extremely consonant third octave, No. 16—but amounts to denying the difference between the top and the bottom of the form on the grounds that there are plenty of boys forming a transition.

What rendered atonality respectable was the strength of Schönberg's early atonal music: some magic moments of suspended tonality in the First Chamber Symphony in E major (1906) or, in the Second String Quartet, the instrumental introduction to the Stefan George setting "I breathe the air of another planet" (part of the cycle *Die Langenden Gärten*); the harmonically altogether indefinable Five Orchestral Pieces (1909) and, above all, *Pierrot Lunaire*, settings of poems by Albert Giraud for reciter and chamber ensemble, which are among the most powerful monuments to Expressionism in any of the arts.

While these works exerted a decisive influence on Berg and Webern, Schönberg himself evidently chafed at the epigrammatic style that he considered was imposed on him through the loss of the tonal *aide-mémoire*. It was to counteract this handicap that the conservative revolutionary, as he has justly been called, looked around for an alternative cohesive and thought he had found it in his "method of composition with twelve notes related only to one another," where one permutation of the notes of the chromatic scale that is specific to a given work is being reiterated throughout it, albeit in any of the four forms: original, inversion, retrograde, and retrograde inversion, each being allowed to start off on any degree of the scale and thus making a total of forty-eight rows. These are considered to represent merely different aspects of the basic row and are to be rhythmicized ad libitum.

Of several fallacies invalidating the system, the chief one lies in the further proviso, designed to insure a work's ultimate unity, that chords must be derived from the row by sounding some of its notes simultaneously rather than in sequence. As I have pointed out elsewhere, such chords belong equally to a number of different note rows, the number growing ever larger, the more notes go to make up the chord, until the ultimate of 479,001,600 rows is reached to which a chord comprising all twelve notes of the scale may belong. Add to this that the system has nothing to say as to whether or no the intervals formed by simultaneously traveling melodies are to count as part of chords, and that dodecaphonic theory—unlike Schönberg's defense of atonality—does not come *after* the event but tries to shape it, and it becomes clear that the success of such a work is in inverse relation to the rigor with which the composer abides by the rules.

It is tempting to consider whether, quite apart from the immense influence wielded in their respective fields by Schönberg, Marx, Freud, and Einstein, and wholly irrespective of ultimate merit, there might not be a common denominator in their mode of thinking, a certain intrepidity, perhaps, in the face of paradox, seeming or real: the equiponderance of consonance and dissonance, simultaneity and sequence; the inevitability of a revolution that yet has to be fought for; an infant's sexuality without the wherewithal; the existence of waves in a nonexistent medium?

It might well be thought heart-rending that during a summer holiday in Traunkirchen in 1921, when Schönberg first told a pupil of his conception of a twelve-note system, he added that he had made a discovery that would "insure the supremacy of German music for another hundred years." For barely a month earlier a Vienna newspaper reported that Schönberg had decided to depart from another Austrian holiday resort rather than produce his certificate of baptism, as requested by the local council which had resolved to bar Jewish tourists (having had a Jewish upbringing he was converted to Protestantism, on theological grounds, at the age of twenty-four). I can, incidentally, testify to Schönberg's speaking German with a broad Viennese accent, utterly un-Jewish—hence Webern's amazement on learning, years after he had become his pupil, that the revered master was a Jew—and shining brightly through his English on a record in Volume III of his Collected Works, issued by CBS, where he is heard talking to Halsey Stevens about the paintings produced during his Expressionist phase.

Schönberg was not the only German or Austrian Jew whose tragically unreciprocated loyalties were eroded when the region's latent anti-Semitism turned into the open threat of Hitlerism. "It was a dream," he wrote in 1923, when with admirable dignity he reprimanded Wassily Kandinsky, the pioneer of abstract

RIGHT: His parents in Eiger, Bohemia, were so poor that he was raised in one room with seven siblings, but by the time he was four years old, Rudolf Serkin could read music and play the piano. At twelve he was guest artist with the Vienna Symphony, but then studied for eight years before beginning a concert career in 1920. His wife is the daughter of the great violinist Adolf Busch. His son, Peter, born in 1947, made his piano debut in 1959 and also has a brilliant concert career. Photo by Erich Hartmann.

BOTTOM, LEFT: A pioneer of polytonality, Darius Milhaud (1892–1974) composed more than four hundred works in virtually every style and medium. Fleeing France in 1940, he became a professor at Mills College in Oakland, California, and continued to teach there and at the Paris Conservatoire until his death. He was born and raised in Aix-en-Provence, where his family, members of the Comtadin Hebrew sect, had prospered for many generations. Photo by Alfred Eisenstaedt.

BOTTOM, CENTER: Daniel Barenboim gave his first piano concert in Buenos Aires in 1949—aged seven. Two years later his parents, both accomplished musicians, took him to Salzburg to further his studies and then settled in Israel. Daniel continued his international studies (composition with Nadia Boulanger in Paris, violin at the Santa Cecilia Academy in Rome), and then returned to the stage as both a pianist and conductor. He married the British cellist Jacqueline du Pré in June 1967 in Israel, where they had rushed to perform during the Six-Day War. Photo by David Hurn.

BOTTOM, RIGHT: Born in Ekaterinoslav in the Ukraine in 1903, Gregor Piatigorsky became an American citizen in 1942, head of the cello departments of the Curtis Institute in Philadelphia and at the Performing Arts Academy, Los Angeles, California, and is now a professor at the University of Southern California. His fame is worldwide; he has appeared with all the major orchestras in the United States, Europe, and the Far East. Photo by Arnold Newman.

art, after rumors had reached him that this kindred spirit had become involved with anti-Jewish trends at the Bauhaus—"It was a dream, I am not a German, not a European, but a Jew—we are two kinds of people, definitely." And after his official conversion to Judaism as a political protest on being dismissed, in 1933, from the Prussian Academy of Arts, he wrote to Berg from Paris: "My return took place long ago." The reference is to the first drafts, in 1922–23, of his unfinished opera *Moses and Aaron* and of the spoken drama *The Biblical Way*, in which the nondenominational religiosity of the text he had written for *Die Jakobsleiter* (1913–1917, unfinished oratorio)—"a materialist's, communist's, atheist's search for God"— is channeled into reflections on the specific relationship between God and the Israelites and into a concern for Jewish nationhood, an ideal, he wrote to Webern in August 1933, to which he intended from then on to devote all his energies.

The first fruit of fervor thus unleashed was the "Kol Nidre" of 1938, when Schönberg joined the handful of Jewish main-stream composers who in the twentieth century resumed the practice, never abandoned in the Christian tradition, of complementing their secular works with an occasional liturgical setting: the *Sacred Service* (1932) by the Swiss-American Ernest Bloch, whose fame rests, however, on the cello rhapsody *Schelomo* (1916); or the "Chants de Rosch Haschanan" (1933) and "Kaddish" (1945) by the Frenchman Darius Milhaud, whose *Poèmes Juifs* of 1916 may well have been written for more innocently musical reasons—such as no doubt also account for his famed integration of jazz into the ballet *La Creation du Monde* (1923)—than the "Hymne de Sion" of 1925.

Schönberg altered the text of the Kol Nidre so that the voiding of "all vows" taken during the preceding year refers exclusively to a conversion to Christianity. It is the most musically committed of those works of his American period (from 1933), where he can be seen wearing a tonal hat—a curious recidivism, due by no means only to the pecuniary hopes of a freshly arrived emigrant, but to a deep-seated nostalgia for pastures never finally forsaken. Every bar of the "Kol Nidre" is derived motivically, by way of a pendant to twelve-note technique, from the traditional melody. Yet the idiom—for all its Wagnerisms, and with the "cello sentimentality" of the *concertante* "Kol Nidre" (1881) by the (non-Jew!) Max Bruch not nearly as thoroughly "vitriolized away" as Schönberg imagined—does not set off any Judaic associations or indeed show any awareness of the Hebrew chant on which it is based, and the same is true of "De Profundis." Schönberg dedicated to the new state of Israel this last completed composition (1950); here he decided against the use of chant material but did set the original Hebrew text and studied its inflections.

All the more remarkable, then, if in Schönberg's instrumental twelve-note compositions one does here and there perceive Hasidic echoes—for example, in the slow movement of the Piano Concerto and Fourth String Quartet or in the opening of the Violin Concerto. The tragic tone of voice contrasts significantly with the phantasmagoric hallucinations of the free atonal period, notably in the symbolist drama with music *Die glückliche Hand*, based on Schönberg's own and utterly obscurantist book; or, again, with the hectic study in *Angst* of the monodram *Erwartung* (1908), set to a libretto written to Schönberg's specifications. It strikes one as a musical version of Edvard Munch's "The Scream," which Schönberg may indeed have seen at the Vienna exhibition in 1904, since the painter Gerstl, a friend of Schönberg and his first wife, greatly admired the Norwegian Expressionist.

Like the periodic thematicism which Schönberg, once dodecaphony had been established, immediately took up again (so different from the attempts, in his freely atonal phase, to bypass form and engage in unstructured, direct composition), those traditional mood contents of curiously mixed Romantic and Hasidic provenance signify a becalmed return to his late-nineteenth-century beginnings: the hunger for modernity appeared to be stilled and his career's revolutionary quota fulfilled (though fears of falling behind the avant-garde were never quite absent).

Composer of four Broadway hit musicals (*On the Town, Wonderful Town, West Side Story, Candide*) and of classical symphonies, conductor of the New York Philharmonic and other orchestras, a television personality by virtue of his Young People's Concerts, a concert pianist, an early sponsor of the Israel Philharmonic—too much for one career, but Leonard Bernstein thrives on many careers. The son of Russian immigrants who settled in Lawrence, Massachusetts, he has rarely been out of the news since November 13, 1943, when at the last minute he replaced an indisposed Bruno Walter as conductor of the New York Philharmonic. Movie fans know he composed the score for *On the Waterfront*. Photo by Alfred Eisenstaedt.

The operation of dodecaphony did not preclude the creation of some profound episodes: the pensive, forlorn cadenza linking the adagio to the smiling finale theme of the Piano Concerto, the andante of the Violin Concerto and the grandiose return of its rondo theme, the other-worldly Third Variation of a set ingeniously based on the folk song "Aennchen von Tharau" in the Chamber Suite op. 29. But Schönberg's luckless, innate tendency to regard certain imitative, corresponsive formations as carriers of symphonic argument—an odd trait, in evidence as early as the Chamber Symphony—is being aided and abetted by twelve-note methods that would endow these practices with additional significance, or so he thought—with fatal consequences for the work concerned.

Hence this phase of Schönberg's creative life is likely to be remembered chiefly for music that is linked to a significant text: political in the "Ode to Napoleon" (1942), where Byron's poem is viewed as a prophetic anticipation of Hitler's doom; and, perhaps, in "A Survivor from Warsaw," where Schönberg's own somewhat melodramatic text is based on an eyewitness account; or, indeed, philosophical in the operatic torso *Moses and Aaron*. This subject may well have been selected as a scenically effective setting —Burning Bush, Descent from the Mountain, Dance around the Golden Calf—for this clarion call to Jewry in the face of the swastika's ascent; but in the event it gave rise to an "opera of the mind."

The Bible's casual hint at Moses' "heavy tongue" sparked off the scheme to symbolize the antithesis between thinker and popularizer, between the purity of an idea and its corruption in being realized, by having Moses engage in speech song while the eloquent public-relations man Aaron is made to sing. Speech song had continued to fascinate Schönberg from its straightforward occurrence in the oratorio *Gurrelieder* (1901) and the problematic instructions he gave for its execution in *Pierrot Lunaire* right to

Two days before the Nazis arrived, she left the Paris Opéra-Comique, where she had sung the title roles in *Carmen* and *Mignon*, each more than two hundred times; she found refuge in the United States. Two years later, with her singing in Toscanini's performance of Berlioz' *Roméo et Juliette*, Jennie Tourel (1910–1974) really arrived. She joined the Metropolitan Opera, the faculty of the Juilliard School of Music, gave numerous recitals, and in 1946 became a U.S. citizen. The mezzo-soprano was born in Montreal, Canada, of Russian parents, who shortly after her birth moved to Paris. Photo by Arnold Newman.

RIGHT: Belle "Bubbles" Silverman made her radio debut at three on *Uncle Bob's Rainbow House*, at six won a Major Bowes Amateur Hour contest, and at seven appeared in several movies. *The Cresta Blanca Hour* and the Rinso White commercials had their limits, so while at Erasmus Hall High School in Brooklyn and in the Professional Children's School, she began daily voice lessons, which led eventually to her stardom at the New York City Opera in such roles as Maria Stuarda, Lucia, and Manon. The long-awaited debut of Beverly Sills at the Metropolitan Opera House in 1975, forty-three years after her first stage role, was the most exciting musical event in New York for many years. Photo by Alfred Eisenstaedt.

Weehawken, New Jersey, does not conjure up images of the dance, but it was where Jerome (Rabinowitz) Robbins began his career in ballet. The chorus of Broadway shows and summer work at Camp Tamiment were prelude to his debut as a solo dancer in *Petrouchka* (1942) and choreographer for Leonard Bernstein's *Fancy Free* (1944). He staged the dances for *Call Me Madam* (1950), *The King and I* (1951), and *West Side Story* (1957), and created new dances for his own company, Ballets U.S.A. and for the New York City Ballet. He was both director and choreographer for *Fiddler on the Roof* (1964). Photo by Martha Swope.

To be a ballet star, one had to be Russian, so London-born Alice Marks (1910–) adopted the stage name Alicia Markova and danced with all the major ballet companies—Diaghilev, Vic-Wells, Ballet Russe de Monte Carlo, from 1925 to 1941. She was prima ballerina of the Metropolitan Opera for six years and director of that dance company for another six years. Since 1970 she has been professor of ballet and performing arts at the University of Cincinnati.

OPPOSITE: Her family background is rich in artists. Her mother and uncle are movie actors; another uncle had been a leading dancer of the Bolshoi Ballet and is now its ballet master and choreographer. Her sister and two brothers dance with the Bolshoi. Born in Moscow in 1925, Maya Plisetskaya has been the prima ballerina of that company for fifteen years, winning the Lenin Prize in 1964 and holding the title of People's Artist of the U.S.S.R. She is considered Russia's finest dancer, and by many the finest dancer in the world. Photo by Martha Swope.

the last psalm. But it is used most meaningfully and provocatively in *Moses and Aaron,* where it helps to illustrate Schönberg's contribution to the philosopher's ancient "inner-outer" problem: nothing less than the proposition that there can be such a thing as an unsayable thought is implied by Moses' final, despairing "O word, thou word, that I lack."

Of Berg's dodecaphonic works at least one, the Violin Concerto of 1935, has survived him. As in the case of atonality, both he and Webern had to overcome considerable qualms, but it was Webern who came to see in the system not merely a unifying device but a central aspect of a work's beauty and the stuff from which to create a novel, spare poetics. Of the three neo-Viennese styles, it is proving the most attractive to current taste.

The only acolyte to break away from dodecaphony and, generally, from atonality was Hanns Eisler (1896–1963). Considering the endearingly Oedipal upheavals that rocked his relationship with Schönberg right to the end, one wonders whether in his youth they may have played some part in driving him into the arms of Bertolt Brecht. This dramatist's combination of socialist realism and alienation effect inspired by far the finest of Eisler's music and that of two other Jewish composers: Kurt Weill's sensationally lucky throw, the *Dreigroschenoper* ("Lehár yes, Weill no," Schönberg is supposed to have remarked); and the snappy, ironical, grossly underrated couplets that Paul Dessau (born in 1894) wrote for *Mother Courage* and *The Caucasian Chalk Circle* and Eisler for *Schweijk in the Second World War.*

Schönbergian note-rows continue to be widely used, notably by Luigi Dallapiccola (born in 1904), while their structural potentialities are being further explored by such composer-theorists as the American Milton Babbitt (born 1916). Even Stravinsky, after decades of neoclassic hostility, turned into a serial convert in his old age on becoming conversant with Webern's music and growing aware of an aesthetic affinity.

"Serial" in this context is a term used misleadingly though not anachronistically, for it had long since come to denote a phenomenon that far transcends dodecaphony and represents the most fateful influence wielded by Schönberg, however innocently, because well-nigh posthumously. If his system concerned itself exclusively with the ordering of pitches, Pierre Boulez and Karlheinz Stockhausen—bright young sparks reacting at the end of World War II against the fascist repression of modernism and fired by admiration for Webern's poetical systematics and for the experiments of their teacher, Olivier Messiaen, in which rhythms were treated in their own right—proceeded to apply the Schönbergian principle to durations and, in due course, to intensities, modes of attack, and all manner of parameters, retaining all the time, unbelievably, the sacred but by now utterly meaningless number 12.

In total serialization, the individual note no longer functions as part of a musical thought; it is, on the contrary, the unpredictable meeting point of pre-compositionally fixed parameter rows, so that only its pitch is meaningfully related to other pitches, its duration with other durations, its intensity and timbre with other such, and, moreover, "meaningfully" only in a serial sense. One could have predicted, and I did in fact predict, that a system which to such a degree either fetters a composer or, if he wishes to remain creative, forces him to deceive himself by breaking the adopted rules was bound to collapse before long, and that such bankruptcy would lead to a sellout, to the clownish chance of John Cage and to mystical methods of composition either by fluidum emanating from a composer like Stockhausen—who contents himself in "From the Seven Days" with giving verbal instructions: "Play in the rhythm of the Universe, play in the rhythm of your atoms"—or by sheer, unpremeditated collective improvisation. Such trends flourish in a soil defertilized by the mistaking of anti-elitist aims for an obligation to turn anti-art. It was through Schönberg that the Jews, who had only just been in on the alpha of Western music, played a decisive part in shaping its funereal omega.

Rabbi Haimel Going to Seek a New God—a woodcut by Arthur Kolnik.

The Violinist

Yehudi Menuhin

So significant is the proportion of violinists with international careers who are Jewish that the specification of "Jewish violinist" may appear to some people as totally superfluous, as may indeed the further qualification "Russian," however many permutations and connotations are added thereto, such as American-Russian-Jewish, or American-Russian-Jewish-Swiss (as in my case of honorary citizenship of that good land), or Russian-Jewish of Israeli birth or subsequent citizenship; but the overriding and all-prevailing factor remains that the international virtuoso violinist's voice, transmuted though it may be via Stradivarius, Guarnerius, or Amati, bears beneath the musical sound more often than otherwise the hidden accent of the Russian-Jew. This said, as much to stand as a statement of fact as for an *apologia pro vita mea*, I do not have to add as further proof of my credentials that, like English tweed, Spanish leather, German diesels, or Japanese cameras, I also carry a ubiquitous trademark, that of the Russian-Jewish violinist, albeit somewhat far removed from the born-and-bred-in-Odessa classic patent. For it is quite a distance from the rich Ukrainian plains where my father was born, or from the Crimean paradise where my mother first saw the light of day, to New York, to which their separate ocean-crossings carried them and where finally—to prove the proper destiny of the long trip—they married and I was born. As a result of this fortuitous beginning, I might humbly claim a wider perspective on the subject not vouchsafed the original article.

It happens that this is a propitious moment in history to write about the Russian-Jewish violinist for he is actually fast losing his international monopoly—not his quality, but certainly his old long-held supremacy—as more and more violinists from Asiatic countries and all manner of gentile fiddlers from various lands fill the field.

The almost total monopoly of the solo field (with the notable exceptions of Georges Enesco, Zino Francescatti, Joseph Szigeti, and Jacques Thibaud) by the Russian-Jew is a fairly recent development and stems from many factors, which I will attempt to analyze in due course: but at the moment I would like to touch upon that wonderful era in Italy when the violin reigned supreme in the hands and the creative minds of such violinist-composers as Geminiani, Locatelli, Corelli, and Vivaldi. Hand in hand with this extraordinary flowering of the violin as *the* musical voice went the work of those great violin-making families of Cremona: Stradivarius, Guarnerius, Amati, Grancino, Guadagnini, and so many others. Nor has the flower faded, for both the literature and the instrument still represent today the most valuable part of the violinist's baggage.

The violin reached its apogee in Italy in the seventeenth and eighteenth centuries. Never since then has the violin dominated the musical scene, for it had to make way for a harmonic development more suited to the keyboard than to the four strings of the violin. Concurrently with the Italian evolution another musical evolution was taking place north of the Alps, which reached its first peak in the works of Bach and later developed into the violin concertos of the Romantic period.

It was most probably from Italy and Germany that the Jews, expelled from one country after another and wandering eastward, brought the violin. We can assume, perhaps, that this migrant urban people of the Book must have drawn as much from the *musique savante* of Italy and Germany and other European countries, where musical literacy and violinistic proficiency had reached such high levels, as from the folkloristic and improvised performance of village and itinerant gypsy fiddlers whose neighbors they became.

There is a museum of folk instruments in Moscow, an amazing collection, that includes an extraordinary variety of crude (some less crude) yet most imaginative violins, hewn and put together by village craftsmen and used for village community purposes. When I visited there, I suddenly realized that the violin is more than just that polished, cultivated instrument on which I interpret the great classical works. Nor is it one people's instrument. It belongs, in fact, to the peoples of the world—certainly to the peoples of Eurasia. It is man's most intimate musical companion.

In the same way as the violin itself has evolved from a folkloristic and rough-hewn object into the most beautiful, delicate, and cultivated of all instruments, so the unique character of the international Jewish violinist, and specifically the Russian-Jewish violinist, stems from the fusion of the cultivated and the wild, of the studied with the improvised, of the urban with the nomad, of the rooted with the exile.

As with the vine, of which the cultivated variety has continually to be regrafted onto the wild, the blossoming of music in Europe was a result of the simultaneous presence of conservatories of music, with their great pedagogues, and of gypsy encampments. We need only recall the violinists of Hungary, Rumania, and of course Russia; and conversely, by the same token, the withering on the vine of violinists in Germany, a country well endowed with conservatories but singularly lacking in gypsy encampments. As Germany became ever more collectively disciplined, it lost the solo violinist—the individual *par excellence*.

I like to think of the rich soil of Eastern Europe as the conjunction of musical streams flowing from many directions: the music of the gypsy violinist whose tribe had left India, its land of origin, to roam from the Volga to the Danube; the monodic chants of the cantor and the muezzin; the music brought to Turkey and Hungary by the west-bound Mongolian hordes—a music entirely different from that of the gypsy (it is in fact the foundation of Hungarian folk music)—and played on a small, crude two-stringed fiddle with the bow entwined between the strings, no doubt for greater portability; and the cultivated music from Western Europe, where a contrapuntal style had been evolved more suited to communal ritualistic and religious observance. Music became enshrined in the noble chorales, the hymn, congregational harmony, and structurally it evolved into fugal form and the counterpoint of many voices.

Eleven-year-old Yehudi Menuhin played the Beethoven Violin Concerto with the New York Symphony at Carnegie Hall, and two years later, on April 19, 1929, played concertos by Bach, Beethoven, and Brahms with the Berlin Philharmonic, Bruno Walter conducting. His first world tour (1934) consisted of 110 concerts in 63 cities, and during World War II he gave more than 500 concerts to U.S. and Allied servicemen. Between concerts he lives in his native California or at his homes in Gstaad, Mykonos, and London. His sister, Hephzibah, also a prodigy, is a concert pianist. Photo by Clive Barda.

OVERLEAF: A New York street scene. Photo by Ken Heyman.

Having cast a wide glance over the background, let us return to our central theme, the Russian-Jewish violinist, and try to fathom why the violin became so much a part of his people's life.

Although the Jews sang, as I know from my own father and his innumerable and wonderful Hasidic songs, there was no established secular communal art form in Jewish life through which one could express oneself or exhibit one's emotions. Certainly the idea of a theater or an opera ran against orthodox tradition. Therefore the Jew had to find a very personal instrument, one not exactly and literally his own voice, for that might be misinterpreted, but a tool that he could wield and transform into the image of his own voice, sufficiently anonymous to be universal.

Also, the Jews had no territory; they not only had no homeland, but they were not allowed in Russia to own or to work land. As we know from the birds and bird song, the music they make is meant to proclaim their dominion over a certain territory they call their own. The violin, too, is a conqueror of space and sublimates the territorial imperative. The individual violinist proclaims his dominion over all that comes within earshot of his music, over his listeners' hearts. He subjugates the space that carries his vibrations, and he continually reasserts and renews his claim over new space. The touring virtuoso conquers new territory with each performance, and he thus fulfills both the territorial and the migratory instincts of a nomad, exiled people, as the bird does for its kind. How much more would the violin appeal to a people like the Jews, without a land or in exile, than it would to the established, rooted, host population! How much more would it mean to them! The piano stands immovable, rooted in space; the painter is linked to his easel, his studio; but the violin is as mobile as the violinist's heart, as flexible and as adjustable.

Music, through the medium of the violin, describes a universal human state, communicates automatically, transforming the subjective into the objective, depersonalizing the vibrations, and allowing them to penetrate, in the same way as those astonishing cosmic rays, all material objects and obstacles. Violin sound, more than any other, conveys a deeply subjective message anonymously and persuasively, for the violin is both separate from the body and yet part of the body. Vibrating with, yet almost free of, the body, not gripped, but held in delicate and subtle balance, it bridges the gulf between the single and the universal, between one man and all men.

The Jew, longer than any Western peoples, has had a deep awareness of universality, whether in the concrete form of suffering or in the abstract form of the metaphysical. So often the abstract—whether symbol, numeral, ritual, theory, conviction, or dogma—blinds us to the reality of suffering, to the pitiful and hopeless human condition. But the history of the Jews has made them a people generally quite as familiar with pain as with mathematics, with God as with man. In fact, the traditional Jewish approach to God is not so much in the form of prayer as in the form of a dialogue, and this dialogue can be a musical one. God, the stern Father who sometimes even repents of his own mistakes, is a presence one *might* influence, persuade, cause to change his mind and think it over, if only to give us poor sinners another chance.

The Jewish violinist is able to combine the greatest respect for the symbols of law and convention—in this case the composer's notes and notation—with the most powerful and communicative expression of the human condition. It is no wonder that in a world growing both more urban and less rooted, more literate and less wise, the Jewish violinist—urban, errant, literate, and possessed—should serve a catalyzing, unique, and essential function. He also brings to his performance that thirst for improvisation which is imprisoned in the written or printed text, and he somehow provides a feeling of improvisation and inspiration in performance that comes of that continuous fire, the fire of yearning and nostalgia, of passionate longing, of self-expression, of self-fulfillment, of ambition, of emancipation, which he carries within him.

A love of improvisation, which is also characteristic of the gypsy—and, of course, is prominent in Indian classical music—has never been lost to the people of the Book. This, combined with the fact that the Russian-Jewish violinist studied musical texts as intensely as the Talmudist studied his verbal texts, made him an extraordinary interpreter of the classical European heritage. In general, he has tended to play the music of the great composers of the Romantic movement, for the Jew is romantic at heart. The violin became his theater, his opera, his novel, his total expression, and his bridge to the world.

It is interesting to analyze the technical points of violin-playing common to the Jew and the gypsy, and also in a way to the Indian violinist—although the latter plays the instrument quite differently physically, squatting with legs crossed, with the violin head propped on a big toe and the violin resting against his chest, and in an entirely different style of music, melodic rather than harmonic, a classical music rather than a simplified folklore. They have all mastered the glissando effect and the vibratos, which enable them to approximate the human voice. They all use the quarter tone—vibrato-glissando—the note not absolutely in tune with the tempered scale or with the perfect interval, the note that is a cry and a sigh.

Even during the driest period interpretatively, 1920 to 1930, when interpretation became literal and a minimum of personal impulse was allowed the interpreter, the Russian-Jewish violinist never succumbed rhythmically to the mechanical metronome or, in quality of sound, to the desiccated "melba toast" approach. No wonder, then, that the public preferred him to the dry-as-dust or academic musicians.

Until recently the Jewish violinist has been the solo virtuoso spokesman, the unrepentant individual who reached out to the world at large. Others carried on the musical traditions of particular cultures; they had roots in the traditions and were quite at home in the country of their origin, and consequently never had the urge, were never motivated, to reach out to the universal, to bridge the gaps between human beings, between groups, to express something common to all men and all women.

Now, as the study of the violin is increasing throughout the world, in an era when frustration and alienation are becoming world-wide, the Jewish solo violinist is withdrawing to a certain extent from the field, not only because he is being outnumbered, but because there are other avenues of expression open.

The Russian-Jewish violinist has only recently become interested in the literature of chamber music, for at the Moscow conservatories, which were his supreme training ground, it was then not part of the curriculum. I remember when I was a boy in San Francisco, just beginning to play the violin, I was introduced to Mischa Elman. My teacher, Louis Persinger, and my father brought me to meet the great man at his hotel. This must have been in 1922 or 1923. After I had played, there were a few flattering words, followed by an uncomfortable silence. Finally, to break the ice, Persinger asked Elman if he had heard the great Casals recently. Elman brushed this aside, saying, "Yes, of course, Casals is quite a good musician, but after all he is only a cellist!" At that time solo cello performances were rare, and most cellists were members of orchestras or chamber groups. The Jewish solo cellist has only relatively recently appeared on the scene with Gregor Piatigorsky.

In Germany, Austria, and Hungary, where chamber music has always been a vibrant musical tradition, the virtuoso string quartets of international fame were almost exclusively Jewish. Playing chamber music was the leisure-time activity of many middle-class families, Jewish and gentile.

Great violinists presuppose great teachers, and there have been many well-known Jewish violinist pedagogues. Joseph Joachim (1831–1907), a composer as well as a solo violinist, taught Martin Marsick (1848–1924); Karl Wilhelm Henning (1784–1867) gave lessons in Berlin to Felix Mendelssohn; Bunzl, himself a pupil of Wilhelm Bernhard Molique (1802–1869), taught Henri Marteau (1874–1934).

The greatest and most famous was Hungarian-born Leopold Auer (1845–1930). From his teaching emerged Jascha Heifetz, Mischa Elman, Toscha Seidel, Efrem Zimbalist, Cecilia Hansen, and many others. Auer's method is still largely dominant in Russia although he left there in 1918 and went to the United States.

This tradition was replanted in the United States, where Naum Blinder, Josef Gingold, and Ivan Galamian (Armenian) gave us a new generation of violinists, including Isaac Stern.

Carl Flesch (1873–1944), too, was born in Hungary. He taught in Budapest, Amsterdam, Berlin, and Philadelphia (at the Curtis Institute); he bequeathed us Max Rostal—an outstanding teacher active in England, Germany, and Switzerland—and the violinists Henryk Szeryng, Henri Temianka, Yfrah Neaman, Ida Haendel, and Simon Goldberg.

May I be allowed a short biographical digression with the excuse that I do belong in the category of the title of this chapter? I hope the reader will forgive me if I indulge in a sketch of my own unusual influences: if for a Jewish violinist they seem typical, it is only a sign of the times. My own masters happened to be all Christian: Louis Persinger, an American, was concert master of the San Francisco Symphony and leader of the Persinger Quartet. He studied in Belgium with Eugène Ysaye. His father was not a concert master but a stationmaster or railway switchman in a Colorado town. Among his many brilliant pupils is my distinguished non-Jewish contemporary Ruggiero Ricci. However, it is not quite correct to say that *all* my teachers were gentiles: my very first, with whom I stayed for nine months when I was five, was Sigmund Anker, "anchored" in the ghetto, or at least in the Jewish quarter of San Francisco: his was a typical forcing-house for the offspring of aspiring "Konzertpapas" and "Konzert-mamas." From personal experience I must report that almost all the Jewish pedagogues I have known or met were solo-career-oriented: however understandable, this is a pity, for it accounts in part for that self- and soul-destructive sense of failure among the thousands of fiddlers who did not reach the summit and who finally accepted reluctantly an orchestral chair or membership in a string quartet.

And then there was Georges Enesco, perhaps the greatest musician I have ever known, inspired and at home in every style, with a colossal memory: he knew literally all the compositions of Bach, all the operas of Mozart, all the works of Beethoven, Wagner—he could sit down at the piano and play any one of them, and sing or whistle the parts he could not reach with his fingers. He never forgot anything he had once heard or studied. He was a magnificent conductor, and the musicians of the Philadelphia Orchestra still remember him. He was an outstanding violinist; played the cello; drew caricatures; spoke English, French, German, Italian, and Rumanian; and was a great composer. He was supremely cultivated but never lost his roots in the Rumania of his childhood. His extensive knowledge of the spirit and idiom of his native land and the gypsies gave him the faculty to ignite musically every note he touched, every sound he made. And he looked the part: he had the aspect, nobility, and carriage of a lion. When at the age of eight I first saw and heard this inspiring and romantic figure when he played in San Francisco, I knew I wanted to study with him. He played the violin with an authority, an abandon, a meaning, a fire, that left me transfixed. Three years later I began to study with him in Paris, and in Rumania at Sinaia in the Carpathian Alps, where for the first time I encountered the gypsies. It was in Sinaia that my father made the discovery that led me to my present train of thought: he rediscovered many of his traditional Hasidic songs in the nostalgic songs of the gypsy violinists whom we heard.

It was Enesco who sent me to Adolph Busch, feeling that I was almost too carried away by that improvisatory gypsy approach and needed the discipline of the very classical, strict, and severe German tradition. With Busch I learned a respectful and precise reverence for the composer's intention as written down, but at the same time he communicated a sense of German exaltation and philosophy, and I have since evolved by the interaction of these two basic human impulses—freedom versus order. That was my first understanding of the noble German tradition of performance which reached its epitome in Wilhelm Furtwängler and is still with us in Wilhelm Kempff, the great pianist.

My list of those I have learned from and who have given me inspiration should include not only my formal teachers but also the violinists who deeply influenced my life and my playing, and among these are many Jewish violinists. From my earliest age and for many years it was that perfect and immaculate performer, Jascha Heifetz, whose recordings were a challenge and an example to me. Later it was Fritz Kreisler (no one seems able to confirm whether he was indeed Jewish or not), from whom I tried to learn the grace and the rhythmic inflection and accent of the Austrian lilt. I never missed an Elman concert, and I tried to emulate his wonderful, luscious sound: his recordings of the slow movement of Lalo's *Symphonie Espagnole* and his recordings with Caruso still ring in my ears.

I am indebted and grateful to countless musicians, Jew and gentile, for their particular insights: the French elegance and economy of Thibaud; the electric, galvanizing impact of Arturo Toscanini's conducting; the shaping of a melodic phrase, Bruno Walter; the living majesty of Wilhelm Furtwängler's interpretations; the severity of Karl Muck and Felix Weingartner, conductors; the unfailing musicality of the conductor Antal Dorati; the delicacy of Walter Gieseking; the brilliance of Vladimir Horowitz on the

336

piano; the command of pianist Arturo Michelangeli; the ebullient and natural spontaneity of pianist Artur Rubinstein; and among the composers, Béla Bartók, Ernest Bloch, Igor Stravinsky, Frank Martin, and others.

Then, of course, Israel too has been part of my background. My parents met there when it was still Palestine. My father had gone there as a little boy to join his grandfather in Jerusalem, and I still have numerous relatives there. Perhaps all these elements outside my immediate inherited background have served to heighten and render even more universal those Jewish qualities of performance which enable the Jew to interpret every tradition, be it German, French, Spanish, Scandinavian, English, Italian, or American.

No musician could feel comfortable in a world that excluded or degraded any human race, religion, or nation. Fortunately, for the musician, the world already exists as it should be for all humanity, and none of us would conceive of a musical horizon today that did not include all musicians—performers, composers, conductors, teachers—from all lands and all peoples. This widening and growing evolution in music explains the multiplying diversity of styles among Jewish musicians as among all others.

The Russian-Jewish violinist as he emerges from the conservatories in Odessa, Moscow, and Leningrad, from those of Tel Aviv or Bloomington, Indiana, is still vaguely recognizable as a species. But for how long?

I believe that the Jew, by sublimating the drive for territoriality and possessions, thus appeasing man's overpowering, compelling urge to control and dominate, sublimated the equally strong human urge to weaponry by adopting humanity's supreme nonaggressive tool, the violin, which, unlike most other tools— the hammer, the ax, and so forth—is not murderous by origin. Is it because the Jew has been forced into these sublimations that he has adopted the violin in such numbers, the melodic instrument *par excellence*, and has, on the whole, produced proportionately far fewer murderers (and sportsmen) than his fellow-subjects or fellow-citizens?

Now that the territorial and weaponry urges are satisfied in Israel, will those ancient Jewish virtues that have yielded the sages, prophets, rabbis, philosophers, poets, scientists, violinists, bankers, business-men, and good family-men—will these remarkable sublimations of normal urges still occur in the same proportion to the population; or will these qualities become submerged in middle-class affluence? This has not happened during the first twenty-five years of Israel as a reborn state. The wave upon wave of new immigrants, and the scores of brilliant violinists fresh from the forcing-houses of perennial Russian despair, have diluted the crystallization of the new patriotic requirements with the old Jewish stuff. But under the pressures and requirements of national survival—the pressures of sheer physical survival both in alliance with and in opposition to nature—will the Israeli people be able to maintain the values of their ancient heritage?

The Jewish-Israeli pilot or farmer may dance and sing, but I wonder if he will play the violin. Perhaps, and not necessarily professionally, but in enlightened awareness, just for the love of it. Perhaps the sons and daughters of farmers, scientists, biologists, will take up the violin, King David's harp, and speak of a new awareness of God.

> Blessed is the people that know the joyful sound:
> They shall walk, O Lord, in the light of thy countenance.

Remembrance of Jerusalem

Elie Wiesel

In the beginning there was Jerusalem.

The sound coming from the mountains, the mysterious and languid call. The continuous dazzlement within a changing framework. The song so near and yet so far. The accumulated silences wrought from words. The joys and the surprises which make you breathless.

Miraculous city stretching toward heaven: I remember it with the same clarity and intensity as I remember the child I was who carried it. It seems to me that I uttered its name before I could utter my own. A melodious and beguiling name conjuring a kingdom both familiar and unknown. A name to soothe and a name to set the heart on fire, particularly in the evening twilight, at the time when children are afraid to be alone. I remember the humming of a lullaby, I remember being taught a prayer. I used to close my eyes and, rising in a dream, see a city where all the people were princes except for a few men who were enlightened beggars or mad beggars with a burning, haunted look. I would go forward toward them, holding my breath.

I could guess the name of the place but could not place it. I knew it was Jerusalem, but I did not know where it was. A child's fantasy? An old man's dream?

"Wherever I go, I follow the road to Jerusalem," would say Rabbi Nahman of Bratzlav.

Often destroyed but nevertheless indestructible, often desecrated but always sacred and supreme, this capital city of Jewish survival has two faces, two destinies.

Earthly Jerusalem, heavenly Jerusalem. The one, visible, suggests mourning and lamentation. The other, invisible, brings peace and rejoicing. They meet in the man who seeks them within himself, in his innermost being, where the light of heaven and that of the abyss met, where tears of joy and tears of despair are reunited.

"Jerusalem," would say my grandfather, crying, crying with all his might. But my Master, he, he was saying "Jerusalem," laughing. He too with all his might.

In a book with torn, yellowing pages I was shown the drawing of an immensely high wall with, at its feet, a few melancholy pilgrims, meditating. "This is Jerusalem," I was told. From then on I was convinced that the place existed only in books and that it was in books that I had to seek it.

Prayer books, books of legends, full of signs and symbols. Books ancient and books eternally new. Jerusalem: the heart of the world, the soul of this heart. Everything is there. Promises and memories. From bygone days and for next year. David and the Messiah. The great adventure, the great expectation. Jerusalem: the light which at night lights the traveler's way, the shadow which weighs heavily as he goes.

All is reflected on Jerusalem. Exile and home-coming. Starting point and finishing line. The history of the Jews would not be Jewish—or would not exist—without this city, the most Jewish city in the world and also the most universal.

The child I was loved it more than his birthplace. I belonged in Jerusalem. I walked through its narrow streets, I lost myself in its sounds. And its joys and its sorrows were, by turns, reflected in my spirits.

A custom: at the end of a meal my father would watch to see that the last knife was removed from the table. This was the reason: in reciting the customary blessing in which Jerusalem was mentioned, there was a risk that the grief-stricken Jew would take the knife and plunge it in his chest. It was better that this temptation should be removed.

A recollection: at Passover, Shavuot, and Sukkoth, as I was trying to slip through the tight ranks of Hasidim to get nearer to the rabbi, a Talmudic anecdote used to spring to my mind; according to this, during national pilgrimages in the days of the Temple no one complained about the lack of space. Such a miracle hardly ever occurred with us: it was stifling. Had it ever happened in Jerusalem? Not at all, replied those critical, emancipated minds who did not believe in miracles in the true sense of the term. Then what explanation did they have for the Talmudic statement? Very simply, there was not enough space in Jerusalem, in Jerusalem, too, it was stifling—but there were no complaints. Poor censorious, argumentative people. . . . They did not understand that there indeed lay the miracle: uncomplaining Jews!

Another recollection: on the ninth day of the month of Av, we were weeping about the destruction of the city of David. Day of fasting and mourning. We wore patched clothes and walked barefoot and stooping. Sitting on stools or even on the floor, we read the graphic descriptions realistically portrayed in the Talmud of the fall of Jerusalem. Bewildering scenes that chilled the blood. Kamtza and Bar-Kamtza: a silly story of revenge that ends in a bath of violence. Nevuzradan, Aspianus, Titus: history of cruel conquest inscribed in the ashes of time. Yokhanan ben Zakkai and his disciples, the story of a flight that turns into a new beginning. Driven away from their burning city, the Jews shall live in graves for the next twenty centuries. And carry with them the memory of this kingdom.

"Jerusalem," my Master was saying, laughing. "Jerusalem," my grandfather was sighing, crying. An offering from God to man, a sanctuary erected by man in honor of God. Both are called to dwell therein in fear, joy, and expectation. So spoke my Master. Or was it my grandfather?

A few maxims: why was Jerusalem destroyed? Because the people did not respect their sages. Or, because its people had lost their sense of decency. Or yet again, because its people hated one another for no reason.

I was more concerned with the destiny of this city than I was with my own. I moved among its inhabitants, I blessed them. I talked to them, I listened to them. I envied them. I drew from their memories to enrich my own.

An image: as the enemy legions prepare to burn the beleaguered capital, four angels descend from heaven and . . . set it on fire. As if to show the impotence of men against the city of God: only He is capable of reducing it to dust. And even He did not succeed. Beyond defeat, Jerusalem imposes itself on the generations by resisting oblivion and death. It survives its murderous conquerors.

Another image: from the depths of the burning Temple, young priests emerge who, having interrupted the sacred service, climb to the roof and speak to God: we could not safeguard Thy dwelling, we could not protect Thy sanctuary, we therefore return the keys to Thee. They throw them toward heaven— and a fiery hand takes them and carries them away.

I used to condemn the young priests. Their gesture seemed childish, melodramatic, and above all convenient. Why did they return the keys? Why did they give up fighting? They would have done better to speak more aggressively, with more determination: Thou art free to renounce Thy dwelling and even to sacrifice Thy priests, but the keys belong to us as we belong to Thee! We shall keep them even in defiance of Thy will. But later I saw the fire taking them and carrying them away: they were the keys to the Temple. And I ceased passing judgment upon them.

The shrine at the Dome of the Rock—Jerusalem. Photo by Richard Cleave.

OVERLEAF: The moon rises over a modern Jerusalem. Photo by Werner Braun.

A story: at the end of the siege of Jerusalem, once defeat was consummated, God ordered the prophet Jeremiah: go, call Abraham, Isaac, and Jacob, tell them to come, for they know how to weep. Jeremiah had to obey. He went to call on the three patriarchs and gave them the message but did not state the reason. When they asked why does God want to see us, he replied, I do not know. He was frightened, explains the Midrash. Jeremiah was frightened that the patriarchs would hold him responsible for the national catastrophe, for not having quashed it and even perhaps for having survived it.

Nowadays the survivors identify themselves with this unhappy prophet. They live in the continuous fear of not knowing how to weep, really, as they should. And then they carry with them a feeling of guilt, they feel the guilt of having survived. Each one of them has seen the death of Jerusalem, each one of them blames himself for having escaped the flames.

We know the words of Jeremiah, but we do not know his silent thoughts. It is a pity. They are part of Jerusalem just as much as the rest—and perhaps much more.

"Jerusalem," would say my grandfather with a sigh. And quoting from the Talmud: having lost his way, the traveler need only direct his thoughts toward Jerusalem. Landmark in time and beyond time. Jerusalem informs, attracts, and encourages. And gives a purpose to life. And yet . . .

I remember my first visit to Jerusalem. It was night. Late. Very late. We had just landed in an accursed and unreal kingdom. Barbed wire, barbed wire as far as the eye could see. And flames, immeasurably high flames piercing the dark sky. Around me friends and strangers, who like me were looking for a sign, a marker, to help us find our bearings. In vain. Those prisoners who were screaming, those officers who were watching them, this stifling smell, dogs barking, cries heard from afar: a sight that did not fit any memory or any dream.

But others were leaving the train. The crowd was becoming thicker. Men, women, and children coming from every country, from every social class, speaking many languages, I could see them converging on this place, dominated by a powerful fire, a voluminous fire from another age, and suddenly an idea crossed my mind and made me stagger: it is Jerusalem! Here is the fulfillment of the promise! The Messiah has come and the Jews, scattered across the world, breaking away from their exile, breaking off from their lowliness, are coming to him to salute him, thank him, and bless him! And they shall wipe away their tears! And they shall wait no more! The gathering together of those who were scattered is *here!* Here is Jerusalem, both earthly and heavenly, calling and sheltering its children who have come to glorify it and love it at midnight.

"Let all men become pure and righteous and the Messiah shall appear," would say my grandfather, sobbing. "Let all men sin and the Messiah will draw them to Him," would say my Master, laughing.

And I remember my second visit to Jerusalem. It was on an autumn evening beneath a leaden sky, in Moscow. I thought I was dreaming, for by its extent, by the number of participants, and by its dynamic strength, my imagination was wholly captivated.

The dream began at sunset. The center of the capital suddenly moved from Red Square to the narrow street where the synagogue was situated. Jewish youth began its march. All the roads led to the same place. Students and workers, schoolboys and soldiers, boys and girls, they were coming in bands or in groups of two or three, happy and hesitant, their hair windswept, their eyes apprehensive, they all poured into the crowd which was welcoming them with loud shouts. Some had brought their accordions, others their guitars, ready to answer the same call.

How many were there? Thousands and thousands. The road was too narrow to contain them. In the fury of the dance, they seemed to float on air, like figures from a Chagall painting, wringing themselves from the shadows, rising above the buildings, above the city, as if they were climbing an invisible ladder, Jacob's ladder, leading to heaven—if not higher still.

I had not felt so strong, so proud, for a long time. Drunk with my dream, I joined their ranks, amazed, moved, and bowled over by this exuberance, by this fervor that I was picking up through all my

Photo by Ken Heyman.

senses. I let it carry me far into the past, into the future, walking on clouds, while luminous waves were carrying me to other shores, other experiences, where everything inevitably ends with a miracle.

There and then I was forgetting that it was the eve of Simchat Torah, the Feast of the Law, the festival that was celebrated in Moscow as it was celebrated nowhere else. I could see myself in Jerusalem, a pilgrim among pilgrims, jostled and hustled by the human whirlpool—the people returning to their land and their city, sovereign in their joy as much as in their sorrow.

"He who mourns the destruction of Jerusalem shall rejoice in its resurrection," would say my grandfather, quoting from the Talmud. And he would add: he who does not identify his grief with that of Jerusalem shall not share in its joy.

And I remember my third visit to Jerusalem. Beginning of June 1967. The fighting is still going on in the country. Snipers suddenly appear here and there in the very suburbs of the capital. So what! It does not stop people from running to the old city. Armed warriors and dumfounded Talmudists, contented tourists and emaciated dreamers, old people and children, I see them and I try to place them, men and women, all the survivors from all the hells, and among them the unlucky and the victims—all the faces from every fate, I see them running breathlessly, running toward the millennial district and its blind houses, its dilapidated façades and menacing roofs. On arriving before the Har Ḥabayit, before the Wall, suddenly they all stop just like children frightened of awakening.

I remember the quality and the density of the silence falling upon us; no one dared interrupt it. Then, after an endless moment, some started to pray, others to weep. And I was saying to myself that this sight was not new; that I had already shared it elsewhere, in another life, timeless ages before, long ago and far away.

In a flash not far removed from pain, I see again the rejoicing of youth in Russia, its exalted dance; and I also see the arrival in the universe of darkness, of the procession of condemned men and women. And I see once again the little town from where we came, the little town we left forever. I see it with a piercing clarity—the children with whom I went to school, my neighbors, my heroes, my friends—and I have never before felt so close to them. And suddenly everything is clear in my mind: it was necessary for Jerusalem to have been destroyed in the past, to bring us closer to those countless little Jewish towns annihilated through the hangman's will.

It is a fact: just as I have never remembered Jerusalem better than in the little town where I was born—Sighet—similarly, I have never remembered Sighet better than when I was in Jerusalem.

In Jerusalem one weeps and one laughs and one sings differently from anywhere else. One feels privileged coming into contact with a past that is mysteriously alive. In Jerusalem one is ceaselessly turning round as if to see invisible friends and companions, fallen on the way, victims of bad luck or misfortune. What did I do to deserve that which was denied to them?

My grandfather used to dream of Jerusalem. My mother used to pray for Jerusalem. My Master lived and died every minute for Jerusalem. And yet I can see them and I pity them as I pity myself. Now I know where Jerusalem is, but I no longer know where I am.

So, I take a sheet of paper and scribble a wish and I place it in one of the clefts of the Wall. Everyone does it, and I do not want to be different, not now. You are not supposed to tell the content of this kind of prayer, but I will all the same. I wrote: "This is my third visit to Jerusalem; I wish that I may not forget, not ever, the first two visits." And within myself a voice said, Amen. And this voice was not mine.

"Do not seek Jerusalem outside Jerusalem," my grandfather would say, crying with all his might. "Do not try to find Jerusalem far from Jerusalem," my Master would say, laughing with all his might.

But what are we to do, we who have unlearned the art of laughing and the art of crying?

Stephen Aris

Stephen Aris's avid interest in the economic activity of British Jewry took root during his stint as a junior reporter for *The Times* of London. A founding father of the sociological magazine *New Society*, he joined *The Sunday Times* in 1964, where he helped to launch *The Sunday Times Business News*, subsequently becoming its foreign editor and chief features writer. Author of *But There Are No Jews in England* and co-author of *Watergate* (*The Sunday Times* account of the scandal), Mr. Aris now lives in New York as *The Sunday Times*'s resident correspondent.

Chaim Bermant

Lithuanian-born and graduate of the Glasgow Rabbinical College of Glasgow University and the London School of Economics, Chaim Bermant has written an admirable total of sixteen books; among them are *The Cousinhood, Diary of an Old Man, Israel* and *The Last Supper*. He is a former features editor of the *Jewish Chronicle* and has been a schoolmaster, economist, and television scriptwriter. Mr. Bermant's most recent work, *The Walled Garden*, is a study of the Jewish family.

Richard Crossman

The Right Honourable Richard Crossman (1907–1974) began his long and distinguished career in the services of the British government in the 1930s and later acted in a variety of capacities: member of the Malta Round Table Conference, Minister of Housing and local Government, Leader of the House, Lord President of the Council, and Secretary of State for Social Services, including the Department of Health and Social Security. He also served as an editor for the *New Statesman*, wrote several books, including *Palestine Mission, Government and the Governed*, and *Myths of Cabinet Government*, and edited the *New Fabian Essays*.

David Daiches

A Fellow of the Royal Society of Literature, Professor David Daiches has been with the University of Sussex since 1961. Prior to that appointment, and since, he has accepted a number of the many invitations he receives to lecture, bringing him to American universities in particular. Apart from his substantial academic associations, in 1943 he served on the staff of the British Information Services and was appointed to the British Embassy staff in Washington, D.C., a year later. He frequently contributes poetry, articles, and essays to a host of periodicals, and is the author of a number of critical studies of English literature, plus two autobiographies, *Two Worlds* and *A Third World*.

Nicholas Faith

London-born and Oxford-bred Nicholas Faith has led a varied and interesting career as film editor and financial journalist, including a stretch as investment editor of *The Economist*. Three books bear his name as author: *A Guide to Personal Financial Investment, The Infiltrators: The European Business Invasion of America*, and *Wankel: The Story Behind the World's Most Revolutionary Engine*. He lives with his wife, four children, and "a large wine cellar" in the suburbs of London.

Philip French

Except for brief periods spent on the staff of the *New Statesman* and as visiting professor at the University of Texas, Philip French has been a BBC producer since the late 1950s. Author of *The Movie Moguls* and *Westerns*, and co-editor of *Age of Austerity*, he has contributed essays to a number of British and American anthologies, equal in scope to those which have regularly appeared in leading newspapers and journals, including *The Observer, The Times, The Times Literary Supplement, Sight and Sound*, and *London Magazine*.

Harry Golden

Harry Golden has served as editor and publisher of *The Carolina Israelite* since 1942, and has written an impressive number of books—*Only in America, For 2¢ Plain, The Golden Book of Jewish Humor, The Greatest Jewish City in the World, The Israelis, So Long As You're Healthy, Right Time: An Autobiography*, and (with Richard Goldhurst) *Travels Through Jewish America*, to mention only a few. Member of the American Jewish Congress and the N.A.A.C.P., he also contributes his support to the Shakespeare Society of America, the Catholic Interracial Council, and B'nai B'rith.

Albert Goldman

While shuttling between Columbia University, where he was a graduate student, and Brooklyn, where he associated with Lenny Bruce, Albert Goldman developed the split personality that marks much of his writing: one-half New York intellectual, one-half Brooklyn–Broadway hipster. Subsequently he taught at practically every college in New York City, including Columbia's School of General Studies, where he introduced one of the first full-credit courses in Pop Culture ever offered by an Ivy League school, using as his textbook a collection of his own writings on the subject: *Freakshow: The Rocksoulbluesjazzsickjewblackhumorsexpoppsych Gig and Other Scenes from the Counter-Culture*. An active contributor of articles to a bevy of periodicals, he was also the Pop Music Critic of *Life* during its last four years and is the author of the best selling biography *Ladies and Gentlemen—Lenny Bruce!!*

Michael Horovitz

Michael Horovitz has been described by Allen Ginsberg as a "Cockney, Albionic, New Jerusalem, Jazz Generation, Sensitive Bard . . . a popular experienced experimental poet who has worked many years with musicians, read at Albert Hall and many universities including his alma mater Oxford, and edited a fat anthology of Underground Verse [*Children of Albion*] . . . in addition to his own books of high metaphysical poesy . . . ," which include *The Wolverhampton Wanderer, Love Poems,* and *Bank Holiday.* When he's not charging around the globe lecturing, reading, singing, and playing music, he lives with his wife—a poet in her own right—and son Adam in a cottage in the west of England, painting, writing, and editing *New Departures.* This has been dubbed by the *Times Literary Supplement* "the most substantial avant-garde magazine in Great Britain" and has just published its sixteenth birthday number.

Arthur Koestler

Author and adventurer Arthur Koestler served as a Middle East, Paris, Berlin, and U.S.S.R. correspondent before he became a member of the Graf Zeppelin Arctic Expedition in 1931. Back to reporting once again, he was sent to cover the Spanish Civil War for the London *News Chronicle* and was subsequently imprisoned by General Franco. In accord with his active and inquisitive nature, he enlisted in the French Foreign Legion, and then the British Pioneer Corps. In 1968 he was the recipient of the coveted Sonning Prize. Among the great number of books he has written are *Scum of the Earth, Insight and Outlook, Darkness at Noon, Arrow in the Blue, Suicide of a Nation, The Call Girls, The Roots of Coincidence, Thieves in the Night, Arrival and Departure,* and *Gladiators.*

Walter Laqueur

Member of the Royal Institute of International Affairs and the American Academy of Political and Social Science, Professor Walter Laqueur has been the director of the Institute of Contemporary History and Wiener Library in London since 1964. Recently he also occupied the chair of Professor of the History of Ideas at Brandeis University, was Professor of Contemporary History at Tel Aviv University and visiting professor at the University of Chicago, Johns Hopkins University, and the University of Reading. His books include *Confrontation: The*

Middle East and World Politics, A History of Zionism, and *Struggle for the Middle East: The Soviet Union and the Middle East.*

Edward Lucie-Smith

A native of Kingston, Jamaica, Edward Lucie-Smith came to England in 1946 and has lived there ever since. After a period in advertising, he turned his creative talents toward free-lance writing and has published more than twenty books to date, including *A Concise History of French Painting: From 1350 to the Present, Eroticism in Western Art, Symbolist Art,* and four volumes of verse. Current projects include a book on early photography, *The Invented Eye,* and another on contemporary artist–craftsmen, *The World of the Makers,* illustrated with his own photographs. His art criticism has appeared in London's *Times, Sunday Times, New Statesman, Listener,* and many other magazines and periodicals.

Yehudi Menuhin

World-renowned violinist Yehudi Menuhin began playing at the age of four and officially introduced his expertise to the world three years later when he debuted as soloist with the San Francisco Orchestra. Since then Mr. Menuhin has performed with the world's foremost orchestras and conductors. As a consequence of his vigorous desire to expand the repertoire of violin concert music, he has introduced rare and important works of both classical and modern masters. Béla Bartók's Sonata for Violin, as one example, was composed especially for him. In 1957 Mr. Menuhin initiated his own yearly summer music festival in Gstaad, Switzerland, which is still most active, and he continues to make world tours every year.

Sir Rudolf Peierls

Sir Rudolf Ernst Peierls has been distinguished with numerous honors throughout his career, notably the Royal Medal of the Royal Netherlands Academy of Sciences, the Max Planck Medal of the Association of German Physical Societies, and the Guthrie Medal, I.P.P.S. In addition to his association with other organizations, he is a member of the American Academy of Arts and Sciences. Author of *Quantum Theory of Solids,* he was a member of the governing board of the National Institute for Research in Nuclear Science from 1957 through 1962. Prior to that he was involved with the Atomic Energy Project in both Birmingham, England, and the United States, and was Professor of Mathematical Physics at the University of Birmingham (1937 to 1963).

Leo Rosten

Member of the American Academy of Political and Social Science, the American Association for the Advancement of Science, and the National Council of the Authors League of America, Leo C. Rosten (pseudonymously known as Leonard Q. Ross) has successfully intermingled his two outstanding careers as author and political scientist. In the world of screenplays he is credited with *The Velvet Touch, Walk East on Beacon,* and *The Dark Corner;* his books include *The Education of H*Y*M*A*N K*A*P*L*A*N; Hollywood: The Movie Colony, the Movie Makers; The Joys of Yiddish; Leo Rosten's Treasury of Jewish Quotations;* and *The Washington Correspondents.* In addition, Mr. Rosten is the recipient of the George Polk Memorial Award and the Freedom Foundation Award.

Ronald Sanders

Son of a Tin Pan Alley composer and arranger, Ronald Sanders has entertained a lifelong interest in music, both classical and popular. On another note, he taught history at Queens College in New York City for seven years, with time off for sojourns in France (on a Fulbright Fellowship) and Israel. For ten years he was an editor of *Midstream*, a monthly Jewish review; at present he is writing full time. He is the author of three books: *Israel: The View from Masada; The Downtown Jews: Portraits of an Immigrant Generation;* and *Reflections on a Teapot: The Personal History of a Time;* and the co-editor (with Albert Fried) of *Socialist Thought: A Documentary History.*

Isaac Bashevis Singer

Isaac Bashevis Singer was associated with several Hebrew and Yiddish publications in his native Poland before he emigrated to the United States in 1935. Having settled in New York, he joined the *Jewish Daily Forward* and published his book *Satan in Goray* the same year. Since then his book titles have steadily increased and include *The Family Moskat, The Spinoza of Market Street, The Slave, Mazel & Shlimazel or the Milk of a Lioness, In My Father's Court, The Manor, The Séance.* He won the National Book Award in 1970 for *A Day of Pleasure: Stories of a Boy Growing up in Warsaw,* and in 1974 for *A Crown of Feathers and Other Stories.* He lends his name and support to the American Institute of Arts and Letters, the American Academy of Arts and Sciences, and the Jewish Academy of Arts and Sciences.

Peter Stadlen

After completing his studies in music (piano, composition, conducting) and philosophy, Peter Stadlen set off on his professional career as concert pianist (which was to continue for twenty years), playing to audiences throughout Europe and the British Isles. Among his world premiere performances were Webern's Variations, Opus 27 (Vienna, 1937), and Schönberg's Songs, Opus 48 (London, 1952). In addition to his BBC talks and numerous published articles, Mr. Stadlen taught modern piano music at Darmsstadt Internationale Ferienkurse für Neue Musik, lectured at the University of Reading, and was a visiting Fellow at All Souls' College, Oxford, from 1967 to 1968. Since 1959 he has been the senior music critic for *The Daily Telegraph* in London.

George Steiner

Paris-born George Steiner is the author of *Tolstoy or Dostoevsky; The Death of Tragedy; Anno Domini; In Bluebeard's Castle: Some Notes Towards the Redefinition of a Culture; Language and Silence: Essays on Language, Literature, and the Inhuman; Extraterritorial: Papers on Literature and the Language of Revolution; Fields of Force: Fischer and Spassky at Reykjavik;* and *After Babel.* In the past he served on the editorial staff of the London *Economist,* and as a member of the Institute for Advanced Study in Princeton. Recipient of the O'Henry Short Story Prize, The Zebel Award of the American Academy of Arts and Letters, and a Fulbright professorship, George Steiner is also a Fellow of the Royal Society of Literature, Extraordinary Fellow of Churchill College, Cambridge, and Professor of English and Comparative Literature, University of Geneva.

Elie Wiesel

In 1956 Elie Wiesel left his native Rumania and emigrated to the United States, where he has lived and worked ever since. Member of the United Nations and Foreign Correspondents associations and the Authors' League, Mr. Wiesel has been the chief foreign correspondent for *Yediot Aharonot* in Tel Aviv since 1947, and a staff member of the *Jewish Daily Forward* since 1957. His most recent book titles include *Ani Maamin: A Song Lost and Found Again; Beggar in Jerusalem; The Jews of Silence; Night, Dawn, the Accident: Three Tales by Elie Wiesel; The Oath;* and *Souls on Fire.* To add further to his laurels, Mr. Wiesel has received the Jewish Heritage Award and the Prix Rivarol.

Picture Acknowledgments

American Institute of Physics–Margrethe Bohn Collection, 300 t
Authenticated News, 233 bl
Clive Barda, 317 t, 331
The Bettmann Archive, 69
Black Star: Agip, 278 tr; James Caccavo, 34; Howard Coster, 166 l, Franz Goess, 49; Claus Meyer, 234 l; Nora, 190 br; Owen, 277 r, 313; Dave Rubinger, 40–41; Flip Schulke, 190 l; Ted Spiegel, 17, 18–19; Burt Stern, 193
Black Star, London, 179 l, 314
Boston Celtics, 191 tl
British Museum, 22 r
Camera Press, London, 97; Godfrey Argent, 304; Donald Cooper, 180 tr; Colin Davey, 96 b; Robin Douglas-Home, 317 m; Tony Prime, 133; Peter Sellers, 185; Shepard Sherbell, 216 b; Chris Smith/*Observer*, 130; Ullstein, 300 bl; Patrick Ward, 148, 151 r
Columbia Pictures Industries, Inc., 238–239
Culver Pictures, 23, 32–33, 137 l, 158 (3), 160 (2), 161 b, 164 t, 164 m, 165, 167, 169, 200 r, 201 t, 204, 206, 210 (2), 221, 223, 230, 277 l, 278 br, 280 (3), 315
Dominic, 317 b
Alfred Eisenstaedt, 110, 135, 137 r, 139, 163, 171, 177 t, 207, 293, 296 (2), 297, 301, 312 r, 320 bl, 323, 325 b, 337
John F. Fleming, Inc., 265
Friedman-Abeles, 168 b, 173, 174 (2), 175 (2)
The Frick Collection, New York, 268
Lee Gross Associates: Marvin Lichtner, 181; Mary Ellen Mark, 176; Alan Pappé, 218
Ken Heyman, 332–333, 346–347
Al Hirschfeld (The Margo Feiden Galleries), 226 (2), 227, 228 (2)
Horst P. Horst, 278 l, 279
International Fund for Concerned Photography: Micha Bar Am, 2, 48, 52 (2); Alfred Bernheim, 281; Werner Braun, 342–343; Boris Carmi 50–51; Richard Cleave, 341; Izis, 54; Bhupendra Karia, 45; Zvi Orron, 27; David Perlmutter, 53; Abraham Soskin, 24–25; Roman Vishniac, 14, 15
The Israel Museum, Jerusalem, 329
Janis Gallery, 267 t
The Jewish Museum, London, 118 b
The Jewish Museum, New York, 118 t (2), 119, 120
Jill Krementz, 183, 283 (3), 286 t, 287 (2), 288
David Levine (New York Review–Opera Mundi), 72–73 (5), 182
Bernard and S. Dean Levy, 270 t
Jerry Lewis Enterprises, Inc., 231
The collection of the Library of Congress, 136, 159, 200 l
Magnum; Eve Arnold, 184 bl, 235; Cornell Capa, 108, 116 t, 282; Robert Capa, 10, 38–39, 39, 82–83, 87 l; Henri Cartier-Bresson, 8, 46, 96 t, 126, 145, 240; Bruce Davidson, 286 b; Elliott Erwitt, 116 b, 177 b; Leonard Freed, 11, 47, 58–59, 63; Burt Glinn, 187, 217; Philippe Halsman, 189; Erich Hartmann, 320–321 t; David Hurn, 320–321 b; Elliott Landy, 196; Inge Morath, 290; Marc Riboud, 90–91, 344; Dr. Erich Salomon, 162; David Seymour, 260–261, 273; Dennis Stock, 141, 192, 234 br, 316
The Mansell Collection, 38, 311
The Metropolitan Museum of Art, New York, 245
Museum of the City of New York, 30–31, 31, 57, 164 b, 201 b
The Museum of Modern Art, New York, 267 b (gift of Philip Johnson)
The National Gallery, Washington, D.C., 246 b (Chester Dale Collection), 246 br (gift of the Joseph H. Hazen Fdn., Inc.)
National Portrait Gallery, London, 22 l
Arnold Newman, 43, 134, 146, 150 (2), 151 l, 153, 154, 155, 156, 172 b, 180 tl, 248, 254 (2), 255 (2), 272 (2), 291, 321 br, 324 r, 325 t
New York Public Library Picture Collection, 65
Perls Galleries, 247 t
Pictorial Parade, 95 b, 143, 161 t, 168 t, 180 b, 216 t, 224 t, 225, 233 tl, 233 r, 234 tr; Central Press, 93; *London Daily Express*, 236, 326 b; *Paris Match*, 300 br
Paul Popper Ltd. (Popperfoto), 64, 161 m, 166 t, 305
Punch, 149
Radio Times Hulton Picture Library, 77
Morris Rosenfeld & Sons, 194–195
Charles E. Rotkin, 144
Israel Sack, 270 b
Vidal Sassoon Inc., 131
Scala Fine Arts Publishers, 266
Peter Simon, 252 b
Snark International, 12, 86
Sherry Suris, 37, 87 r, 219
Martha Swope, 326 t, 327
United Press International (UK) Ltd., 78
Douglas Villiers, 61
The Whitney Museum of American Art, 246 t, 247 b
Wide World Photos, 92, 94 t, 94 b, 95 t, 170, 172 t, 184 br, 190 tr, 191 bl, 191 r, 211 (2), 213, 263, 271, 275, 302–303, 324 l
Woodfin Camp: Thomas Hopker, jacket; Marvin E. Newman, 20, 117
I. Zafrir, 252 t, 253
Zionist Archives and Library, 13
Source Unidentified, 25 b, 29, 68, 179 r, 184 t, 205, 222, 224 b, 310 l, 310 r, 312 l